ENGLISH TRANSLATIONS OF

ALAIN CHARTIER'S

Le Traité de l'Esperance

AND

Le Quadrilogue Invectif

VOLUME I. TEXT

EARLY ENGLISH TEXT SOCIETY

No. 270

1974

University College, Oxford MS. 85, fol. 1

lynn which nounbreth the ster
rea Allas with grette peyne
knowlift thou thin owne de
dis for to gouerne but oon
erthely body which is in co
parison a litell worme of pe
erthes Wherfor sette god a doon
with the state of Realmes
With the transmutacon of
powers for ther is no realme
but his that is pmanent
stable

Who that
seethth wele thr
ough knowlege
the ordinaunce of Jugemen
tis the alliaunce the durpurg
the constaunce and theabun
daunce of hith purbeyan
nce Wherof all goodnes is
drawen owte ought sette no
doubte vpon the divine sub
staunce for he avaunceth him
self to ferre by presumptio
us trust which puttith hym
self in so grette an ouir pude
and ought tobe blamed but
god hath sette his markis in
the cirsute of hevenes by

meruelouse duysing and grette
maistrye andir that the rthe
comprisid for to scheue the
ensaumple of submission
Will that it suffice vs to looke
vpon the firmament which
shynith bright and there we
shall see a proef of the infinite
powere

God diffende
that I shulde dou
bte in his power
for his rewardis
and his punycons be doon
to the creatures afstir their
worldly dedis allas I perive
right wele that it turiuen
tith the ffredome of oure
cristendome Wherfor I ple
yne to his mercy and to pe
in whoise vertu is mevite to
preserue and areyse and I
mervaile that his piety strec
chith nat vpon his cristen
people sore ouirthrowen

If thou mervaile
vpon theoppressions of Jus
tice peyse agenist that the
grette largresse of his graces

FIFTEENTH-CENTURY
ENGLISH TRANSLATIONS OF
ALAIN CHARTIER'S
Le Traité de l'Esperance
AND
Le Quadrilogue Invectif

EDITED BY
MARGARET S. BLAYNEY

Published for
THE EARLY ENGLISH TEXT SOCIETY
by the
OXFORD UNIVERSITY PRESS
LONDON   NEW YORK   TORONTO
1974

Oxford University Press, Ely House, London W. 1

GLASGOW NEW YORK TORONTO MELBOURNE WELLINGTON
CAPE TOWN IBADAN NAIROBI DAR ES SALAAM LUSAKA ADDIS ABABA
DELHI BOMBAY CALCUTTA MADRAS KARACHI LAHORE DACCA
KUALA LUMPUR SINGAPORE HONG KONG TOKYO

ISBN 0 19 722272 2

Printed in Great Britain
at the University Press, Oxford
by Vivian Ridler
Printer to the University

CONTENTS

FOREWORD

THE Introduction, Explanatory Notes, and Glossary of these editions will follow in another volume.

I take this opportunity to express my indebtedness to Dr. Albert C. Baugh, who suggested the need for these editions; to the late Miss Dorothy Everett and to Professor Norman Davis for their kind help and encouragement; to Miss Kathleen Lea for her constant support; to Mr. Neil Ker and Dr. R. W. Hunt for their assistance with the manuscripts; and to the Librarians and Staff at the Bodleian Library, the British Museum, the Newberry Library, the Sion College Library, and St. John's College (Cambridge) Library.

Much of the work on these editions was done while I had a Fulbright Fellowship (1951–3) and an American Association of University Women Fellowship (1963–4), for which I am grateful. I also appreciate the time allowed me on a sabbatical leave from Highland Park College.

Finally, I am grateful to an understanding daughter and to many good friends, especially Gretchen Ladd and Jane Cobb.

NOTES ON THE MANUSCRIPTS AND THE TREATMENT OF THE TEXTS

IN the second half of the fifteenth century the same author translated Alain Chartier's *Le Traité de l'Esperance* and *Le Quadrilogue
Invectif*, translations edited here and referred to hereafter as the
R versions. (He also translated Chartier's *Dialogus familiaris amici
et sodalis.*[1]) These R translations were widely enough copied in the
last quarter of the fifteenth century, for five manuscripts, one a
fragment, to have come down to us:

R Rawlinson A 338, which contains only *The Treatise of Hope*
   and *The Quadrilogue Invective* but has been chosen as the
   copy text because it is less corrupt as well as more complete
   than the other manuscripts;
N Newberry f. 36, Ry 20, which contains all three translations
   complete except for a short passage at the end of *The
   Treatise of Hope* but is the most corrupt manuscript;
S Sion College (London) L. 40.2/E. 43, which contains all three
   translations but omits almost two-thirds of *The Treatise of
   Hope*;
J St. John's College (Cambridge) 76 D 1, which contains all
   three translations but has lacunae;
C B.M. Cotton Vitellius E. x, which has only a short fragment of *The Treatise of Hope*, published among the works
   of Sir John Fortescue under the title *Dialogue between Understanding and Faith*.

Another translator's version of *The Quadrilogue Invective*, presented here in parallel text with the R version, is taken from

U University College MS. 85, the only known manuscript of
   this translation.

The manuscripts will be described more fully in another volume.
The emendations in R accepted from the other manuscripts
when all these manuscripts agree are placed in square brackets and
are not recorded in the critical apparatus. The corrections in R and

[1] The present editor is currently editing this translation.

U made either by the scribe or by another hand are placed in parentheses and also are not recorded in the critical apparatus unless the other manuscripts have different readings in the R texts. The spellings of the emendations in and variants from R are taken from N, which is more complete than SJC, except when RN agree, in which case the spellings are from J.

In the critical apparatus of the R texts I have recorded only substantive variants, with certain exceptions noted below. Thus, I have recorded all additions and omissions when NSJC differ from R; transpositions, since N especially shows a tendency for such rearrangement of words; and differences in singular and plural forms except when the forms are used interchangeably by these scribes and others (e.g. 'othir'—'othirs', 'folke'—'folkes', 'richesse'—'richesses', 'largesse'—'largesses'). But I have recorded differences in verb forms and endings only when the tense or mood of the verb is changed or when an ending is completely omitted, as often in N. I have not recorded words and forms commonly interchanged by these and other scribes (e.g. 'them'—'hem', 'their' —'hir',[1] 'ofttymes'—'oftentymes', 'parte'—'party', 'pite'—'piete', 'othir'—'tothir', 'whosoeuer'—'whosomeuer', 'a'—'an', 'no'— 'non', 'from'—'fro', 'at the'—'atte', 'among'—'amongist', 'ne'— 'non'—'ner'). I have also generally not recorded certain substitutions of one word for another with the same meaning (e.g. 'wastith' —'westith', 'trustyng'—'trastyng', 'satisfy'—'satify', 'singuler'— 'singler') nor corrupt or unusual spellings (e.g. 'þes'—'þais' N), but I have noted such variations in either the Introduction or the Glossary. In addition, I have not recorded minor obviously scribal errors in the manuscripts (e.g. dittography errors, omissions of a single letter such as 'r', the most commonly omitted letter) nor insertions or cancellations in NSJC, unless they seem to show something about the relationship of the manuscripts or the history of the text.[2]

For the convenience of the reader, the French reading[3] has been referred to as D in the critical apparatus when the manuscripts

---

[1] R prefers 'their'—'them', but NSJC have 'her'—'hem' frequently.

[2] For example *T.H.*, 11/13 hast] RN hath J hath *canc.* hast S.

[3] The French readings used here are from André Duchesne's edition of *Le Traité de l'Esperance* in *Les Œuvres de maistre Alain Chartier* (Paris, 1617) and from E. Droz's revised edition of *Le Quadrilogue Invectif* (Paris, 1950). In the Explanatory Notes in another volume, however, French manuscripts of the treatises are also compared with the translations.

differ in readings or when an emendation may be briefly supported. But fuller discussion of the relationship of the translations to the French texts will follow in the Introduction and Explanatory Notes in another volume.

The paragraphing of these editions is mine, with, however, attention to the French texts. Passages in *The Treatise of Hope* which are verse in the French, always translated as prose in R, are slightly indented in the edition of that work.

I have punctuated and capitalized according to modern usage. The scribal pointing and capitalization, particularly in R, are erratic and sometimes misleading.[1] Where the scribal stops and capital letters have seemed indicative of the translator's intention, however, I have attempted to reflect this intention by modern equivalents. I have been assisted in punctuation also by close attention to the French construction and the author's interpretation of it. I have not retained the frequent separations of 'a yeinst', 'a way', 'by cause', 'hym self', 'afore tyme', 'no thing', and so forth. I have also separated 'shalbe', often written together in the manuscripts. In capitalizing I have considered 'ff' a capital, hence recording it as 'F' if it begins a word which normally would be capitalized in modern English.[2]

I have followed exactly the spelling in R and U, retaining þ and ȝ where they occur. I have expanded the meaningful abbreviations and contractions (including two forms of the ampersand in R) without comment. The scribes in general follow usual fifteenth-century practices in such abbreviations and contractions. But ȝ is used in 'ȝendebus' in *T.H.*, 110/3, as an abbreviation for *us*, and the usual sign for *er* has been used once for *n* in 'men' in *T.H.*, 77/12. The latter may be the symbol of a corrector rather than of the scribe. The line through, or the two dots on each side of, the tail of þ have been expanded as *per* or *par*, according to the most common spelling of the words concerned in each manuscript. þ with the usual sign for *er* above it has been expanded as *þeir* when it is a possessive pronoun and as *þer* when it is an adverb or expletive, again in accordance with the usual, but by no means consistent, practice of the scribes. The loops at the end of plural words have been expanded as *is* in R and as *es* in U, which seem

---

[1] See, for example, *Q.I.*, 134/24-5.
[2] I have recorded 'll' as 'L' in the one place where it occurs initially in 'Liue' in *T.H.*, 103/22.

to be the spellings preferred by the scribes, although the practice of both scribes varies.

Certain symbols of abbreviation or contraction have not been expanded, either because they are superfluous or because it is impossible, especially in R, to tell the meaningful ones from the meaningless ones. In R, for example, there are many flourishes on the scribe's *r*'s, of varying degrees of boldness. Hence, it is impossible to determine when he intended to indicate final *e* by his flourish, except in a word like 'noumbre', where I have expanded. Medially, a nasal sign is expanded only when the extra nasal reproduces the usual scribal spelling; the sign often occurs, however, over the vowel and following nasal consonant where the usual spelling does not seem to demand doubling the nasal. When the same sign appears in R over final *n*, or through the top of *ll* or *th*, I have not added final *e*; and when the sign occurs over final *p*, *pe*, or *pp*, as in 'lordship', 'lordshipe', or 'lordshipp', I have added neither final *e* nor an additional *p*. The scribe of R adds a great many obviously superfluous symbols, as over the ending *cion*, when *i* has not been omitted; over the syllable *aun*, where *au* has already been written; in the tail of *p*, where *per* has already been written out, and so forth. These have been ignored except in words like 'leccon' and 'at', where the abbreviation sign is not just superfluous, but wrong, and where the error has been noted in the critical apparatus. The scribe of R also omits at times necessary abbreviation symbols, as in the *con-cion* ending; these have been expanded without comment.

The arbitrary nature of the policy of expansion of abbreviations outlined above is necessitated (unless one becomes ridiculously pedantic) by a scribal inconsistency not only in use of symbols of abbreviation, but in spelling itself; this is, of course, especially true of fifteenth-century manuscripts. It should be noted that in U, slightly earlier than R, the scribal inconsistencies are much less common.

In emendation, I have followed certain principles as consistently as possible with a view to arriving as near as possible to the original readings in the English translations. I have emended R when the readings in NSJC follow the French more closely, except when the variant involves only the addition or omission of an article or the change of a connective word (e.g. 'and' to 'or'). In such changes the practice of the translator is so erratic in following the French, and the possibility of scribal variation in the French manuscripts so great, that I have usually not felt justified in emending unless the emendation from NSJC is stylistically more in accord with the translator's usual practice. In passages where the translation is so free that comparison with the French is not helpful, I have emended R when the sense of the other English manuscripts is obviously superior or when stylistically the emendation improves the translation, as in maintaining parallelism or following the usual sentence pattern of the translator. Doubtful cases, which I have not emended, are recorded in the critical apparatus and usually discussed in the Explanatory Notes.

When the sense of a passage is corrupt in all the English manuscripts of the R translations or in U, I have emended only when the French supports the emendation and when no corruption in the French manuscripts I have examined accounts for the English corruption; or only when the error may plausibly be shown to be scribal. I have made one exception to these general practices: when the sense of a passage is badly garbled and obviously corrupt by processes that cannot be identified (as a corrupt translation from a bad French original, as an obvious scribal error, as several efforts of the translator to render the same French passage, etc.), I have occasionally felt justified in making a slight change that maintains the original intention of Chartier, although it does not exactly follow the French.

In connection with corruptions carried over from French manuscripts to the English translations, a special problem arises for all editors of translations, a problem which is difficult to solve short of examining in great detail every surviving manuscript of the work in the original language. Even then, when one considers the number of manuscripts which probably existed at the time when any given translation was made (especially if some fifteen or forty have come down to us, as with *Le Traité de l'Esperance* and *Le Quadrilogue Invectif* respectively), one cannot be sure that some of the corruptions are not derived from a lost version.[1] Such a problem exists in the present works where many corrupt French readings in the manuscripts examined can be shown to have resulted in corrupt English readings. This difficulty has necessitated a rather

---

[1] It is, of course, possible that one may be fortunate enough, as Dr. Bühler believes he has been with *The Dicts and Sayings of the Philosophers*, to discover the exact manuscript from which a translation was made.

arbitrary decision about a policy of emendation, a policy adopted with the recognition that some emendations may unknowingly correct errors in the French originals from which the translators worked, rather than errors in the English manuscripts.

Proper names furnish an excellent example of this problem. There are many corruptions of proper names in the English manuscripts. Some of them—for example in *The Treatise of Hope* 'Achilperich' (65/30), 'Althinus' (102/22), 'Detharmich' (84/12), 'Marcus Tucius' (76/19), 'Nusye' (89/23), 'Paphagonye' (89/23), 'Policitatus' (86/5), and in *The Quadrilogue Invective* 'Mavlius' (226/30) and 'Staurus' (238/7)—may be traced directly to corrupt spellings in one or several of the French manuscripts, sometimes further corrupted by the translator (as in 'Achilperich', where he tacked the French preposition 'a' on to the name). These I have let stand as they appear in the English manuscripts and in the French original. There are other corruptions, however, for which there is no evidence in the French versions I have examined, and which scribal error in the English manuscripts might easily explain. These I have emended: in *The Treatise of Hope*, 'Foreus' to 'For[on]eus' (59/4); 'Myntoue' to 'Myn[er]ue' (86/31); 'Nestoryue (? ne)' to 'Nestoryu[s]' (89/19); and in *The Quadrilogue*, 'Lucius' to 'L[iv]ius' (234/23). There are other examples of this problem besides those related to proper names: e.g. the variation between 'sa' and 'ta' or between 'son' and 'ton' in the French, despite the sense requiring one or the other, and the corresponding variation between 'the' and 'thi' in the English; the omission of subject pronouns or relative pronouns in the French and hence in the English, and so forth. Thus, it is important to remember that some emendations made when all the English manuscripts seem corrupt must be viewed in the light of possible corruptions in the French manuscripts used by the translators as well as in terms of the inaccuracies of English scribes.

SUMMARIES OF *THE QUADRILOGUE INVECTIVE* AND *THE TREATISE OF HOPE*

Le Quadrilogue Invectif, written by Chartier in 1422, and *Le Traité de l'Esperance*, begun about 1428 and left unfinished, are reflections of a period when the fortunes of France, and more particularly of the Dauphin Charles, looked especially dark. The years 1422–8 saw the increasing discouragement and confusion of the French people of all estates because of the great victories of Henry V; the Treaty of Troyes; the deaths of both Charles VI and Henry V; the rivalry of the weak Dauphin, surrounded by self-seeking counsellors, and the infant Henry VI; and the ever-growing disorders in ordinary daily life, brought about by famine and by the ravages of English troops and of mercenaries hired by the French. It is out of such an atmosphere that both French works grew.

The English translators' interest in these two works is understandable not only because the histories of England and France during Chartier's time were inextricably bound together, but also because conditions within England itself during the second half of the fifteenth century, when the translators were at work, made Chartier's observations about and criticisms of his own country cogently applicable to the confused state of affairs in England during the Thirty Years' War.

The Quadrilogue is concerned entirely with the French situation of Chartier's time—its causes and its effects—while *The Treatise of Hope*, in its attempt to offer consolation to the people, deals not only with the spiritual significance of the tribulation of France and the necessary acceptance of God's scourge, but also with a vast number of the political, religious, and philosophical themes discussed widely in the Middle Ages. Both works are cast in the form of dream visions, in which allegorical figures carry on dialogues heard by the author.

The prologue of *The Quadrilogue*, a discourse on the rise and fall of cities and states according to God's will and a reflection on the state of France ('la main de Dieu est sur nous'), is followed by the author's falling asleep in the midst of an inward struggle between hope and despair. In a dream vision he sees a sad and ill-treated lady, symbolic of France, surrounded by her three sons—Nobility (or Knighthood), Clergy, and People. France reproaches her children for their cowardice, ambition, and disordinate living, and for their lack of knightly perfection, prudence, and loyalty. In reply, the character representing the people complains that he endures the hardships of the evil conditions in France and should not suffer the blame for the evils as well. He also bitterly criticizes Knighthood for not fighting in the people's defence. Knighthood defends himself against the charges of People and attacks him for misusing and not recognizing the prosperity of peace and hence for constantly seeking change, for failing to support the men of war, and for living in a manner beyond the proprieties of his estate. But People has an answer to that: he declares that, since the people live by the example of their betters, the nobility and clergy have made the people what they are. After another rejoinder by Knighthood, Clergy, who before has remained silent and pensive, discusses the state of France in terms of the three things necessary to a prince who wages war—wisdom, money and goods, and obedience. In showing that the Dauphin does not have those three necessities, Clergy finally points to the failures of all three estates in their patriotic duty. A brief comment by Knighthood is followed by France's appeal that the debate be ended. She then asks Chartier to record all that he has heard for the edification of the French nation.

The Treatise of Hope deals with some of these same themes in a more general and philosophical way. Champion says, '*L'Esperance*, c'est le testament de Me Alain, et peut-être aussi celui de la pensée du moyen âge'.[1] Modelled partially on Boethius' *Consolation of Philosophy*, *L'Esperance*, in prose broken by passages of verse (translated as prose in the English), opens with the author's dream vision of himself on a bed of sickness and sorrow, tormented by Melancholy and harangued by Indignation, Distrust, and Despair. With the words of these three, Understanding is awakened and ushers in to the author Faith, Hope, and Charity. Then follow the two dialogues between Faith and Understanding and between Hope and Understanding, which make up over three-quarters of the treatise. (We must assume that Chartier intended to conclude with a dialogue between Charity and Understanding.) In these dialogues the author writes about topics which range from the justification of the divine punishments then befalling France, to the condemnation of Mohammed, the evils of the court, the relative values of reason and faith, the benefits of prayer, and the degenerate living of priests.

[1] *Histoire poétique du 15e siècle* (Paris, 1923), i. 149.

THE TREATISE OF HOPE

A TRANSLATION OF
ALAIN CHARTIER'S
Le Traité de l'Esperance

From Rawlinson MS. A 338

[The Auctour]

Inn the tenthe yere of my sorowfull exile aftir many troubles and aftir many mortale perillis and the daungers which I haue passid vnto this tyme, thankid be Allmyghty God. And nat long agoo syn I / redde in the Cronicles, ther I sawe the grette dedis col. 2 of the olde faders which war the furst founders of the noble 6 realme of Fraunce, tha[t] habounded in grette vertues and were veray possessioners of the same and aftir their decesse lefte it to their successours, which tooke grette heede to their doctrynes and good maners through which thei grettely incresid the 10 realme and made themself to be worshipd, louid and doubtid both beyond see and on this syde. Thei wer iuste in their dedis; thei socourd their frendis; thei punyschid the evile doars and feers ayeinst their enemys, brennyng in wourship, and takers of grette and high enterprises, lovers of vertue, repre- 15 vers of vices, regnyng rightfully, fortunat and [glorious], and ayeinst all inemyes strong and victorious. That tyme thei regnid in grette prosperite for bycause thei louid equite and iustice, and aftir their grette victories lefte their realme in glorious prosperite. / And thes good fadirs, [that] were born before vs, f. 34 in that [goode] tyme lyuedin honorably and endurid all [the] 21 cours of their age bothe in seuirte of their bodyes and reste in their courages.

But O allas we caytifis, borne in a evile hour and vndir suche [a] desteny that in our tyme is fall the grette pryce and 25 noblesse of Fraunce, which is to our wourship a grette repryef, for somtyme it was noble, free and blessid, and nough it is boonde, confusid and in maner dispeyred, and we dryvin into exile and disperpuled. And so we be experte in our myschevis and euery day we lye in sorowis and sighinges, in pouerte 30 chasid owt, and worste of all we shamefully fall in age. Also we be in deserte, mystaken, naked and disherited for because we do nat right nor loue nat trouthe. Wherfor in our herte we haue

1 The Auctour] NSJ *om*. R *see n.*   2 sorowfull] soroull J   3 aftir] *om*.
NSJ   5 syn] sith J   8 their] the N   9 to] of NSJ   12 beyond]
beyende N byyende S beyend þe J   14 ayeinst] ayen J   16 glorious]
NSJ gloriously R glorieux D   21 the] NSJ their R   23 courages]
contrees J   30 lye] lyue NSJ   33 herte] conscience (*ins.*) J

grette remors for the tyme that we haue lost and also we be
conquerid and our frendis slayne. And that is for to come we
cannat knowe but that we lye in maner of / an hope.

And whanne I was in my flowres, for the aquitale of my
5 youth I wrote plesaunte dictees, and now must I drawe me
to othir werkis with herte sorowfull, owt of which may issewe
no ioye, but peyne, feer, pouerte, losse and doubte, that
environith all my thought. Wherfor I may haue nothing
but vndir their daunger. And so I must nedis chaunge my sen-
10 tence, for in me is nothir witte ne vndirstonding for to write
but onely as I knowe. For the grette sorow that durith so longe
annoyeth me in suche wisse that in my yong age it makith me to
waxe olde and of leene natur and woll nat lette me lyve my
right course. And so with trouble and sorow I haue begonne
15 this booke.

[Item the Auctour]

I(n) this heuy and sorowfull thought, which at all tymes is
present in my herte and berith me company both at my rising and
goyng to bedde which causith the nyghtes to be / to me full long and
20 noyouse and my troubled life, which hath long tyme travailed
and diffouled my symple vndirstonding, which [is] so ouircome
and environed with displesaunt frenesies that I can do nothing
wherthrough I may haue any conforte. Yet nat long agone the
memory of thingis passid, the vgglines of the disposicions that be
25 nough present, and the horriblenes of perillis that be for to come
renewid ageyne my sorowfull grevis, my dull ymaginacions and my
power fayled of seuirte. And so I aboode as a mane confusid, the
visage [wexith] blemeshid, the wittis troubled and the bloode
medlid in the body. And as I laye in this poynte came toward me
30 an olde woman all owt of aray lyke as she hadd sette nothing by hir
habite. She was leene, drye, ryvelid, with a pale colour bloo as leed,
and swollen. Hir loking was downwarde, hir voice trou(b)led and
hir pace hevy. Hir heede was wrappid in a [suyled] kerchif like / as

3 that] whan N　　lye] life N lyue SJ　　maner of an] *om.* N　　5 must
I] *tr.* N　　9 their] þat J　　14 course] cource J course *canc.* cource
S courte N　　17 In] NS n *orig. square* A *with illuminated* I; *cross bar canc.*
R An J　　thought] though J　　19 to be] be SJ　　to me] *om.* N me D
21 is] *om.* RNSJ est D　　28 wexith] N wexit J woxit S *om.* R　　33 suyled]
NSJ suyvelid R sale D *see n.*

it had ben through suotte and asches, and hir body was cladde lyke as
it had bene in a thredebare mantille. And whanne she was come
vnto me, withowt sayng of any wourde she sodeinly embraced me
within hir armes and couered both myn yghen and my body with
that vnhappy mantelle, and with hir armes she streyned me so sore 5
that me semyd myn harte had ben as (in) a presse. And with hir
handis she helde myn hedde and myn yghen all downward and hid
in suche wise that I had neythir leyser to here ne see. And as a man
vanischid or in a swowne I was take and brought into the lodging
of infirmite, and ther I was caste on a bedde of anguisch and 10
maladye. Yet Vndirstonding, the yong and wele-avised bacheler,
folowyd me somtyme nygh and somtyme ferre lyke as God had
geve me the queynttaunce. But this woman gave me suche vnhappy
drinckis which cast me in a frenesie and suche mysknow/lage that f. 35
the wise Vndirstonding, which at this neede conduyted me vnto 15
the bedde where I lay and ther he abode beside me as a man that
had be from hymself or like as he had ben in a litargie. And aftirward I vndirstode that this olde woman was callid Malencolye,
which troubleth mannes thought, dryeth the body, corruptith the
humours and febelith the spirite sencetif, and bringith a man in 20
langour and so to the dethe. Aftir hir doctrine haue ben and oftintymes by the high wittis and the grette vndirstonding of persones
and excellent men gretly troubled and made derke aftir the havnt-
yng or exercyse of to depe and diuerse thoughtis. For the fowir
sensuall vertues that be within man which we call sensetiffe, 25
ymaginatiffe, estimatiffe and memoratiffe be bodily vertues which
stret[c]hen to euery [parte of man], and thes may be hurte by to
ofte or in to strong werkis which man labourith sorar thanne nede
ys / to acheve, like as among the .v. wittis that be withowte, the col. 2
yghe is troubled whanne it lokith vpon to grette a bryghtnes or by 30
moche reding or ellis setting his sight perfectely vpon smale thingis
that be plesaunte to the lust of man or vpon different fygurys.
O thou caytyf nature humayne, borne to peyne and to travaile,
clothid in body freele and vayne, tendir, sympyll and vncerteyne

1 through . . . asches] drawen oute of the asshes NS drawen oute of asshes J
lyke] *om.* NSJ   2 a] *om.* N   4 within] in NSJ   4–5 and 1 . . . armes]
om. J   12 had] hath N   16–17 that . . . from] owte fro N oute of SJ
25 man] a man N l'homme D   which] *om.* N   26 bodily] *om.* N corporelles D
27 parte of man] SJ part of a man N man of parte R   30 to] the N trop D
a] *om.* N   34 body] both *add.* NJ both *add. canc.* S

and lightly ouirthrowin, [thy] thoughtis put the owte of vertu;
thy folishe witte noyeth and in manere sleeth the; it bringith the
owte of knowlage. And in lasse thanne thou be holpyn by vertu
of the hevyns, thou maist nat lyve in helth.

5 [The Auctour]

f. 35ᵛ Thus troubled in my body and in my thought, I lay / revercid
vpon that noyouse couche wheras I haue abydin many dayes sithin
with a faade mouth and a fayled appetite, and aftir that, longe
fastynge, sharpe sorow and hurting of my brayne, which Dame
10 Malencolie turmentid with hir harde handis. And as I lay thus I
felte quake, remeve and opyn þe parte that was in the myddis of
my hede in the regyon of ymaginatyffe, which some men call
fantasye. And at the same hou[r] on the lefte parte, which was the
derkest place of my bedde, presentid themself thre horrible sem-
15 blaunces and fygurys of women passing feerfull to loke vpon.

[Deffyaunce]

The furst of them bore in [her] hande a cofre of iren shete with
double keyes, which she helde streightly in hir honde. An on hir
col. 2 shuldirs she / bare a peyr of beseges; and the besege that hyng
20 bifore was full and that hyng behynde was voyde. She was also
girdid with on girdill and trussid with anothir, and on bothe
gyrdillys (hynge) purses and litill (bagges) full of diuerse thingis.
And yette she had hir handis vpon hir baggage as a woman that
doubtid euery man and like as she woulde flee. Hir loking was neuir
25 stedfaste [ne] vpright toward the hevene, but behynde and asyde
she caste allway hir yghen like as she hadde be affrayed. And in hir
behavinge ther was no maner of reste nor stablenesse in [hir]
constaunce, wherthrough myght right wele be knowen the suspec-
tion of [hyr] harte.

30 [Indignacyon]

The secounde was Indignacion. And she was cladde in a shorte

1 thy] *corrected from* by S by NJ be R Ton D   2 in manere] *om.* S
sleeth] slees S flees N *?* fleith J   2–4 it . . . helth] and to mysknowing bryngeth
the Being of so pore strenght and vertu If off heven þou be not vpholde In the
strenght þou be full colde S *see n.*   4 the] thi N   11 þe] the *add.* R
13 hour] NSJ hous R   14 themself] hymself J   14–15 semblaunces]
semblauntes N   16 Deffyaunce] *om.* R *glossed as* mistruste NSJ   20 that] þat
þat N21 girdid] gyrd NS gryd J   girdill] grydyll J   25 asyde] a saide N
26 allway] *om.* ND   27 hir] NSJ their R   28 wherthrough] it *add.* N
knowen] *om.* N   28–9 suspection] suspycyon N susspessyon SJ   29 hyr]
NSJ their R

mantelle, and vndir the same, as [it] had be a thing hydde, she helde
on of hir armes couerid, with / the which she helde a passing sharpe f. 36
whippe like as she had thought to haue do vengeaunce or hurte to
some persone. The tothir arme was discouerid oute of hir mantelle,
wherein she helde a peire of tables that war opyn, in which she 5
redde for hir remembraunce the vnkyndenesse, the fawtes and þe
iniuryes that war done vnto hir. Hir visage was rede and enflammed,
and hir yghen sparkeled as the fyer. Hir lokyng was merveylously
sharpe. The herte and the body was (so) swollin with despite and
felonye that it wolde haue broken in (lasse) than it had be avoydid 10
with chydyng and repreves, like as must that is put into a tunne
and for lake of attendaunce breketh both his barris and dryvith
owte the bong.

[Desesperaunce]

The thredde was discheuele and hir gowne was slitte byfore on 15
the brest. Hir yghen war like as (they) had be half dede and holow.
Hir colour was all / fadid. And on hir arme she bare a towaile, hir col. 2
here abowte hir necke and (a) knyf in hir hande.

And as sone as these thre abhominable monstres hadde appered
before me, the seconde had suche desire to repr(o)ve me by hir 20
mouthe, which was full of pride and ryotouse wourdis, that the
haste that she made for to speke suche wise brake hir voice and
bablid with hir tonge. And the multitude of repreves and euil
sayingis that she enforced hirself for to haue shewed owte of hir
appostomed courage lette echon othir lyke wise as a preese of 25
people that make haste to go owte at a streight wiket. Thanne she
beganne to reason me withowte abydyng or somonyng her fellawes
and reprevid me with an high voice sayng thes wourdis followyng:

[Indygnacion]

O thow vnhappy and in euil tyme borne and as a / parsone caste f. 36ᵛ
owte, naked of goodis, forsaken of thy freendis and cast away on 31
euery side or parte through the aduersite of fortune, what counseile
castest thou to take to conduyte thy life and thin estate from
hensforth, or what foly hath moevid the hensforwarde for to drawe

3 haue do] do (*damaged MS.*) N   8 the] *om.* N   10 haue broken]
abroken N   11 into] in NSJ   12 his] the NSJ la D   17 fadid] fade
NSJ   20 suche] a *add.* NSJ   23 repreves] *2nd* e *made* o *by hand that*
ins. o *in l.* 20 R   27 reason] with *add.* N   28 reprevid] *2nd* e *made* o;
cf. l. 23 R   followyng] *om.* NSJ   32 side or] *om.* NSJ   the] *om.* N des D

to courte or to royall paleys or to serue in the office publique, seyng
that thou arte neuir avaunced ne profited therby? Thou hast lost
also the tyme of þi most vertuouse youthe and thi labour wasted
in vayne. And nough it is come to that poynte that thou abidist
5 nothing ellis but pouerte and perill. In lasse thanne thou dedist
pourvey for thyself, whanne the tyme of plente was, of suche thing
as was necessary to mannes sustinaunce, hough shalt thou do in
a leene tyme, in a harde tyme and in a pore tyme? For and the
col. 2 courte haue mysknowe thy seruice and the / vnkynde men forgoten
10 thy goode dedis, houg canst thou thynke that thou myghtest from
hensforth do any profight to the comon wele or to thiself whanne
the goode dedis and þe evile be sette like and no difference saue
only that by longe vsage malice hath the gretter entre and the
gretter boldenesse? Hast thou forgoten courte and hast thou so
15 long asaiyd it? At the lest wey thou shulldist haue born awey the
fruyte suche wise that be knowing of the same thou shuldist haue
lerned for to fle it and eschewe it. Vndi(r)stondist thou nat wele
that dissimulacion hath so long tyme occupied the yates and the
entrees of the courte of princes that trouthe, [þat] hathe so long
20 knokked at the dorre, may haue non entre to schewe the comon
wele? Hast thou forgoten Lucan, which taught the on a tyme that
auctorite of courte may neuir suffur to have a fellaw and that /
f. 37 [betwene] glorie and envie is perdurable and mortall werr? Remembre the that the liff of courte is of the nature of folis and
25 wanton women which cherisch more them that come last, and love
them more fervently that diffame them and pill them thanne suche
as best louith and seruith them. But and thou wolt know fortune
and the variablenesse that is at all tymes in courte, ther shalt thou
fynde hir; [ther she dysportes hir; þer shalt þou fynde hir] turn-
30 ynges returned; ther she makith hir chaunges and entremedelynges.
For at some tyme she takith hir disporte for to make a caytyf that
he cannat knowe hymself; a myghty man she makith soo prowde
that he can knowe nothing. And suche as be cherischid abowte
princes she settith them so on hight that she fillith theme full of

---

1 the] thyn J   2 thou 1] om. N   arte] wast NSJ   2–3 lost also] tr. NSJ
10 thynke] than add. NSJ   12 evile] dedys add. NSJ   13 that] om. N
14 hast thou 2] hast NSJ   16 that] þat þat NS   be] the add. N
17 Vndirstondist] Vndistondist (i. canc. er ins.) R   18 that] om. J   tyme]
me add. N   23 betwene] NSJ biveyne R entre D see n.   26 them 2]
om. N   31 takith] take N   31–2 that . . . knowe] which knowe not N
32 soo] to J

veyne glorye and of pompe that (they) can nothir knowe God ne
man, and aftir that she lettith them falle and vnmakith them and /
suffirth them to lyve in grette shame and soore annoyed of their col. 2
lyves. Sometyme she estraungeth suche as war right nyghe; somtyme she reprevith suche as hath estraunged themself. Somtyme 5
she takith the litill goodis away from the poore people to encrese
the riche mannys treasour, and sodenly she departith that treasour
so that ther restith nothyng but a bare place or a voyde. Somtyme
she fedith the yghen of foolis which stondin in grette ryalte whanne
thei loke byhynde them and seen a grette rowte follow them and 10
at euery wourde bowe downe. Anothir tyme she makith them
walke alone and had in disdayne of suche as aforetyme bar them
vp with blaundisshing wourdis. If thou haue the corage or power,
to speke more propyrly, folish presumpcion of thiself, to wille to
putt the in prees vnto the daungerous dongeon wher Dame Courte 15
[retrayeth] vnto hir secrete / place, knowe for certeyne that the f. 37ᵛ
wiket is so litill, the plancke so streight and the diche vndirnethe
so deepe and the wynde of Envye rennith in the same with grette
blastes that othir at the entre or at that ysswe þou maist be hurte
withowte helth or ellis fall withowte any arysing. But the vanyte 20
of worldly wourship and the delite þat mannys power hath oon
ouir anothir make the folish thought alwey to desire for to entre
into thexperient periles, like as the birde that fallith into the nette
wheras he hath seen othir take byfore him. Wherfor me semith
that the day of thy departing from the scoole of science for to entre 25
among the people that be full (of) worldly ambicion was nat [to]
the most profitable. For whanne thou war in thy scoolis thou
haddist delectacion of spirit, rest of herte, plesaunt ocupacion,
honest pouerte, litill richesse, sevir gladnesse, desire of mesure and
content with a litill. / And now thou hast failid of fraunchise and col. 2
put the into seruage, from suerte into daungier and so into suffryng 31
of ambicion; and thy good fortune is suche wise cast into this
tempest that thou liest floting as doth a shyppe which bi force of

1 nothir] neyþer N nott J   2 she] om. J   5 as hath] as haue SJ þat
hase N   estraunged] enstraunged N   6 takith] away add. NSJ   away]
om. NSJ   7 mannys] godys and add. N see n.   departith] departed N
8 ther] om. J   a bare . . . voyde] a voyde place NSJ see n.   13 power]
and add. NSJ   14 folish] folyseth SJ   16 retrayeth] NSJ retaynith R se
retrait D   vnto] to J   place] places N   19 that 2] the NSJ   24 othir]
othyrs SJ oþer bryddes N   27 thy scoolis] the scales J   28 haddist]
om. J   spirit] and add. N om. D   30 thou hast] tr. NSJ   31 the]
om. N   into 3] vnto NSJ   32 good] om. NSJD

the wynde is dryvyn vpon the londe and so perishid. Thou seest
wele that euery man aparte serchith for his saluacion and euery
man gadirth what he may lyke as all thing war abandoned and lost.
O vnhappy aventur, thou cannat cast thiself owte, but be as a
5 partener of this perille, but thou arte neuir fellawe of the profite.
What shalt thou say of thyne acquayntaunce and nough nat
acqueyntid, which thou hast seruid as thi frendis saue only (þat)
the name of frendship hath be comon to them and to the, and the
veray frendship hath restid only in the? For the lawe of frendship
f. 38 woll euyr that the availe or profight that / cometh therof be
11 retournable and ought to retourne to hym from whom it come be
like kyndnes. Now is thyn goone withowte retournynge of which
we spake. But the lawe of frendship which was vsid among the
auncientis is long syn revokid by Dame Courte. But and þou wold
15 knowe the frendis of thy mayntenaunce, furst thou must putte the
in peyne to knowe þi fortune, for she and thy frendis be mesurd
[both] by on mesure and of lyke endurynge. Thy dedis shall be
right wele alowed if ther be any wourthy to be remembrid, but
with suche loenge I suppose thou wolt be wery. And notwith-
20 stonding that thy loose and thy glorie be grette, yet þat availith
nat the all only; for ouir that thou must haue bredde or ellis thou
myghtest dey for all that lawde, and anothir waxith fatte in
repreueable werkis.
    Wherfor iuge thy dedis by othir men and thanne shalt thou
col. 2 knowe that the issew of thy case is above all othir / thingis right
26 doubtable, seeng that so many of the olde auncientis and wise
philosophers which haue resisted ayeinst fortune by wisedome, yet
cowde nat they eschewe withowte deth the grette mysauenturis of
courte. Noote Senecke, how for all the grette doctrine and seruice
30 that he ded to Nero, yet he made hym to dey bleding in a hote
bayne. What rewarde also had Tullius for all the offices that he
had in the cite of Rome, which by his witty excercyse diuerse tymes
savid the said cite? Yet natwithstonding he was by Anthony cruelly
beheded. Demostenes also, prynce of fayr language and mirrour
35 of eloquence, ought nat be forgoten for the Athenyences, which
oftymes by his fayre language and wisedom sauid their city. Yet

    5 arte] wast NSJ   8 them] hym N   10 that 1] SJ om. N þat add.
R   14 wold] wilt NSJ   17 and of] of an N   shall] schul S shuld N
18–23 but . . . werkis] om. N   19 loenge] lowynge J   24 thanne] om. J
28 mysauenturis] myssauntres J   31 bayne] bathe N   31–2 for . . .
Rome] om. N   33 said cite] Cite Rome N   34 prynce] om. N

for all that for envy they put hym to deth. Also Boece may be to
vs anothir ensaumple for to moche loue that (he) had for the
diffence / of the comon wele. Yet was he by Kyng Theorich put f. 38ᵛ
in prison with grette peyne, wher he compiled his *Booke of
Consolacion*, and so endid his dayes in wretchid pryson.   5
    Wher is that herte that cowde holde hym content with so many
vnkyndnesse and so many seruices with(owt) a rewarde? Thy
corage ought to be passed for to suffre seruice, pouerte and travaile
in peyne. Hough may thi tonge be withowt clamour and withowte
complaynyng whanne the mouthe in the which it restith is famischid 10
for defaulte, and othir plenteously fedde withowt deserte with
suche goodis as thou supposid to haue deserued? O thou infortunat
man, which hast passid the daungerous wayes and the anoyeng
watchis, and othir also which haue borne vpon their shuldirs the
hevynes of theire exile and travailed in pouerte for the wele pub- 15
like, which your troughe ought full li/till to preyse forasmoche as col. 2
ye be for the same diffowlit, sette at nought and nough in captyuyte.
Wherfor the wordis of Tholome may well be shewed afore yow at
this tyme, which said this wise: 'I holde hym well blessid', said he,
'that retchith neuir vndir whose gouernaunce the realme be 20
guyded.'
    Who may wryte or suffice to tell what owre humaynite desirith
to drawe to hym by waye of myschief? For angre is to vs a
martirdome; it noyeth vs to chese; favoure, hate or angre, to
thenke, to do or to say anything that is trouthe. Also infelicite 25
and aduersite withowt auctorite maketh a man bolde to dispice
othir that be bettir thanne hymself. Also necessite in begginge
puttith freelte in perplexite, which empeyrith the witt of man. /

[The Auctour]   f. 39

Whanne that she, more by angre thanne by reason, was so 30
straungely moevid to speke the chaffyng and felenouse wourdis,
hir voice byganne to faile, but hir will was to haue said worse.

1 that] *om.* N   2 to] þe (*corrected from* to) N   3 by] the *add.* N le D
6 herte that] *om.* N   7 seruices] servyce J   10 the mouthe] thy mowth J
la bouche D   in the which] wher in NSJ   11 defaulte] of mete *add.* N
plenteously] plenvously N   deserte] deseruyng N   12 supposid] supposest
N   13 hast] hath J hath *canc.* hast S   19 said 1] in *add.* N on *add.* J
20 be] his N   24 vs] *om.* J   angre] hangyr N   28 of man] *om.* S
30 that she] *tr.* NSJ   31 straungely] straungly N strangly S strangely J
32 to haue] haue SJ   said] more *add.* J

Thanne the furst of this wom[e]n, aftir that she had cast hir feerfull
looke abowte hir to see that no straungier was ther nygh for to her
hir sayingis, she, with a lowe and a trymblyng voice, beganne to
speke suche wourdis as followe:

5   [Deffyaunce]

Iff mennes thoughtes war turned into a high voice and the
lamentable workis of the comon wele wer put in lamentacions, our
erys shuld be astonied and owr hartis abaschid to her the sorowfull
affliccions and the pituous pleintis of the good Frenchmen, for in
col. 2 townes and in the opyn wayes men shuld / her nothing ellis but
11   cryes, wepyngis and deepe sighes, which in this present tyme
murdirth and sleth [pryuely] mennes corages wheras thei be hid.
For now euery man perceyvith ther ruyne and ther comon dis-
enheritaunce and euery man holdith downe the hede abiding their
15   persecucion, like them that dwelle togedir in a howse that fallith
and canne fynde no meane to scape owte nor fynde the meane
hough it myght be kept vp so as thei myght dwelle therin.
Telle me, thou man which art dispurveyed of all helpe and
destitute of socoure, what meane canst thou fynde to haue a seurte
20   of thy sustinaunce or wher maist thou pitche thy tente seuirly?
If thou woldist do trewely for the comon wele, thy power is litill
and thi travaile shal be but in vayne, seyng that euery man racith
f. 39ᵛ   away his parte and makith his fardell for to goo his waye. / A, Lorde
God, who cowde haue supposid or demed that euir any man shulde
25   haue seene iustice thus put abak, which is the most pr[i]ncipall
piler of the comon wele? Now is it so vndirmyned that it hath but
fewe stayes to ber it vp, which be rotid with corruption suche wise
that [with] the powr comon wele they make the priue richesses.
Yet it myght happe that among all thy confusid thoughtes thow
30   woldist chese to lyve solitary life, and sodeinly [thi] spirites myght
be withdrawen to the occupacion of publique thingis as a thing
brought agayne to thyne olde custome. Thanne is this nothing ellis
but as a dreme wherof the dedis passe away in dremyng. But hopest
thou thus to scape away from the handis of fortune? Nay, for I

1 this women] NS thees women J this woman R   3 hir] om. J
8 astonied] astoned NSJ   10 the] om. NJ   12 thei] om. NSJ
13–14 disenheritaunce] disheritaunce NSJ   15 fallith] down add. N   16 scape]
escape N   22 racith] rateth J   24 euir any] euery N   28 comon]
people add. canc. R   33 a] om. N

woll that thou knowe that she entendith more to make thes cour-
tiers to feele mischieff / and mysery thanne othir for because thei col. 2
purchase largely the prosperites of fortune, and thou hast seen that
the lowest and penyble degre of perverce fortune is to haue ben
happy. 5
Whider shalte thou goo than or in what seure and agreable place
canst [þou] fynde to drawe thiself vnto? Thou wottist wele that in
citees is for the no good abyding seeng that thynne estate ys grettely
abatid or rebatid, which were nough right peynefull amonge the
riche citeȝeines the to suffre daungerouse indigence. And yet that 10
more is, thou canst nat lyve in them withowt feere, but at euery
crye or noyse thou shalt wene to be supprisid outhir by enemyes
or by the inconstaunce of the prive courages, wherof the dis-
purveyd comynges ben at this day right doubtfull. For in the feldis
men darre nat come withowt his harte shal be afrayed seeng that 15
force and the sworde reignen / by auctorite of violence and no man f. 40
dar be so hardy to gette his livelode in them for feere of his life.
The champaine cuntreis may be likenid to the see wherin euery
man hath as grette lordeship as he hath power to labour therin.
So thanne nowadayes the naturall lordis haue lasse power ouir 20
their livelode thanne the ravinours straungiers, of whome the londe
is sowen as it war full of langustes, whiche through their grette
companyes wasten the regions and makith them falle into deserte.
Wherfor I conclude, seenge the feldis may nat be enhabited, that
the citees through the prykke of hungre shuld be enfamyned. 25
Constreynt of hungre maketh the wolues renne owte of the woddis
forasmoche as necessite surmowntith nature and of veray force it
causith hym to renne owte from his rewlis and to forsake his law/is. col. 2
And if thou noote wele thes thingis foresayd it must nedis follow
that many diuerse inconuenientes nat able to be recouerid of very 30
force must nedis falle, lyke as in thi reason thou maist right wele
see by these premisses. Wherfor I wold avise the to flee owte of
this mystye tyme which (is) full of pestilence and duelle with a
straunge nacion. And this may be to the a reasonable counseile
accordyng to thensaumple of Anthenor and Eneas, which escapid 35

6 seure] suerte N   7 wottist] wost NSJ   9 abatid or] *om.* NSJ *see n.*
11 nat] no S   13 courages] courage J   wherof] wherfor N   16 by]
be J be *canc.* by S   17 so] *om.* NSJ   in] on N   21 their] the N
ravinours] ravenous NSJ *see n.*   25 shuld] shul SJ   26 renne] to
renne N of 2] *om.* N   28 to forsake] forsaketh NSJ   30 inconuenientes]
inconveniences N   32 by] *om.* N   33 with] NSJ within (in *ins.*) R

from the fyre of Troye and the sworde of the Grekes. Remembir
the also on Virgile, which by þe space of vij yere was putt owt and
banischid. Yet his eloquence may be to the expedient. Allas yet on
the othir party ther be so many anguisches which stoppe soo moche
5 thi passages that þou art ferde to take any passage vpon the for it
f. 40ᵛ is greuouse to be maynteined. Yet must / thou lyve in a straunge
nacion like wise as thou wer bo[r]ne to begynne a newe prentishode
both of maners and of life, sorowyng whenne thou remembrest on
thi naturall cuntre, which alweyes restith prentid in thi courage,
10 [and yet shal þou allway compleyn the ruyne of thi nacyon for the
straungers shal make of the a specta[c]le of mokkery, a man sus-
pecte], and as a man [þat] hath mysguydid himself and so chacid
away, forsaken in cites and in townes, and art ashamyd for the
destruccion of the londe, bering therfor a blame of which thow
15 maist nat do withall. And th(u)s thou shalt dwelle like an [esclaue]
in bondage and thy renowne shall lye in the daungier of straungiers.
What availith to holde oure peece and nat speke of this perille?
For what party that euir thou go, the infortune of the cuntre shall
pursewe the and abate thi good name and empeche thi seurte.
20   Anothir discomforte ther is which I may nat hide. For anguysch
col. 2 for[seen] is as it wer half passid. Wher/in must be reuercid all the
werkis of this present tyme to þe contrarye, which hath brought
you shortly to the myschief that causith you to flee, wherethrough
ye fall as a man that sette not by hymself or recrayed in the seruage
25 of your enemyes like as þe partriche which in fleing from the horse
necligently fallith into the tonelle. And suche as be nowe which be
willfull hastinese chesen to transporte themself vndir the power of
enemyes may wele be likened to Calcas, which, for the aunsweris
that he had in [Delphos in the] temple of Appolyn of the destruc-
30 cion of Troye, made him turne to the Grekis, to whom was likened
a Romayne named Acuron, which feerfully left the liberte of his
cite for to flee the fortune and power of Cesar. But the issew of
f. 41 their werkis damned their inconstaunce, for thei fonde / their deth

---

4 party] side N   6 thou] _om._ J   7 borne] NSJ bowne R ne D _see n._
9 alweyes restith] _tr._ NSJ   prentid] enprentyd NSJ   courage] mynde N
11 spectacle] SJ spectale N   15 thus] NJ thys S _2nd minim of u ins._ R
esclaue] NSJ estlauene R   16 the] _om._ N   18 cuntre] contrary N
pays D   19 empeche] emperch J   21 forseen] NSJ for sithin it R
preueuë D   25 partriche] partryke NSJ   29 he] she J   Delphos in the]
NSJ the Delphes in R   31 the] _om._ N   32 and] þe _add._ SJ   33 thei]
thy S

wher thei supposid to haue had their seurte and wente ther way
spotted with vntrouth to ther perdicion.

Now avise the wele whiche parte thou oughtest to chese or what
consolacion or redresse knowest thou hope to fynde in suche perplexite. For frendeship is withdrawen and euery man callith it to 5
hymself only, closid in his herte withowt departing. Thei that be
riche in themself ben powr to othir men. The helpe and conforte
wexith all dull. The witte failith me and my wourde also. And I see
nothing ellys but that God hath forsaken and forgoten Frenschmen.

O Creature which arte pardurable, O Sapience inestimable, 10
O Trinite estable, which arte of powere incomperable, so fulle
of bounte that no man can comprehend, and knowest all
thinge withowt any techinge, Thou maist yeve and take away
/ and Thou cowdest make with[oute] any ensample [takyng] col. 2
the hevynes in which no man can fynde defaulte. Thou 15
madest also the corruptible erthe, and by charitable and am-
yable love Thou formed man aftir Thyne owne semblaunce
and put in him [a] spirituall and a quike sowle ioyned to a litle
hepe of asches and woldest that oon shulde be with that othir
an putte in them the vertu of vndirstonding. Tho(u) gauest 20
him also wille and mynde to remembre on thingis passid. Thou
suffrest him also to be chaungable, his fortune to be variable
and his life myserable, also on euery parte lokyng whanne
warre shal be made vpon hym. And to resiste he is but feble
and tendir. So Thou suffirst him to be ouircome with sekenesse 25
and passions, which maketh his witte feble to vndirstonde the
resonable iugementes. But Thi myghty helpe, Thy veray true
science, Thi redoubtid iustice and the grace of Thy / socour f. 41ᵛ
may defende all. And he woll attende to The and nat to be
ouircome nor yolden, but mavgre fortune kepe himself from 30
mysdoing, his merite shal be moche the more alowable and
also more agreable to Thy pleasur.

[The Auctour]

And as my powre fantasie was thus tourmentid with diuers

5 it] *om.* J   9 forgoten] the *add.* SJ   10 O 1] Ryme *ins. on line above* S
pardurable] parduable S *2nd* r *ins.* J   11 estable] euer stable N   13 take]
and take *add.* R   14 any] *om.* J   17 Thou] he NSJ   Thyne]
his NSJ   18 a 2] *om.* J   19 that othir] the tothir NS toþer J
20 them] hym NJ   Thou gauest] he gaue NSJ   23 myserable] mesurable J
24 made] *om.* J   26 witte] more *add.* NSJ   28 the] the *add.* R   Thy]
the J   31 the] þer N

consideracions, I drowe to my mynde the wourdis of the prose
afore rehercid, debating in myself all the consideracions of the
same, wherein I founde nothing ellis but contrariousnes. Thus I
abode longe, supprised with vayne thoughtis and as a man affrayed
5 withowt ordir. Thanne forthwithall avaunced hirself the thridde
lady which apperid to me in manere of a visione, hiding hirself
behinde hir fellawes. And sodeinly she come towarde me and with
col. 2 an high voyce cryed, speky/ng to me vndir this fourme:

[Desesperaunce]

10   O thow foole which arte disseyvid through the vanite of this
shorte life and [take] thy plesaunce to lyve here in langoure and
in anguysch, I haue mervaile why thou arte pleasid with suche
thingis as turment the, for and thou woll nat leve it with thi good
will thou shalt forgo them magre thyn hede. What is thi lif worth
15 whanne thou canst gette nothing ellis but myserie, which growith
with thi yeris and enforceth itself ayeinst the seeng that thy power
waxith feble? Thyn age [falleth] now into declyne, and the vnhap-
pines of thy nacion doth but now begynne. What thinkest [þou] to
see for to lyve lenger? Nothing ellis but deth of frendis, rapyne of
20 goodis and wasting of feldis, citees distroyed, lordeshippis ouir-
f. 42 come, londis desolate and put vndir / seruage. What cowdist thou
lern by thi wysedom henseforward but onely to playne, to sighe
and to chaunge nurture vnto vnconyng and wourship vnto repref?
Thow Nestor, which aftir the stories lyvid to the noumbir of CCC
25 yeris and was partener of the grette prosperite of Grece, yet he
sorowid in his natur that he had endurid so longe as for to see so
oftintymes deth of his frendis and of his neyghbouris. Wherfor me
semith thou shuldist take litill hede to lyve seeng that thy cuntre
perischith afore thyn yghen and that fortune [allso] (takith) awey
30 the hoope and the solace of thi life. Thencke non othir that by thi
lyving in this mortall season thou shalt haue non other fruyte but
longe tyme to be vnhappy. And for to dey it wolde preserue the
from the feling a thousand tymes on a day suche thinges as in maner
is worse thanne the deth.
col. 2   O hough many [high] hertis of grette / men excercisid of worldly
36 infirmites which wilfully chesin to dey for eschewing to live in

1 my] *om.* J   8 spekyng] spekyd N   11 take] *om.* RNSJ prens D
12 thou arte] *tr.* N   17 falleth] NSJ waxith R tourne D   22 thi] the J
26 endurid] dured NSJ   33 on] vppon J

seruage. The vertuouse Caton killid hymself for eschewing the
tyranny of Cesar. Mitridate also—he that was Kyng of Pont—aftir
that he had ouircome many batailles, and many countrees made to
him tributarie, killed himself with a swourde whanne he failed to
fynde his deth by poison by the vsing of a medicyne which aftir- 5
warde was callid aftir his name; for it pleasid hym rathir to dye
with his own hande by homicide thanne Pharnates, his sone, which
conspired his deth, shulde reioyse himself to haue soiled his handis
in the blode of his fadir by vnkyndly natur. Haniball also, which
gretly rebatid the glorye of the Romayns that aforetyme helde the 10
monarchie of the worlde, through his grette / manhode, [thei] war f. 42ᵛ
fayne to kepe themself within the bowndis of their wallis. But aftir
that his fortune was tournid to infelicite, he bar in his ryng venyme,
and whanne he was in distresse of his lyfe, he bar on honde he was
slayne by venyme to thentent that the Romayns shulde nat take a 15
glorye for the kyllyng of so grette a duke. Iugu[rt]he also, which
by force and subtilte rewlid the grette lordeship of Affrike, whanne
he was in the prisons of Rome avaunced himself to abreggein the
sorowfull tyme of hys captiuite. Nero also tourned the swourde
towarde hymself to theffusion of his propir bloode and to thentent 20
þat the swourdis of Virginyus and of Galba, which pursued him
to the deth, shulde haue no power to slee him. Yet in a more freele
natur thou shalt fynde exsaumples of women [þat], for to abregge
their deþe, / haue founde remedies ayeinst their sorowfull life, like col. 2
as did Lucresse for the shame that (s)he had whanne hir chastite 25
was brokyn. Dido also was sorowfully constraynid for to lose hir
plesaunce, and the wif of Kyng Syphace chase rathir to deye in
liberte thanne to live [vndre the Romans] in seruage. Wherfor
thanne wolt thou watche in this sorowfull mischief and live wissh-
yng thy dethe? Euery day the chiualry of thi cuntre is perischid and 30
deyen; the studiauntes ben distroyed; and the clergie is disparpulid,
oppressed and as a thing voyde; and the moderate rule and honeste
of the churche turnith as the tyme is turnid, that is to say,
in disordinaunce, nycete and wantonnes. The citeȝeines ben

2 he] *om.* NSJ   5 by 2] thurgh NSJ   11 through] for N   thei] N
om. RSJ   14 honde] þat *add.* NSJ   16 kyllyng] sleyng N   Iugurthe]
N Iuguche RSJ   17 grette] *om.* NSJ   18 abreggein] abregge in RSJ
a brygge in N   20 to 2] for NSJ   22 the] *om.* J   24 haue] *om.* N
25 she] NJ s *ins. on line* R he S   27 and] to be *add.* N   Syphace]
Cyphax N   29 thou] wylt þou *add.* J   30 thy] after N   31 disparpulid]
dyspapulid and (and *canc.*) J disparpulyd and N   32 a] *om.* NSJ

dispourveid of all maner hope, and the knowin of lordeship is
made derke through the derke clowdis of this myshevouse fortune.
f. 43 Ordre is tourned to confusion and the lawe / is turnid into vnmesurable violence. Lordship and wourship fallith; obeisaunce noyeth;
5 pacience la[kk]eth. So all fallith and synkith into the derknes of
ruyne and desolacion. Curcid be that remembrance which sterith
the to haue will to reserue thi life seenge that thou fallest amo[n]ge
so many tempestes and myserable abhominacions, for the pryme-
temps of thi best and ioyfull dayes is past, and whanne yowthe
10 faylith thanne begynnyth angre and syghing thoughtis. Wherfor it
is bettir that thou lette go a litill space of thy short age thanne
whanne thou arte olde fall into pouerte; for ther is no mysery more
sharpe [nor] a more inpaciente seekenes thanne a man to suffur age
and pouerte bothe at ones, for pouerte may nat norisch age and age
15 may nat endure pouerte. Wherfor I avise the to breke the lyeine
col. 2 of thy lif which kepith / the in [þis] bittir thralldom and deliuir the
shortly from thes infinite myschevis by oon mischief, through
which at one tyme thou maist escape the grette daungiers of fortune, and forgette all thyng forasmoche as that erly or late þou
20 must nedis dey.
    O Lorde God, hough may it be þat man woll do so moche
amysse and by errour mysmake the noble lawe of natur, which
takith so grette heede for enduryng of the same, that for his
worldely dedis, which allway hath for to make newe, now woll
25 he vndo himself by dethe and discomfiture, by iniury or by
faulte of enduringe? Whi brekith he the iointur of so noble a
creatur which God made aftir His figur aftir the ensaumple of the
Trinite oonly to plese him, and with his witte medelid mesur?
f. 43ᵛ Allas that man gothe for owte of / natur that through filth puttith
30 his soule in aventur seeng that falce fortune may cause his body
to be disfigurid. That is to say, as whanne a man procurith
murmur ayenst God and his sainctis, which causith a man to
forgette charite and drawe himself from the glorie that is alway
dueringe, and falcely [is] forsworn and gretly forfettith ayeinst
35 the creme of his bapteme.

3 into] vnto J   3–4 vnmesurable] vniuersall N desmesuree D   5 lakketh]
SJ laweth RN fault D   7 amonge] NSJ amomge R   13 nor] NSJ thanne
R ne D   14 norisch] suffre J   15 the 2] thy N   23 takith] take N
26 iointur] ionctoure NSJ   a] om. N   27 figur] and add. N   31 as]
þat N   33 forgette] foryuge SJ foriurer D   35 creme] sacrement N
cresme D

[The Auctour]

Through the haynous, hiduous and sharpe wourdis these thre
seducyous and dissaiveable ladies had blyndid and turned vp so
downe my reason in suche wise that almoste I was brought to the
mate of a dedlye frenesye, having my life in suche an hate that I 5
wischid to have be dedde. Seyng that, feble Natur, which was
abatid by malencolye and sorowe, beganne to tremble (and) quake
ayeinst the horrible feere of dethe / as she that myght nat suffre ne col. 2
here the violence and the destruccion of hi[r] corage and of hi[r]
werkis but alwayes made redy and susteyned vttirly with hi[r] 10
power that [that] seeke fortune with hir lamentable contraryousnes
hath fordoone, for to make vs endure our litill rightfull peryode.
With that she enforcid hirself so gretly that all hir veynes, senewis
and musculles [moved], that through hir shaking and betinge she
awooke Vndirstondinge, which lay sleping by me, and put so 15
strongly vpon hym that sodanly he vpsterte, his yghen but half
opyn, and with tremblyng wourdis he ganne to speke as aftir
followith:

[Vndrestondynge]

O very God, what dremyng fantasies hath in suche wise ouir- 20
come me that I haue thus forgotin myself and lefte the coundite of
the, man, which our Lorde hathe put into my kepynge? /

[The Auctoure]   f. 44

Upon thes wourdis, turnyng his yghen toward þe derke corner
of my bedde, he sawe the thre infernall massengeris which [had] 25
spoken with me byfore. Thanne he drowe nere, cryinge on this
wise:

[Vndrestondynge]

O man, what thynkeste thou? Turne towarde me and avise right
wele in what daunger thou fallest and prey Allmyghty God to be 30
þy keper from all evyle thoughtis and from temptacion of the

2 haynous] *om.* NSJ   5 a] *om.* N   dedlye frenesye] *tr.* N   7 malen-
colye] merencolye SJ   sorowe] I *add.* N   8 the] the *add.* R   9 hir]
his RNSJ *see n.*   hir] his RNSJ   10 hir] his RNSJ   12 litill] *om.*
NSJD   13 veynes] hir *add.* NSJ   14 musculles] *om.* N   moved] *om.*
RNSJ esmeut D   15 sleping by] slombryng besyde NSJ   16 vpsterte]
styrt vp N stert vp SJ   17 opyn] vppyn J   he] she NSJ   20 dremyng]
drenynge SJ   26 on] in NSJ   28 Vndrestondynge] NJ *om.* R feyth
add. above S

devile, and looke thou suffre nat thiself to be ouircom by thes thre
cursed enchaunteresses, for the more that God hath sent the of
vndirstondinge, the more shalt thou be punyschid if thou wolt
sewe their oppynions. For and þou take good heede thou maist
5 clerely vndirstonde that the names of those ladies be of wondirfu[l]
col. 2 condicion, for the furst of them is callid Indig/nacion, the second
is callid Diffidence, and the thredde is callid Dispeyre of thingis for
to come. They war made and norishid in the derkenes of helle;
they be enemyes to the peace of concience and aduersaries to the
10 saluacion of mannes sowle.

[The Auctour]

Thes wourdis he beganne me sodanly [yn] to trouble, but I, as
a man hevy with ouirmoche slepe and owte of apetite through the
bittirnesse of poysons of Malencolye, and I, that aftir all this
15 trouble in my mynde as a man soore in manere noyed and loste,
cowde nat inprynte his wourdis in my thought, nor by their
semblaunce thei cowde nat wele be brought vnto my remembraunce, for my visage was turned and my fantasie fermely sette
towarde thes three monstres vnto the tyme Vndirstondinge drowgh
f. 44ᵛ himself towarde þe / parties of my mynde, and with a grette might
21 for to shewe me a clerenesse of light he openid a litill wiket of
which the boltis war waxen rousty with foryetfullnesse, through
which entird evin forthwith thre ladyes. And þe oon of them was
right curteis and wele-countenauncid, which hadd long tyme musid
25 how she myght haue entird in at that wiket, but their was no man
to opyn it. Yet Vndirstonding, which opynned the wiket of my
mynde, knewe them nat at their comyng in. For yet at that tyme
his yghen war swollen as a prisoner that comith owte of a derke
prisonne and sodeinly brought into a cler son. And through thentre
30 of these ladyes the place was made clere with light, but the yghen
of seeke Vndirstondyng war repressid, for the [li]till vertue of
col. 2 feblid sight, which was hurte through / the derkenesse of errour,
might nat susteyne to endur so grette a light. And therfor Vndirstonding kest downe his looke towarde my bedde and towarde the
35 litle corner whereas stoode the thre damnable lyars, suche wise that

1 ouircom] ouer (*end of leaf*) J   5 wondirful] NSJ wondirfur R   6 con-
dicion] condycions J   12 beganne] to *add. ins.* N   14 of poysons] *om.*
N des poisons D   17 wele be] *tr.* N   19 tyme] þat *add.* NSJ
21 wiket] wyked J   25 in] *om.* NSJ   29 thentre] the entres N *sing.* D

he cowde nat turne himself towarde the ladyes nor them receve and welcome as it apperteyned to the keper of a seeke bodye, but alweyes abode in a shamefastenesse-mysknowliche vnto the tyme the furste of these thre ladies by [hir] swete wourdis made him bolde. And she with hir humble auctorite and most auctorised 5 symplenesse this wise beganne hir sentence:

[Feythe]

O thou resonable Vndirstonding, ymage of the Trinall vnyte, clere, shyning, comyng owte of the Springe of life, the bryght beeme going owt from / the fulfilling light of the soueraigne Sunne f. 45 of which noone may flee the hete, beshynyng the body of man 11 forasmuch as it enlumynith the derknesse of dedly men, thou arte create by the soueraigne Werkman which may nat faile, of whome the prouidence watchith euirlastingly ouir His creatures, and His fair hevinnes turnith the influence and shewith withowt seacyng 15 the clerenes of light aboute the erthe. Now thou arte ioynned to man for to governe [the] Party Vegetatyve by dwe ordir and the apetite sensitif by royall lordeship. And the poletike Nature, that God hath yevin the to helpe, is nat ydill in his commission, but by the fair vertues that [he] shewith euery man in his ordir shulde to 20 continewe mankynde in studye and to conserue the indiuiduale suppositif. For the Power Vegetatif restith neuir, with hir dough- tirs, Nutrityve, Formatyve, Assimylatyve and / Vnitive, which be col. 2 continually werking in their forges in which bellowes blowen by [the] spirituall membris of life, of moeving and of knowlage in 25 reparing the hurte of the radicall humour whereof parte consumith and wastith at euery moment. And thou that arte most perfecte of all creatures, and now hast left thy werke all brokyn and thine office withowt excercice as voide, and by necligence let fall the perdurable sowle into perille, which is moche the losse where[of] gretter thanne 30 of the mortall body. And knowest nat thou that the high Maister of werkis, whose prouidence makith nothing in vayne, which hath

2 a seeke] *tr.* S   3 a] *om.* N vne D   tyme] þat *add.* NSJ   4 hir] NSJ their R   6 symplenesse] symplesse SJ   9 shyning] *?* browgh *ins.* *above* S *see n.*   10 owt] aute N   12 enlumynith] enlymyneth SJ   arte] were NSJ   14 euirlastingly] euerylastyngly N   15 hevinnes] *om.* J 21 indiuiduale] indyvyde N   22 Vegetatif] vegetavyue N   neuir] *om.* N 28 brokyn] to broken NSJ   29 the] þi J   30 whereof] where is RNSJ *see n.*   32 which] he *add.* N

putte the in mannys body to excercise the and to do[mp]te sensuall
appetite and by discipline bring it ageyne to reason? And if the
passiones of man stonde ayeinst it, so moche is the victorie more
f. 45ᵛ gloriouse and thi me/rite more preciose, for thexcellence of vertu
5 is peysid aftir the difficulte of his werke and suche thingis as be
withowt peyne and daungiere owght nat to be rewardid nor haue
thanke therfor. The preif of this was yevin to the by [the werke and
doctryne of] my disciple Seint Pawle, which was the herawlde and
publischer of my comaundementis an taught the also that in seeke-
10 nesse and perill is the perfeccion of vertu, for (in) seekenesse toke
he his delite and his glorie for the consequence of the rewarde by
the seurte of the divyne grace, which failith neuir to traveling men
at their nede. For He that made the made the nat for thentente that
thou shuldist be perischid, but for to helpe the and to redresse thy
15 freelte through the myght of His grace, which thou maist neuir
col. 2 deserue but onely by travaile and meritoryous werkis. He ope/ned
by His spirituall power the yate through the which opyn the
fleschly worlde may entre into the blissid life, which yate is litle and
streighte. And who that woll come in that yate muste stowpe,
20 humble hymself and bowe his membris in mysease and anguysche.
But the yate through which men passe into perdicion is large and
opyn and men may lightly entre in by a double yate, of which the
one yate is working of synne and þe othir omission of good dedis.
Why suffirst thou thanne thi knowing to be blynded in þe clowde
25 of thi mortale body through the humayne passions and to fall with
the hevy weight of carnalite, which is cast downe through the
hurtelingis of fortune, whereas thou shuldist loke vpe, arise and
drawe ageyn thauncient masse of thi humayne body, inclinid to
vice and infelicite by pride and synne, renewid in purified spirite
f. 46 and parti/cyp[a]cy[o]ne of grace? Wherfor do thi devir and lete nat
31 that body which is bounde to the worlde drawe the with hym to
pardicion. But loke thou make watche and harken vpon the keping
of thiself, for in tyme of tribulacion the fruites of merite wake

1 the 1] *om.* N te D   dompte] doubte RNSJ dompter D *see n.*   6 nor]
no J   haue] no *add.* NSJ   7 to] *om.* NSJ   10 and] in *add.* NSJ en D
11 the 2] hys J du D   13 thentente] þat ententt J   16 meritoryous]
merytory NSJ   17 the which opyn] which NSJ   19 in] at *add.* NSJ
20 humble hymself] humbley and meke hymself N humilier D   23 þe othir]
the tothir is NS þat oþer is J   27 arise] and ryse N & ressourdre D *see n.*
30 particypacyone] N particypcyune R partycypcyun S partypcyun J   31 the
2] *om.* J te D   to 2] vnto NSJ   33 merite] mercye J mercy *canc.* meryte
N merite D

ageyne, through which the tresurs of glorie be made opyn to them that lyve in travaile, and thei that be chargid with good dedis shall come to the yates of grace.

[The Auctoure]

Undirstondinge with good entent harkened thes wourdis, that be 5 right grette and high techingis, wherby he knewe veryly þat thei came from the skole of the Maister that made them, for euery thing turnith lightly to his principle and holdith by naturall inclinacion the point of thende suche wise as the Creatour hath ordeynid them. [Than] the confusid and / shamefast of his defaulte humbled hym- col. 2 self redy to receyve correccion and doctrine, and as he was thus 11 ashamed callid to himself ageyne all his mighty officers which were disperpulid and troublid with worldly desirs. And forthwithall he suspend þe commyssion of thre sistirs, of which the oon is callid Demonstratyue or serteyne, the othir Dialetique, dowtfull, and the 15 thryd Sophistique, dissaiveable, and put them holy vndir the obeisaunce and fredom of the divine Feith.

Thanne this lady sawe that he was sumwhat withdrawe from his contrariousnesse and humbled hymself to hir swete wourdis. Thanne she confortid hym through the assuraunce of þe divine 20 mekenesse, which at no tyme closith hir lappe from them that woll at any tyme returne to hir. And as she leyd hir honde vpon the yghen of Vndirstondinge, / his sight beganne to wax clere so that, f. 46ᵛ through the vertu of hir and through the divine tokenes and hevenly ornamentis that she ware vpon hir, he knewe visibely that it was 25 Feithe. And the furst token that she bar was an olde booke of which the coueryng was of a derke colour, portrayed with diuerse signes and figurys ceryously entremedled; and this she bar close and folden vndir hir arme. And this was the Penta[t]heuke of Moyses, which was the figure and the shadowe of the feithe, of which the 30 light shynith eternally in the divine predestinacion from the begyn-yng of the worlde. The secunde token was anothir booke with sevin

---

5–6 wourdis . . . right] om. NSJD   6 veryly] right wele NSJ
12 officers] J omits from here to p. 27, l. 30 simplenesse   13 troublid] trembled N
see n.   14 thre] their N trois D   which the] tr. N   15 Demonstratyue]
Demonstravyue N   or serteyne] ins. above as gloss S om. ND see n.   dowt-
full] ins. above as gloss NS   16 dissaiveable] ins. above as gloss NS   21 them]
hym N   woll] wyl S while N   22 leyd] hir sonne vppon add. N om. D
25 hir] om. NS   26–7 of which the] the which N   28 close and] om. N
clos & D   29 Pentatheuke] NS Pentacheuke R   30 of 2] the add. N

claspis of yren, but it was writyn with the blode of a Lambe
withowt spotte, which was wourthy to opyn this booke through
the vertue of His passion, which she helde in the tohthir hande /
col. 2 opyn so that a man myght clerely rede therin the alliauneces and
5 the reconsiliacions of God to man and the degre of the wasching
away of synne with the promisse of helth and glorye. The thrid
token was a crowne of golde with xij rich flouris sette by ordir aftir
their digniteis, of which som wer so high that (þei persyd) the
hevins; othir ther wer that war meane, and the remanaunte wer
10 lower thanne the othir, like as the divine ordinaunce hath sette
euerych in diuerse degreis, lyke also as the avision of the laddir
which apperid to Iacob was sometyme figurid, of the which some
of the raungis passid þe hevenys, some touchid the erthe and some
meeve bitwene bothe. And these betokene the xii articles of the
15 feithe. The furst of thes forsaid percid the hevenis vnto the contemplacion of the divinite and of the trynall distinccion of persones
f. 47 in the vnyon of oon beyng. The / othir restin in the mydde waye
touching the merveillous misteries of the incarnacion, of þe passion,
of the resurreccion and thascension, which touchithe [next] to our
20 humanite and shewith vs the mortifieng of synne by the viuificacion
that man receivid whanne he was ioyned to the Godhede and to the
lif of grace through the dethe that God suffird in divine vnite with
mannys natur. But the last of the thre is shewid oonely to the
perfeccion of mannys life through the infusion of the Holy Goste
25 by gyfftis of grace and by the addressinge of our werkis to helthe
and to glorie in the power and merytes of holy chirche, foundid
vpon the feith of the holy apostils at suche tyme as the two keyes
of hevyn war yevin to Seint Petir. That oone keye was the key of
discrecion for to discerne the vnworthy from the wourthy, and
30 the othir was the key of iurisdiccion for to absolue and bynde as
col. 2 Goddis vicarye by divine / e[x]cercise in erthe, approued bothe in
hevine.

1 claspis] clapses S clapses *canc.* claspes N   was] was *add.* R   4 alliau-
neces] allyaunce N *pl.* D   5 degre] *see n.*   8–9 persyd the hevins] per-
ceyved not the highnes N tresperçoient les cieulx D   9 war] wher so (so
canc.) N   10 sette] hem *add.* NS   12 Iacob] which *add.* N   12–13 of
. . . raungis] to the xij articles of the feith of the which ladder the rowndys som of
them N   13 raungis] rungys S   hevenys] and *add.* N *om.* D   13–15 and
. . . feithe] *om.* N   14 betokene] ben S sont D   20 viuificacion] vivifacion
(*written over* visitacion) N   27 the two] ij N   28 That] The NS   30 absolue]
assoyle NS absouldre D   31 excercise] NS ercercise R

Thanne Vndirstonding was grettely confortid of his sorowe whanne he vndirstoode by so clere tokyns þat which he had so ofttymes lerned of holy chirche, which he had seruid and wourschippid in his secrette meditacions, and abode to be enlumyned by hir and to be cast owte of the dowbtis which prickid hym and to be alightid of the grette charge through which the mortall body was diffoulid with opyn and prive tribulacions. Thanne Feithe beganne to reioyse in spirite whanne she vndirstoode the conforte of this newe merite.

[Vndrestondynge]

O thow high vertue divine, vndir whome studie, witte and doctrine be enclined to vndirstonde the highly; O light which enlumyneste whanne reason failithe and vnwourthy op/pinion for to yeve helpe to mannys vndirstondinge and putte hym owte fro the combraunce of the flesche, which troublith his iugement by his inperfection and settith his entent in argumentis full of decepcion. But thi grette perfictnesse surmowntith the opinion and yeuith a firme helpe wheras the herte is determyned in God, which examinith all thingis, of whome comith all conynge, as the sprynge, the foundamente, the roote, and the stronge medicyn which purgith the spirite by divine powere and yeuith hym a high power ouir his propir felinge withowte taking of any othir foundament, silogisme nor argument, but oonly by the plaace of auctorite which lieth nat, in whom we tristen all; for withowt th[e] we canne have no lawe, religion nor deuocion to God. But we beleve withowt seyng vnto the fruycione of His benigne mageste by thi provisioune. /

f. 47ᵛ

[The Auctour]

col. 2

[By this modulacion or song Vndrestondynge remembrid the high laudes of Dame Feyth, beseching hir of help ayenst the assawtes of Dyffydence, of Yndignacion and of Despeyre. Feith, on the tothir side, list to serch oute the causes whi mannys vndrestondyng was lette, and vppon the infirmyte of a seeke [body] she asked certeyne demaundes.]

17 the] all N *om.* SD   20 sprynge] is *add.* N *om.* D   foundamente] to *add.* N *om.* D   23 nor] or N   24 whom] whan N   tristen] trusten N   25 the] tho RS *unclear* N toy D   27 provisioune] prewysyn NS
33 body] S *om.* N corps D

[Feythe]

O thou Vndirstondinge, figure or patron of the Trinite, which
by the three powers, that is to say, knowinge, will and mynde,
ooned in the substaunce of a sowle, whom by the creatures in this
5 visible worlde thou knowist as by refleccion in a derke mirrour, as
feithe enlumynith her the invisible werkis of God which aftir the
glorificacion shal be seene face to face, hast nat þou mynde of the
othe thou madist me whanne thou receyuedist the holy bapteme,
where thou forsokest all pompes and decepcions of the enemy and
10 of the flesche and dedicatist and consecrat oonly thiself to the
seruice of God?

[Vndyrstondynge]

Yes, lady.

[Feythe]

15 Dost thou beleue that my vertu may ouircome all temptacions
f. 48 and conquer all world/ly passions and to escape þe tormentis, the
grette peynes and temporall affliccions, and that withowt me it wer
vnpossible to get the grace of God?

[Vndyrstondynge]

20 [Ye], I beleue this saue I wolde be more perfectely enformed by
the how the to(r)mentis and passions myght be ouircome, for here-
vpon lieth the weight of my charge vndir which my powr power
is feblischid. Wherfor I haue nede of helpe and supporte in this
behalue grettely.

25 ## [Feythe]

I woll schewe the by exsaumple of thingis don in dede, which
is of gretter preeffe thanne by dissaiuable argument. And furst of
Abrahaum, which was iustified by me. He was so stedfast in his
beleue that he submittid the piete of natur to the obeisaunce of the
30 feithe whanne he wolde haue sacrificed his son for to obey that God
col. 2 that he beleuid on. And so natur was / ouircome in ouircomyng of
his affeccions through humilite of the feithe. And so she was wil-

---

7 nat þou] *tr.* N   8 othe] þat *add.* NS   15 temptacions] tenptacion N
17 grette] *om.* NSD   and 1] the *add.* NS   18 vnpossible] ympossible NS
20 Ye I] S   I R   Y N *see n.*   21 and] the *add.* NS   24 grettely] *om.* NS
31 that] on whom *add.* NS   beleuid] leuyd N   on] *om.* NS

fully constreyned to that which by hir wille wolde be constrayned. Noe also, warned byfore of God by amonicion and garnischid with seurte of the feithe, gatt suche grace of our Lorde that he vndirstode the fury of God and of the floode, wherevpon he lette purvey the arche for his saluacion. So whanne he wndirstoode this perill, 5 through his trewe feithe it was eschewed. Also the people of Israel through their true feithe passid drye through the Reede See, which for lacke of the feithe drowned the Egipcians. Wherefor lette vs come to the tyme of grace and vndirstonde the reuelacion of the divine secrees which wer somtyme hidde and couerid vndir the 10 cerimonies of the Olde Testament. And if we devoutely thincke thereuppon ther is nat so harde ne mysbeleuing an harte but it / ought to be rauischid through the wondirfull and merveillous f. 48ᵛ misteries of the Cristen feithe, through which the mekenesse of precheours hath ouircome the mageste of kingis; likewise the 15 symple ydiotes haue confounded the subtil(i)te of philosophirs; also þe tendir virgines and freele seruauntes haue ouircome the felony of tyrauntes; and so the wisedom of the world is turned to dispreysable folye. Also our Lorde made by my hande an cheef through which natur hathe lost his ordir and mannys estimacione 20 yelde himself confusid, whanne she sawe that my power was coundited by inpotente humylite and my witte by humble and symple ignoraunce. And thanne was the vayne life of the worlde putt vndir and the feblenesse of them that livid in mekenesse was strengthid in vertuys, for the martirs ouircome their persecutours 25 whanne thei suffird dethe, and / through dethe men haue fonde col. 2 thentre of perdurable life and triumphe vpon the mysbeleuyng men. Nero, Dioclisian, Domycian and Maximian, which helde the huge monarchies of the worlde, enforcid themself to put away the name of Cristendome by force of dethe, and through simplenesse 30 and humilite the feithe was enhauncid; for their swourdis shedde thinnocent blode of martirs through which was tempird the morter of þe high belding of holy chirche. Now by the tyrauntis dede and their renowne turnid to shame in this worlde and also damned perdurablely. But the seinctis lyvith in hevyne in eternite with 35 grette lawde and deuocion. And in erthe [the] meke men haue

12 ne] so *add.* NS   19 dispreysable] desperable N desprisable D   an
cheef] and chef N   20 hathe] *om.* NS   25 strengthid] strenkyth N
26 suffird] suffre N   29 huge] *om.* NSD   30 simplenesse] J *resumes here*
31 feithe] it *add.* NSJ

disfacid the prowde men, and suche persons as war put abacke and
kept vndir be now arraysid into the high troones from whens the
prowde men be fall. Thempir of Roome, which by force of armes
f. 49   made somtyme the vniuersall / worlde to tremble, now is it brought
5   lowe by simple preching vndir foote. Wher is become also the riche
paleys of þe cursid Emperour Nero? Forsothe there stondith now
the devoute chirche of the curteys and meke prechour Sainte Petir.
Lo thanne me semith that þes proves ought suffice inough to the
to knowe my vertue and to trust in my victorie, which may ouir-
10   come all mannys passions and resiste ayeinst all these myschevous
tempestes of the worlde.

[Vndyrstondynge]

O thou charitable lady and excellent mastresse, which surmown-
test the naturall comprehencion of my thought through thyn high
15   techingis, thi miraculouse exaumples and crafty workingis, forasmoche as mannys witte folowith nature in his werkis, but the divine
col. 2   arte, of which thou arte instrument, / passith ferr the othir inas-
moche as thou kepest it subiect and chaungest his rewlis and his
lawes by spirituall power, which passith the bowndis of his commis-
20   sion. Wherfor I feele wele that our naturall witte in þe power that
is lymytid to natur may nat touche so highe and infinite bounte in
lasse that it be by a vertue above natur longing to the highe power
divine. Wherfor, lady, haue compassion and pite of my infirmite
and take hede of the inportunite of this feble body, which holdith
25   me in maner as I wer faste in sto(k)kis so that I may nat come to
perfect knowlage, but drawith me to inperfeccione. O lady, excuse
me to Almighty God, which hath sent me suche a fellawship; also
and if it pleasith the put awaye a doubte which is to me right hevy
and answer to this question. Syn it is so that thy vertue is so grette
f. 49ᵛ   that by veray feithe is put away all / contrarye affeccions, all tribula-
31   cions and all hasty anguschis, why woll God thanne in such a
Cristen realme, in which thi name is susteyned and thi power
exaltid, suffre to reigne so grette persecucion and myserabill
adue(r)site?

2 now] newe J   4 is it] *tr.* N   5 lowe] and *add.* NSJ   also] *om.* N
15 thi] by J   20 witte] is *add.* N *om.* D   22 that] than NSJ   highe]
om. N haulte D   23 of] on NSJ   25 to] þe *add.* N *om.* D   27 me
1] *om.* N moy D   28 and] *om.* N   pleasith] please NSJ   put] to put N
a] *om.* N vn D

[Feythe]

Bi thi question vpon a compleinte I haue vndirstonde the wounde
of thi sorow, for thou wottist neuir whi thassemble was made
bitwene the perdurable sowle and the mortall body, but woldest of
right chalence that the body shulde euir abyde in seurte. Nay not 5
so, for the body is but an herberow of thy pilgrymage and is yevin
to execute thi vertue and to preve th[i] constaunce. A crowne ought
not to be yevin but to hym that is victorious; so thanne no man
may haue victorye in lasse thanne he haue an enemye. And therfor
the / repugnaunce is avauncement to thi merite and the noyaunce col. 2
therof is the doublynge of thin hyre. The body desirith to haue 11
reste in the worlde, and hit was ordeinyd for to labour. It sechith
the delytes and the eases, and the kyngdom of hevene wolde be
goten by force, by violence of peyne and of affliccions. It drawith
the through his grette peyse vnto the deepe derkenesse of helle, and 15
yette thou maist by prikkyng areise it above the hevenys and
accompanye it (to) the glorye of finall resurreccion, like as it hath
accompanyed the in the peynes of this life. Thanne put away now
thy folisch presumpcion and vayne compleynte, and I woll retourne
to thi question fermed in thy mynde by devoute consideracion that 20
He which made all withowt any nede of helpe and withowte any
request of any [othyr] manys cowncell, but only for to shewe the
largesse of His bo/unte, to the helpe and gouernaunce of (all) f. 50
vniuersall realmes and also of parsones, which by His prouidens
adressid all thingis to thende for thentent that He made them for, 25
in lasse thanne their disordinaunce breke it and putte it owte of
ordir. For I woll thou knowe that He neuir compassid this crafty
worlde in His eternall thought ne formed it nat so ordinatly in
noumbir, peyce and mesur by so iuste proporcion that nothing can
be amendid in the workemanschip therof, and aftirwarde sette it at 30
nought as a thing lefte withowt gouernaunce or patron. Nay forsothe, He entendid neuir so to do, but in the euirlasting throne of
His eternyte hath an ententif regarde vpon þe mutacion of temporall lordeshippis and chaungith their fortunes, ther tymes and

---

2 thi] the N ta D   4 woldest] þou *add.* N   5 chalence] chalenge NSJ
6 but] not but N   7 thi] NSJ the R ta D   10 noyaunce] noye/ J
12 for] *om.* J   13 and the eases] *om.* J & aises D   14 of 2] by NSJ *see n.*
22 any] *om.* NSJ *see n.*   othyr] SJ *om.* RN   autruy D   but] both N
26 thanne] þat N   31 a] *om.* N   32 the] *om.* N du D   throne]
thorne J

their placis by diuerse habitacions and many small pathwayes
col. 2 subtilly entermedlid, which drawen to the grette high/way of the
souereigne god and to the loving of the Creatour lymited by His
euirlasting abidynge, which mayntenith their mutacions and diuer-
5 sitees and also theire moevingis, and to diuerse estatis shewith the
magnificence of His glorye. Who may thanne vndirmyne that
Workeman whom neuir man taught? Or how may a man repreve
theffecte that cannat vndirstonde the preef nor þe cause? What
hast thou yevin to God for thi creacion or wherin maist thou repreve
10 Hym though He chaunge in the suche as He hath made withowt
the? The potter makith of a lumpe of erthe diuerse pottis, som to
serue for clennesse and som for filthe; yette whenne hym listith he
brekith them if thei be nat made aftir his plesaunce; and no man
of right may aske whi he doth so. Is it conuenient that the axe shall
f. 50ᵛ rise ayeinst the carpenter or / the hamour to rebell ageinste the
16 smyth and followe his own appetite rathir thanne the profigtht of the
werke? Kingis be instrumentis of the divine ordinaunce, and thou
wolt mak reasons for them ayeinst Hym that made reason and Causer
of the cause of all causes. Seeke wele in thi feble papir and examyn
20 the compte of their offices where the diffaulte is, and seeke not the
diffaulte in the perfite bounte where no faute may be. Nor aske
non accompte of the Maistir vnto the tyme that compte must be
made, but suppose that His science is infallible, His providence
inevitable and His wille rightwisenesse. Thanne shulde thy powr
25 capacite be as a thing not vndirstonding for to get the estimacion
of His infinyte power nor thi sight might nat suffice to susteyne nor
to see the clernesse of suche a light.
col. 2   O thou soueraigne Sapience depper thanne þe / erthe and more
high thanne the hevenes, which mesuredest the tyme and assigned
30 to euerything his bowndes, where is he that woll put hym in preefe
of Thi iugementis or who can see byfore what shall fall of Thin
entencions? Thanne thou creature that wolte serche so ferr byfore,
go vp to the firmament and descende agayne downe into the deepe
derknesse, call to the agayn the thingis passid and avaunce the
35 thingis that be to come. Discouir also the myxtion of destenyes;
embrace thordir of the causis, the noumbre of theffectis, the mesure

2 to the] drawen to the *add.* (drawen to *canc.*) N   3 god] goode S   to]
om. N en D   6 vndirmyne] vndyrnyme S   7 Or] O N   9 hast
thou] *tr.* N   17 be] the *add.* NSJ   21 diffaulte] fawte NSJ   23 His
1] this N sa D   25 a] *om.* N   29 mesuredest] mensuredyst J

of tyme to the conclusions of their endis; and [then] dispute ayeinst
the Maker which hath their ordinaunce regestird in the booke of
His secretes. Yet it is bettir to the to withdrawe thi dissaiveable
subtilte and knowe thiselfe thanne for to travaile in vayne, as for
to laave the deepenesse of the see, to mesur the hevenes and to 5
stryue with / Him which noumbrith the sterres. Allas with grette f. 51
peyne knowist thou thin owne dedis for to governe but oon erthely
body, which is in comparison [but] a litell worme of þe erthe.
Wherfor lette God aloon with the state of realmes and with the
transmutacion of powers, for ther is no realme but His that is 10
permanent and stable.

Who that sechith wele through knowlege the ordinaunce of
iugementis, the alliaunce, the duryng, the constaunce and the
abundaunce of (þe) high purveyaunce wherof all goodnes is
drawen owte ought sette no doubte vpon the divine substaunce, 15
for he avauncith hymself to ferre by presumptuous trust which
puttith hymself in so grette an ouirpride, and ought to be blamed.
But God hath sette His markis in the circute of hevenes by /
meruelouse diuising and grette maistrye, (and) (v)ndir that col. 2
therthe comprisid for to schewe the ensaumple of submission, 20
and will that it suffice vs to looke vpon the firmament, which
shynith bright, and there we shall see a proef of the infinite
powere.

[Vndyrstondynge]

God diffende that I shulde doubte in His power, for His rewardis 25
and His punycions be doon to the creatures afftir their worldly
dedis. Allas I perceyve right wele that it turmentith the fredome
of oure Cristendome. Wherfor I pleyne [me] to His mercy and to
þe, in whoise vertu is merite to preserue and areyse. And I mervaile
that His piety stretchith nat vpon His Cristen people sore ouir- 30
throwen.

[Feythe]

Iff thou mervaile vpon the oppressions of iustice, peyse ageinst
that the grette largesse of His graces / that be vnknowen. f. 51ᵛ

1 tyme] tymes N *pl.* D   9 Wherfor] Therfore NSJ   11 and] nor NS
ne D   12 Who] Ryme *ins. above passage* S   14 abundaunce] haboundaunces N *sing.* D   15 owte] owthe N   18 of] *om.* N   19 and vndir]
and *ins.*, v *made from* a R   20 the] *om.* NSJ   21 it suffice vs to] is to vs
sufficyent vn to N   vpon] on SJ   22 we shall] *tr.* NSJ   26 to] *om.* N
30 sore] so NSJ

[Vndyrstondynge]

That oon and that othir ought to be remembred, but yet His
mercy is above all His othir werkes.

[Feyth]

5   What wolt þou say and the vices of thy realme make it vnwourthy
to haue mercy?

[Vndrestondynge]

I trust suche wise in [hir] grette bounteousnesse that she woll not
entrete vs aftir our diffautis but aftir hir pite suche wise that our
10 vnwourthy diffaultis take not away from hir the dignite of hir
foryeuenesse.

[Feythe]

Hir mercy and hir iustice have peace togedir, and though she do
col. 2   iuste punicion yette is she neuir the / more vnmercyable ne the
15 more vniuste in hir mercyfull indulgence.

[Vndyrstondynge]

I haue trust in hir mercy, but in hir iustice I haue a maner of
grugginge.

[Feithe]

20 Thenke on thy wikidnesse and thou sha[l]t knowe the equite of
hir iustice. Thanne shalt thou vndirstonde hir iugementis inas-
moche as thou knowist thyn owne diffawtis and apperceyvest thyne
offences.

[Vndyrstondynge]

25 This conclusion is to me full derke.

[Feythe]

By this propo[si]sion may be vndirstonde hir declaracion: for
who that woll discerne the statis of creaturis by the Creatour
begynnith to highe and may nat perfourme his begynnynge no

8 hir] NSJ their R   bounteousnesse] habovntevousnes (ha *perhaps canc.*) N
10 of hir] *om.* N   11 foryeuenesse] foryevenesses NSJ   15 vniuste]
inyuste N   20 shalt] NSJ shast R   22 thyne] tyme N   23 offences]
offence N *pl.* D   28 the 2] a N   29 no] nor NSJ

acheve thendinge, but only by the perfeccion / of the creature, f. 52
which susteynith their feblenesse and correctith their errours. And
if thou wolt holde this humble ordir in our processe, I woll yeve
the a clere vndirstondinge and assoile thy questions.

[Vndyrstondynge]   5
I wolle accepte suche fourme as thou semest moste doctrinable.

[Feythe]
Lo, here is she that most is proporcioned to thy might, for bi
th(e) mynistracion of bodyly vndirstondinge and bi the likenesse
of materiall thingis thou muste make thi course [to the] spirituall 10
thingis.

[Vndyrstondynge]
O lady, performe suche thinge as þou hast begonne and thou
shalt fynde me ententif and redy to lern.

[Feithe]   15
Thanne at this tyme woll I helpe / myself with the holy Bible col. 2
and also by ensaumple of othir thingis I woll assoile the question
which holdith the in the errour aftir thine affeccion.

[Vndyrstondyng]
Be it as it pleasith the, for it is so wretin that in our propir dedis 20
we haue dissaiveable opinions and an vncerteyne sentence.

[Feythe]
Iff we beleue that therthely powers weren stablischid by the
power of heven, we shulde as wele beleue that He which made them
maintenith them or if Him list canne vnmake them, for all maner of 25
thingis haue of oon maner cause their being and their durynge. But
who that wold say that lordshippis goten by violence with the
mighty men of the powr men shulde long stonde withowt subuersion, it shulde seeme, though it tourned, it wer no mervaile, for it

---

1 creature] creatour NSJ *probable om. here* RNSJ *see n.*   4 thy] the N
10 course] courte N   to the] NSJ *of* R aulx D   16 woll I] *tr.* N
18 affeccion] J *omits from here to p. 50, l. 7* synne *see n.*   20 our] *om.* N
nos D   23 Iff] C *begins here*   25 if] he *add.* C   Him] self *add.* NSC

C 7740   D

f. 52ᵛ is foundid vpon a wikkid begynnynge and / rathir it ought to be callid tirannie thanne regn[e].

Wherfor let vs beleve that Saul was the furst kinge which God furst stablischid to whom He gaue the ceptre of power and the
5 vnccion of grace for the gouernaunce of His people. Yet notwith-stondinge for his diffences our Lorde put away the realme from his heyris and chaungid it vnto Dauid, which reigned ouir þe people of Israel vertuously and left it aftirward to Salomon, his sone, which helde it peacibly aftir his dissease vnto the tyme that fleschely
10 delectes peruertid his wisedom. For as sone as he enclined from the lawe of God and sewid his owne pleasurs, forthwith our Lorde areisid ayeinst him [newe enemys. Yet notwithstondyng at that tyme the opyn werre was not reysed ayenst hym] for the merites of his fadir. But the diuine furour turned vpon his sone Roboam
15 and toke away the tenthe parte of his lordshipp and the hertis and
col. 2 the obeisaunce of his subiectis, for he disdeyned a/yeinst the coun-seille of his wise people and he dispreysid hit and followed thappe-tite of his desiris and thopinion of fooles which were but yonge and of no grette vndi(r)stonding.
20 O ye erthely kyngis, which sitte in youre trembling chayers and haue commaundingis by auctorite disseyveable vpon the people peruertible, lothe to lerne your [leccons] of the Kyng of hevene, which [sitteth] in perdurable trone, of which the realme may neuir chaunge nor thauctorite therof may neuir be agaynsaide. But your
25 realme failith with your life and His realme lordeshippith [o]uir the life and deth. Ye regne ouir the subiectis and bonde men and He regnith and commaundith ouir the kyngis. Ye make in the worlde lawis transitories but His perpetuall lawe vnbindith your lawe (and byn)dith your powers. Lefte your yghen and meke your hertis to
f. 53 lerne of His doctrine which by Hym alone / the kingis may reigne,
31 seeng the furst kyng that He made and stablischid He toke away

2 regne] N reigne C reygne *canc.* regne S regns R   6 diffences] offenses C
9–10 fleschely delectes] flesshly delytes NS flessly delites C   11–12 pleasurs . . .
newe] SC *om.* N newe *om.* R   11 forthwith] forwyth S   16 disdeyned]
disdeyne N   17 he] *om.* NSC   18 and 2] *om.* N   20 sitte] *om.* N
20–2 and . . . lothe to] ly *add. after* disseyveable R and haue commawdyn by
auctoryte dysseyvable ly vppon the peple pevertybloth S and haue commawnden
by auctoryte deceyvable ly vppon the peple and þer fore N *om.* C *see n.*
22 leccons] leccions R lesson NSC *sing.* D   23 sitteth] NS *om.* R *burned* C
siet D   24 be] *om.* N   25 ouir] NSC euir R sur D   27 commaundith]
commawndyd N   28 lawe 2] lawes NSC *pl.* D   29 Lefte your] lyfte vp
youre SC lyft ye vp N   31 stablischid] stabyssheled N

the ceptre and lessid his obeisaunce by the thridde parte and with-
drowe his subiectis in tokyn that your reigne here beneth is nothing
ellis but a commission reuocable at the pleasure and conseile of
above. And to thentent that the wourship of her charge shulde
make them nat to mysknowe Himself, He punyschid the furst of 5
His makinge afftir the grette diffence that he had done for declaracion of the furst institucion of realmes vpon the deuoir and condicion of kingis that be vnhappy. For the crowne is full heuy to suche
kingis as slepe [in] vayne glorye and make themselfe dronken in
pride as whan thei mysknowe their humanite and vsurpe vpon the 10
divine power. For the feer that his people and subiectis haue of
hym for his grette power makith him to forgette the dreede which
he shulde by reason / owe to Almighty God. And thus thei take col. 2
vpon theim suche honour that thei ne may neuir gette ne kepe at
thende. Suche make of the royall see a chayer of [pestilence] and 15
the pride of their enhaunceyng is the sentence of their ruyne, for
suche royall seegis synkyn vndir the man that is ouirchargeid with
synne and his chayer reuerceth vpon hym the sorer forasmoche as
the dedis which long to the crowne be nat wele supportid and
maynteined according to his office. Ensaumple of Nabugodonosor, 20
which was so high reysid in pryde that he made hymself be wourshippid as a god, but oure Lorde brought hym so lowe that he
fedde hymself with bestes. Knowe for certayne that the yghes of
God waken ouir the synnes of realmes for to chastice them or to
subuerte them. Arte not thou remembrid how it is wretin that 25
lacke of / iustice and vntrewe dedis make realmes redy to be f. 53ᵛ
chaungid, which is oftentymes seen, and bringith theim lowe
through the grette weight of synne. For synne is so foule and of so
falling a condicion that it drawith vnto hym myserye and seruage
and his delyte is alway accompenyed with vnhappynesse and pur- 30
sewid with peyne. And so the diuine iustice, which is rightfull, may
nat suffre suche kyngis to reigne ouir the people forasmoche as thei
be seruantis vnto synne. And therfor Almyghty God transportith
the realmes from honde to honde.

1 his . . . parte] the obeyssaunce of the thyrde NC the obeysaunce of thrydde
S au tiers amoindri son obeissance D   6 grette] *om.* NSC   diffence]
offence N   had] hath N   10 mysknowe] mysknowlegh N mysknowleche S
mysknowlage C   12 for . . . him] *om.* C   13 thus] this NS   14 ne 2]
nor NSC   15 pestilence] NSC pestitilence R   18 reuerceth] reverteth C
20 his] the NSC   21 high] *om.* N   22 a] *om.* C   23 yghes] yys S
yys *canc.* yghes N   24 to 2] *om.* NSC   25 not thou] *tr.* NSC

[Vndyrstondynge]

Whanne our Lorde liste to punysch men for synne, what is the cause þat He diuerse tymes puttith them in hondis of gretter synners thanne they be?

5

[Feythe]

col. 2   In that is schewid / His iustice for the more turment of the synner, for like as by synne he is reysid vp ayeinst the meeke and benyngne lordship of Almyghty God likew(y)se by punycion is he cast downe vndir the harde tyrannye of synne. For he that woll

10 putte all erthely thingis vndir hym must furste submitte hymself to God, and in contrarye wise whanne man mystakith hymself ayeinste God it makith man subiecte and bonde to all thingis. For as oon yron filith anothir, so a synner chastiseth his symblable and becomyth an instrument of the divine iustice. The fyle werith and

15 aftir þat is leyde asyde as a thing nat profitable. Yet through amendement of the maister werkeman the yron is made able for to file and so brought ageyne to profight. The fadir othirwhile takith the rodde to bete his chylde, and in his betyng the rodd brekith,

f. 54 and aftir whanne he [is] appeacid he / takith the rodde and (c)astith

20 it in the fyir. So vndir this maner our Lorde holdith His chapitre and His reformacion, and who that woll not lerne of His discipline may holde hymself closid from grace. The naturall sonne is betyn of his fadir within the howse whenne he trespassith. But the hired man is vttirly put owte of the howse whanne he trespassith, with-

25 owte any stroke. And who that redith Ysaye may fynde ensaumple of these wourdis and notid in story how the realme of Assiryens was the skorge that God ordeined for His chi[l]dirn of Israell. Thanne aftirward He brake þat skorge and distroyed the realm of Assury and chaungid that lordship to the Perces and the Medes

30 and made Babilone (inhabitable) and deliuerid His people from servage and sette them in liberte.

3 in] the *add.* NSC   6 more] *om.* N   7 and] the *add.* N
9 downe] *om.* N   10 hym] he *add.* C   13 symblable] semable N
19 castith] c *ins. on line after erasure* R chasteth (h 1 *canc.*) N   24 whanne
he trespassith] *om.* NSC *see n.*   24–5 withowte any] withouten NSC
26 realme of] *om.* N Royaume des D   27 skorge] k *ins. on line after
erasure* R scorge N scorge *canc.* skorge S   28 þat] the C   29 chaungid]
chaunge N   30 inhabitable] NS *ins.* R inhitable C   His people]
om. C son peuple D

[Vndyrstondynge]

Thanne syn it is so that aduersite of realmes ben execucions of
diuine iuge/mentis through the mysknowlechinge of kyngis, what col. 2
is the cause thanne that He suffirth the powr and lowe subiectis
bere the penaunce for othir mennys synne and why woll God putt 5
vpon newe turmentis ouir the travaile of their laboure?

[Feithe]

Holy Scriptur wittnessith that for synnes of a kyng the people
be oftyntymes punischid and for the synne of the people kyngis be
deprived and put downe. 10

[Vndrestondynge]

Theffecte of this I knowe by ensaumple. For whanne Dauid hadd
synned, many of his people dyed therfor. And on the othir syde for
thoffence of people Kyng ȝedechias was punyschid by God, that
is to know, he was take with Assyriens and his yghen putte owte 15
of his hedde. Nowe wolde I fayne / knowe the cause of these two f. 54ᵛ
punycions which semeth to me shulde be as a rygoure in the divine
iustice or ellis it shulde seme (þe) text war nat true which seith that
the son shall nat bere the iniquite of the fadir and that euery man
shulde bere the peyse of his owne fardell. 20

[Feythe]

The werkis of God ouircometh our iugementis an iugeth them,
and His infinite power iustifieth all His werkis in doyng them, for
He (is) a iustice of Hymself. Yette for the ease of owr ignorauns
He lefte vs His wourdis in Holy Scriptur, which may nat fayle, and 25
by them wele vndirstonde, we may by [His] iustice iuge the
stablischinge of kyngis, which is foundid for thoccasion of synne
in the people. And we war all iuste and trewe, we hadde no nede
to feer lordeship. For as the Apostle wrote to the / Romayns, 'The col. 2
kynge is nat the feer of wele-doers but he is dredefull to them that 30
done amysse, and the lawe was nat made for the rightwise men but
it was made for the synners.' Also it must be vndirstonde that

2 is] not *add.* N *om.* D   4 that He] *tr.* N   14 people] the N
subiects D   Kyng] *om.* C Roy D   18 which] that C   that] *om.* C
20 owne] *om.* N   25 lefte] *?* lost N   27 thoccasion] the occasion NS
the *om.* C la D   28 And] for and S And *canc.* For and N   29 the 2]
om. N aux D   32 the] *om.* N aux D

through the inportune request of the people was grauntid them
furst a kynge. Yet our Lorde sente vnto His people by Samuel and
schewid them the corrupcions and the infeccion that evil kynges
spred among the people through þeir vicious ensaumple. And nat-
5 withstonding that, yette wolde they nedis haue a kinge.

O Lorde God, how that realme shinith bright where ther regneth
a vertuouse and a Catholike kynge. Certainly like as the faire sonne
that castith his bright bemes vpon therthe, through which is
voydyd away the derke mystis, and makith the day to shewe more
10 cler, so in lyke wise the rightwise kynge confoundith and destroyeth
f. 55 all maner of wyk/kednesse through the foresight of his wisedome
and dressith all maner of thing to honeste for the honour of his
renowm. But O allas in contrary wise who that canne ymmagine or
thenke the poyson and the venyme that the wicked and the vicioue
15 kynge soweth in his realme! For the wickednes descendith from the
grette to the smale. Thanne the people sewen the fortune and lyve
aftir the patron of their souereigne. The schrewed kynge makith
his subiectis nyce and owte of mesure. For looke wher a prince is
withow(t) wisedom there be the people withowte discipline, for and
20 a booke be falsely wretyn it shall make the reders for to erre, and
he that wrytith aftir that booke ioyneth false vpon false. So thanne
the kynge is the booke of the people wherein thei shulde lerne to
lyve and amende their maners. But and the originall be corrupt /
col. 2 thanne by the copyes vntrewely wretyn. For the corrupcion that
25 descendith from the hede chavefith the lyvir, chargith the harte and
filith the stomacke; it stoppith thentrailes and alterith all the body.
Like [wise the] vices that rebounden vpon the subiectis peruertith
the ordir, troublith the offices and empeirith the condicions of all
the estates of his people, for the sekenesse that comyth from the
30 hede causith all the membirs to be troublid. Nowe all kyngys take
hede to this, for and thei knewe that in theire wickednesse honged
the synne of the people thei wolde enteirly kepe their dignite above
all othir and thei wolde be vertuouse above all othir.

Now here it followith whethir the kyngis were stablischid to

1–2 them furst] to hem N   2 by] was N   3 that] the *add.* NSC
4 vicious] vycons S   9 voydyd] avoyded N   more] *om.* NSC   12 of 1]
om. NC *erased* S   13 or] and C   14 the 4] *om.* NSC   16 to] and N
aux D   17 souereigne] souereyns NS *pl.* D   18 and] NSC *canc.* R
For] *om.* N   20 the] *om.* N   for] *om.* NSC   21 he] thei NSC ceulx D
wrytith] wryte NSC   25 chavefith] chavfeth S and chaveth N   lyvir]
it *add.* NSC   and] yt NSC   28 offices] office NSC *sing.* D

thoccasion of synne of the people and at their requeste and whethir
the subiectis doubtyn the synne of the kynges through / which   f. 55ᵛ
hurte may come to eythir party, but he that synnith most, eithir
the kyng or the people, is most wourthi to be blamed and on that
party ought rathest to tourne the vengeaunce. For the nature of 5
shrewed men is to be seruaunte to peyne and bounde to correccion.
And syn it is so that their euyll inclinacion may not kepe them in
rewle in lasse thanne they haue a kynge, it is reason that thei suffir
the charges and affliccions that growen owte of the vices of kynges.
And the kynge also shal bere the offences of (his) people forasmoche 10
as his dissoluc[i]on of vices is openid amonge them and through
necligence that he doth not his peyne to enhaunce vertu and
repreve misdedis, which is the begynnyng of their dissordinaunce.
Wherfor princes ought to be gretly moevid to discipline, to good
maners and to vertue seenge that their goodnesse / may profight col. 2
to all the people, and on that othir syde their iniquite may noye 16
euery man. For the good that is most vniuersall and comon is most
excellent, and in contrary wise the evile more damnable, lyke as by
oon manere of discipline schewith twoo contraries. And the wise
man seith that to such folke shal be yevyn right a scharpe and a 20
harde iugement, namely suche as sitt in the high seeges. And [thei]
that be smale and powr shall haue their peyne made swete with
mercy, but þe grette shall feele the myght of stronge turmentis.

O ye kynges, harke what the grette Kynge hath ordeined for you.
He hath ordeined you honours and magnificences. But looke ye 25
love vertu for ye haue it to thentent that ye shulde serue Hym
with(owt) hom ye cannat kepe them certainly. Vertu that comith
from hevyne where perdurable thyngis dwellyth holdith the grace
and the semblaunce of the good/nesse of his natiuite, and therfor f. 56
she makith the powers to endure and suche as woll followe it 30
makith them stedfastly abyding in their seurte. But who that is
borne of this lowe fragilite vndir the passion humayne is variable
and makith werkis þat be nat durable and draweth them to the falle

1 whethir] *om.* N   2 the 3] *om.* NSC des D   through] the *add.* C
3 synnith most] *tr.* NSC   4 be blamed] bere the blame NSC
7 inclinacion] inclynacions N *sing.* D   9 charges] charge NSC *see n.*
and] the *add.* NSC *om.* D   10 offences] offence NSC *sing.* D   11 through]
the *add.* NSC   13 is] *om.* N   dissordinaunce] deshordenaunces SC
see n.   16 noye] to *add.* NSC   20 to] *om.* N à D   27 withowt] owt *om.*
NSC   hom] hem and yf ye serue hym with hem NSC *see n.*   28 dwellyth]
dwell C dwell yn NS   33 makith] his *add.* NSC ses D

through þe feble impotencie of that thei came fro, for euerything
tournith agayne to his principle. And who that woll nat begynne
his werke vpon vertuouse affeccions nor condidith it nat by lyne
and vndir mesure of reason, may well be likened to hym that
5 bildith his howse vpon a falce foundement and conditeth his werke
in manere for to schewe, but nat to endure. And what beawte
apparent that the bilding schewith, yet it woll encline to his furst
beyng, that is to say, fall vnto ruyne. Remembir the on þe sentences
col. 2 that thou fyndist / in writing and on suche thingis also as thou hast
10 seene in experience, and thou shalt see them accorde in this
byhalve. For the glorye of euile princes and the reising of their
digniteis is as the fire that is withinne flex or tough, which litle
while durith. For noweadais thei woll vsurpe and take vpon them
auctorite and power nat dew and blynde themself suche wise in the
15 vanite of their fortune and be so stonyet in the grette bruyt of their
worldly worshipis þat thei may not her the schewingis of reason.
Wherfor their estate may nat stonde ferme, for thing that lightly
comith lyghtly goth. And trees that beren hastily, both the fruyte
of them is lasse and also thei (dure) nat so longe as thei that haue
20 longe attempraunce and wele-tilled, which receyue their norisching
of the heete of the sonne. Therfor thou seest but fewe or non reigne
f. 56ᵛ longe of suche / as through pride and synne avaunece themself to
high gouernaunces, for as sodeinly as thei aryse to the high pompes,
as sodeinly thei fall from their estate, their name pirischith, þeir
25 goode gothe away and their lignage fallith from their enheritaunce.
Dauid dissimelid nat the meruelouse iugement whanne he said,
'I haue seen,' quod he, 'the euile men areised on highe as the high
cedre, and whanne I was past and comyng homwarde ageyne I
sawe nothir roote ne braunchis.' Wherby thou maiste see that the
30 grette realmes and myghty powers that be occupied vnrightfully
and wrongfully condited may neuir stonde stable nor acerteyned,
but it drawith the kyng and the realme to peyne and to dethe,
which is the rewarde of synne, as saith Seinte Paule. And this

2 tournith] returneth NSC   his principle] ther pryncyples NSC leur
principe D   3 affeccions] affeccion NSC *sing*. D   nat] *om*. C   8 senten-
ces] sentence N   12 digniteis] dignite C indignee D   15 stonyet] stvnyed
S stonned N   the . . . their] their gret N le bruit des D   16 her] ther *add*.
canc. R   18 And] the *add*. C les D   20 norisching] nvreture S nutriture
N   21 of the 1] þurgh NSC   23 gouernaunces] governaunce N *pl*. D
25 from their enheritaunce] into disherytesone NSC *see n*.   27 areised]
reised C   highe] height NS heith C   28 was] *om*. N   29 braunchis]
braunche NSC *sing*. D   Wherby] by N   that the] *om*. N comme les D

rewarde ought to be gevin aftir the qualite of theire desertes. The
iniquite of / a prince, which is a publike persone (thorow) whose col. 2
misdedis fallith oftintymes vniuersall sclaundir and grette hurte to
the people, causith hym to haue generalite of peynes aboue all
othir.   5

O ye kynges that be closid in this lowe worlde whereas
Almighty God hath sette both ende and terme which no man
may passe, your power may not be stablishid in lasse thanne God
aff[e]rme it through wose handis [ye] must nedis passe. Wherfor
thanne do ye engrosse vp the grette hepis of thes wordely goodis 10
vnrightfully to the grette noye and trouble of the powr people
seyng that ye be of suche a seede that ye must nedis passe awaye,
and your power shall be all tobroken and fewe teeris or non shal
be shedde for you in lasse thanne your herte be firmely sette on
God, which bindith and vnbindith? For / aftir your passage ye f. 57
must make acompte. Wherfor it is necessarye that reasone passe 16
your desiers suche wise that it may be confourmed to Godis will.

[Vndyrstondynge]

(F)ayier doctryne and deepe instruction may be gadred owt of
thy wordis, but yet I haue a scripyl vpon the divine iustice foras- 20
moche as it punyschithe the iuste and trwe men with the synners
and puttith thinnocentis and wikkid people as all one. Allas hough
many iuste and peacible creaturis haue borne the peyne and the
angwisch of this werre. Also howgh many men of honest living
haue suffird shamefull dethe and moche good truely goten haue 25
ben wickedly ravischid and take awaye. I see the noughty and
reproueable people hepid with richesse, / and the good and honeste col. 2
people beggars and nedy. Also chastite that hath be kepte in
wourship now is it constreyned and brought vnto myschievouse
vylaynye. So thanne through myschief, necessite and owtrage man 30
cannat haue that is his nor no good dede may receyve the rewarde
aftir the vertue therof. But strengthe makith the right aftir his
owne propir opinion, and ouirpride vsurpith to haue wourschip

3 misdedis] dededs C   4 peynes] peyne NSC *sing.* D   6 O ye]
Ryme *ins. above passage* S   9 ye] NSC it R vous D   10 thanne] *om.* N
11 vnrightfully] vnryghtfull N   noye] noyeaunce C   12 that ye 2] as NSC
17 wise that it] which þat it NS as C   confourmed] con *burned* fermed C
19 Fayier] F *made from illuminated* I R   21 it] is *add.* R   and] *om.* N
25 shamefull] shamfully (y *perhaps canc.*) N   haue] hath C   32 the 2] *om.*
NSC vn D   33 propir] *om.* NSC

withowt any deserte. Where is thanne the divine iustice, or to what tyme is she reseruid whanne she may nat helpe vs nor amende our myscheves whanne we haue most nede vnto hir?

[Feythe]

5 Yff youre felicite were oonly in the goodis of this world and your being fyxid withowt abidyng of an higher life, thanne wolde I

f. 57ᵛ thenke that there were grette / apparence in thine argument. But the very rightwisenes is finall punicion of them that be damned, and the rewardis of happy folkis is nat to be gotin in this worlde.

10 For who that seethe the evil dedis vnpunischid and the good dedis eville rewardid among therthly people may wele thinke þat their is anothir thing through which all is refourmed by egall iustice or ellis the same Iuge that mainteignith vs in this dedly world war nat rightfull to euery man. And by this argument diuerse enforcid

15 themself to shewe the perpetuite of the sowle, the resurreccion of the body and þe generall iugement. But it ought ynogh suffice to euery man suche thinge as the Creatour hath liked to shewe by me. Yet of the comon synnes her byneth men see allday erly or late ensaumple of Goddis indignacion and execucion of peyne vpon the

col. 2 same. For whanne the prowde men / be sodeinly reysid on hight

21 thanne soone aftir they haue the grette fall and the goodis that be euile gotyn drawith þe getter to mysease and perille, for as they come so thei go and levith himself or his heyers in shame and in pouerte.

25 ### [Vndyrstondynge]

Thestate of iniquitees lett them be whereas God and fortune woll, for of their hurte and peyne is but litill harme. But vpon affliccion of the good and rightwise men I wold faine be answerid.

[Feythe]

30 Canst thou, as thou supposest, knowe the iuste man from the euile or synner and be incerteyned of secrete thoughtis which God hath reseruid to Himself? For the punicions of men be nat allway

f. 58 done at tyme of the trespasse, but our Lorde oftintymes, / whanne

---

11 their] thyn N   12 is 2] his N   17 shewe] schewed S   18 Yet] but C   21 the 1] a N   23 and 2] or N & D   27 vpon] the *add*. NSC   28 the good and] *om*. NSCD   faine] *om*. N   31 euile or] *om*. NSCD   of] the *add*. NSC du D   33 the] *om*. C

a man doth good dedis, taketh vengeaunce vpon the mysdedis
which be passid and foryetyn. Man ought to be redy to receyve the
grace of correccion of penaunce, and God chastiseth hym sonneste
whanne He fyndith hym best disposed to receyve it. His wisdome
and His iustis is kept so longe through His grette piete and grace 5
that He tarieth longe to chastice the ev[i]le folke in trustyng of their
amendement. And on the othir parte He woll rewarde the good
[but He abydyth] for to preve their suffraunce and to encreasce the
perfeccion of their merite. But He recompensith His abiding by
augmentacion of grace or ellis by engruggement of peyne. The 10
fysiciane gevith not the seke man to drinke aftir the appetite of his
thirst but tarieth and abidith a dew hour (for) the profight of his
welefar. And though so be that the pacient grugge and conpleyne
vpon his fysiciane bycause he leueth hym sweting in grette peyne
of the heete, / yette for all that the wise phisiciane woll nat graunte col. 2
his requeste, for suche a compassion resemblith rathir to cruelte 16
than to piete. And this ensaumple leith Seint Ierome right
scharpely in the prologge of the prophecye of Abacuc, which, in
stryving with the hasty desyers of man contrarie to the tarieng and
longe suffraunce of the iugementis of God, formed this question 20
oftintymes to God contrarie to his owne helthe. For He which hath
yeve tyme and place and knowith whanne His helpe [and] His
socour or His chastesinges be most to oure welthe departith theme
nat at our eleccion nor in the howirs of our desier but to His
resonable wille and to the profecte of our perfeccion. Wherefor 25
abasche the no more though thou see hym which thou takest for
iust suffyr peyne, for thou knowest nat what spirituall wynnynge
reboundith from thes temporall hurtes or harmes nor thou knowest
/ nat also what synne is hid in suche as thou reputest to be iuste. f. 58ᵛ

[Vndyrstondynge] 30

Salomon yaue vs for a rewle that men haue turment by the same
thinge of which [they] did the synne. Thanne hough may it be that
suche folkes be punyschid that neuir bare office nor neuir war
callid to counseile for the comon wele?

6 evile] NSC evlle R   8 but He abydyth] *ins.* S *om.* RNC *see n.*
the] their C leur D   13 that the] *om.* N   14 fysiciane] for *add.* NSC
15 graunte] all *add.* NSC   18 the prologge of] *om.* N ou Prologue des D
20 iugementis] iugement C *pl.* D   22 and 3] NSC or R & D   24 desier]
desires N *sing.* D   28 or harmes] *om.* NSCD   32 they] C he RNS
33 war] *om.* N

[Feythe]

Thine erroure is foundid vpon ignoraunce for thou wenest that he allon doth offence to God that opinly puttith synne in vre. Nay certainly it goth othirwise thanne so, for the consenters or suche as
5 haue power to resiste and do it nat and suche as blandisch in the
col. 2 fortune of synne / and sewe the bruyte and folowe the vanytees therof bene parteners and norischers of synne and yeve a grette boldenesse for men to do eville and to continewe in the same. Ha, Vndirstondinge, if thou knowest them which so longe tyme haue
10 dissimiled the iniquitees through which the corrupte pestilences ar growen amonge vs by suche as haue honourid the vaine glorye, and auctorisid the iniquitees of suche vntrewe people and shadowed them in their pride, þou woldest say that their be but fewe that may wasche clene their hondis from the spottis of this myschief. And so
15 the Frenchemen haue yeuin vp the honour to vsurpid estate and to the goodis that ben rauischid and nat to the vertu. Why do ye apply yourself to the greef of youre coragis and worship and plaece suche which through their shamefull enterprises and your folische suff-
f. 59 raunce be reisid to / auctorite withowte deseruyng of merite?
20 Thanne hough may ye be put owt of blame seeng that ye haue committid your poletik rewlis to the manere of an ydolatrie which corruptith your maners and peruertith your polecie? Who is he tha(t) aftir [theis] defaultes may iuge hymself wourthi to escape the comon peyne of your realm? For some lyue in grette synne, (and)
25 [some] in dissimelynge hath yeuen preuy consentement to the euile and to the mischief; and some there be that wolde nat resiste ayeinste comon infeccion which gaue occasion to the encresinge of grette hurte and to the multipliynge of euile doers. Othir ther be that encline and cherisch in doyng reuerence to the myghty men
30 which be full of wantonnes and yeuith them corage to [life]
col. 2 viciously and through their fals conforte taketh away the shame of their vnhoneste nycete and / owtrageousenesse and causith othir men to favour them and sewe the same rewle. Yet I tell the that, amonge othir, some vertuous men oure Lorde taketh owte of this

4 othirwise] another wise C   6 synne] and yeue a boldnesse for men to do euile and to continewe in / the same *add*. R   the bruyte and folowe] *om*. N   7 grette] *om*. NSC   8 do] to N   10 iniquitees] C *ends here*   pestilences ar] pestylences ys S pestilence is N *sing*. D   11 vs] namely *add*. NS   12 iniquitees] inyquyte N   15 yeuin vp] yelden NS rendu D   23 theis] NS his R ces D   27 ayeinste] ayent the S the N 29 doyng] gret *add*. NS   30 life] NS *om*. doo *ins*. R   33 that] þat þat N

worlde for because they shulde nat be infecte by the contagiouse-
nes of othirs, or ellis He deprivith and takith them away by affliccion and by egyr peyne to thentent that the vanite of delices brynge
them nat in amonge suche evil folkis. Also beleve that þe divine
clemence suffirth the viciouse men to lyve othir for to abide their 5
correccion or for to make them vertuouse through the prykkinges
of thes myschevous people. Wherfor hereaftirwarde le[eu]e this
question and suffice the to rest and abide in this holy and meke
thought that the infinite Trouthe which by our good dedis may nat
be amendid nor by our diffaultes empeired, but taketh ouir all 10
maner of people egall and rightfull iustice nat onely by vs / nor for f. 59ᵛ
vs but by thessenciall perfeccion of His naturall bounte.

[Vndyrstondynge]

I am contente to obey to thi holy submission. Nevirthelesse I
mervaile whi oure Lorde suffirth His holy chirche and His ministirs 15
sacred to be in this wise diffoulid and nat sette by accordinge to His
ordinaunce. Wherfor and it shulde nat displease [you], I wolde
fayne enquiere the cause of (this) mischief, for it greuith me sore
whanne I see the preestes which be dedeifyed to God and the holy
monkes and the holy clergie mokkid more thanne any othir people 20
and their goodis taken from them and abandoned vnto rapyne.
O thou soueraigne Herdeman, thou mightest, and it wolde please
The, preserue Thi chirche and Thy shepe from violence of the
werre like as Thou hast diffendid and put sentence in Holy Scriptur
that whosomeuir touche them to/uchith the appill of Thin yghe. col. 2

[Feythe]
26

Malachias the prophete shall asoile the this question, through
whose mouthe our Lorde kest His cvrse vpon þe iniquite of euile-
livinge men of the chirche, sayinge to them in this wise: 'The
mouthe of preestes springith abrode science and doctrine which 30
ought to yelde acompte of the good o(b)se(r)uaunce of the lawe.
For the preest is as a sharpe messaungere of the victorious Lorde.
Wherfor ye preestes that haue goon owte of the right waye and
sclaundre the people through the [euyl] ensaumples (of) your vices

---

7 thes] the N des D   leeue] NS lerne R laisse D   14 to 1] *om.* S
15–16 ministirs sacred] *tr.* NS   19 dedeifyed] dedicate N   21 abandoned]
habounded N   23 The] to *add.* N   33 ye] þe N vous D

and broken the covenaunte of holy clennesse which ye promised
vnto me, therfor I iuge and say that for the transgression of your
holy estate ye shal be brought lowe, defowlid and put vndir; euery
f. 60 man shall ouirerenne you and dispreyse you / as for the most shame-
5 full people of the worlde.' The(se) be wourdis diuine and now thes
cases be comown and þe peyne execute and [the] prophecie verified. Ne seest thou nat þe prowde pompe, the vnstable ambicion
and the shamefull maners of suche as call themself ministers of God
and now be seru[au]ntis vnto [the] worlde, hauyng alweys a regarde
10 to the fruytes that growen of benefices, and leve the seruice of God
and sette nat by the helthe of sowles, but committe to othir men
that be nat substanciall the occupacion of their offices, but the
profightes thei witholde to themself. Thei wandre abowte in the
del(y)tes of this worlde and putte themself in the vanitees of
15 temporall courtes and to lay occupacions, and to þe, Lorde of
hevyne, to whom thei wolde be called vicaries vpon erthe, letin
Thy chirche alone. O very God, me shulde nat so boldely axe so
col. 2 perilous / a vicariage and execute it so necligently. And I merveile
hough a man may take pride and presumpcion by the dignite of
20 benefice while he disdeyneth to do the devour of his crafte. [Allas
yet nat] onely in the mystaking of that they haue nat done their
devour in their duete ne sacrifice, but thei be ashamed to were the
habyte and kepe thestate of their professione. Also they thinke
shame of the ordir [of] which they desyird and [preysed] moche
25 the profight. Than syn it is so that they honour nat their dignite
of benefice, who shall honour them? If thei disdeyne the holy
preestehode, who shall alowe and susteyne this holy office whanne
thei that haue take it vpon them be ashamed therof?
O modir, holy chirche, thou arte foundid in humilite, which is
30 the furst stoon of Cristis edifice, and kepte by humilite vndyr the
drede of Almyghty God. [Thu art reysed on heyght ouyr all the
worlde but now for the pride that thu art yn ayenst Allmyghti
f. 60v God] thou shalt turne into pardicion vndir þe / worldely people.
Somtyme the ministers and prechours of the feythe were martired
35 in scheding of blode, and now thei be gaderers of goode and

9 seruauntis] NS seruuantis R   12 nat] no N   substanciall] S for
add. ins. R to add. N   offices] office NS sing. D   15 lay] laycall N
16 vpon] the add. N om. D   erthe] and add. N   19 presumpcion] N Allas
yet nat add. RS   20–1 Allas yet nat] misplaced above RS om. N   25 they
honour nat] their honoure and N   26 of benefice] om. NSD see n.   29 arte]
were NS   30 edifice] edifyeng N

laberers of therthe. The holy conuersacion that was somtyme in cle(r)gie moevit the couragis of princes and conquerours for to enhaunce the chirche with grette and noble yeftis, but the dissolucions that now regnith in the clergie maketh euery man bolde to ravische and to take away suche as longith vnto them. O thou poete of Florence, and thow wer on live in thes dayes þat now be, thou mightest fynde matir inough to write ayeinste Constantyne, whanne, in the tyme that religione was most obserued, thou dourst repreue him in thi booke, of the venyme that he had sowen in holy chirche and the poyson through which it shulde be destroied and desolate; and the case was this—forasmoche as he gave furst / (e)e(r)thely possessions [to the chirch] which othir auctorised doctours gave him therfor a grette lawde. O poete, what moeuid the to blame [or reprefe] this Catholike emperour? For nothing ellis but for the cysmes or discordes, disordinaunces and iniquitees which we may see growinge in the chirche through thabundaunce of richesse that restith in the clergie, which be norischars of ambicione and envye, like as fattenesse norischith the fyre and oyle or touch the flambe. And though so be the receyvours of these goodes be abusid and mistake themeself, yet I saye not that the charite of the yever shulde be cast awaye and takyn as for a synne. But the punycion of the synne ought to turne vpon them that be abusers and nat to hym that gave it to a good vse seynge that necessite and lacke of suffisiaunece myght enduce theme to synne or to this entent that the symple pouerte of the chirche were nat to lightly diffoulid through / temporall power. Yet trewe it is that he gave nat these goodis to man, but he gave them to God. For it is the patrimonye of the chirche which our Lorde conquerid with His preciouse blode through soroufull and grevouse passion oonly. And of these goodes the preestes have dispensacion and ministracion, of whom our Lorde woll aske acompte, namly of suche as wolde take and ocupy them as their owne goode and with the same mak riche their kynne and encrease their temporall patrimonye.

col. 2

f. 61

5

10

15

20

25

30

1 in] the *add.* NS 3 enhaunce the] S *ends here* 6 on] a N 8 in] *om.* N 15 or] *om.* ND disordinaunces] dishordynaunce N *pl.* D 16 growinge] growe N thabundaunce] haboundaunce N l'abondance D 18–19 or touch] *om.* ND 19 so be] þat *add.* N 22 be abusers] abvse such goodys N 23 to 1] *om.* N 27 them] it N 28 the chirche] Crist N crucifix D 29 through] his *add.* N sa D and grevouse] *om.* ND And] *om.* N 30 the . . . ministracion] which prestees haue be dispensours and take mynystracion N *see n.* 31 wolde] will N

O holy prophete Dauid, thou sawest wele this abusion byfore in
spirite whanne thou spackest to suche as vsurpin the saintuarye of
God and take it as their owne heritage. Thou dedist liken suche
men to a whele which turnith the parte that is above downewarde.
5 He likneth them also to reede which may nat stonde firme ayeinst
col. 2 the blowing of the wynde. Nough is thy worde / confirmid in dede,
for the g(r)evis and the oppressions of the clergie of Fraunce, which
þou, Vndirstonding, bewailest, and the persecucion of preestes, of
which some be slayne and some chaced owte, berith recorde.
10 Nough God forbede that suche confusion multiply worse ouir His
chirche. And for certaine this present state shewith following—
aftirwarde which is right doutefull seing that the synne of the
clergie provoketh so largely the indignac[i]on of God and draweth
to them hate for mysguyding of the lawes, which hath more
15 helpears to the mischief thanne aduersaries. And though so be that
the roote be bareyne, yette the braunchis and the bowes extende
in oothir places. And euery man wolde take from the chirche suche
as thei neuir gave him. The owtragious wantonnesse and nycete
f. 61ᵛ of symple prestes brought in this wounde into the chirche and / the
20 necligence of the grette prelates makith it growe and endure ouirall.
For thei flee from the holy Counseiles like as euile childern flee
from the scoole. Yette moreouir thei wolde be dredde and fynde
light causes for to yeue sentence and cursing ouir the people as for
smale dettis and othir light occasions. But þei doubte nat the sen-
25 tence of the Euirlasting Preest that may bynde and assoile, which
offird His body and [His life to] His Fadir for our synnes. We may
see now that all ordir and reule of holy preestehode is turned vp so
downe, which is a hevy thing, for the prelatis lyven as people
exempte from their estate and from the feere of God. Yette at the
30 leste weye I wolde have them to knowe that Ihesus Criste is their
soueraigne Lorde and Bischope of the chirche, of whom the testa-
col. 2 ment was humilite and charite, from whose iugement / no man may
appele. Thanne shall come vnto their mynde þe reuelacion of
Ysaye, which highly cursid the pastours that fedde non othir but

5 them] hym N   to] the *add.* N le D   8 Vndirstonding] vndystondest N
Entendement D   9 berith] þou berest N   10 confusion] such *add.* N
11 shewith] the *add.* N la D   14 more] mo N   18 him] þerto N
owtragious] outrage N   19 into] to N   20 it] to *add.* N   28 thing]
possible om. here RN *see n.*   30 their] the N le D   31 Lorde and]
om. ND   32 was] of *add.* N de D

hymself; for thei shulde (fere) the grette myschief that God hath manaced them.

Nough I holde my peace and speke not of symonyes nor of the vnlawfull contractes, for and it were recited it wold make [the ayer] derke. Yette I woll nat holde with promocion of suche as be nat wourthi, for it causit realmes to fall in grette repreef. O Lorde God, what merveile is it though thei feele the debilite and the hurte therof seing that kyngis procur suche promocions through which their realmes lak counseile and their doctrine as a spectacle of iniquite and spectacle of ignoraunce? Now hast thou satisfaccion of thy doubte and from hensforthe thou maist pleyne [lesse] the shame and vexacion of the clergie if so be thou wolt say that the state of dignite maketh the / grevousnesse of thoffence.

f. 62

[Vndyrstondynge]

Yette remayneth the doubte of the violacion of þe chirche and the polucion of holy places of which the iniurie is to God and nat to His ministirs, for the iniquite of viciouse preestes causith not the diffoulyng of the holy temples.

[Feithe]

Nowgh woll I sende the ageyne to Ezechiell and there shalt thou reede the vanite of preestes which wexe prowde whanne thei had rewle in the temple and delited them in suche wourshippis as war dewe to Almighty God and vsurpid His power and ware punyshid in (þe) same wheras thei toke their vayne glorie. For the dyvine punycion suffirth the holy places be diffouled for to abate the violent pride of them that take away the honoure and lordeship through the grette height of pride. Yet not/withstonding, the divinite of Hym that is Almighty abidith vndefoulid and the dignite of halowid places may nat be apayred through the indignite of men. Wherfor if polucion or sacrilege be done in the temple, the concience of the dede-doers is furst polute and their feithe diffoulid. So the spotte therof shall nat reste in the chirche, but it shall reste in þe sowles of synners which doo the dedes, for the fowlenesse and the vilany therof restith vpon them that be culpable.

1 hymself] hemselfe N fere] *ins. on line after erasure* R be affraied with N
4 the ayer] N their yghen R l'air D 5 with] þe *add.* N la D 10 thou]
om. N 11 lesse] *om.* RN moins D 16 the 1] *om.* N la D 25 be] to
be N 26 lordeship] wurshipp N seigneurie D 30 the 1] *om.* N ou D

O ye Cristen [men], whom Criste hath chosyn to be parteners
of perdurable lif and bere the holy merke of bapteme and the signe
of Ihesu Criste, which is your God and your Maister, hough dar
ye be so bolde to diffoule the thing that He hathe lefte you her
5 benethe for your sanctificacion and for the remembraunce of Hym?
Wher haue ye the herte that movith you or foote that may bere /
f. 62ᵛ yow to entre by violence and by synne into the place wherein ye
shulde be puryfied of synne? It is the withdrawte of them that be
repentant, and nough ye make a howse of wiked counseill. Ye take
10 fro God, that all commith fro, the thing that He hath withholde
and sacred to Himself for His parte. Wherefor He woll close from
you that ye shall nat be parteners of His grace. And I haue merveile
hough the sacrid hondis may obbeye to a wicked herte for to
execute so grevous a misdede whereof the iniurye longith directly
15 to Almighty God and hough any creature dar presume to make any
suche rebellion ayeinst his Creatoure which is Allmighty, namely
in the house that is of so grette vertu.

I will that all menne knowe—namely Frenchemen—that the
disknowlege of Almighty God and favte of iustice have causid the
col. 2 vnlawfull cus/tumes of sacrilege. Lerne, if ye know it nat, that this
21 offence only is inough to confounde and bringe to mischief realmes
and lordeschippis, to distroie and disparple hoostes [and] bataillis,
and for the synne of oone make all his fellawes vnhappy; for
thoffence is so damnable that it takith away grace suche wise that
25 men shall (haue) no power to do wele. Pompey, afftir all his grette
victories, stabelid his horse in the temple of Salomon, and aftir that
he neuir did good to the comon wele nor honour to his name, and
from that tyme forth he had neuir victorye but allwayes discom-
fitoures and at the laste a shamefull deth. Heliodorus also, which
30 cam to robbe Go(d)dis temple, was smetyn with Goddis punycion
afore all the people. Anothir named Antioche, which was a dis-
poyler of temples, the woormes ete him, his fleshe turned into
f. 63 grette styncke and rottid as he went vpon the / erthe. The realme

1 Criste] god N Dieu D   2 of 1] the *add*. N *om*. D   5 sanctifica-
cion] satisfaccyon N sanctification D   7 synne] J *resumes here*   13 sacrid]
sacry J *see n*.   15 any 2] *om*. NJ   16 namely] the *add*. NJ   22 and 3] N
om. RJ & D   24 grace] in *add*. N   27 neuir did] *tr*. NJ   the] *om*. N
28-9 allwayes discomfitoures] *tr*. N   29 laste] dyed *add*. J *om*. D   Heliodorus
also] *tr*. N   30 Goddis 1] the NJ le D *see n*.   31 Anothir] þer was *add*. N
Antioche] Antioce N Anthyoce J   32 fleshe] rotyd and *add*. N   33 grette]
om. N   vpon] on J

of Assiriens also was translatid to the Parseantes and to the Meedes
in the ende of Balthasaris reigne for the sacrilegis of his fadir.
I cannat say to moche ayeinst this horrible misdede, of which the
offence is to God only, and He hathe reseruid the vengeaunce only
to Himself. For religion is of so grette excellence that oure Lorde 5
punyschid suche as did hurte vnto the temples of paynems. Notwithstonding thei wourshipid ydoles and vayne thingis yet He
wolde nat that hurte ne violence were done to suche placis as were
dedicat by them, which thei made vndir title of the deite, which
thei wourship as Almighti Go(d). And of this the Gaules had 10
experience aftir the takyng of Roome whanne thei wolde haue
distroyed the temple of Appolyn [in] Delphos, wheras thei loste
the grette parte of their people and many of the genti/les wer ther col. 2
distroyed. Many suche exaumples maist thou lerne of Valere. And
if thou take good heede in tyme to come, thou [shalt] see all suche 15
fall into miserable lif or ellis dye a shamefull dethe, for thei be
closid from [the helpe of] Almighty God through the noyaunce of
that synne.

The holy Cristen feithe was somtyme figured in the table
which our Lorde toke to Moyses. The othir lawe was erthly, and 20
this lawe was heuenly, holy and reconsilenge, physycian of synne,
ferfull of damnacion, abiding the glorie and the comyng of the
grette Iuge, which shall geve a sentence diffinityue, ayeinst whom
no man may stryue, but take it for perpetuall iugement. And ther
shall euery man vndirstonde the rewarde; suche as he hathe 25
deseruid it / shal be egally mynistrid vnto them. For ther pride f. 63ᵛ
shall haue a fall and the meke shall stye to hevene. There (shal)
iustice be opened and poorte recouerid and malice discouerid,
(which) [aftyrwarde] shall neuir be couerid from rightfull iustice.
The worldely welth shall turne into losse, and equite shal be 30
made open, and expertely knowen to euery man the light of
iustice. Wherefor it is (noo) right that man shulde enquere by
presumpcion to moche vpon divine prouidence. But clerkis
which that haue science, witte or grette experience, prelacy or
audience, if thei axe Godis propirte and will nat kepe humble 35
pacience nor continence in religion and feer in concience, their

6 vnto] to J   7 yet] þat N   8 as] þat J   10 wourship] wurshipped
N wurschypt J   this] *om.* N   12 Appolyn] Appolynye N   in] and
RNJ en D   16 miserable lif or] grete mysery of N   21 physycian]
man N Physicienne D   24 for] a *add.* N   26 ther pride] *tr.* NJ
33 vpon] the *add.* NJ *om.* D   34 or 2] and NJ & D

trespas is the more, for thei synne themself and make sclaundir
in othir men, and thei breke the comaundemente of God wherof
our Lorde woll question them at the day of dome. For the
col. 2   Gospell saith hough it is necessarye to suffre / dissclaundir, but
5   yette beware, who doth that dede.

[Vndyrstondynge]

Though so be that thy holy resolucions haue meked my thought
to vndirstonde and feele the dyvine iustice, yet wolde I fayne knowe
hough the punycions of the parties of our realme dureth so longe
10   and euyrmore encrescith all this xxᵗⁱ yeris and more.

[Feythe]

Tell me how longe it is nough agoone that the princes and the
people of Fraunce beganne to tourne [their] hartis to vnclennesse
and polucion from their honorable life, and aftir that I woll answer
15   the.

[Vndyrstondynge]

I confesse wele that in oure dayes we haue seen but fewe that
haue kepte honest life or clennesse in conscience, but euery man /
f. 64   applieth to the auctorite of his power and haboundaunce of their
20   goodes aftir thappetyte of their vayne desyre rathir thanne to their
owne estate.

[Feythe]

Thanne synne it is so that owr Lorde hath so long suffird your
obstinate maners and abyde the amendment of your dissolucions,
25   why shulde nat ye than susteyne the equyte of His iustice? I see
wele your will is that He shulde suffre you to lyve in wikkidnes, and
may not suffre Him to do iustice and rightwisenes. His correccions
noyeth you as sone as ye fele any touche of them, and yet (He)
suffrith from tyme to tyme or He punyce your defaultis. But and
30   thou looke wele abowte, thou shalt wele fynde that the synnes haue
moche lenger dured thanne þe penaunces, for they beganne longe
col. 2   afore the peyne, and yet notwithstonding the chas/tismentis thei
multiplye and endure at this day. Thou woldest that [God shuld]
withdrawe His scorge from the synners, and thei woll not with-

10 yeris and more] yere NJ   13 their] NJ our R leurs D   17 I] om.
(*illumination error*) N   18 or] nor NJ   20 thanne] *om.* N   28 them]
hym N   31 penaunces] penaunce N *pl.* D   33 God shuld] NJ *tr.*
(*double lines before and after* shuld *perhaps indicate change in position*) R

drawe their hertis from synne. Hough shulde thei thanne be
wourthy to haue His peace that prowok [Him] at all tymes to
stande in gretter indignacion? The oxe that stryvith ayeinst the
prycke is gladly double prickid, and who that resistith ayeinst
discipline and dispreysith correccion shal be dispreysid of the cor- 5
rectour. For and so be that the sonne taketh the rod of his fadir in
his honde by rebellion, thanne woll the fadir take a staff that is
moche harder and forgetith the chastesing of discipline through the
rigour of punycion. Our Lorde by the mouth of the wise man
spacke, 'Lette theym witte that sette His doctrine at nought and 10
dispreysid His chastesingis that He woll laugh at their mortall
myserie and / mokke at their sodeine confusion.' f. 64ᵛ
Wherfor ye Frenschemen, take heede and remembre hough ye
haue lyued syn the deth of Kyng Charles the Fyfte of that name,
which lefte the realme full of all plente and voide of enemyes. Haue 15
ye well vsid the prosperite that your predecessours getten by excercise of noble werkes and by the vsage of vertu? Nay, the successours leese it for they sette not by doyng of good dedis forasmoche
as thei be abusid of their grette power. God yaue them grace
through the meryte of their good fadirs, and He hath taken it away 20
from the childern which gon owte of the fadirs ligne through their
demerytes. Youre grette cheueteynes noughadays studyen by envye
hough thei may enbrace the grette lordshippes, namely suche as by
olde auncetrye shulde be patrones of all wourship and mirrour of
perfeccion, and nough be thei the shewers / of pride and the col. 2
outereres of enuye. And the agid folkes make themself subiectes 26
to ambicion for to surmounte eche aboue othir through pryde; and
the yong lerne to corrupte their condicions for lacke of doctryne
and dissolute company, for nough thei haue so taken the prynte of
light will that thei dispose them to live like galauntes in ydel prodi- 30
galite and array themself lyke iouglours—that is to say, in disordinat
arrayment. And their vnatemprid corage cannot be hidde vndir
their disguysid habites, but make the nyght of the day and the day
of the nyght in fortefying of their shamefull plesaunce. Hough kepe
thei thexcellence of lordeship or the dignite of prynces? In nothiing 35
elles saue the [name] only, which is feynte and vayne, whose werkes

2 Him] *om.* RNJ le D   5 dispreysith] despeyreth N mesprise D   11 dis-
preysid] depreysed N   at] and N   16 ye] *om.* NJ   16–17 excercise] exer-
cises N *sing.* D   19 as] much as *add.* N   them] hym N   25 thei the] thee
(*final* e *perhaps changed to* i) N   28 yong] men *add.* NJ   35 thexcellence]
þe excellente J   or] of N   36 the name] *om.* N name *om.* RJ le nom D

appere shamefully. Yette woll thei gladly receue the reuerences and
f. 65 the feere of subiectis with the profy/tes of therthe, but the dedis of
good gouernaunce and the charge of tranquillite and iustice thei
haue cast from them. Hope thei to kepe and rewle lordeship ayeinst
5 nature of lordeship and regne ayeinst the will of the Kyng of
Kynges? Nay it may not be, for all power comith of God, and þe
princes be the ministers and the instrumentis of holy prouidence.
What shall the werkeman do with the instrument whanne it is nat
profitable to his werke but ley it away and take anothir? So thanne
10 thou, mortall man, wylt gouerne Goddis people ayeinst His will
not dreding His myghty power. Wherfor He woll yeue the a fall
mavgre thin hede and yet He woll not call the.

O ye men blyndid in wourship, having lordship and dominacion
ouir the [pore] people and trwe subiectis, and ye yourself be ser-
col. 2 uantis to iniquite and vices, thinke not the / contrarye but the Lorde
16 that made you to be borne yevith you gouernaunce of lordeshippes,
and only He that canne make you retournid into dust and into
wormes mete canne take all thes from you—rychesses and glories
that ye mysvse in this worlde. O ye kynges which bere ceptre and
20 crowne in this worlde, what avauntage haue ye more thanne a powr
shepeherde, or what hathe nature yeven to you or to your fadir
more thanne to othir men save oonely that God hath sette in you
by prevelage of grace? For all ye be of oone sede and entird into
this freele life nakid, and owt shall ye go agayne dispoilid, foule and
25 abhominabl[e], and thanne haue ye nought to take but oonely the
wayes of your trespasse and nought shall ye bere away but the
spottis of your diffaultes or the merite of your vertues. And yett ye
f. 65ᵛ woll vyolently vsurpe to ex/ercise the divine office, and turne it vnto
pryve glorye and to your plesaunce and profight suche as is stab-
30 lischid to the honour of God and for the profight of all the people.
What is lordship? [Noþing elles] but auctorite humayne vnder the
power of God stablischid to kepe the lawe [to] the comon wele and
the peace of subiectis. Neuirthelesse ye vse it othirwise, for ye make
therof a violent bruyte and mesprision to Almighty God, redy to
35 breke the lawe for delyte of pryve raveyne to the grette trouble of

5 the Kyng of] *om.* N 7 of] the *add.* NJ 10 man] þat *add. ins.* J
17 and . . . retournid] and oonly he and he allso that can make you to return N
oonly he and he þe also can make yow returne J 25 abhominable] NJ
abhominably R take] to *add.* NJ 26 and] nor NJ ne D 27 merite]
merytes J *sing.* D 28 vnto] ynto J 32 to 2] J *om.* RN à D 34 mes-
prision] myspreysing N God] and *add.* NJ *om.* D

subiectis. Wherfor I suppose it semith to you that lordeship is as moche to say as a power to do evil witheowt eny punycion. Wene ye [to] holde of God by parag and to departe with Him that hath no peere? Ye owe Him both seruice and feithe as His creaturis and also as His ministers and as (a) gaarde vnto His people and to kepe 5 rightwisenes as / a commyssioner and a ministour. And ye do not so He will withdrawe His fee and revoke your commyssione and will putte your wikkidnes into perdicion and take His vyneyard to othir vynours which shall in suche wise tille them that thei shall bere there kyndely fruyte in dewe season. The lordis that come nough by 10 enheritaunce were furst bygonne by forme of eleccion and through their vertuouse excellence were chosen and abled to haue suche dignite, and aftirwarde to their next heyre by permission of the people. What was this thanne? Nothing ellis save þe confidence of nature and hope of honest nortur and the holy doctryne of good 15 frendis, for naturale vertu procureth semblable effectis to their cause and of good faders be engendird the good childirn. The wisdam and the feere of worshipfull kyndred is comonly shewed owt / of their generacion through vsage of good doctryne and frequentacion of high werkes. And this wise diuerse comontees 20 haue accepted heyers in reemes as for the most perfight and semblably of the vniuersall regimen which cometh all owt of hevene where it beganne and whereas multitude shal be brought to the vnite of a symple and vndeui[d]ed power. Othir ther be þat be exaltid to lordeship and chosen for their vertue, and suche be called 25 principally Aristogracye, which is as moche to say as powere of vertue, which sometyme the senatours (of Roome) vsed and the Venycians also at the institucion of their Duke. Some ther be also that be gouerned by persones enstablischid to rule for a certayne tyme, which haue power to guyde the comonalte by myghti 30 auctorite, euery man aftir his degre; and vndir this forme the Florentynes institute their / princes by the wise counceill of the olde fadirs. And this power is callid polytyke[ly] Thy(mo)tracye, whiche some, for doubtefull vnstablenesse of ofte chaunginge their

col. 2 (line 5)
f. 66 (line 19)
col. 2 (line 32)

3 ye] *om.* N   to 1] N *om.* RJ þat *ins.* R *see n.*   God] to *add.* RNJ   6 mini-
stour] 'mynystroure NJ   And] if *add.* NJ   9 vynours] vynerous NJ
15 and . . . nortur] *om.* N   17 the] *om.* N   24 vndeuided] NJ
vndeuined R indiuisee D   27 Roome] Romen N   29 enstablischid] estab-
lysshed NJ   30 comonalte] comonte NJ   31 vndir] after J   33 power]
counseyle J *om.* N puissance D   polytykely] polytyke by RNJ politiquement
D   Thymotracye] Thymotratye N *see n.*   34 for] the *add.* NJ la D

rewlers and to þentent also to avoide occasions [of] divisions of
chesinges and parcialite of gouernours, lefte that and loued better
to continewe, by order of nature and reule of doctryne, their lordeship in a wele-rewled house and vndir gloriouse kynderede thanne
5 ofte to fall in murmoure and rumoure of mutacions, discordes and
envyes. And ayeinst thes thre spices of polecye be raysid vnlawfull
vsurpacions, which is contrarye and grette hurte to the realme:
Tyranny, Aristogracye, in which fewe men will reule by iustice,
Oligracie, Tymotracie and Democracie, which shulde gouerne the
10 vniuersall people, ys now withowt ordre.

f. 66ᵛ   O noble house of floure-de-/lyce, which haste engenderid so
many myghty men and florishid through the renowne of thi
gloriouse kynges of longe continuaunce in oone bloode and oone
manere of people, but nough wher is bycome the honorable
15 magnificence of thin estate? Where is become the laudible ordinaunce of lyving, þe shewyng of honeste, the countenaunce of
corage and good maners, and high herte to take vpon them entreprises suche as thine auncesters lefte to their successours? Chastite
is corrupte, which was sometyme wonte to holde thine abyding
20 certayne. And noughadayes men norishe lordes sones in delites and
nycetes as sone as thei be borne; that is to say, as sone as thei can
anything speke thei be brought to scole of foule wourdis. Some be
wourshipid in their cradils, and aftirwarde thei vse them so that
col. 2   thei canne nothir / knowe themself nor othir. Who be thei that be
25 abowte þem that may iuge himself owt of presumpcion? For many
of þem entre in by fauour which can nothinge enforme them in
connynge nor vse them to do any goode werkes. Seest þou nat
hough disordinaunce hath suche a wise putt polecy owt of reule
that princes take their preve eases and acustome [hem]self to necli-
30 gence wheras thei shulde travaile for the comon wele? And so thei
take their pleasur like as thei wer borne to do nothinge ellis but ete
and drinke, and yette woll looke afftir grette reuerence of the people
and (no)thinge do therfor. Yette ther is more, for at this day their

1 also] so add. N   avoide] voyde NJ   of 1] om. RNJ de D   3–4 lorde-
ship] doctryne J seigneurie D   12 myghty] myghten J   the] om. J
15 become] allso add. NJ   16 countenaunce] contynuaunce J constance D   20 lordes] lorde J   delites] delyces N   22 to] the add. NJ
la D   26 can nothinge] tr. NJ   27 do] om. N   27–8 nat hough]
tr. (// may indicate change of position) N   28 a] om. NJ   29 hemself]
hem NJ self R   32 and 2] om. NJ & D   woll] thei add. NJ   33 their]
om. N

[renneth] a folische langage in courte seying the grette estates shult
nat lerne lettur and taketh it for a shame that the nobles shulde
othir write or rede. Allas, who may speke of gretter folye or opyn
a more perilouse erroure? Certainly / he may be wele callid a beste f. 67
that glorifieth himself to be likened as a beste, that is to say, as a 5
man that hath non vndirstondinge and yette woll yeve lawde to his
own diffawtes. The priuelege of mannes nature is to moche forgoten whanne they woll lyve bestially in ignoraunce, for if man
haue excellence in vndirstondinge more thanne bestes than me
semes he that hath lordeship and reule ouir the people ought sur- 10
mount in conning aboue othir men. Thanne I cannot repreue him
that saith, 'A kynge that is withowte letturature is like an asse
crowned.' For it is no doubte that lordeship and seruage be stablischid by the lawe of reason and not by the yeftis of fortune.
Thanne and so be that all be egall in humanite, as wele in genera- 15
cion as in birth, me semyth that suche as haue by the lawe pre-
eminence to governe ought to haue by excercise perfeccion of
knowlage and vn/dirstonding. For it is clere thing that lordeship col. 2
and seruage be institute by statute humayne, for this begynnith in
them in the faculte of Dame Nature. For thei that haue wretyn to 20
vs before *The Polesyes* haue shewid vs by conclusion that men by
theire vndirstondinge ben abled within themself by nature to haue
gouernaunce and lordeship, and the rude people, which haue their
vigour in their bodily strenght, be putt down and yeven to naturall
seruage lykewise as þe mortall body is subiect to þe perdurable spirit. 25

And thou wolt knowe whereof this ianglyng and lesynges cometh,
thinke that evyl officers may not abyde with a wise prince, for an
vntrew seruaunt desireth allway to haue an ignoraunt maister. For
vice is foundid vpon ignoraunce and norischid vndir the shadow of
derkenes, but trouth requirith the know/lage and the light. Folish f. 67ᵛ
guyding of a powre man stretchith no ferther but to hymself, for 31
othir men take but litill hede to diss[ei]ue hym, but a prince that
hath non vndirstonding troubleth thestate of euery persone and is
as a shelde to the euil people and a couertoure of synners. Wherfor
he that hath all in rewle ought to haue vndi(r)stonding in all 35

1 renneth] NJ remainnith R court D   seying] that *add.* NJ   grette]
as *add.* R *see n.*   2 lettur] lettrure NJ   4 be wele] *tr.* NJ
12 letturature] lettrure NJ   17 to 2] *om.* NJ   18 is] a N ys a J   22 within
themself] with hymself N   30 requirith] knowlage *add.* R   the 1]
om. NJD   the 2] *om.* NJD   Folish] the folyssh NJ la D   32 disseiue]
NJ dissolue R deceuoir D   34 as a] as J a N

thynges. Also he ought to [be] custumed in reding and haue a witte
to eschewe inconuenyentes. All thes ar sittyng to a prince which
euery man desirith to yeve attendence to thentent that thei might
be of gretter auctorite or ellis supprise him by malice. And [þerfore]
5 that person that stondith in ieoperdy of the grettest falle ought of
reason to haue vndirstonding aboue othir that he fall not in perile.
Othir ther be that for lightnese of speche and faute of vndirstonding
fallen in the sentence of the wise Plato, which said [that he] helde /
col. 2 all lordeshippes and comon weles for happy whanne the wise men
10 of grette vndirstonding haue the gouernaunce therof. Salomon, the
grette, wise kynge, made herein a grette profe whanne he wrote so
many bookis of Holy Scripture, which by his wisedam of vndirstondinge distroyed all iniquite and cast owt of his realme in his
tyme all mischief and discorde. [Avicenne] through his profounde
15 vndirstonding atteyned to secrettis of nature and left you the fayre
(distincions) of Philosophie and Phisike [in his Booke of Canons.
He was prynce of Baaly. And his envyous Avereys coment on
Arystotle was a Duke of Grece.] Iulius Cesar, which was fortunate
to victories and gloriouse in thempyre, was not he an oratour and
20 an excellent philosophr? We fynde his oracions in writinge and the
werkes of [astrologie] by him were amendid. And if the stories be
trewe þe *Mageste* and othir principall bookes of the hevinly sciences
f. 68 ben attrybute to Tholome, Ky/ng of Egipte, which assembled the
noble [librarie] in his cuntre, which no manne coude esteme the
25 noumbre of volumes. Mydrydates also, that was Kyng of Pont,
comprised so many sciences that he spake xxij langages and yave
them to xxij nacions þat were vndir him. Knowest þou not hough
in his furst yeris the vij artes wer callid liberall forasmoche as the
princes and the fre people studyed in them? And on the othir side
30 the high men, which [first] stablischid principalitees and made
lawes through which þe worlde is gouerned, gadred togedir clerkes
and wise men and mighty councellours to be conseruatours of the
lawe and yave them high and mighty power. Yette thei wer mor
assured of ther connyng than of their powere, for connyng of itself

1 and] to *add*. N   2 thes ar] þis is NJ   4 ellis] to *add*. NJ   6 to] *om*
NJ   8 that he] *tr*. RNJ   9 happy] happly J for *add*. R   14 Avicenne]
A vice thanne RNJ Auicenne D   21 astrologie] Aristotle RN Arystole J
Astrologie D *see n*.   22 sciences] science N *pl*. D   24 librarie] NJ
libraries R *sing*. D   29 studyed] dyd studye J s *canc*. dyd studye N
31 gouerned] he *add*. N   34 of 1] to J   34–p. 59, l. 1 of itself is] is of
itselfe NJ

is mighty to gete and encresce power, but powere withowt wisdom
is as a bowe withowt a strynge and like / also as a fayre arme wele- col. 2
shapen of flesche, boon and synewes whose myght is withdrawen
through power of the palsy. Whanne Ligurgus and For[on]eus in
the tyme of Grece, and sithen that tyme Iustynean and othir 5
Emperours of Roome, had stablischid the lawes, thei reseruid vnto
the princes for to declare and susteyne them, for and if it had ben
othirwise it had be but in vayne, for the lawe that is wretyn is in
himself but a ded thyng and withowte myght. But the prince and
the lawe togethir maketh it to lyve quykly and refreschith the 10
spirite of the lawes, which yevith them power and vertue; and so
through good guyding of the prince the lawes may be made quycke.
Thanne synne it is so that in the lawes and the wrytingis restith the
prudence of man, me semith that it wer not sittyng that he which
is the lif of the lawe and redressing of worldely wisedom / shulde f. 68ᵛ
be a foole or a man withowt vndirstonding. And yette by the lacke 16
of this knowlage the princes wolde lyve as lordis ouir the people
and thei be subiectis to vices. They haue misknowen their soueraigne Kyng perdurable, and He hath made them to be vnknowen
of their temporall subiectis. Thei wolde putt downe mannes reason 20
in fulfillyng of their worldely desires, and He hath putte them
downe vndir the reason eternall.

O ye Frenchemen, ye take in custome to blaspheme the name of
Hym to whom all the worlde ought to bowe their kne, and He
through vsyng of His iustice hathe putte yow in blame and repref 25
of nacions and maketh your bodyes and your hedis enclyne byfore
youre enemyes. The owtragiouse lyfe is turned vnto the miserable
dethe. The voluptuouse vanite is a streyte prysone. / The feerce col. 2
pride is turned into lowly and plyaunt seruitute. Knowest thou now
hough necligence, which is stepmodir to vertu, drawith man to a 30
lowe renown and makith [hym] vnworthi to haue rewle of lordshippis? In like wise vnhappy ignoraunce is vnperfite in himself,
and in his werkis febl[e] and [impotent], and leuith the knowlage

2 as 1] like N om. J comme D   3 flesche] and add. NJ & D   4 Foroneus]
Foreus RN Floreus (1 perhaps canc.) J Phoroneus D   5 Grece] grete Iulius N
Grecz D   sithen] syn NJ   6 vnto] to NJ   7 if] om. NJ   9 him-
self] ytself NJ   10 it to] yt J to N   11 spirite] spyripte N   13 lawes]
lawe N pl. D   and] yn add. J om. D   14 that 1] om. NJ   18 subiectis]
subiect NJ pl. D   19 hath made] had N   27 vnto] to N   28 is]
as add. NJ   29 now] nott J or endroit D   30 man] a man N   31 hym]
J om. RN   33 feble and impotent] NJ feblith and impetentith R impotente D

of God and of his office as an vnresonable beeste. And therfor his
delite, his suerte and his grace levith him, and peyne, shame and
miserye pursewith him vnto his shamefull ende.

[Vndirstondynge]

5   Yet returne to the first request from which me semes thou art
somwhat goon owt of the way, and shewe me what is the cause of
the longe duryng of our grette eviles.

[Feythe]

f. 69   Thanne excuse if thou canst your harde and / long obstinacion
10   afore or thou accuse the prolonginge of thy Iuge. And if He delay
longe to be peaced ye delaye lon[ger] or ye repent yourself. His
hande is al[way] redy bent to smyte till His people returne ther face
[towarde Hym]. Feer and humilite getith grace and mercy, and
misknowlage of God procurith murmur, myschief and vengeaunce.

15   ### [Vndyrstondynge]

What othir persecucions knowest thou that ha[ue] dured so
longe, that by them aftir Catholike introduccion we ought lerne to
kepe and suffre in so longe continuall sorowes in exemple of longe
pacience?

20   ### [Feithe]

Hast thou nat redde that þe people of Israell were in deserte the
space of xl yere for their contradiccions and murmur through which
they procured the indignacion of God, namely suche as caused the
col. 2   ru/moure and disobeysaunce? Wherupon the texte said that thei
25   shulde neuir entre into þe londe of promission, but suffrid by
divine terminacion the deth oon aftir anothir in deserte till the
people were clensid. And aftir that our Lorde putt His people in
possession of the heritage that He promisid them. As in othir places
of Scriptur men may fynde inough of like sentence, and among all
30   other specially in the transmygracion of Babilon, which for blas-
phemyng [of] the name of God, preuaricacion of the lawe and
infeccion of ydolatrie, Ieremye by the decre of hevinly iugement

---

1 therfor] for N   10 Iuge] iugement N iuge D   12 alway redy] NJ
alredy R Tousiours D   ther] hys J   16 haue] NJ hast R   18 longe 1]
tyme add. N   22 murmur] murmurs NJ pl. D   26 terminacion] deter-
minacyon NJ   31 God] and add. N om. D

shewed in Ierusalem that the princes and the cheueteynes of the people, the olde fadyrs and the grette men of the lynage shulde be take and brought prisoners into Babilon, their temples shulde also be dispoylid, and the people chaunged vndir the seruage of straungers, like as it fell aftirward. But whanne þe / people re- f. 69ᵛ tournid agayne owt of bondage vnto fredom, from the aff[liccion] 6 of Babylon vnto the tranquyllite of Ierusalem, and specially suche as blasphemyd God, whethir thei euir come ageyne into their cuntre? Nay. The persecucion dured vnto the tyme that the cursid generacion wer exteynte and voydid owt of therthe. And the chil- 10 dern that had lerned to travaile in vexacion and pacience recouerid the merites of grace and as trew chi[l]dern of Israell entrid the heritage of their fadirs. The durynge of this plage lastid longe like the age of a man, that is to say, the noumbre of lxx yere to thentent that the evile people durynge that tyme shulde deye in caitifnes. 15 And thanne our Lorde restored His londe with newe people whiche were examined in aduersite. This same persecucion diffaced thini- quitees and made preef and confirma/cion of the good dedes. And col. 2 this was couenable for two causes: for divine iustice berith witnesse in exterminacion of repreues, and the soueraigne goodnesse of yong 20 men is to represse their willfull desire through constreynte of peyne in their yong yeris, beryng the yocke of subieccion in the heete of youthe.

Concidre the infortune and discordis nough present, and thou shalt fynde semblable thinges according to the same. Hough be it, 25 it is not myne entent to remembre them þat be gylty in this poynte, which applye themself to myschaunce and to dispurveyed dethe. But wold God that thingis suche as noyen to the lyvers may be profite to the succeders and that this scorge myght the shortlyer be abriggid and mercy more ney you in the lawe of grace thanne was 30 to the people of the Iewys in the lawe of rigour. And this may come through youre / contricion and the mekenesse of the euyrlastyng f. 70 Fadir, whiche syn the passion of Ihesu Crist hath more withdrawe His f[ur]oure thanne His benyngnite and in the humanyte of His

3 shulde also] *tr.* J   6 affliccion] N affeccion RJ affliction D *see n.*
8 their] own *add.* NJ   10 exteynte] extyncte N   14 noumbre] space
(*ins.*) J   17 persecucion] perfeccion N   19 witnesse] wytneth J   20 good-
nesse] goodes J bien D   21 through] the *add.* NJ *om.* D   22 their] her
(*corrected from* yer) N   25 semblable] semablelye N   25–6 it, it] yt NJ
28 thingis suche] *tr.* NJ   30 ney] nere NJ   31 this] tyme *add.* N
om. D   34 furoure] favoure RNJ fureur D *cf. p. 62, l. 17*

Sone hathe avaunced His mercy to the Cristen people, which He
withdrewe from the childern of the Olde Testament.

[Vndrestondynge]

To put away the remenaunte of myn doubtes and confirme my
5 thought in feer, shewith that we suffre is divine punycion and that
it shulde not be yevin to fortune nor to the power of mannes myght
nor of worldly enterpryses.

[Feythe]

There be many thinges that [openly] ar shewed in that maledic-
10 cione which shall (make) the certeyne of that thou sechest. For
thefficient causes [of euery thyng] shyne in theire effecte, and the
col. 2 huma/yne demonstracion begynnyth in [in]perfeccion by the acci-
dence and by the inperfight effectes. But I woll not reste at thi
discordes, for argumentis and silogismes be closid owte of my
15 boundes. And therfor I woll returne and shewe what the holy
prophe[cyes] techith vs. And there I fynde that ther be thre principall thyinges that yeve tokenyng of divine furour ouir euery nacion
and the wrath of God ayeinst lordeshippes. The furst is whanne the
harme and the persecucion begynneth in the souereignes and in the
20 princes, and the hedes ben furst smeten and diffaced by vncouen-
able deth or put from wille and power by vnhappy iugement of this
worlde. Dauid said vnto God: 'Thou hast smeten the hede in the
house of the evile man and vnknyt the foundament of his strenghe
vnto his necke. Thou hast cast Thi curse vpon the ceptrees and
f. 70ᵛ vpon the cheueteynes / of men of armes.' The secunde token of the
26 divine iugement shewith himself whanne men fall in disknowlage
of remedy in aduersite, takyng no hede in what case and perill thei
stonde, in their aduyce troubled in neede, counseil incerteyn and
wandryng abowte in necessite. O thou celestiall Ysaie, which in the
30 lawe of Moyses haddest a Cristen spirite, it semed as thou haddist

5 is] of *add*. NJ *om*. D   7 enterpryses] empryses N   9 openly ar]
openly be N openly ys J ar R *see n*.   11 shyne] schynen J shewen N
reluysent D   12 inperfeccion] NJ the perfeccion R imperfection D
13 not] now (w *ins*.) J ne D   16 thre] the N   17 furour] NJ *corrected
from* fauour R *see n*.   20 and the] and that N and þat þe J & que les D
vncouenable] yncouenable N vncouable J   21 and] or J & D   24 curse]
curses N   25 men] of men *add*. R   27 and] or J   28 incerteyn] vn
certeyn J in Certeyn R vncerteyn N   30 as] at NJ

rathir be a wryter of Euaungeles thanne a shewer of prophecyes, for thou wrotest clerely this demonstraunce in the peresecucion that thou shewdist in Egipte, of which Abbot Ioachym and othir holy persones haue syn that tyme exposid [for] Fraunce, saying this wise by divine power: 'I woll amate youre hartis within youre 5 entrailes, and I woll ouirthrowe your counseyll and put in you a spirit turnyng and variable and withowt constaunce, and I woll make you / walke as a dronken man which losith the vndirstonding col. 2 and the vertu hough he shulde guyde himself.' Thriddely may a man perceyve the swourde of Godd whanne it is reysid ouir the 10 lordis and the lordshippes whanne through the steryng of foreyne enemyes cyuyle discordes ben ingendred in realmes, which causith oftetymes that their is no resistence. And certainly theuidence hereof hath opynly be shewed, for men may see that within the high paleyces grow and encresce grette discencions and pryue 15 diffiaunces. For the venym and thinfeccions of cyuyle discordes was ordeigned by God to put away pryde of worldely highnesse and to thentent also as suche as surmountid othir by suche ensaumple shulde putte downe themself in humilite vndir God and so to be brought ageyne to [the knowleghe of] their freele 20 powere. And this is ratified to vs in the Gospell, which shewith desolacion to diuerse realmes.

Applye nough thes [signes] / to thi matere and take hede what f. 71 mervelouse pestilence and what spede of condemnacions ben fall vpon þ[i] princes and on the high persones, and many men be 25 perischid and dede, and the glorie of lordeship is turned into captiuite and myserye in a shorte space. Where is nough a noble house in Fraunce that may say [itself] quyte owte of the daungere of prison or exempte from the hevynes of this new dethe? For in all the parties of the londe the castellis be enhabited with wedowes 30 or desolate wyues of prisoners; the lordshippis be in the handis of childern [and] fadirlesse. Yette and any be lefte of estate that is of age to rewle lordeshippis, diuerse of them lacke þe dignite and the

---

1 of 1] the add. NJ om. D   4 exposid] expowned N exposée D   for] NJ from R pour D   9 shulde] om. N   15 discencions] dissencyon N pl. D pryue] pryvate N   16 diffiaunces] diffyaunce N pl. D   discordes] discorde NJ sing. D   17 highnesse] rychesse N haultesses D   18 as 1] that NJ 22 desolacion] desolacyons N sing. D   23 signes] NJ thi/nges R signacles D what] þat J quelle D   25 þi] NJ þe R tes D   28 itself] om. RNJ se puisse dire D   the] om. N   daungere] daungers NJ pl. D   30 the 2] þis J   32 of estate] om. N en estat D   33 dignite] dygnytes NJ pl. D

vertu of lordshippe. And yet thei be more redy to make vncouen-
able charge thanne to yeue any confort. Yet shortly in all estates
col. 2 the wourshipfull men worke thexcellentes and the / witty excercyses,
the corageouse and the manly men in armes and wourthines be
5 withdrawen from you, furst oon and sithin anothir. For ther is
abiding but small noumbre of perfight men, but ther is lefte a
multitud of powr, [of] nedy and of dispurveyed people withowt
power and withowt herte. And yet with more your infelicite is
suche that though so happe any man among you dispose himself
10 with a corageouse herte by good inclinacion or grace for to do wele
in sustentacion of the werres, anone God and fortune sufferyth him
not to endure. And so I see nothing that may surely stonde with
you that may be hoope of your arysyng. And among all thes
anguisshes and in the grettest constreynte of your nedis, your
f. 71ᵛ hertis vanish and / lette yourself fall to the daungers of fortune as
16 symple seruauntes, and thus ye perishe, not rekkyng, wilfully,
wittingly, withowt putting of any heede to your counseile. [The
language of the prophete may wele be verified in you, which said,
'Ye shall speke moche] and He shall nothing do. Ye shall make
20 many counseils, and your counseillis shal be but vayne, variable
and disperpulid. And ye shall procede in your dedis as the blynde
man that gothe gropyng abowte the walles and wote not wherby to
holde nor in what place he is.' And this wise do ye, for your
counseils be withowt liberte and withowt ordre, your opynyons be
25 aftir your affeccions, your conclusions withowt [areste], and your
ordinaunces withowt any effecte. Suche thinges falle to you as God
discryvith by the voyce of Isaie, vpon suche as wolde not be
chastised like as aftir foles: 'Comaunde and comaunde ageyne,
col. 2 abyde and abyde ageyn, now on this syde, now / on that syde. This
30 is the way whereby ye shall fall bakwarde, and men shall trede vpon
your feete. In a latche shall ye be taken and perischid through your
variable counseile and fawte of constaunce.' Moreouir it is fallen to

---

3 thexcellentes] þe excellences J excellence N   5 sithin] syn NJ
6 abiding] abyden NJ   but 1] a add. NJ   8 herte] The language of the
prophete [prophetye N y *perhaps canc.*] may wele be verified in you which said
ye shall speke moche *add.* RNJ *see 17–19*   10 do] *ins.* J *om.* N   12 to]
om. NJ   16 wilfully] *om.* NJD   17–19 The . . . moche] *misplaced
above* RNJ   21 shall] schul J shuld N   23 holde] hym *add.* N   ye]
the N   25 affeccions] affeccion J *see n.*   areste] NJ reste R arreste D
26 ordinaunces] ordynaunce N *pl.* D   27 not] to N   28 foles] folowes NJ
see n.   29 syde 1] and *add.* N *om.* D   31 feete] takyn *add.* NJ
latche] lacche N laithe J   shall ye] *tr.* NJ   32 fawte of] faute J de D

yow as to men that ben acursid, which be so vnhappy that ye may
not lyve togedir, but distroye eche oþer and a[ne]auntise your
werkes more by your debate thanne by the sworde of your aduersaryes. Ye study how eche of you may put owt othir, and ye slepe
in the putting owt of your enemyes. Ye haue malice and enterprises 5
ayeinst your neyghbours, and ye be necligent and symple anempst
your persecutours. Ye may not endur oon of you with anothir, but
ye may suffre to be disherited and brought to myschief by your
enemyes. What thing may helpe hym that liste to noye hymself?
Or hough may a cite endur which is beseged / withowt and werre f. 72
within?   11

By suche significacions ye may knowe that the hande of God (is)
ouir you, for aduersite me semeth cannat amende you and travaile
gevith you no poynte of knowlage. What shall a man thinke in you
whanne ye putte your glorie and apply your stvdye most diligently 15
to the ruyne of your prosperite and the ouirthrowyng of your
power? But your hertis be so bathid and inprynted with murmours
and pryve discordis so that vnto the tables and beddes of theyme
that ete and drynke and slepe togedir is the suspecion couerid and
the trust failed. Ye aske of God peace by rancour and requere His 20
mercy with the sworde in the hande. Ye wolde be belouid withowt
charite, and ye wolde abide in surete withowt goode feith. Why
shulde [God] kepe (you) from þe enemyes that ye lose your owne
self? What humilite might ye kepe in the happy / tyme whanne   col. 2
your presumpcions and your rumours growe nowe in your mis-   25
cheves? Your wourship perischith sith your wourthines beganne
to byte eche othir, kyssing, as dogges and cattes of a caitif corage,
and leve the proteccion of the comon weleth. Certainly in this age
may wele be confirmid the vision that the Quene of Saba [shewede]
to Achilperi[c]h, the fadir of Clouys, vpon the generacion of   30
Frenchemen, which I reporte me to the texte of your olde cronycles,
which ye may rede and knowe, also in othir stories if necligence
make it not. Rest vpon thes poyntes. And from hensforth revoke
not nor be not in doubte but the wrathe of God hanghith ouir you,

2 aneauntise] aneentyse NJ avauntise R aneantissez D   6 anempst]
ayenst NJ   11 within] hemselfe *add.* N hymself *add.* J *om.* D   12 suche]
om. N ces D   17 with] withyn NJ en D   23 God] NJ he R Dieu D
you] *om.* J *see n.*   þe] your N   ye lose] list to lese N   25 presumpcions]
presumpcion N   your 3] awne *add.* N   27 caitif] þe *add.* N
30 Achilperich] NJ Achilperith R Chilperic D *see n.*   33 not. Rest] J no
Rest N not rest R   34 but] þat *add.* NJ   wrathe] wrethe NJ

C 7740   F

which distryneth you above the fortune of tyme and is more grevouse vnto you thanne the owtragiouse ambicion of theym that make you warre. /

f. 72ᵛ

5 Thow that art turmentid with aduersite, both with the fleshe and the worlde, and temptid with the evill spirit, which is alway redy to disceve the, loke thou present thiself fermely, both body, herte, trust, conscience, power and hole entente, to the goodnesse of the most excellent Lorde, before whome all thing is presentid and nothing absentid. And ther is the way of helthe. Ther euery

10 herte is content and [peesed] which sorowith and bewailith the offences done to his Maker. And one thing I lette the witte: that armes, subtiltees nor good nor nothing that any man may haue, withowt Hym is but a thin(g) voide and of no substaunce. For ther (is) neithir feere ne affeccion that may move Hym from

15 doyng of rightfull iustice though He be long or slowe in the

col. 2 doing. But who that woll receve / councell and clerely vndir- stonde hymself must put away pride and purvey that it hurte him not. Thanne he, so doyng his devoir, shal be abled to receve the vij yeftis of the Holy Goste, which bringith in [grace] shortly

20 to all meke folkes.

[The Auctoure]

By thes solucions and Catholike shewinges Vndirstonding abode aswryyd, yolden vnto reste of his concience, for owte of his secrete thoughtes wer putte away all murmours and grugynges ayeinst þe

25 diuyne iugementis; and þe feere of God, which was hid among these murmours, and for Feith was half put in and half owte, abode alone victoriouse in the discrescion of Vndirstonding. Yet he of newe thought to aske a newe demaunde vpon þat that was to come of his premisses in [this] sentence: /

f. 73

[Vndyrstondynge]

31 O lady, which barest in thyself the fygured dignites of the Holy Gost and through holy symplenes hast powere of divyne message

---

7 herte] and *add.* N   8 before] to N   10 peesed] NJ pleacid R r'apaise D   13 but] as *add.* NJ   18 devoir . . . abled] meryte shalbe redy and able N *see n.*   23 aswryyd] assured N answyryd J assoulagié D 24 grugynges] grucchynges N   26 half 2] put *add.* N   27 victoriouse] victoryously N   28 was] new *add.* N   29 this] NJ the R ceste D 31 barest] berest N beryth J

to conforme the creatures vnto the knowlege of þe Creatour with
tvnges and wourdis more persyng thanne swerdis, the dyvision of
the sowle which is ioyned to the sencetif body, and that the spirit
may be areysid to God by spirituall grace and with fyre embraced
with trewe love and feere of Hym that hath callid vs vnto His 5
frendlyhode to make Hym anamowrid vpon vs furst. And this that
is fall to vs makith me at this tyme haue the lesse weyght forasmoche as thou hast clerely shewed me the dyvine equyte and the
iniquyte of oure humayne offences. Wherfor me semeth he that
hath shulde not vnwourthily suffre the peyne that prowdely hath 10
committid the desert. But lette se nough what maner of allegeaunce
/ wi[l]t thou [yeve to oure litle feblenes, or what comforte yn tyme col. 2
to come or what hope of allegaunce wylt thu] promyse vs seing that
thi Maister and our Iusticer hath made vs to be parteners of His
goodenes and to be brought to His clemence and hatith nothing 15
of His werkes, owt of whose goodnesse may issewe non evyle.
Wher shall we become or what ende woll He sette vpon our soroufull myscheves?

[Feythe]

Let suffice the that I haue said and constreyne me not to enbrace 20
othir mennes offices, for though so be that my sustirs and I be
alyed and that our begynnynge and ending be ooned in one cause
efficient and fyniall and our meanes conioyned inseperable, yet this
question longith to my sustir Hope, of whom thou shalt fynde the
answere. 25

[The Auctoure]

Aftir thes wourdes Dame / Feithe kepte cilence and gave place f. 73ᵛ
vnto hir sustir Hope for to speke, as to hir that dressid [the] spirite
to vndirstonde by desirous confiaunce suche thinges as we ought
furst to vndirstonde by entere feythe. For drede gothe byfore the 30
hope, and the stedeffastnes of hope is foundid in the stedefastnes
of goode beleve. And þerfor feythe is callid substaunce, that is, the
foundement of thinges esperable and the argument of thinges
which may not appere by mannes reason, forasmoche as it hath no

---

1 conforme] conferme NJ confermer D *see n.*   4 with] a *add.* NJ *om.* D
12 wilt] NJ wist R   14 Iusticer] iuge N iusticier D   21 sustirs] sustur J
pl. D   23 inseperable] ynceperable J yncrepable N   25 answere] answerd
N la response D   28 vnto] to NJ   the] hir RNJ le D   29 confiaunce]
confydence N   31 of hope . . . stedefastnes] *om.* N

foote nor substaunce which may be founded vpon manes reason. Neuirtheles by hir stedefast cleving she liftith the beleve of man above his own knowlage, and on that parte which is made by experience or by dryfte of arguynge [the] rewarde ceseth and the

col. 2 perfeccion of the holy feythe. So beleve is by / ensaumple com-
6 parable to (a) byrde callid alerion or a merlion, which hath no feete to go on the grounde, but all hir movyng is on hir wynges, which enhaunce or lifte hir vp into the eyre. Thanne in hope we abyde those thinges which by feyth we beleuen.

10 And what is hope? Nothing ellis but a certeyn abyding of the blissidnesse that is to come by the grace of God and by premission of holy merites. Trewe it is that we may hope in som thinges here byneth as the grace of God, Is helpe and the benefice of His proteccion and sustinaunce, and all thes thinges be nothing ellis

15 but oonely meanis to come to the blissid ende and perdurable glorye. Thanne syn it is so that the petyte hope restith not vpon these thynges here byneþe, but oonely make waye towarde the soueraigne goodes above, which euery man ought to seche and is thende of all abyding and inclynacion of all thinges creat, yet I

f. 74 say / that all oure worldely abydinges ben callid hope forasmoche
21 as theire endes here bynethe subaltare stretchith to the (f)inall and infinyte ende and be parteable to His bountie of which all othir particulare endes take thaire name and their goodnes. And who that trustith in God shall haue helth and victorie. Also hope may

25 right wele conforte vs in the lowe thinges forasmoche as thei may be likned [to] the thinges above, for all thinges were made of God and for God, and by God thei haue their abyding vndir God and their reduccion into God and their blissidnes with God.

This ordre Dame Feith stablischid amonge the vertues in send-
30 ing the knowlage of the last question to hir suster Hope. And she as an officere of a Prynce of ordinaunce, through whom all werkes ben ordinatly rewled, kepte hir place and toke vpon hir withowt

col. 2 envy or pryde the / office for to speke, whych Feyth lefte hir by

---

1 substaunce] the *add.* NJ   2 liftith] lyftyfe N   man] a man N
6 alerion or] *om.* NJ   7 hir 1] *om.* J son D   on 2] vppon NJ   8 or]
canc. and *ins.* N   11 and] *om.* N & D   13 Is] hys (*corrected from ?* ys) J and
his N *see n.*   15 ende] *om.* N fin D   18–19 is thende] yt ys ende J *see n.*
21 subaltare] and *add.* N   finall] *cross stroke of* f *ins.; scribe mistook word for*
small R   24 trustith] tresteth J   helth] helpe N santé D   and] or J ou D
27 and for God] *om.* N & pour Dieu D   28 into] vnto N   blissidnes]
blessedhede NJ   32 rewled] and *add.* N *om.* D

humilite and by ordynaunce of wourship. For the goodnesse of
vertues discorde neuir but accorde, good with good and trouth
with trouth. But amonge the vices there is contrariousnes and
debate, and puttith euery herte in trouble whereas it restith.
Slowthe will slepe and take no hede; and couetise sechith travaile; 5
and hasty wrath, ryotes, noyses and cryes; and lechery yevith
counseile to blaundischynge, to flattre and to disceyve. Thanne let
vs see here the mervaile of divine werkes. We fynde that all that
is of God kepith an ordynaunce and all that growith of synne owt
of arraye into a confuce wandryng and to volucion turneth, all 10
disordinat.

Thanne Hope drough hir towarde the bedde and sodeynly withdrewe hirself ageyne. But as sone as Vndirstondinge was warre of
Hope, his spiritis ioyed, and dressid hym vpwarde and lifte vp his
yghen / ententyfly to see, abyding hir conforte. This lady Hope had f. 74ᵛ
a lawghing and a ioyfull visage. She bare an high looke. Hir speche 16
was agreable. And in oone of hir hondis she bare a boxe of cipres
full of oynement confecte with promysses sometyme made to the
fadirs by the prophetes an to vs of the wourde of Goddis Sone;
and this was the bawme of consolacion of Holy Scr[i]ptures, which 20
hathe norischid vs in hope and aswagith the sorowes and angwysshes of the wo(r)lde. And in the tothir hande she helde a turet
of golde with a gossehawke theron, whose beeke was fastened
within the hevenes closid within þe seurte of the depe mercy of the
Creatoure. And forthewithall this lady opened the boxe owt of 25
which come so grette a odour that it persid me evin to the herte,
which surmounted the stynke þat the thre fantasied ladyes / had col. 2
lefte me in byfore. Thanne myght Diffidence and Dise[s]peraunce
no lenger endur that deliciouse flauour which was contrary to their
natur, as tryacle vnto venym, and drowe abacke into the shadow 30
of þe curteyne of the bedde as thei wolde haue hydden themself.
Thanne Vndirstonding, confirmyd by Feithe and somwhat towched
with swetenesse of the oynement that was in the boxe and also of

1 by] the add. N om. D   6 wrath] wrethe NJ   8 see] and add. N
10 volucion] þat add. N   12 hir] nere add. J   15 see] the add. N om. D
abyding] and add. N om. D   18 to] of J   19 of 1] om. N   21 aswagith]
aswaged N   sorowes] sorowe J pl. D   22 a] þe J   23 of golde with]
of gold of J of N   theron] om. NJ   fastened] fycched NJ fiché D see n.
26 a] and N   28 Thanne] Then ne J Thu ne N   Disesperaunce] J
Diseperaunce R Desperaunce N   30 as] was J comme D   tryacle] is add.
N om. D   32 Thanne] thou/ne J Thou ne N

thapproching of Dame Hope, which Feith at that tyme had let him haue the knowlage of hir commyng, byganne to say these wourdes:

[Vndyrstondynge]

O lady, full of socoure, spryng of conforte, refuge of all sorow-
5 full, right happy and ioyfull is to me thi comyng, for in a gretter aduersite thanne this thou myghtest neuir socoure me thanne owt
f. 75 of the sorowe that I haue ben in syn / thi longe being hens. But now through thyne approching I fele myself arysing owt of the shadow of deth into þe clerenesse of lif. O hough wele it apperith that thou
10 were born in good place and ysewed owt of the founteyne of life, for withowt the þe life of man were but as an ymage of deth and lyke as a body withowt soule, as lyfe withowt lyving and as deth withowt deyenge. By the is ouircome the wrechidnesse of the worlde amonge which all othir counseile failith. Thou abidest
15 allway in the felde and art neuir ouircome, but withstondest the myschevese of þe vnhappy folkis so that thou neuir levist them vnto the tyme that [thei yeld] the spirit, and though othir vertues departe yet thou abidest alone ayeinst all evill fortune. But who that lesith the may holde no vertu. Thi grette myght maynteyneth
20 the vigour and the spirit, and it may not be take away [with
col. 2 strenketh] nor be withdrawe / by violence. The only erroure of thought and fawte of feith maketh [þe] to leve them which ayeinst nature leve themself and stryve to vnmake in himself that nature hath made by the vertue of hir Maister. Why hast thou thanne thus
25 wise lefte me, and why hast thou be soo longe from me? For through thy longe taryenge I was allmost fall into the pytte of dispeyre seynge that I had no signe nor apparence of thy comyng. For the maners of man nor the state of things present shewid me no manere significacion of þe. Wherefor I was aba[ndened] and
30 thought that the habitacion of this oure realme was from the at all poyntes entyrditid by God as a londe condemned and cursid vnto þe tyme that Feith lyfte vp hir spirit in contemplacion of the mercifull power of aboue, which hath brought the hider. For by

1 which] wyth J que D   2 the] om. N   6 thou] thaw N   thanne 2] om. NJ   17 thei yeld] NJ thou yeldest R   23 himself] hemself J   24 the] om. N la D   thus] this NJ   25 soo] thus NJ   26 into] yn NJ   27 nor] of (corrected from nor) N   29 significacion] signefyaunce NJ   abandened] J abashid R ashamed N habandonne D   32 Feith] which add. NJ

the meditacions and the perseyvinges of / heere benethe I cowde f. 75ᵛ
not atteygne to vndirstonde by any demonstraunce thy comyng
ageyne. And syn it is so that þe grace of God and the merite of
Dame Feith haue the rewle of the, I pray the approche to me that
I may enbrace the in myn armes, for it sufficith me not to see the 5
with myn yghe aferre, but it is to me behovefull to towche the and
my feblenesse to leene vpon thy myght. For and thou susteigne me
I may not fall in discomforte, but thou wolt bere me vp by stable
consolacion. And suche as ben in tempestis of the see cry to the to
socour them from the wyndes and the wawes. Suche also as bene 10
in stokkes and irens cryen to the for helpe. And thei may not disavow the nor mystrust the which among their turmentes gon
abowte deyeng in their avowes and complaintes. And it be so that
in rvyne of body and of goodes yet thou mayntenest and redressest
the spirit by the yefte / of God, which woll [not] vttirly cast downe col. 2
that He made withowt rysyng ageyne, helpe me ayeynst this infor- 16
tune in tyme of necessite. For among the grette dredis and the
vncerteyntees is the preeff of good hope more shyning and more
laudable. Lerne me to conceve somthing which may confirme my
infirmite and wher I may fyxe myn entent for to come among the 20
vertues present.

[Hope]

What folissh thought or what light disiounte hath causid the to
mysteppe owt of the ordre of spirituall vndirstonding? Were thou
made man [for to] serue sensuall passions or for to refrayne them? 25
Hath not the commiccion of man his comunycant beyng with the
stone(s), his lyvyng with plantes, his feling with beestes, and his
vndirstonding with angelys? Mankynde takith all his commyxtions
of the elementis, both corrupti/ble and passible, excepte the, which f. 76
comest into the body by infusion of the hevenes to be aboue all 30
othir parties þat be medlyd with the elementis, to which thou
oughtest not to be subiecte nor divided, but thou oughtest to reule
them and drawe them to reason by obeysaunce. Take hede what
wourship nature gaue the whanne he formed the body of man,

---

1 and the] and *add.* R   3 þe] *om.* NJD   the] *om.* N   5 it]
þat J   me not] *tr.* N   14 yet] thou J *om.* N   16 rysyng] reysyng N
18 vncerteyntees] nown certeyntees J   21 vertues] vertuous N   26 com-
miccion] *extra minim in* mi J con/mii(?u)ccyon N   27 plantes] his felyng
with plantes *add.* N   29 passible] possyble J passibles D   32 to 1]
om. NJ

whose visage is dressid vpward toward the hevene in signe þat
thou oughtest to reigne therin, which art comen owt of the celestiall
growinge. Thes othir bestis ben shapen and the hedde downwarde
and their membres stowpyng towarde therth, and man goth vp-
5 right and the visage reysid towarde the hevene vnto which the
soule stretchith by naturall appetite, for ther is his furst howse, his
assuraunce and his last refvit; it is the pales of Hym which brought
the forth from Him, the for to reduce or bryng ageyne to Hym,
col. 2 forwhy the dyvinite is ouir all by / present being and power and
10 inhabiteth the hevene by glorye and by superexcellence. Who may
thanne remeve the in erth from thi trust seyng that thi hope is
foundid in hevene? O alas, why dost thou mystrust Hym in whom
abidith eternally vnvariable seuir[te] and certeinte thoroughly
establischid? He hath not formed [the] by hevynly grace to difforme
15 the by the corrupcion of this worlde, but thou art reformed by Hym
in confirmyng the to Hym. Thinke not that He woll faile the at
nede, but He woll socour the of His piete if thou wolt retourne to
Him in humilite. For it is nedefull to the to trust in Hym of suche
thinges as thou maist not have withowt Him. Take vpon þiself the
20 occasion of thi doubtes and grugge not at His statutes nor haue no
suspecions of His promisses, for the hevene and therth ben transitorye, but His wourde shall neuir be fals nor voyde, nor He woll
f. 76ᵛ neuir make vayne the / pur and perfight hope of theym that right-
wisely put trust in Hym.

25   O ye wery and recrayed people, fall from vertu, and haue [not]
lerned to suffre, and all suche goodis as ye haue hadde, which
war receyved by grace, ye haue to sone put them owt of your
knowlege, takeyng no hede from whens þei cam, which is displeasur to Allmyghty God. And whanne fortune touche[th] them
30 anything sharpely thanne fall thei in erroure. But thei that wisely
take hede to their diffaultes and repent them ben right wele
purveyed of hope.

[Hope]

Like as Holy Scripture is sowen all abowte with preysinges of the
35 olde fadirs for the stablenesse of hope, and hough many tymes also

2 to] *om.* NJ   5 vnto] the *add.* N   8 the 2] ther N   10 hevene]
heuyns NJ *pl.* D   13 thoroughly] thurgh N   14 establischid] enstablisshed
N   17 socour] suffre N   23 perfight] of *add.* N   29 toucheth] N
touched RJ   35 also] all N

is brought to mynde the glorye and exalta/cion yevin to God for col. 2
benefyttes of grace [abydin] by hope and yolden by effect. The
patriarkes were not sloughe nor ovirthwart to suffre nor grevid to
abyde, for God woll neuir be forgetefull to socour nor make His
promisses voyde. Was Abraham voyde of his hope whanne aftir so 5
many yeris passid his lignage multiplied vpon therthe as the gravell
of the see, owt of which ben issewid many generacions? Dauid
mistrustid not Goddis helpe in veyn, of the blissing þat was yevin
to his sede, for his childern regned aftir hym ovir his people and
of his ligne was born the Saueoure of the worlde. Thou hast redde 10
hough the childern of Israel atteyned, aftir their travaile and annoye, through hope the londe of promission. And through hope
also thei came agayne suffering grette tribulacion by the space of
lxx yeres in the seruage of Babilon, and aftir that were re/storid f. 77
vnto the cuntre of peace, except suche as were vngarnisshid of feith 15
and voyde of hope and had no stronge corage for to endur the
lenghe of good abiding, but feble hertis not putting themself to
vertu; wherefor in the myddis of theire wretchidnesse endid their
dayes and closed themself away from the fruyte of hope. Symeon,
that was right wele norisshid, wold not for nought lyve so longe in 20
hope, in his olde age abiding the reuelacion which was shewed him
by an angell that he shulde not dye vnto the tyme that he hadde
seen the Saveour of the worlde. And so he lyvid many yeris in hope
or he dyeid, and at the last his entent was fulfilled.

Wherefor opyn thin eres and here the voice and the trumpe of 25
divine proclamacions, and thou shalt [alweys] here speke of me.
For amonge the commaundementis for to do wele ben medled the
a/monicions of good hope. The Creatour for to make men be col. 2
excercised in vertu yevith þem othirwhile sharpe aduersitees, and
for to stere them to perseueraunce He ioyneth to them the oynne- 30
ment of hope; for the sharpe pricking withdraweth the delites
transitories, and the oynnement draweth him to meritorie dedis.
Aduersite kepeth that thei fall not through delites vnto perdicion,
and I susteyne them suche wise that thei shall not be cowardes in

1 to 1] þe J   2 benefyttes] benefyces NJ benefices D   abydin] NJ abyding
R attenduz D   4 nor] or N   5 promisses] promys N   11–12 and
annoye] om. N & d'enhan D   13 tribulacion] trybulacions J pl. D   15 the]
their N   16 voyde of] om. N vuidez de D   22 vnto] to N   25 of]
the add. NJ des D   26 proclamacions] proclamacion N   alweys here] J
a voice here R her a voyce N tousiours D   28 for] om. N   32 transi-
tories] transitorye N   33 not] om. N

tribulacion. Many a tyme David sterid himself to abide longe in
abiding and to susteyigne vertuously the dedis of penaunce suche
as pleacid God to charge vpon man; for to say trouthe his werke
is like for to be wevid of my stuff and the leest of his webbe was
5 myghtily strengthid with beleve. Wele it apperith, for by ofte
praising and remembraunce of my name he shewith it þat he woll,

f. 77ᵛ hough so it be, that the stedfastnes of hope be en/prynted in the
herte of man, of which he was purveyed for to profight to hymself
and geue ensaumple to othir. In him we fynde the yeftis of connyng,
10 of feer, of wysdam, of pyte, of strengthe, of vndirstonding and of
counsaile, which ben the plentuousnes and þe largesse of the Holy
Goost. By conyng he knewe the vncerteyne hopes of this worlde,
and by wisedam the certeyne abiding of hevenly goodes. Feer
makith him retourne to himself that he may know his freelte. Pite
15 makith him enclyne to considre by compassion thinfelicite of othir
men. Strengthe yevith him vertu to resiste perseuerauntly all
worldely temptacions and stedfastly abyde the divyne consolacions.
Vndirstonding yevith him light to discerne the corruptable goodes
from the perdurable goodes, and counseile yevith hym to chese the

col. 2 most helthfull party. Wotest thou not wele / that this Dauid was
21 a man chosen of God and l[o]ved among the people? Yet notwithstonding he was preved by many temptacions and fownde stable in
feithe and sure in hope. In hough many maners was he in perill of
his lif, and by what grace was he preseruyd? What tempest rose
25 ayeinst him whanne his son Absolon drough his people in rebellion
ayeinst him? What angur suffrid he for the prodiciouse occision of
Abne[r] and in the discorde of Salmon and Adonias, his two
sonnes? Yet amo[n]ge all othir goodis restid with him hope, and
had it allway in his herte by confort and in his mouthe by doctryne.
30   For and his people and his techinges may not suffice the, looke
how Scripture confortith the vpon þe long abiding of þe only
alightyngys and socours of God, in comparynge the divine suffer-

f. 78 aunce to a longe / slepe. The devoute soule that is troubled in the
worlde callith his spouse sayng in this wise: 'Sir, whi slepist thou?

1 tribulacion] tribulacions N *sing*. D   2 to] *om*. J   3 werke] werkes
NJ *sing*. D   4 for] *om*. NJ   leest] lyest NJ   5 myghtily] myghty N
6 þat] att *add*. J   7 be 2] is N   7–8 the herte of man] his hert N
8 of 2] þe *add*. J   9 and] to *add*. NJ   11 largesse] largenes N   15 him]
to *add*. N   20 helthfull] healfull NJ   21 loved] NJ leved R aimé D
25 in] to N   27 Abner] NJ Abnee R Abener D   31 long] vppon the
add. long vppon the *canc*. N   32 alightyngys] alightnynges N

Awake and forgete (not) [our] powr and feble impotencie which hathe nede of thy socour.' But aftirwarde it is founde in the text that our Lorde did wake owte of His slepe, which is as moche to say as syn the tyme that He promisid His people that wer turmentid and wele prouid in their stable sufferaunce, in þis similitude He 5 puttith in vre the re(me)dies of consolacion and the exploite of His misericorde which aforetyme was suspendid and (brought) vnto a slepy reste. Yet to the same purpose thou shalt finde that our Saveour lyked to slepe [yn Hys bote] vnto the tyme that He was waked by His Apostulis, and aftir that He was awaked He blamed 10 them for their litle feithe and reprevid them for þeir doubtfull trust. For which cause He wolde slepe amongst the wawis of the see, this Lorde, which alway waketh vpon the gouernaunce of sees and lon/des; for certeyne He had not so muche nede of slepe as the col. 2 discipules had of good doctryne, but rathir sought their owne rest 15 thanne His and their assuraunce in God rathir thanne His recreacion by slepe.

O ye Cristen men, which haue so muche avauntage of grace and knowlage above all othir creatures and be callid all to His [high] perfeccion as to perdurable glorye and to the yeftes of blissidnes, 20 both of body and soule, hough maist thou norisch so the lechery of worldly þingis tha[t] sorowe of lesing therof discouragith the so that þou leuest me? Who hath mouid þe to do so grette iniury to Allmighty God as for to be in w(y)ll to distroy by dispeir His werke that He hath made for to trust in Him? He hath mekid Hym vndir 25 Hymself for to araise þe aboue thiself. He offerith and presentith the grace of His glorie, which of thiself thou art not of power to gete [by] merite. Whi wolt thou vnmake / in thiself that thou neuir f. 78ᵛ madest of thiself? Thou oughtest not to turne the blame of thyn iniquite in repreef of His mercy. Also it sittith the not to iuge vpon 30 Hym that shall yeue true iugement vpon the. For He knowyth thyn entre and thyn issew afore ere thou were made, and yet thou takest

1 not our] NJ nour (not *ins.*, n *changed to* y) R   and 2] a *add.* N *om.* D
2 is] was (*ins.*) J   9 yn Hys bote] J is his bote N is but R en la nasselle D
10 waked] awaked NJ   12 amongst] amonge J and monge (nd *perhaps canc.*) N
13 gouernaunce] governaunces J *sing.* D   15–16 their . . . thanne 1] on þair rest
and N   18 and] a N   19 callid all] called also J allso called N
20 the] *om.* N aux D   22 of 1] theis *add.* NJ   þingis] goodes NJ deliz D
that] thanne R than the NJ   24 werke] werkes N *sing.* D   28 by] the
RNJ par D   28–9 neuir madest] *tr.* N   31 knowyth] knowe N
32 ere] or NJ

vpon the to haue a knowlage above the providence of His ordinaunces for to com. Endure with Him that maketh the to dure and
be not recraied ayeinst Him that made þe. Alas, whom shalt thou
profite if thou be ayeinst God and discordest with thyn owne self?
5 Right a grevouse counseyle Dispeyre gaue the whanne for a litle
disease of thi liff maketh the to take the way of euirlastynge deth.
He is to moche vnknowen by man which hath willid to make Him
knowen to a Cristen man. For ther was neuir lawe had his God so
famylier nor so nygh him as hath the Cristen lawe. He list to take
col. 2 mankynde to [be] His partenere / by compassion and to be socoure
11 by grace to thine infirmite. He hath accompenied nature humayne
to the diuinite to thentent that thei shulde be reisid eternally aboue
the heuennes. In what dost thou mistrust amonge mannes humayne
impotencyes sith that humanyte is ioyned to Allmighti God? Para-
15 ventur thou mightest be meved by abhominacion of thi liff by
ensaumple of othir which haue slayne themself with their owne
hondis for the displesure of their owne liff, like as may be shewed
before the of the wise Caton, that wilfully killid himself. Also ther
may be layed afore the Marcus Tucius, which wilfully [l]epte into
20 the depe pitt at Roome. Also a man may shewe the occision that
Lucresse did on hirself for shame that was done vnto hir vnlaw-
fully. But suche argumentis ben disseyveable and full of guyle. Yet
suche argumentis and fawtes yevith vs not ensaumple of dissceyv-
f. 79 ing but it is a gretter ensaumple to vs for to flee it thanne to / sewe
25 it. Yet I say the that this argument which procedith by semblaunce
or semblable comparison may be asoylid by similitude, for the
Cristen feith hath yevin the provision of so high an hope that the
paynemmys and the ydolatres may not atteyne. Somtyme olde men
sought their felicite in humayne vertu and their finall glorie in the
30 during and multiplighing [of] their worldely renome. Wherfor them
semed that suche as slough them by magnanymyte lyveden by
lawde of mennes memoryes and by the reders of storyes and lefte
to oþer men ensaumple of high courages as though thei shulde nat
sette by the deth. But I say that thei that war n[e] wourthi to
35 conceve the blissidnes of the othir life and the good fortunes of
theime that be chosen within theimself, thei arestid and assistid the

1–2 ordinaunces] ordenaunce N   7 hath] haue N   14 impotencyes]
ympotencye N pl. D   19 lepte] llepte (ll made from k) R   20 at] of J de D
the 2] om. J   25–6 semblaunce or] om. NJD   28 Somtyme] the add. NJ
les D   29 humayne] humanyte NJ   30 of] NJ in R de D   34 war ne]
warn R worn J wer N

blyndenesse of their abyding to þe praysing of vertu and to the
erthly wourship. But syn that tyme God is bycom man, which
through the medlyng of His deite with humayn nature hath made
vs parteners of the dyvyne counceyllis and discoue/rid the secretis col. 2
of Paradise, which war [hid and] conseled from the prophetis of 5
othir lawes. He hath reuertid and made voyde the mortall hope and
the temporall vayne glorye of this liff, for which som killid themself and perischid and mystoke themself constaunt in aduersite, for
to enhaunce oure hope above all mortall rewardis and more higher
thanne erthly worschip can bryng of thoes discordis. What if the 10
myscreauntis thanne gafe themself to the dethe by folisshe hope to
purchece them a name among men or for to eschew shame in their
lyving? Thou that hast achyved the yssue of true hope more opynly
thanne they, thou oughtest not aftir theim to desyre worldely vanite
nor to doubte the fowlnesse of this liffe, and thou oughtest not to 15
lerne the maner to wirche in their exaumple, but the behovith to
make the prynte on a higher patron and to desir thi liffe not
praysyng it, nor dispysing dethe withowte desyring. Thi liffe was
stablisshid for to deserue a good deþe, and thi liffe was ordeyned
for an / entre of a bettir liffe. If thou avaunce thi deth thou drawest f. 79ᵛ
abak from the meryte of thi lyffe, and if thou haue (in) cherte the 21
keping of thy liffe thou shalt begynne to dye aftir thi deth. Thanne
dispose thi liffe othirwise thanne the paynemes did and make the
redy to lyve aftir the deth, and lette Him alone with thi liffe which
assigneth the houres and termes and the bowndes of all thynges. 25

It is a thing to sore aventured to take an vnnaturall deth for
a lawde which litle durith and soone fallith, for lawde that is
procured and disfigured by suche manere of deth is soone made
derke and lightly goth away. For through foryetfullnes, [detrac-
cion and vnmesurable envy] is rebatid worldely honour, but the 30
pured bountie yevith suche mesurable rewle to all men that it
may not faile.

[Hope]

I woll shewe the a doubte wherein many folkis ben wrappid and 34
[will] trust withowte hope and vsurpe my name and werkis / for col. 2

1 blyndenesse] blyndnesses NJ   6 reuertid] reuersyd NJ   7 temporall]
om. N temporell D   10 thoes] theys NJ   11 myscreauntis] myscreaunce N
14 oughtest] owyst J   15 fowlnesse] feblenesse J vilté D   16 lerne] lere NJ
21 abak] bak NJ   24 the] thi N   25 and 1] the *add.* NJ   27 litle]
whyle *add.* N   29–30 detraccion . . . envy] J and vnmesurable detraccion R
detraccion and vniuersall [*extra minim in* niu] envye N *see n.*

nought, and suche put in theire hertis vayne ententis, taking my
shadowe and levin my light. And thus thei serche their confort by
false singnes and fynde their discomfort in the way of trouthe. And
whanne thei be fall through their folisshe emprise into erroure,
5 thanne thei say that Hope hathe disceyvid them through trust that
[þei] had in hir. But and I war disceyveable I shulde not be seruaunt to Hym which is the right way, the pure trouthe, the veray
liffe and the souerayngne wisedome. Wherfor I woll lette [the]
knowe [whiche ben] the countirfeted hopes that bryng men to
10 confusion with lawghyng chere by maner of feyned consolacion
and folishe trust evell foundid [which] drawith them to sorowes
and wepinges.

The furst bastard hope is callid presumpcion. This maner of
hope begilith suche men as entende to gette good which thei not
15 deserue. Thei wolde haue grace withoute meryte and fryte withowte
laboure. Thei may be likened to him that openeth his mouthe and
closith his hondis and wolde that the mete shulde entre into his /
f. 80 mouthe withowt any labour, for him thinkith it is to grette a laboure
to lift his hande to his visage. But lette them wele knowe that oure
20 Lorde helpith not effectually suche as noye themself through their
owne defaulte, for He is the soueraigne Werkeman and man is but
a shewer of his werkes. And if thou lette thiself fall and sette not
by thiself He woll lette þe fall whatsomeuer thou arte. And who
that woll helpe hymself by merite He woll socour him by (His)
25 grace. Hast thou herde at any tyme in the writyngis of paynemes
þat their goddis gaue euir any socour to the lachesse and slewgh
people? Reason wolde that their requestis sholde stonde in vayne
in lasse thanne thei dede their devour to pleace their goddis, as in
watching, in counceyllyng and doyng of good dedis. To suche men
30 thei graunte propirly their desyirs. And syn it is said thus of ydolles,
what shalt thou thinke of Almighty God, which is so iuste that He
col. 2 castith not away His benefittes in vayne nor departith His / largesse
withowt deseruing? Softe slowthe is right an harde steppemodir
and a perylous aduersary, and though so be she be contrary to all

1 vayne] thoughtes and *add.* N *see n.*   2 levin] leue N   3 way] *om.* NJ
of] the *add.* NJ   4 emprise] empryses N *sing.* D   6 þei] J he RN   and]
om. (*perhaps ins.*) J se D   9 countirfeted] countyrfete N   11 which
drawith] J withdrawith R withdrewe N tirent D   13 The] Thy J La D
14 gette] grete *add.* N *om.* D   18 thinkith] þat *add.* NJ   19 them]
hym N   26 slewgh] slow NJ   28 thanne] that N   30 said thus] *tr.*
NJ   34 so be] þat *add.* NJ

folkis yette I wote wele she is a very enemye to youthe, in which
season is the tyme of labour suche wise that whanne thei come to
age thei may lyve honestly. Wolde God that ye Frenchemen war
nat anoyed through this sophistyk hoope and that ye wolde leve
your vnprofitable fantasies, for chalenging of good vre withowt 5
deserving cometh more of presumpcion thanne of hope. And so
hoope is frawded by too ferfull and symple mekenesse, and lachenes
of courage decresed from goode beleve. Hoope and feere is in maner
oone ayeinst anothir (but not all contrary, for feere is a yefte of the
Holy Goste), which may dwell togeddir subiecte in oone howse. 10
For hope reysith a man to trust vpon his propre myght by confydence of the divine bounte, and feere maketh him retourne to
haue himself in a doubte through consideracion / of his freyle f. 80ᵛ
nature. But feere that cometh of humayne compassion, which more
propirly is callid drede, is a mystrust of the herte which makith a 15
man dredefull to trust God. Yet euery man may wele truste in
grace more thanne he can deserue, and more feere of punycion than
the divine mekenesse woll yeve him. But the good hope ought be
so wele assured (þat) ther shulde be no manere doubte of dispeire.

Anothir manere hope ther is vnperfecte which othirwise is callid 20
defectife for fawte of a suere foundacion, and suche as afferme
vtterly their desyers in variable thingys and sette ententiffly theire
hope vpon the vncerteynte of þe worlde. What manere surete may
be had in suche thingis as be doubtefull ? Who woll seke surete wher
no suerte is ? Hough mayst þou be born vp with that thing þat may 25
nothir susteyne the ne maynteine the ? I say not that in thingis
worldely oon ne may abyde by hope relatif, but neuirthelesse so to
abide by determinacion substantyve. And who / so trustith othir- col. 2
wise but by re[lat]ion to the hevenly hope he fotith on yese of oone
nyght or he lenyth to a staff of wekyrs. If thou assur the in 30
strenghthe of body, of anothir feere [he fereth], the age, which
approcheth to the, crepyng, and a lityll fever shall take away the
[comforte] of thi hope. If thou delyte of thi beavte the ioye thereof

1 is] om. J   2 labour] such of labour add. N   3 ye] the N ? þe J
5 vnprofitable] inprofitable N   7 lachenes] lachesnes NJ   8-9 in . . .
feere] om. N   17 than] om. NJ   20 is 1] þat is add. NJ om. D   vnper-
fecte] imperfite NJ   which othirwise is] oþer weys N   21 fawte] defaute
N a favte J   suche] possible om. RNJ see n.   22 vtterly] outturly J om. N
23 manere] of add. NJ   26 the 1] om. NJ   29 relation] rebellion RNJ
relation D   on] non N   30 assur] assureth N   31 the] om. NJ
33 comforte] NJ fever R confort D   delyte] the add. NJ

shall endur the but awhile. Othir ther be þat trust in theire goodis,
but what thing is worse thanne money, which comonly is groced vp
by vntrouþe of the getters and is kepte through mistrust of the
holders? Yette the nature thereof is to shrincke away as dothe the
5 watir and to be sperpuled lightly like quycke siluer. It makith warr
and diffyith him that kepith it, and studieth alway hough it may
haue newe maisters and to be lodged in new purses. Wolt thou
thanne put thi trust in suche thing as breketh the feith of all the
worlde? On the othir party thou wolt say þat thou art myghty of
10 frendis and gretly allied. Yet ware thou take not the staff instede
f. 81 of the potence, / and bewar also that the pricke of thi frendis entre
not into thi hondis. For there be diuerse that trustith in the loue
of princes and on theire fortunes, and to suche people the wourdis
of Dauid ought inough to suffice, which defendith euery man that
15 thei shulde not put theire trust in princes nor in the sonnes of men,
which may yeue non helth.

The thrid vnlawfull hope disseyvith the foles, which be called
opinatiff. And in this manere of hope resten the ovirprowde men
which yevith auctorite to their own propir wittis and obstinatly
20 beleven their own counceylles, trusting theire own braynes, and
govern themself vndir [the hope of] their own thoughtis. In this
disseyte liyth the [height] of mannes foly, which assayith by in-
moveable obst(in)acion to chaunge thingis from their propirtees,
and wene to make of wille, reason; of oppynion, connynge; of argu-
25 ment disseyveable, shewyng; and of folissh thought an hope that
may not faile. Thanne is the cowarde ravisshid in this [dreme]
col. 2 which weneth that / he is made for to teche all the worlde, and him
semes that his answeris ben lawes imperiall and his fantasies sentence of the gospell. And whanne he hath all don, his hope is lyke
30 a fyre that is made of heerdis; his witte is turned to nought and as
a dreme of a man that hath slepte. Thanne he lerneth that more is
worth; that is to say, he serchith othir mennes counseile by doubtefull humi(li)te rathir thanne to stryve with his own by ovirgrette
pride. A man aloone may be kyng ovir othir men, but he may not
35 regne oonly by oone mannes wisedom, for suche thing as per-

1 endur] dure NJ   ther] they J   4 shrincke] strynke J   couleur D
10 ware] þat *add.* NJ   11 potence] potente NJ   12 hondis] honde NJ
14 to] *om.* NJ   22 height] hope RNJ   comble D   28 answeris] onwers
NJ   fantasies] the *add.* N *om.* D   32 serchith] secheth J   othir
mennes counseile] counsell of oþer men N   33-4 ovirgrette pride] ouyr
pride NJ

teigneth to many ought be comowned by many for the gouernaunce
of a hede alone. For the discrecion of gouernynge growith of many
wittis in whom the wittes ben departed that longe to so high a
mysterye. And thou wolt aske what is the wisedam of kynges, I
answere the on this wise: that it stondith more in good beleving of 5
counceyll thanne himself to / yeue good counceyll. For good coun- f. 81ᵛ
ceylling accordith to euery persone, but to chose to counceill þe
wele and to chese of othirs witte counceill profitable longeth to him
that ought to here euery man and for euerych to putt in vre. Moreouir I telle the that the maners of a king be more accomplisshid in 10
a prince that is symple in himself, abiding the disciplyne of good
counceyll, thanne in a prince that is subtyll and willfull. For to vse
of propre witte, it is inough to singular lyff and religiouse, and to
gouerne himself to the iugement of the more parte, it is the guyding
polityke and cyvill. And that þat is said kingly in cyvill guyding it 15
may be applied of comen counceyll and secrete, which ought not
to dispraise the grosse vndirstonding of seruauntis nor the avise of
the comensales of their householdis.

Come [w]e ageyne to that hope which to opinion holders and
obstinates is hope opynatyffe, holden as a mayde that is holden by 20
trust. A, it is / daungerouse to vndi(r)stonde to be wise withowt col. 2
teching and by to moche truste to himself to mystrust of God. But
the moste shamefull thing is obstinate abiding in errour and to will
rathir to lese himself thanne to amende. Who that hath a fall and
rysith ageyne hath lasse shame thanne he that lieth in the myre and 25
may not for shame aryse. For good avisement is more lawdable
thanne viciouse fawte is repreveable. For humayne inperfeccion
may lightly faile, but discipline and correccion ben werkis dyvine.

What is the cause the people of Iewes be so long tyme in disper-
sion and put bak? Nothing ellis but for obstinate beleve and hope 30
opynatyff. Thei haue mysknowen their Savioure, and thei say also
that thei abyde the comyng of [Messyas] which is com allredy, and
beleve not that shall fall vnto them. Wherfore do thei desyere Him
seynge that thei haue refusid Him? Or hough may thei abide [the]
comyng of Him which thei haue mystaken, seyng that their hope / 35

2 many] my NJ   5 on] om. NJ   8 othirs] ordres N   witte] wytty N
counceill] the wele and add. the wele canc. N   14 the 3] om. N au D
17 avise] advises N sing. D   19 we] he RNJ Reuenons D   to 2] the
add. N aux D   20 mayde that] maydyn N   22 of] om. N   24 a fall]
om. N   29 cause] þat add. NJ   31 their] the NJ le D   32 Messyas]
NJ him R Messias D

G

f. 82 is voyde and their beleve in vayne forasmoche as thei wolde not
meke their witte to the veray vndirstonding of Scripture. Their
curse is grette whanne thei seche thentente of thauncient volumes
and woll not vndirstonde them, and the maisters of their synagoges
5 norishith them forth in abusion and turnith vp so downe the sentence of Scripture for to turne away their people from veray con-
uersion. For contrary opynion hath suche wise peruertid their hope
that thei deyne not enclyne [þai]re vndirstonding to the sense of the
lettir, but thei dar wele shewe the textes and take away the trouth
10 of the prophecyes and contryue the exposicions aftir their will.
Alas, and thei woll nat be redressid by the Bible, of which thei have
diffouled the sentence, at the leest way let them be remembird on
their longe seruage and on the peynes of their myserye. And if thei
woll not beleve the wourdis let them beleve the dedis. Loke and
col. 2 thou shalt / see that it passith a thousand thre hundred and liiij
16 yeres syn thei were exiled and dryvyn owte into diuerse countres
as a people reprevid and in bondage. And wheras thei hadde somtyme the holy vnccion for their kyngis it is nough cessid. The
ceptre of Iuda also is translatid vnto othir lordeschippis. And by
20 the visions of their owne prophetis it is clerely shewed that Messias
is come; yete thei abide Him, and so thei may long. He woll neuir
more be conuersaunt with mankynde nor come among vs ageyne
as a redemptoure, but He woll come in His divine maieste and [as]
a doubtable iuge. Moreouir thei affirme that whanne He comyth
25 He shall reise all the ded bodies of the lynage of Iuda and forthwithall woll make them dwell togethir vpon erthe in grette prosperite; and for bycause that thei haue this fantasy the doctours
s[e]yne that thei be brought lowe and vndir in their mysbeleve.
f. 82�v For through the hope of / temporall resurreccion thei be confortid
30 to lyve in exile and myserye, abiding the tyme to be brought owt
of seruage and that bothe the quycke and the dedde myght assemble
togedir in their owne countre. But who that takith good heede
therof hough thei diffoule þeir owne wittis and study to knowe that
may neuer be. And yete thei woll vsurpe vpon their true sayingis

2 veray] *om.* N vray D   3 thauncient] þe auncyent J aunncyent N
6–7 veray conuersion] the very trew conuersacion N   8 deyne not] disdeigne
to N ne daignent D   þaire] NJ youre R leur D   9 textes] of the lettyr
add. N *om.* D   10 contryue] conceyve J controuuees D   11 and] þat N
25 reise] areyse N   the 2] Iuda (*canc.*) J   26 woll] *om.* N   28 seyne]
NJ sayne R *see n.*   32 countre] courte N   33 therof] heerof NJ
that] þat *add.* N þei *add.* J   34 their] the NJ   sayingis] seyeng N

of prophetis and applye them aftir their owne fantasies. Ezechiell
and othir speke wele of the resurreccion fynall where all shall aryse
to saluacion or damnacion at thende of the worlde. But the folissh
Iewes turn their wourdis vp so down and thincke that the resurreccion of men is non othire but whanne thei be areysid thei shall lyve 5
togedre her in this worlde, which is a intollerable frenesy and a
thing inposible, for all the erth of þis worlde myght not suffice to
enhabite and to labour for þe sustinaunce of them that ben / dedde col. 2
and on lyve of the lynage of Iuda. Moreouir Ieremye and Ysaye
prophecied of the seruitute and captiuite of Iewys and shewed the 10
restitucion of their liberte and hough thei shulde come ageyne into
their cuntre. Thei lost also the reedificacion of the temple and the
reno[v]acion of the Holy Cite aftir the pestilences. These two
prophetis had this vision, but it was accomplisshid in the lynage of
Ieconyas, which aftir the transmigracion of Babilone the Iewes, 15
that war put in seruage by the space of lxx yere, were restored
ageyne in peace vnto the cite of Ierusalem and restored the temple
ageyne and made vp ageyne the wallis of the cite through [the]
witti excercyce of Neemyas. And nough at this houre the fooles
confort themself in thes prophecies which ben passid and abyden 20
the promyses that ben payed afore to the good men, for which it
was spoken of aforetyme. The vnhappy masters of their lawe
promyse their people liberte and re/stitucion of their cuntre through f. 83
their writingis which thei mysvndirstonde and glose it aftir þeir
owne entent, but their entent is fawty, for thei reioyse them aftir 25
the false interpretacion of the lettir and their predecessours haue
hadde the veray fruyte. And so through opynatyffe hope thei abide
in myscheve and seruage and as people that be blynde. For synne
the tyme that Titus distroyed the cite of Ierusalem, the xl yere aftir
the passion of Criste Ihesu, wheras he solde xi hundred thousande 30
Iewes and a hundred and fyfty thousande slayne, as Iosephus
recytith, syn that tyme thei hadde neuir amonge them spiryte of
prophecye, vision, reuelacion nor non othir divine visitacion as thei
hadde before or thei fell in this incredulite. For the consummacion
of Scriptures and the visions of prophetis toke their ende in Ihesu 35

2 aryse] ryse NJ   6 her] *om*. N   9 on] a NJ   13 renovacion]
reuocacion RNJ renouation D   pestilences] pestilence N *pl*. D   16 the
space] trespace N   21 payed] doon N payées D   23 their 1] the N
24 mysvndirstonde] vndyrstond N   25 fawty] fantycy (cy *ins*.) J faillie D
28 and 1] yn NJ   as] a *add*. N   30 Criste Ihesu] *tr*. NJ   33 as] like
as NJ   34 incredulite] credulyte N   35 of 2] the *add*. NJ

Criste, and He, that is fulfillid with perfightnes in all thing, atteyned
the perfeccion of the prophetis wh/anne His divine light toke away
the clowdy light of inspiracions prophetikis, like as a grette torche
makith derke the clerenesse of a litle candill. And if thou aske a
question whi that God made not vttirly an ende of these fals(e)-
beleveing people like as He did of Sodom and Gomer I wolde
answere and say that it hath liked Him to suffre them to live in
miserye as men that haue yeven themself to myschief and to be
blamed withowt tyme of mynde for their cursed errour and in
exsaumple of sclaundre to the lynage of all their generacions. For
at all tymes thei rede and study on the fables in a booke callid
Detharmich, which thei haue contriued of tales ayeinst the Cristen
men, but notwithstonding their reding thei shall fynde that thei
live myschevously and aftyr their deth to be damned in lasse thanne
by meke thought thei retourne to knowe the veray hope and to
knowe also þe / spirituall sence of the letter more thanne aftir the
flesche. For the serymonyes of the olde lawe was the shelle of the
note of which the Cristen lawe [in] the plenitude of tyme was closid
wherof the kyrnell myght not be tasted in lasse thanne the shelle
were brokyn. Thanne syn it is so that men may not come to the
kernelle withowt brekyng of the shelle, the Cristen thanne ought
of reason to leve the olde cerymonyes and the byndyng of trouth,
which was couertely hidde kepte vndir by figure, and lette the
childern of Iuda kepe the shelle and the barke, which sufficith them
through their opynatyue hope. But the childern of Ihesu Criste by
adopcion shulde haue the kernelle.

He that hathe yeven lyff to all men and hath power above
reason, which [yeveth] to all folke His plentuouse grace wherin
He gave a preciouse gyft, He shewed al/so by His prophetis
thingis that war to com, (or)deined the lawe by proporcion and
condicioned it with many cerymonyes, peynted with right troub-
louse colours (and) pregnabull wourdes, for to restreyn þe grette
offenses, promising on the othir party by figurs and holy visions

---

2 the 2] *om.* NJ   3 of] his *add.* R des D   prophetikis] prothetykes N
12 Detharmich] Detramyche N Detharnach J *see n.*   13 shall] shulde N
15–16 to knowe also] allso to knowe N   17 the shelle of] to shewe
N   18 in] and RNJ en D   20 were] was N   21 withowt] the *add.* N
22 byndyng] byndynges NJ   23 kepte] *om.* N   24 them] *om.* J leur D
26 shulde] schul J shall N   27 yeven] yeve J the N   28 grace] yeuith
add. ins. R   30 com] and *add.* NJ   ordeined] o *ins. on line after erasure,*
r *made from* i R   32 pregnabull] pregnaunte NJ

and by vnfeyned hope to haue ioye aftir our compleyntis [and o]pteyne grette rewardis. And whanne the tyme was come He kepte His couenant so that all is come, litle and moche, which He kepte close vndir covert of the Olde Testament. Now man haþe made couenaunt with God and fully come to Him, and God is bycome man wherthrough the busshement is disclosed and cerymonyes opened that byfore war covertly closed [like as the redde rose is closed] within a grene budde. The Olde Testament purposith, and the Newe previth it by exposicion vpon the grette texte. The toone lawe promisith, shewith and disposith; the othir contentith and restith. The furst lawe dressith and ordeynith; the othir lawe accomplisshith and / fulfillith and maketh an ende and settith his merkis. The oon sowith; the othir repith. The oon punysshith; the othir pardoneth. The oon causeth merite; the othir rewardith. The olde lawe yevith the leves; the othir bo(d)eneth and florisshith. The oon bourieneth and waxith grene; the othir vendengith and tvnnith, and abandoneth both rynde and leeffe and gaderith the fruytes that ben assigned, which longe agone war predestinate by the prophetis, which war hidde vndir courtynes by fygure and nough thei be determined, opened and made clere and disclosed from the courtyne. And so the power of prophetis is endid, and the vnwourthy Iewes abide in their folishe obstinacie.

[Hope]

[Y]et restith the fourth poynte of dispeyred hope which I cannot name save onely it may be callid frustratyve. And this maner of hoope noyeth them that be light of beleve, trusting that suche / goodis shulde come vnto them which thei shall neuir obteyne. There suche men resten that trust to moche in their good fortune and on þe happe which thei haue hadde aforetyme. Othir ther be that be not ferre from suche folyes, for thei doubte so moche the fortune of their enemyes that their hertis faile them for to take eny enterpryse vpon them lyke as fortune war onely made to sewe the wille

1–2 and opteyne] NJ apteyne R et attaindre D   2 He] a NJ   4 the Olde] *tr.* N   13–14 merkis . . . pardoneth] *om.* N   14–15 the othir] the tothir N to tothyr J   16 bodeneth] d *made from* t R boteneth NJ   florisshith] florysshneth N   17 abandoneth] habundeneth N   19 agone] *om.* N   21 opened] *in position of catchword on f. 61ᵛ, not repeated on f. 62* N courtyne] curtynes NJ   25 Yet] NJ Let (*illumination error*) R   29 There] Therfor N Là D   33 made] for *add.* NJ

of othir men. In this Iulius Cesar failid, which often committid his
bataillis and the perile of his lif vnto fortune more thanne vnto
reason, for he trustid that she durst not faile hym. Aftirwarde aftir
all wepyns of the worlde discomfite, in Tessalye was he throwen
5 vndir and deed in a counceyle by writing poyntelles. Policitatus,
the tyraunte, trusted so moche in fortune that he caste his ryng into
the see trustyng that by fortune he shulde have it ageyne, for all
thing come vnto him lyke as desired, but afterwarde he felle vnto
myschieff and thanne hanged. Through this maner of disseyte
f. 84ᵛ beganne / the synne of ydolatrye among þe people whanne Nynus
11 let make an ymage of golde for the memorye of his fadir callid
Belus and comaunded the people to wourship it as a god, wherthrough men that were feble of witte and light to myschevous
exaumples which aftirwarde toke in custome to wourship and pray
15 to the ydoles and to make ymages to suche as dyd them good and
of suche as had ben of myghty power in their dayes. And thus came
vp in vsage the ydoles of the paynemys, and, by the commemora-
cion of the ydoll Belus, made name their ymages Bel, Bell, Ball,
Belphegor, Baalyn, Belzebub, and aftirwarde othir names aftir the
20 folishe thoughtis of them which gave þemself to suche fantasies.
For the rude and vnexpert people vndirstode at that tyme by their
naturall institucion that of dewte thei shulde do wourship to euerything perteynyng to the divine power. But forasmoche as thei wist
col. 2 not propirly to whom thei shulde / or ought to do the perfeccion
25 of this honoure which longith to the deite, thei gave it to men which
in their tyme lyved in worldely auctorite and in dignite above
othirs. For at that tyme the symple people myght not haue knowlage to atteyne to an higher perfeccion thanne of Iupater, which in
þat age was a kyng and through suche foly aftir his dethe was called
30 a god for bycause of the magnificence and deliciouse lyving þat he
vsed in his realme. Also a lady of Athenes named Myn[er]ue was
enhaunced as a goddes for certeine craftes that she founde. Appollo

1 Iulius] *om.* NJ   often] oftentymes NJ   2 perile] pepyll J   4 all]
all þe N allso the J   throwen] thrawe J thrawe downe N   5 deed]
dyed N   6 tyraunte] tyraune N   7 the] *om.* N   that by fortune] be
fortune þat N   8 as] he *add.* NJ   vnto 2] to NJ   9 this maner
of] maner of his N   11 callid] named NJ   13 light to myschevous]
lyghte to myscheves J lyghtly disposed to all myschefys N faciles à perni-
cieux D   14 in] to J the N   15 to 3] of NJ   18 Bell] *om.* NJD
see n.   20 suche] *om.* N telles D   23 But] and J Mais D   24 shulde
or] *om.* NJ   to 2] *om.* NJ   25 gave] haue N   27 not] nought J
31 Mynerue] Myntoue RNJ Minerue D

also was deified for his excellence and for the me(r)velles that he
dyd on mannes body through the crafte of medicyne. Thes multitude of people wer grettely vnwise and sore disseyved for to aske
divine helpe of them that were ded and to seche diuinite wher
humanyte [was fayled and] corrupte. Me thinkith thei ought to 5
haue but litle truste to be spedde of their requestis whanne thei
pray humbly [to hem] which thei themselffe / gaue the auctorite. f. 85
And yet thei attended to receyve goodis and the vertues of suche
as had no power but through them. Thanne whereas thei made
them, it was to inprofytable and to superflue a thing that men 10
shulde require and pray to suche one of necessite which thei themself haue made a god, and haue nede of his power to whom thei
themself gaue the myght. And for to say trouth, the begynnynge
of the paynemes supersticion cam furst by ty(ra)nnye of suche men
as made themself or their predecessours to [wurship hem be force] 15
and drede, and aftirward this novellery turned in vsage, and kept
it aftirward by long continuaunce wilfully which aforetyme was don
by constraynt. For ther is not so harde nor so violent int[ro]d[u]c-
cion but that in lenghe of tyme it shal be brought ageyne to the
semblaunce of natur, nor ther is non so grette an errour but that 20
continuall impression of wourdes shewethe a visage of trouthe. The
childern sewed þeir faders in abusion of the false / godis, and wher col. 2
reason warned theim the feith of ther predecessours scomfite them
by auctorite of doctrine inviolable, also that in the same paynemes
lawe ther was non suffird to disprayse the wourshiping of goddis 25
withowt blame of sacrilege and withowt peyne. And this was the
(cause þat þe) Romayns war so long tyme hardened in their courages ayeinst the doctrine of holy chirche, through which the londe
of the Romaynes was consecrate with the blode of martires afore
or emperours wolde receyve þe name of Cristendome, taking it to 30

2 mannes] mennys N   through the] by N   3 to] om. J   5 was fayled
and] NJ faylith and was R estoit faillie & D   to] om. NJ   6 be]
om. N   8 receyve] the add. NJ les D   9 as] þat NJ   10 to 1] om. ND
to 2] om. ND   a thing] om. N chose D   12–13 haue 1 . . . myght] made
and gafe hem þair power and myght N see n.   12 and] to add. J   14 the
paynemes] þis paynyme J this N ceste D   by tyrannye] by tynnye J om. N
15 wurship . . . force] be forced R be force J wurship hem N adorer par force D
see n.   16 aftirward] aftir N   novellery] it add. N   in] into NJ
18–19 introduccion] interdiccion RNJ introduction D   22 sewed] shewed N
abusion] ab[? v]oysyon (corrected) N   23 them] om. NJ   24 paynemes]
payene J payne N   25 ther] om. N   non] not N   27 so] om. J   29 the 2]
om. N du D   30 or] or þe J þat the N les D   þe name of] om. N le nom D

a crymynall vnstedfastnes and a dispraysing ayeinst their blood and
their auncetrees if thei passed the religion of their fadirs or the
techingis of their soueraignes or of their maiours. Yet synne the
sanctificacion of Roome by veray feith their hertis [were] so en-
5 clyned to their furst accustomed lawe that many of theme said that
thei had loste their prosperite syn thei l[ef]t þe wourshiping of their

f. 85ᵛ [first] goddis, / ayeinst which temptacion and for to make voide in
all poyntes the regarde that thei had to the wourshiping of the false
goddis, Seynte Augustyne compileth þe booke callid *The Cite of*
10 *God* and Lactaunce wrote the voluyme of the *Divine Institucions*,
to the which thow mayst haue a recourse in the pleynnese of this
mater. Trew it is that God, having compassion vpon the humayne
ignoraunce and of their vayne vittis which travailed for nought to
knowe þe divine powere, He of His goodnese liste make Himself
15 to be knowe and shewed in the last age, and for because that man
myght not areyse his iugementis ferther thanne the power of
humayne vndirstonding made Himself man and meked Himself of
His deite, willing to enhaunce humanyte, and toke vpon Him the
freelte of the flesshe withowt leving the eternall diuinite, to thentent
20 that through the vertu of God mankynde shulde be made divine
col. 2 and He which divinly made Hymself man myght be knowe / both
God and man. For [by] similitude and comunycacion all mortall of
mortall nature, thou myghttest at that tyme have seen Him and
herde of divine werkes that war don in mannys body as to beleve
25 and wourship God in His onely essence and infinyte to be knowen
and, as man was, at His dethe withowt power. But nough His deyte
is knowen to man in humanyte, and His humanyte glorifyed and
dred by þe vnyon of His deyte. So by this reason the bestialte of
ydolatrees is gretly reuercyd and confounded, and the Cristen feith
30 gloriousely wourshippid.

Now ye paynemes that be of false beleve, answere me to this
question: whethir is more possible that Allmyghty God wolde
meke Himself to become man or ellis man which is vnmyghty

2 passed] *om.* N trespassoient D　　　　2–3 or . . . maiours] or 2 *om.* J
souereyns and maiours N ne les traditions de leurs maiours D　　　5 accustomed
lawe] customes and lawes N Loy acoustumée D　　　that 2] *om.* J　　　6 their 1]
the NJ leur D　　　left] NJ lost R laissé D　　　7 first] NJ false R premiers D
ayeinst] and yenst N　　　8 the 3] þair N des D　　　9 compileth]
compyled N　　　11 which] the N　　　12 having] haue N　　　15 that] *om.* N
16 areyse] aryse N　　　17 meked] meke N　　　21 He which] which þat N
knowe] beknow N　　　22 comunycacion] coicacyon NJ　　　22–3 of mortall]
om. N　　　24 of] the *add.* NJ　　　27 humanyte 2] is *add.* N

myght enhaunce himself to be God? If thow woldest of men make
goddis which hast no power to make a man of thiself, but beleve
certaynly that God myght make Himself man by His eternall
power, in whom and by whom all þing / is made. Now hath He f. 86
subuertid all thy power and vtterly made [voide] thi frustratyue 5
hope. And syn it is so that by thy litill witt thou hast erred in
thiself to knowe þe wisedome of God, He therfore of His grette
goodnesse hathe callid the to knowe Him by Himselff.

God had welle purveyid for man, which in the birthe of Ihesu
Criste and syn that tyme all þe worlde was bedewed with the 10
sprynge of grace by the infusion and knowlage of one very God.
And by illusion of opynatyff wanhope it was turned vp so downe
by the meanys of the devele, fadir of derkenesse, made Mahomet
to be sett on high through the wourship that he had in this worlde.
And some doctours holde opinion that God suffird it to be don for 15
the punicion of the Emperoure Eraclius, which went owt of þe way
from the clere light of the feithe, to which God had called hym, and
blyndid himself of heresye by adhesion gyven to the herretik
Nestoryu[s], mysbeleving the vni/on of two natures in the person col. 2
of Ihesu Criste. At that tyme was the eyre made derke and that 20
clowdy derkenesse made an obstakill bytwene God and man by the
sedicion of Mahomet, wherthrough Armenye, Capadoce, Solacye,
Pont, Paphagonye, Bythinie, Nusye, Frigye, Lybye, Carie, Lycie,
Mesopotayne, Serye, Fenyce, Pa[lest]yne and a grette parte of the
regions of Ayse and some provinces in Europe toward the west 25
tyll thei came within Spaygne and toward the este vnto Tarace and
Panonye, which war pervertid from the Cristen feith and infecte by
the seede of cenefye an by þis newe secte.

Wherfor it wer necessarye for the Cristen people to knowe by
what malice Mahomet ouircame so moche people and [how] he 30
drowe to him the inconstaunt people through folishe hope. For the
mysknowelage of the flesshely doctrine, well I knowe, maketh the
feithe Catholike to be preysid in the likenes wheras it is emprynted.
Wher/for I tell the that ther war thre thingis through which he gat f. 86ᵛ
audience and by the same drough the people to him. Oone was that 35

5 voide] om. RNJ euacué D   6 by . . . witt] om. N par ton petit sens D
7 þe . . . God] God and his wisdom N la sapience de Dieu D   8 Him]
hymself N   9 had] hath N   13 the 1] om. NJ   devele] the add. NJ
om. D   14 high] heyght NJ   18 of] with N   19 Nestoryus]
Nestoryu[? n]e RNJ Nestorius D   24 Palestyne] N Pastelyne RJ   a] om.
NJD   35 to] vnto NJ

he, which at his begynyng was a dryver of camellys, did so moche
by his disseytis and by the arte of nygromancye that he weddid a
noble and a riche lady named Cadigan, which helde the lordeship
of þe prouynce of Corroȝayne. And as sone as he felt himself wele
5 garnyshid with grette richesse, he conceyued in his hert hough he
myght haue dominacion in the parties of Turkye and Arabie.
Thanne he drough towarde him, what by yeftes and by promesses,
a people callid Robusces and the maliciouse men and suche as war
enclined to myschieff by the constraynte of pouerte, whose owtra-
10 giouse vices war borne owte through his cunduyte, like as a companye of theves, which through their robrye and rapyne war made
col. 2 riche and encresed their people in/asmuche as thei war not
punysshed for their evile dedis. And oftetymes it happid that thei
had good fortune ayeynst them that thei assayled for rapyne, and
15 othirwhile thei war chased and confused by their aduersaries.
Thanne wolde thei ageyne kille and murdir the othir party, what
by tresons and othir [fals] meanys, (so t)hat by processe of tyme
through their cruelte and subtill witte þei bar a grette bruyte and
war sore dredde in the partyes of Asye. Thanne he felte himself
20 mighty through rapyne and vndirstode wele that for his furour the
people feryd him soore, and thought that [h]e s[e]tte on a grette
hight. But whanne he remembird him on his lowe birth it with-
drowe his courage to call himself a kyng, for him thought it
accordid not with his furst office to clymbe to so high a title. Than
25 fell it in his mynde to make people beleve that he was a messinger
sent from God, through which name he was r[e]puted and taken
f. 87 in grette wourship. And / this name he made to be labored by his
factours and allies and by the symple men of Arabye, som for drede
and som by errour and some for fantasye. And suche folke brought
30 vp his name and callid him a prophete, and som of his owne men
in abusing of þe people wourshippid him and flatterid him. And
som durst not say nay in eschewing of his malice. And the rude and
symple people belevid on him through the counterfetyng of a fals

1 which] *canc.* N qui D   camellys] and *add.* N *om.* D   2 disseytis]
conceytes N deceptions D   3 Cadigan] Sadygan J Cadigan D   5 grette]
om. ND   6 haue] gett J   8 Robusces] Robustes NJ *see n.*   the]
þei were N   9 the] *om.* ND   11 rapyne] ravyne N   14 had]
om. N   16 ageyne] *om.* N   17 tresons] treson N *sing.* D   fals] N *om.*
RJ aguet D *see n.*   by 2] the *add.* N   processe] processes J   20 the]
of N   21 that he sette] J that we sitte R to be sett N   24 so] over
(*ins.*) J si D   29 by] for N   32 in] his *add.* N   of] *om.* N   and]
the *add.* NJ *om.* D

myracle. For he had a dowe which he customed to eete peesen honyed owt of his ere, and on a tyme as he was in his predicacion came this dowe and satt downe vpon his shuldir and forthwithall put hir beeke into his ere hoping to have founde hir mete like as she was wounte. Thanne the vnhappy people supposed it had ben the 5 Holy Gooste in likenes of a dove, which by reuelacion shewed vnto him the fals lesingis that he preched to the people through the devellis crafte. And this was the begynnyng / of Mahometis lawe col. 2 or prophecies.

O thou that art disciple of Mahomet, thou oughtest haue more 10 shame than glorie to yeve feith to the doctrine of suche an auctour. Art thou not ashamed to here and beleve as messaunger of God suche one that by rapyne and by ambicion hath vsurpid the name of prophete and the yefte of God, which is contrarie to all suche maner of folkis? For prophecie is shewed among the meeke men 15 and amonge þe innocentes, for the [office] of divine message is neuir yeven to him whose lif is contrarye ayeinst the holy doctrine. A messaunger ought to bere vpon him the token of his maister, but he toke vpon hym Goddis marke which (he) diffowled with the spottis of murdre and trechery. This wise was Mahomet wour- 20 shipped and þe folishe people war abused through which thei did honour and lawde to the maister of dishoneste and to the [con- trever] / of all infamye. f. 87ᵛ

And aftir this he acqueinted him with an evill spirit which brought in his mynde a newe cautele, and thought þat extremite 25 requered nothing withowt debate and the meane waye war best of all othir ways. Thanne (he) thought that he wolde medle his doc- trine with all lawes for to gete people on euery party. Thanne he fonde a maliciouse meane to medle his sayngis party of the Olde Testament and party of the Newe for to gete the favour of the 30 Iewes and the Cristen to his secte. And vntruely he corrupted the sence of the lettir and disfaced the substaunce of all othir lawes and construed it to a fals entente in colouryng of his fals dedis by diuyne auctorite and said that he was ordeigned of God to modre the

ouirgrette rigours and the sharpe ordinaunces of the [lawe of
Moyses] and of Ihesu Criste, which [had] compassion of the grette
col. 2 charge of the people and wold sumwhat enclyne to the / plesaunce
of man. Wherfor He wold enlarge by him the rewle of living,
5 [which was] His messaunger. Thanne he toke of the Iewes lawe
the circumcision and the prohibic[i]on of the fleshe of porke; and
of the Cristen lawe he toke a similitude of baptisme, comaunding
the Sara3ins that thei shulde oftentymes wasshe them in the watir
wenyng by the watir that thei shulde be made clene of their synnes
10 withowt any confession or penaunce; and for bycause that he wolde
not withdrawe the hope of Cristen people from the worlde which
God comaunded, that no man shulde put his trust thereon, promised to his discipulis paradise and manaced all suche that louet
not the worlde that thei shulde haue the peynes of hell for their
15 rewarde. And thus he altird the lawe in entent to have turned them
vp so down, for in the ioye of paradise that was to come he promised
them non othir thing but fleshely delites and concupiscence of the
f. 88 body and of the yghen and delicate metes and / drynkes and feyr
women for to ly by, a grette habundaunce of riche vessels and
20 ryvers rennyng with mylke and hony and all othir worldely delites,
which be contra[r]y to the state of perfec[ci]on and glorye, and
comen to men and to hoggis in thys worlde. And yete thou shalte
not fynde in all the lesyngis þat he made that he promysed any ioye
to the sowle nor no maner yefte of blissidnes, but yevith all the
25 rewarde to the body and to the appetite of the careyne, which is
a roten corrupcion. And aftir his wourdes all suche as lyven in the
delites of this worlde haue their paradise forthwithall in the same,
s[e]ying that he promysith non othir thing beyonde but suche
delicate thingis as may be founde on this side. Moreouir this fals
30 prophete gadred owt of the two Testamentis certeyn abstinences
of mete and drynke and lyeng with women in certayn dayes till the
col. 2 sonne war down, which he callid the Fastes of the Moneþe / of
Rama3an. Also he comaunded fyve orysouns to be saide on the day

---

1 rigours] of the lawe of Moyses *add.* R *om.* D   ordinaunces] ordynaunce
N *pl.* D   1–2 lawe of Moyses] NJ same R loix de Moyse D   4 enlarge]
om. N   5 which was] NJ as R qui estoit D   7 comaunding] to
add. NJ aux D   9 by . . . that] þat by the water N   10 that] *om.* N
21 perfeccion] NJ perfecioon R   22 men] to men *add.* R   to 2] *om.* N
26 aftir his wourdes] after wordes J afterwardes N par son parler D   28 sey-
ing] NJ saying R puis que D *see n.*   29–30 fals prophete] saide prophete
fals N   30 abstinences] abstynence N *pl.* D   33 on] vppon N

and ix knelynges, tweyne in the poynt of the day, tweyne aftyr
mydday, tweyne aftir sonne-settyng and thre aftir souper, on a
condicion that all the nyght aftir thei shulde take their sportis to
eete and drynke withowt sykyng and to take all their pleasur with
women vnto the tyme that the day was so lyght that thei myght   5
knowe a white threde from a blacke. The meryte of this abstinence
ought litle to be preyside which is so sone recompensed by so many
excesses, and the fasting in the day was but litle wourth for the
hope of so foule a nyght that [was] vsed by thes ydolatres in their
fleshely lustis. And yet he abused them by anothir meane for to get   10
them towarde hym whanne he ordeigned the Bahach, which was
a goyng euery yere to the Meke, which was an howse applied for
the reprevable sacrafice of the ydoll Venus; and now it is the /
grettest pilgrimage of the Saraȝines. For ther thei dispuyle them   f. 88ᵛ
naked excepte a litle kercheff that is knyt abowte their reynes, and   15
by deuocion thei cast stones vndir their membres, through which
thei make a gret heepe. And this thei do to the honour of Venus
and of the ydoles. And yet he wolde kepe certeine ydolatres for to
woursship his mastres Venus wheras he shewed his doctryne full
of all dissollucion and filth. Yet his lechery surmounted all othir for   20
he was subiecte and seruaunt to all corrupcion.

O Lorde God, what signes war þes of a prophete? And what
werkes occupied he to be the massaungere of God? Or hough
myght any man be so light of beleve to take suche mokkaryes for
doctryne or suche supersticion for very religion? O thou vntrew   25
Mahomete, thou tokest vpon the to modre the streight comaundementis of the lawe of iustice and grace, but thi moderacions be
turned into / mokkeryes and instede of attemperaunce thou hast   col. 2
put in an owtragiouse extremyte owt of all reason. Thou saidest
that the streyte lawes by the [shulde] be enlarged, and thou hast   30
opened the way [and] abandoned the bridyll to all sensuall appetite.
He purveith evill for the rigour of the lawe that yeveith a lawe to
vnlawefullnes, and suche lawe is contrary to reason which is fauorable to flesshely desir. But hough may any man covenablely enlarge
the lawe in anythinge that no lawe may sufficiently refreyne? Yet   35
it is bettir haue some delite by the streyte lawe thanne by [the]

1 aftyr] in the N apres D   3 to] and NJ   4 withowt sykyng]
om. N see n.   8 excesses] excesse NJ   9 ydolatres] ydolatryes N
11 Bahach] to add. ins. N   12 Meke] parts of k spaced like lr R Melre NJ
13 the 3] om. N des D   17 to] in NJ en D   18 for] om. N   23 Or]
O N   29 put] it add. N   33 lawe] as N

large lawe be put away from vertu. For the flesshe assayeth euir to
gette vpon the bridill of reason, but yet the harde bridill yeveth it
excercise to kepe him from doyng amysse. I wolde haue grette
mervaile of the foule sentence of thi lawe but that the fowlenesse
5 of thi lyving taketh from me the mervaile of thi wourdis, for euery
f. 89 man speketh aftir the habundaunce of his herte. So thanne / thi
living bare wittenesse of thi doctrine, and therfor it was no straunge
thing though thou taughtest othir to abandone themself to glotonye
and lechery and promysed them that thei shulde haue inough
10 therof in the othir worlde, seeng that thiself madest avaunte that
thou haddest by the yefte of God the powere of xl men in thi
reynes for to accomplisshe the werkis of lechery. Also thou tokest
so owtragiouse parte therof that thou haddest at onys xv wyves
and ij chaumberers and taughtest them that war abowte the
15 for to do the same owt of mesure. For nature yevith vnto
man so grette inclynacion to lechery that [yn] lasse thanne the
lawe refreyne them ther shulde be to grette mischieff. And
therfor reason will that the power of nature, which is ample
and common, that it shulde be condicioned aftir auctorite of the
20 lawe. But aftir thin ensaumples thou woldest fulfill the power
col. 2 of nature and vnbinde the power of the lawe. Wh/at is this? Nothing
ellis but a bandon alltogedre and ouir natur to provoke the worlde
to a [superflue delyte] and to a comon lechery. Doth it not suffice
inough to lette nature haue his kyndly course but that it be con-
25 streyned? Is it needefull to awake with grette cryeng in the nyght
them that ben on sleepe for to stere them to the werkis of Venus?
It ought to suffice to haue sowned thi disordinaunce to haue many
women withowt to haue stablisshid to haue forsaken them at euery
occasion for to e[f]tis fill the beddis full of women?
30   O thou foule creature, vnwourthi to knowe the lawe of God,
which maiste right wele be a fellow to hogges and a disciple of
Bacus, wher hast thou lerned that the spirituall yefte of prophecye
was yeven to flesshely men or what reu(e)lacion may come to a
thought wher fornicacion or filthe regneth? It may not be, for the

5 taketh] away *add.* N   6 his] the[? y] N   8 themself] hemselff J
hymself N   9 and 1] to *add.* NJ   11 the yefte] yeftys N don D   13 so]
the N   15 for] *om.* N   16 thanne] þat J   23 superflue delyte] NJ
superfluite R superflu delit D   24 haue] to haue N   25 Is it] *tr.* N
26 on sleepe] asleepe J aslepee N   28 haue forsaken] forsake NJ   29 eftis]
NJ estis R *see n.*   full of] of alle J of awen N   31 of] to N   34 or]
of N & D

spirit of prophecie, that procedith from hevin, is not yeven but onely to suche hertis as be clene and / reisid on hight by contempla- **f. 89ᵛ** cion and browght lowe from the delites of this worlde. And the angellis, massaungers of God, thei be so pure thei appere to no persone but to suche as be chaste. Hough may it be thanne that any 5 man may beleve that the aungell Gabriell shulde brynge to the the lawe whanne thou avauntyst thiself of thi corrupte lechery, of which all the legions of aungellis have abhominacion, and disdeyne at all inordinat filthe and shamefull polucion? That lesing was nedefull to the for to couir with thi shame, for whanne thou fellest 10 in þe falling evill, with which had smytten the Almyghty God, þou saydest that the syght of the aungell Gabryell whanne he appered to the was so bryght that thou mightest not susteyne to stonde on thi feete, which appered visibly vnto the and invisibly to othir folkis. Lorde God, what laughtir and iape war this and the losse of 15 so many sowles had not fallen ther/upon! And what that euir thou **col. 2** say, ther was nethir God ne angelle that euir medelid with suche a devilrye or mokkerye. And it was at Saignys a monke apostata, infecte of the heresie Nestoryne and put owt fro holy chirche, which taught the this cursidnes to sette holy Cristendome in trouble and 20 to do pleasure to the heresies Nestoryne. And he which was well-purweyed in lecture and had but fewe good maners chastisid not his vices by (his sciens but) peruertid his connyng and þe sadnes of his evill lyfe. And he shewed welle that it was a perilous assemble of grette clergy medlid with an evill thought. And this may be 25 likened to good wyne which corruptith and egrith through an evill vessell. He this lerned the: to bete down the booke of Alcoran, wher thi werki[r]s lerned the lectre and vnmesurable wille and receyvid willfull opening and licence to walowe in ther flesshely pleasures and vnrefrayned lechery. And for that thou art redy to / obey. For **f. 90** thou diddest confirme the doctryne aftir their appetite and gavest 31 a famylier lawe to the flesshe, which drowe their hertis to vanyte, which was disceyveable.

1 hevin] it *add.* N   4 pure] þat *add.* NJ   10 nedefull . . . for 1] to the nedefull N   11 which] God *add.* NJ   Almyghty God] *om.* NJ *see n.*   13 the] he *add.* N   15 what] a *add.* NJ   and 1] a *add.* NJ 16 fallen] ifall NJ   18 devilrye or mokkerye] or *om.* N mokkerye *ins. above* devylrye J *see n.*   a monke] a mong N   23 sciens] sentence N science D 24 perilous assemble] perilous *canc.* perveys assembled N   25 grette] *om.* N grant D   27 this lerned the] lerned the this N   28 werkirs] werkis RNJ wer *add.* N adherans D   lectre] lettre NJ   29 pleasures] presurs N 31 diddest confirme] confermest N

Yet notwithstonding all this, thou foundist a thridde meane to gette vnto the people that were feerfull and feble through thi grette manaces and bostingis as sone as thou feltest thiselff mighty and accompanyed with cruell people. For thi writingys bare witnesse
5 that thou was sent in the vertu of the swourde to put to dethe and in bondage suche as wolde not beleve on the, and perfor suche did sewe the for feere, that thou myghtest not turne with thin erroure. But what reuerence may be dewe to a lawe that is brought in by cruelte, or hough may a man have any devocion to be shreven
10 whanne he is compellid therto by force? Certeinly trewe it is that the dignite of oure religion is so free and so noble that it may suffre no violence. And loke wher feith lesith his liberte it lesith his
col. 2 merite. / For God desirith to wynne nothing of a creature but oonely his herte, for He woll not ravisshe nor take it away but
15 rece(i)ve it as yefte forasmuch as (it) belongith to the pure and liberall perfeccion of the holy feithe for to drawe hertis vnto hit by softnes and not by rigour. And therfor the highnes of the Savioure liste to appere in humilite, and in His teching was benigne and not constreined man to come to Hym for feere. For He entird not into
20 the worlde armed with swerdis but fulfillid with vertu whanne He through His digne wourde and meke predicacions and by His holy myracles confirmed and (gate) vnto Him His holy chirche. But Mahomet did not so, for he toke his abiding vpon the introduccion of ydolatrie and helped himself with force of the swourde as
25 ydolatres doon, constreyning the people by stronge manaces and turmentis for to do sacrifice. And this was wele preved by the holy
f. 90ᵛ mar/tirs that endured many mervelous peynes for because þei refused only to offre encence to the ydols. And there was atteynte the probacion of the fals sectes, which might bettir be callid fals
30 thanne trewe lawes and preuaricacion of doctrynes. For where trouthe and reason, which ben the foundacion of the feithe, faile them, thei renne to the swourde in their woodnesse, and so thei helpe themself with suche instrumentis as destroyeth mankynde.

O gloriouse God, Thou hast wele previleged Thin holy lawe
35 Catholike and iustified it aboue all othir lawes. For h[o] that hath any witte or clere vndirstonding may wele knowe that it is rathir

12 it] he J elle D   14 not] no N   ravisshe] it *add*. NJ   15 receive]
take N   as 1] a *add*. NJ *om*. D   19 constreined] constreyn NJ   man]
no man NJ   not] *om*. N ne D   21 meke] holy N simple D   24 helped]
helpe N hylp J   28 to 2] vnto NJ   31 feithe] *om*. N   35 ho] NJ
he R quiconques D

yeven by divine wisedom thanne founde by mannys witte seing
that by it arn put away all filthis; all derkenesses and all opin
iniquites by it arn redressed; and all othir introduccions be confused, vayne and anulled. And if thou woll en/tre in comparisons col. 2
to knowe what thing may be most wourthi in contemplacion, moste 5
iuste in good livinge, moste honest in humanyte, moste reule in
maners, moste profitable to euery man, moste peasable to all folkis,
most garnisshid of good hope in abiding of a souereygne rewarde,
I say that it is the holy Cristen feithe, which is conduyte of all thes
thingis afore rehercid. For loke all the holy Euuangeles, which is 10
the doctrine of oure God and of our Maister, and þou shalte fynde
nothing [yn hem] but good shewyngis of love, of iusti[ce] and of
peece, counceyllis of holy clennesse, of innocencye and helping of
his neyghbour, refusing all dissolucion, all dishonour, all disordinaunce and all iniquite of this worlde, trusting to haue the euir- 15
lasting glorye that is to come. The Euaungelyes accorden all to the
iuste and morall lawes, to þe doctrines of the olde faders and the
honest conuersacion of wise men and to the attem/peraunce of f. 91
lyving. It techith to beleve vpon [o] God alone, which is soueraigne
and euirlasting and of His grace techith man to kepe hospitalite, to 20
haue compassion, to haue mercy and to be cheritable to his neyghbours. His auctorite is neuir derogate of reason, nor His statutes
discorde neuir from the way of vertu. It techith no man to beleve
on (noo)thinge but on suche as may be lawde to Almyghty God
[nor] techith no maner of poynte wherthrough myght growe any 25
fowle sclaundir or wanton ensaumple nor to speke shamefull ne
repreveable wourdes nor do werke that shulde turne to the hurte
of any othir man. If so be that Cristen men be bounde to beleve
on some articles which may not be comprehendid by mannes
reason, therby is knowen the high excellence of their God and the 30
divinite of their lawe, and apperith wele it was not founde by the
erroure of man but yeven by the souereigne Maister, seyng that it
surmountith their in/uencion; but it is doon by suche a foresight col. 2
that all his poyntes ben to the glorie and exaltacion of him that
beleuith therupon. Take good avisement that all the othir lawes be 35

1 by 1] the add. N   2 derkenesses] derknes N   4 anulled] vnabled N
thou] om. N   9 that] om. NJ   10 all] as J toute D   12 iustice] NJ
iusticice R   14–15 disordinaunce] dyscordynawnce J   19 o] J om. RN vn D
20 man] men N sing. D   22 derogate] derrogacion N deriogacyon J
25 nor] NJ it R ne D   26 ne] nor J   27 nor] to add. N   do] no add.
NJ   29 articles] of/tycles J   31 wele] þat add. NJ

ordeigned by man hymself, but thauncient Testament cam by God
to the men by þe ministracion of Moyses. This was yeven by
Go(d)dis own mouthe like as the prophete had said byfore, 'He
shal be seen in erthe and be conuersaund with men.' Haue we not
5   in writing that the philosophirs repreved the paynemes for the
worshipping of false ydoles? And at that tyme by their philo-
[so]phye Socrates, Plato and Aristotyll atteyned to the knowlage
onely of one God, for which opynion Socrates was condemned to
the dethe at Athenes. And it is euident that he and Seint Denys by
10 the preching of the apostle and by the grace of holy baptisme, in
f. 91ᵛ myn advise, shall iuge the philosophie of / the sect of Mahomet,
vnreyned in lechery and owt of all ordinaunce in delites of the
bodye, seyng that all morall sentences damnet excesse and techeth
hough a man shuld be moderate in delites and attemperate in the
15 werkis of the flesshe. Morouir we se hough holy Catholike religion
honouret souereigne diuinite. Hough may a man sette his beleve
higher thanne vpon oon euirlasting God before all thingis, the
maker of all thingis, and myghty aboue all thingis? And so be not the
ydolles nor the newefounde goddis which ben founded through
20 the appetite of man. But the beleving of Him is trewe beleve and
the lernyng of [Hym ys perfyte] wisedome. And if so be that the
Catholikes holde opynion that euirlasting God hathe lyked to
becom man for the saluacion of man, yet suche beleve is no deroga-
cion to His mageste, but it is a highing and a glorifiyng of His
col. 2 humi/lite. But who may repreve Ihesu Criste that He had mysdone
26 ayeinst the lawe of nature seyng He so covenablely stablisshid
nurture modered, and dewe generacion and lawefull? And if His
feith movethe men to abstinence, yet He ioyneth mesure with it so
that through habundance the body shuld not fall in synne, and on
30 the othir syde for lake of sustinaunce it shulde not be made feble.
O hough lityll thing susteynith nature! Certeinly the litill norissh-
ing suffiseth and profiteth more thanne the grette excesse of the
Saraȝines, which is more chargeable to them thanne the fasting of
Cristen men is hurte vnto them; for scarsete is tresoure of helthe,

6–7 philosophye] J philophye R philosophrs (*corrected to* philosophy) N
8 onely] *om.* N   13 seyng] Seenge J se *canc.* Seenge N   morall]
mortal J morales D   sentences] sentence N *pl.* D   14 attemperate] attem-
peraunte N   15 hough] þe *add.* J *om.* D   19 through] be N   21 Hym
ys perfyte] J perfite N prophete and R *see n.*   22 that] þe *add.* NJ
om. D   26 seyng He] *tr.* N   34 tresoure] tresoresse NJ *see n.*   of]
to N de D

and wher the body is lene and voyde the [soule] is full and the witte
plenteouse. Who wolde speke of childern brought fourth and
norisshid, I make euery good conscience iuge that the state of
mariage vndivided and oon bytuene ij persones is Godly / and   f. 92
according to veray love, laufull engendringe, profitable, thoughtfull 5
norisshinge, and necessarye to the good techinge of childern. And
what shall þou deme of the multiplicacion of the women Saraȝines
with oon husbonde and of the diuersite discordable of the childern,
but oonly l[o]ve departed, issue doubtefull, feding of no force,
teching of debate among the sonnes of oon fader, by the which   10
occasion sheding of blode cometh oftymes by the discorde of
brodern in the howses of princes myscreauntes for þe mysknowlage
of the ordre of the priorite of the childern of many [mo]ders?

And þou, which somtyme a viage vpon their marches, hast
knowen of suche lerningis, suffise it to the so moche to have harde 15
thaduersite of lawes whereof riseth the vanyte of sectes and þe
voyde hopes, and by the cleving to of oon hoole holy feith abyde
and stablisshe the to þe trewe and perfight hope. If thou / beleve col. 2
in God assure the in Him. But who that wolde aske from whens
this seurte shuld com, I say that it ought to begynne in the exami- 20
nacion of conscience and trewe entent to do wele. And furst he
must retourne to himself by correccion and put himself in vre to
do his devoure. So by this meane and by non othir thou maist
fynde assured hope. For good hoope is so contraryouse to all cryme
that the soule that is gilty may neuir be assured. Gilt is norise of 25
suspeccion, and the conscience that is full of cryme maketh a
feerefull thought. And so covert offence is wittenessed by the
shewing of feere, and tremblyng membres shewith the sekenesses
and the gref of the harte as a reede visage shewith the shame of
his courage. And know this for certeyn that no man may assure 30
that persone that is affrayed in his owne conscience. For iniquite
is suspecte and a lyer vpon himself, but innocency / is of his   f. 92ᵛ
nature consolatyve.

And put away thanne presumptuouse hope and make thiself

1 soule] NJ body R esperit D   5 engendringe] engendure N engend-
reure J engendrure D   7 the women] om. N femmes D   9 love] NJ
leve R amour D   11 cometh] om. J aduient D   discorde] discordes N
sing. D   12 þe] om. NJ la D for the add. R   13 moders] faders RNJ
meres D   14 a] yn NJ   16–17 þe voyde hopes] hopes which are voyde N
20 I say] isseye N   to] om. NJ   28 sekenesses] seknes NJ   34 thanne]
the N doncques D

wourthi to gette the goodis or thou presume to take them; but tary
not vpon hope that is defectyve nor on the suffrages of worldely
goodis which may not be withholde by the, nor by them thou maist
not be susteyned. Yet I woll gree [þat thu vse] them so that thou
5 be not mocked by them and that þou helpe thiself by them so that
thei noye the not. But looke that thou sette not thi ferme trust on
suche thinges as ben desperate, but make it be seruaunte to thin
hope. Also bewarre and follow not all thin owne willes and opina-
tive hopes. For he that followith his owne propre counceile puttith
10 from himself the counceill of othir men, and he must nedis go
alone owt of the way that is guydid by himself alone. But who þat
preisith othir mennys avise shal be preised with wele-av(i)sed /
col. 2 men, and who that canne applie his witte to othir mennes wisedoms
he shal be trusted of (his) frendis and make his enemyes to bowgh.
15 But aftir (these) thinges kepe the fro wanhope. And if thou wolt
argue thin vnhappynesse by thin fawtis and thin good aventures
aftir the reason of thi cunduyte, thou shalt neuir be disceyvid by
folisshe hope nor supprysed nor dispourveyed for lacke of knowlage. And loke thou take thi good fortunes in humilite, and be
20 feerfull of damnacion, and comfort the evile folkis bi pacience,
which may cause them of amendment, and the good men woll
turne the to helpe and socour and the evill men by pacience of
amendment. Thanne shall the good helpe of seurte turne vnto the
and the evill of prouision. And if thou kepe thes iiij poyntis I woll
25 be nye the, and also thou shalt approche to Him that I am nye
vnto, which is [the Fadre and] the Wardeyn of all good hope and
f. 93 fulfillith the desires of them that stedefastly and rightwise/ly truste
vpon Him.

Iff thou wolt come to the high thinges and retourne from
30 myschef, thou must thinke on thi dedis if thou wolt come to
conforte. And also thou must remembre oone God in thi herte
and suffre tribulacion paciently an sett not thi witte on vayne
thinges nor on fortune, which is [feynte] and may nothing do.
And with othir mennes wisedom helpe thin own and take good

3 thou] ins. J om. N   4 I woll] tr. N   þat thu vse] NJ at R que tu . . .
vses D   5 that 1] om. J   þou] mayst add. ins. J   by 2] with NJ   that 2]
NJ that add. R   6 that] om. NJ   7 it] om. J see n.   to] vnto J
8 and 2] nor NJ & D   8–9 opinative] opynatyfes N   12 wele-avised] wele
ayised N   14 trusted] truted N tristed (corrected from truted) J   enemyes]
frendys N   21 and] þan add. NJ   30 myschef] myschefys N sing. D
31 oone] on NJ see n.   33 feynte] NJ finite R fainte D

heed of him that saith wele. Beleve counseill and kepe it well.
And if thou be angry rest not longe therin. Love and susteyne
the good men, for it shall cause the the rathir to be good. And
loke thou withdraw the from flatterers and kepe wele all thi
frendis. And kepe secrete thine owne counceyll. Beete the 5
hownde nygh the lyon. And thus shuldest thou rule thiself.

[Vndrestondynge]

I fele myself highly / conforted and profytably counseiled through col. 2
thi presentes and speculatyue probacions, for thei be ryght clere
and apparaunt. But aftur the small subtill reasons the grette 10
ensaumples profighten grettely. And let vs receve them agreably
for doctryne and let vs kepe them stedfastly in our mynde. And
who that may not atteyne to knowe by deepe argument must helpe
hymself by entendible ensaumples, which ben comown both to the
symple men and to the wise men, and printe them firmely in th[e] 15
courages for the proporcion and the qualite of singler causes that
we haue with princes and othir aventures. Science tretith not of
singler thinges but leveth them to experience and counseilith þat
thei shulde [werke] by patron and by ensaumple. And of thes thre
thynges I haue specially ado in myn own cause. Wher(fore) I 20
beseche the shewe by othirs what I shuld hoope of myself and that
I may / vndirstonde it by practike in thinges passed and that thou f. 93ᵛ
shewe [me] of my hoope that is for to come.

[Hoope]

Off ensaumples thou maiste [not] faile if thou rede in the holy 25
volumes of the writing of storyes and of the amiable cronicles of
Fraunce and of thi forefaders, that whanne thei war in necessite
good hoope neuir failed them but toke vpon them good courage.
Wherfor thei ought to be had in remembraunce to theire lawde and
for good ensaumple to othir. Remembre the hough Mathathias and 30
his childern the Machabites, which fledde and hid hemself in þe

---

1 Beleve] hys *add.* J we *add. canc.* N   3 cause the] *om.* N the *om.*
4 loke] þat *add.* NJ   9 thi] þe J ta D   presentes] presence NJ *see n.*
and] thi *add.* NJ tes D   10 small] fynall N   14 entendible] entable N
15 men 1] *om.* N   the 2] NJ thi R ou D   17 of] *om.* N   18 them]
it NJ   to] the *add.* N *om.* D   19 shulde] shall N   werke] NJ wake R
besongnent D   20 in] yn in J   23 to come] certeyn N futures D
27 thei] thi N   29 to 1] *om.* NJ   31 Machabites] Machabees N

mountaynes, aftirwarde risen vp ageyne in the persecucion of the
tyraunt named Antiocus. This tyraunt had vsurped and put in
seruage all Iude. He stroyed the lawe and the sacrifices, helde the
col. 2 symple people in subieccion / by force, and suche as warre variable
5 toke them into his fauour by corrupcion. And to the traytours of
[the] people he gaue receipt and kept them for to helpe him through
theire malice ayeinst their owne cowntre and to the distruccion of
their lawe. And thou vndirstondist wele these fewe people that
suche wise war chacid owt of their cuntre through good hoope
10 gadird them togedre and delyuerid theire cuntre and stablisshid
ther lawes by iugemente and powere and put away the traytours
owt of the cuntre. Hough happid it that the men wer of suche
powere which by lyklynesse war withowt remedy? It is to beleve
that thei enforced themself with hope mavgre fortune and made
15 vertue of their necessite and that the diffyeng of mannes powere
turned all their hertis into divine hoope, conceyvid in high courage
and cunduyted by firme hoope, and so made themself that war
f. 94 ouircome to be ouir/comers and the humble folkis [or] suche as war
chaced owt to be lordis and maisters. They callid to iustice suche
20 as had put them owt through owltrage and did rightfull iustice in
all the cuntre and satisfaccion to God and did lawe vpon the
traytours and preuaricatours, amonge which oon named Althinus
and othir that war his fellowes, afftir their extort richesse and
vsurped glorye by treason, made them flee shamefully owt of
25 cuntre. And among the good men Neemias and Esdras may be sett
in ordre, which in þe tyme of theire persecucion conceyvid in their
thought a mervelouse hoope to assemble ageyn the people that war
disperpuled in seruage by the persecucion of þe Assiryens, and put
themself [forth] to redresse and edifie the Holy Cyte and the
30 temple, which was all tobroken. And the good man Esdras traveled
so moche that [he] restored the holy librarye, through which the
col. 2 lawe was renoveled that long / tyme byfore was forgeten and nought
sette by. Hast thou not redde of the wise lady namyd Delbora,

---

1 risen] thei rose N   2 named Antiocus] *tr.* N   3 stroyed] stryed J
destroyed N   sacrifices] sacrifice he N *pl.* D   4 people in] vndre N
5 corrupcion] correccion J corruption D   9 suche wise war] were such
wise NJ   13 lyklynesse] lyknes N   16 courage] corages N *sing.* D
17 so] thei *add.* NJ *om.* D   18 or] of RNJ *see n.*   20 through] their
add. NJ *om.* D   22 oon] was *add.* N *om.* D   Althinus] alchinus J
alchimus N *see n.*   24 of] the *add.* NJ   27 ageyn] agayns J rassembler D
33 namyd] *om.* N

whose abyding was vndir the shadow of a palme tre, rose on hyght
owt of dispeyre in myddis of the people of Ysraell, which by the
space of xx^{ti} yere was persecuted by Iabyn, Kyng of Cananee? And
ayeinst thoppinion of Barach, which at that tyme was leder of the
people, she gatte the victorye of the enemyes and gatte a grette 5
triumphe for the scomfiture of the Cananeys and a grette lawde for
the deth of Duke Cysara. What felle of Gedeon in the tyme of
oppression which was don by the Kyng of Madien vpon Israell?
Did not he discomfite with iiijc men an hundred and twenti thousand and delyuird throught his grette hoope all his people which 10
lay in langour and mysery? Yette was he but a powr laborer, a man
vnknowen, of litill stature and of / lowe birth of the lynage of f. 94^v
Manasse. But wheras the grace of God and the vertu of man ioynen
togedre ther is nothing vnpossible to be don nor vnlawfull so to
hope. And oftymes owr Lorde yevith man suche power that he 15
cannot come in his thought. His ensaumples ben made opyn among
the myracles of my werkis.

Yet it may be that the herte which is enprynted in worldly
mutacions desirith more the witty excercise of man thanne divine
grace. Wilt thou than see thi caas by othir men and compar the 20
aventures of oure dayes with the aventures of our auncient predecessours? Thanne reede O[m]ir, Virgile, Tyte Liue, Orose, Troye
Pompe, Iustyn, Flore, Valere, Stace, Lucan, Iule Ceste, Bru[n]et
Latyn, Vincent [and] othir writers storyes, which haue travailid to
enlonge their short age through the longe and notable renown of 25
their writyngis. And ther shalt thou fynde th[i] dedis and ensaumples ac/cording to the matere, and thou shalt mervaile in thi col. 2
reding hough the dyvine prouidence hath chaunged the myscheves
vnto boncheves ayeinst the estimacion of man. And ther shalt thou
fynde hough Troye was distroyed by Theseus and Iason in the 30
tyme of Laemedon, and yet it was relevid ageyn and sette in bettir
caas thanne euir it was afore in the tyme of Priamus. In othir places
thou maist rede hough Athenes, Lacedemoyn and Thebes war
oftintymes put in seruage, desolate and distroyed in the tyme of
Зer[с]es, of Philipe and of Alisaundre, which aftirwarde risen ageyn 35

1 tre] she *add.* N   6 scomfiture] discomfiture N   7 of 1] the *add.* N
du D   14 vnpossible] inpossible NJ   15 man] a man N homme D
20 thi] thin awn N þin owne J   22 Omir] NJ Onir R   23 Lucan]
Lucam J   Brunet] NJ Brumet R   24 and] *om.* RNJ & D   writers] of
add. N   26 thi] NJ the R ton D   27 the] þi J thyn N la D   31 it was]
tr. J   32 caas] estate NJ   35 Зerces] J¡Зertes R Xerses N   and] *om.* N & D

and wer in grette prosperite and glorie. Also it wold be straunge to
the for to vndirstonde the fortune of Mitridate, Kyng of Pont,
which gate many victories and many tymes was discomfited, for
(whan) thou notist his batelles that wer discomfite and the renewing
5 ageyne of his hooste—this day discomfite and tomorow quickly
f. 95 restablis/shid, it shulde seme to the that the cites war new quykened
ageyne in the feeldes and þat his discomfiture shulde bere the
semblaunce and the pompe of [a] victorye. On the othir party thou
maist be instructe in dyverse volumes of the state of Roome, which
10 by so high and inuiolable hoope was preserved and amonge his
infortunable causes was brought to so high a wourshipe that it was
lorde ouir all the worlde. And who war the founders of þis cite?
Non othir but Troiannes that war discomfited and exiled owt of
their cuntre and chaced aboute [by] tempestis of the see. Thanne
15 it is to beleve that so high a warke had neuir be done nor be
bygonne save only by suche men as war preved in grette necessite.
For the hardnesse of their travaile couraged them to seche a seure
restyng place, and the annoye that thei had in their lowe estate
col. 2 made them so stronge in hoope that aftirwarde thei / cam to high
20 glorye. Was not that excellent cite take by Hanyball, that duke
victoriouse, whanne aftir iiij notable batailles that he ouircam in
fewe days and slough the knyghthode of Roome, he thanne forthwithall pyght his tentis in the thredde medew of Roome? And the
same day was solde at Roome the feelde wheron it stode. And by
25 a firme hoope amonge desperable myseryes that was within the
walles of them that war beseged, of fortune the same man was
founde in the town that had bought the feelde and he was arayed
in the armes of Hanyball. Thanne and thou rede further of the
same thou shalt fynde hough myghtily thei rose vp ageyne and
30 hough ther aduersite turned aftirwarde to grette augmentacion of
their glorye.

What mervaile may a man take of the dedis of Marryus, which
so ofte tymes was dispoyled and put owte of his fraunchise and
f. 95ᵛ sone aftir restored / ageyne to liberte and to the wourship of a
35 myghty duke and a doubt[ed] chevetayn? This was a singulare
ensaumple of happy men which issued (owt) of perverce fortune,

7 ageyne] *om.* N   14 by] NJ the R par D   15–16 be bygonne] begunne N
17 seche] such J querre D   19 so] *om.* N   20–1 duke victoriouse] *tr.* NJ
22–3 he . . . Roome] *om.* N   25 amonge] the *add.* NJ   32 of 1] on NJ
34 to 1] þe *add.* N *om.* D   and to the] to þe J and N & en D   35 doubted]
NJ doubty R *see n.*   chevetayn] chapten N   36 issued] sued N

namly of hym which had nothing left of his fortune save onely his
lyfe or to be in the daunger of seruage or in the perill of deth. For
aftir his scomfitur and his caytifnesse he recouerid ageyne to suche
powere that he commaunded his legions vpon peyne of deth to
make them redy to feyght with his enemyes that war nygh him and 5
so discomfited them.

   Yet I may say the by a persuasion to beholden that thei that arn
meked by frowarde fortune were the occasion of hoope forasmoche
as amonge the extreme periles norisshith and enforcet the highnesse of vertu. And oftentymes mystruste of helpe enforceth nature 10
and fortune to save þem that shulde be perishid. The conquerours
haue doubte allwaye to lese, and thei that haue loste haue hoope
alwey / to recouer. And oftentymes suche as haue the bettir hand col. 2
waxen prowde and forgettyn themself through the delites of their
conqueste, and he that is vndir charpith his wittis to thentent that 15
he myght be releced of his angwysshe. And if he haue no hoope to
come owt of his evile fortune, yet he may hoope that the happe of
his enymye may retourne into myschefe. And to this purpose the
storyes may serue the in which thou shalt fynde many myserable
ruynes and the falling of grette conquerours, and thou shalt fynde 20
but fewe of them which by ambicion, by rapyne and by the owtrage
of pryde that euir their good cam to laudable fyne nor honest issue
of their lewde empryses. Semyramys was the woman that furst
wolde haue conqueryd the Aydes and Ethiope, but hit happid that
she was slayne by Hercules, which was hir owne sonne. He sette 25
the markes of his conqueste in thende of the Occean / See; yette f. 96
was he slayne by a woman with a chirte that was enpoy(so)ned.
Mytrydace also furnysshed many batallis and warred vpon many
provynces, and at thende his owne sonne made warre vpon him
evin to the depe. Philip troubled all Grece and Macedonye and 30
aftirward was slayne by oon of his souldeiours. Alysaunder was not
content notwithstonding he had conquered all therthe, and a litill
venemouse poyson toke awey all the pryde of his courage so that
the body su[f]fised with a sepultur of vi or vij foote for to close
him in. Kynge Ʒerces sembled so grette an hoste that wheras 35

1 of 1] in NJ   of his fortune] *om.* N de sa fortune D   2 the 1] *om.* N ou D
7 that arn] þat are N arn J   12 doubte allwaye] *tr.* NJ   12–13 hoope
alwey] *tr.* NJ   13 as] þat N   15 conqueste] conquestes N *sing.* D
16 angwysshe] angwysshes N *sing.* D   22 nor] or J   24 that] *om.* N
26 thende] of the ende *add.* N   28 and] he N   32 notwithstonding] þat
add. NJ   34 suffised] was suffysed NJ susfised R   35 sembled] assembled NJ

thei cam they dranke the ryvers drye; his ministirs bracke the grette
mountaigne of Athos for to make [a way] ovir the see and that the
shippis myght saile through the same; his navy of shippis couerid
the see named Medtryraine so that thei made a brigge from (þe)
5　toone syde to the othir, by which thei passid ouir. Yette at the laste,
col. 2　fortune turned hir / backe suche wise that he which was vnhappy,
notwithstonding his grette navye and multitude of people, vnneth
myght scape in a lityll vessell. But yette he escaped not the handis
of his prouest, which for helping of himself myschevousely slewe
10　him by treson. What shall we say also of Cyru[s], which shedde
many mannys bloode on the erthe? The Quene Thamarys also
made vs wise of hir ysswe, which (she) ouircam by a grette manhode
and aftir that made put his hede in a disshe that was full of blood
of them that wer slayne, saying thus wise: 'Nough fulfill thi cursed
15　cruelte and staunche thi thirst in the blode of man.' Considre also
vpon the grette dedis of Hanyball and see hough lityll a conclusion
fell therof, which ensaumple may suffice the for all. For that
doubted duke, patron of knyghthode and maister of victoryes, was
so customed to ouircome that him semed to haue ben aboue for-
f. 96ᵛ　tune / and to haue ouircome by force all vnhappynesse, and also
21　that God and the desteneys war sworn to him. But at the last he
fonde himself withowte londe or people, fledde into a straunge
cuntre, chased owt with his enemyes and had in suspeccion with
his hooste and founde no socour in his myserye safe to disface his
25　wille and his soroufull lif with drynckyng of poyson. So thanne it
is no neede at this tyme to multiplye any mo ensaumples, for and
thou take thi leiser to reede Seneck and the tragedyes that benne
in the booke of Iohn Bocasse, which tretith of the fall of noble men,
of the losse of conquerours and of the casting down of them that
30　wold haue rysin ovirhighe. And therfor conforte the in this caas
and thyncke that the bruyt of thine enemyes ys not perdurable
whanne oftentymes aftir such oultragious force the diffoullers and
col. 2　vsurpers vpon othir realmes be confounded and / brought to nought
and the realm at longe goyng shal be le[f]te to þe auncient dwellers

1 thei cam] om. NJ　　ryvers] wer add. N see n.　　bracke] breken N braken
J　　4 named] called NJ　　6 backe] in add. N　　8 scape] escape N
10 him] hymself N　　Cyrus] NJ Cyrue R Cyrus D　　11 mannys] mennes
N　　12 a] om. NJ　　14 of them] om. N　　thus] this NJ　　20 all] om.
N　　22 londe or] om. N pays & D　　25 with] the add. NJ　　26 at . . .
multiplye] to multyplye at þis tyme N　　27 thi] om. N ton D　　31 bruyt]
in þis case add. N om. D　　34 longe goyng] longeyng N　　lefte] NJ leste R

and restith but seeldom to the conquerours. For thei waste their
power and consume their strengh in the excercise, that thei shewe
them by their assaylyng and techeth them to defende themself and
to recover ageyne their victorye vpon the ouircomers so that at
thende the defendours haue fynally the profite and the discipline 5
and thei that war the ouircomers receyve the hurte and the ruyne.

Thanne let vs leve the vncerteyn estate of the fallyng glorye of
them that trouble therthe and let vs reste in the certayne hoope of
suche as amonge the persecucions of the warr attendid haue peace
and in the myddis of their myscheffis hooped to see prosperite and 10
reste com amonge them. Thanne this purpose seruyth to the
ensaumples of which þou diddist requere me, yet and if thou wolt
haue en[s]aumples of a more fresshe memorye leve the bookis and
assur thi creaunce / in the recytacion of thauncient men in whos f. 97
age the realme of Cycille was so troubled by Maynfray and Coradyn 15
that no man cowde vndirstonde any hoope of remedy nor provision
of counseille vnto the tyme that good Charles liked by mervelous
and not supposid prowesse to restablish the said realme vnto his
furst estate. Likewise thou maist here by the reporte of olde men
of þe tempest that was done not long agoo in Castyll by Petre 20
calling himself kyng, and to the hurte of the same realme he callid
to his helpe the paynemes of Affryke and the Englishmen, which
did grette turment by many yeris to the Spaynardis and slough
moche of the people and caused so grette desolacion that the more
party was vnhabited. But yet the knyghthod of Fraunce through 25
power of the divine iustice restored the realme of Castille vnto
peece and sure estate, which lastith yet at this day. Hough many
mortale affliccions / did the realme of Scottis susteyne by the space col. 2
of many yeris in the tyme of Robert Bru[c]e, which at that tyme
was Kynge of Scottes, which may be shewed the by suche as yet 30
lyve at this day. For within this hundird yere the Englysshmen,
that war aduersaryes to the same, [and oþer rebelles longyng to the
same] contryved suche persecucion that he was chased here and
there as a wylde bore through bushes and breres. Ye, so forferth

5 profite] prosperite N prouffit D   6 the 1] *om.* N   9 attendid] to
add. N to *ins.* J   10 in] *om.* J   12 if] *om.* NJ   13 ensaumples]
NJ enlaumples R   14 the] thi N   15 Maynfray and] many/fraye of N
17 that] the *add.* NJ   18 restablish] restablysshed N   23 by] *om.* J
25 through] the *add.* N   26 the 1] *om.* N   28 susteyne] *om.* N sous-
tint D   29 Bruce] NJ Brute R   32-3 and . . . same] N contre *add.*
J & aucuns ses rebelles d'Escoce D   33 contryved] dyd J *see n.*

that aftir the discomfiture of his batailes ther was non othir helpe
but to hide him in deserte places vnknowen amonge þe wilde
beestis. Yit loste he his realme through this? Nay certaynly. For
aftirward he was a victour and bar pesibly the royall ceptre through
5 all Scotlonde.

Yet and thes foren ensaumples may not suffice the, let the
cronicles of thin own nacion serue to thi hoope, which in lyke case
may the more tendirly move the by naturalle affeccion, which of
f. 97ᵛ reason shulde be more conformeable to thi / thought forasmoche
10 as the certeinte ther(of) is knowen. Remembir thiself hough
Chelderych, the thirde Kyng of Fraunce, was chased in(to) Loreyne
and depryved of his royall crowne, and yet aftirward the French-
men restored him ageyne to his grette honour and glorye; and had
a sone named Clouis, which was a strong [and] a myghty kyng and
15 the furst Cristen that brought to his subieccion all the londe
betwene the Ryne and the mowntaignes called Pyraynes. Hast thou
forgeten the piteouse aduersite of the good Lowes, which was sone
and successour to the grette Charlemayne, as well to the realme
of Fraunce as to þe Empyre? O hough lamentable and perylouse
20 thing was it to the realme whanne the iniurye and shamefull desti-
tucion of so grette a prince if he had not be restored ageyne.
Certeinly a more oultragiouse shame cowde not haue ben thought
col. 2 thanne to disapoynte his kyng from all auctorite / and shamefully
to kepe him from his honour and his estate. Lo, this was don
25 withowt cause to this good Kyng and Emperour. Yet though this
dede was iniuryous and hedy of itself the condicion of them that
war doers therof was more [byttyr and] displesaunt in regarde
thanne the othir, seyng that his own childern and suche as he had
honoured with yeftis and graces wer gilty of this cryme. O ye
30 owtragious childern, hough durst ye, seyng the fresshe memorye
and lawde of the gloriouse Charlemayne, attempte so shamefully
the wourship of your fadir? It was grette merveile that þe excesse
of your vnkyndnesse did not put away the large mercy of the
piteouse Emperour, for aftir that he was restored to his furst estate
35 by the divine grace of our Lorde, he shewed himself to you as a

---

1 batailes] bataile N *pl.* D   2 hide him] hide hyde N   4 royall
ceptre] *tr.* N   7 case] wyse J   10 as] at NJ   12 and 1] the *add.* N
14 named Clouis] name Cloyus N   strong and] J strong man and N strong
R   15 the 1] he J   Cristen] crystened N   to] vnto NJ   londe] londys
N *sing.* D   16 thou] NJ not *add.* R *om.* D   22 haue ben] abeen N
25 this 1] hys J cestuy D   26 was] were NJ   34 aftir that] aftirwarde N

naturall fader and hadde pite vpon you and forgave you your
oultragious offences. And aftir the suffryng of all thes sha/mes and f. 98
repreves he lived in grette magnificence and deyed in good renown
and lefte vnto you bothe [the] Empyre and the realme of Fraunce
in pesible possession notwithstondyng all the vnkyndnesse shewed 5
before.

On the tothir syde yf þou woldest mysknowe the ferefull tempestes, the clamours of the people that fledde awaye and the plente
of bloodeshedde of dede men lying on hepys, and hough the
rychesse was take awaye, and the brennyng of the howses whanne 10
the Gothis, the Vandres, the Huns, the Sarsines and the Danys
entird into Fraunce, thou maist yet at this day haue grette prevys
by the chirchis which at that tyme war cast down, destroyed and
brente, and by the translacion also of the holy bodyes and wourthi
reliques from oon cuntre to anothir wherof som cam neuir home 15
ageyne. And thou shalt not fynde hough any remedy myght be
founde at that hour / saffe only by the meryte of holy persones and col. 2
[by] divine myracles. And to vndirstonde that this was trwe, the
cite of Orliaunce myght not escape by any maner of power of
armes from the hondis of the Wandresse save only by the prayer 20
of Seint Aignein, through whose vertu þe Wandres (resyn) vp and
war slayne and chased away from the cite withowt the honde of any
man. Paryes also was preseruyd in his bondis by Seint Genouyeue.
Likewise fell aftirwarde of the cite of Toures by the merite of the
gloriouse Seint Martyne, which wold save his good cite. Harke 25
hough paciently and in the drede of God Seint Lyeu mayntened
himself ayeinst Athila, [the Kyng of Huns, in the tyme of hys
persecucions, and thu shalt fynde humble doctrynes and profytable
obeissaunce. His legend reciteth how the] holy man opened the
gatis of his cite [to the tiraunte Athila], which was a myscreaunt 30
and sparid neithir yong ne olde and had with him many moo
thousandis of men thanne owr princes may haue nowadayes of
hundredis. Whethir did this holy man opyn the / ȝatis of his cite f. 98ᵛ

2 suffryng] sufferynges J   7 yf] om. J se D   woldest] wylst N
8 the 3] gret add. NJ   9 bloodeshedde] blodeshedyng N   10 the 2] her N
11 Danys] which long agone add. NJ om. D   13 cast down, destroyed]
destroyed cast down NJ   16 myght] cowde NJ   17 persones] men N
19 any] no NJ   of 2] om. NJ   20 only] but add. N   prayer] praiers N
pl. D   24 merite] merytes N pl. D   25 gloriouse] man add. N om. D
27–9 the Kyng . . . how the] NJ ayeinst whom a R see n.   28 doctrynes] N
doctryne J sing. D   29 opened] made opyn NJ   30 his] the N la D

more for favour of any man or for drede of any man? We may be
sure that he did it for neithir. For the tyraunt named himself
Athila, sone of ȝendebus, nurisched in Gudy, lorde of therthe,
dredde through þe worlde and scourge of God. And whanne this
5 holy bisshop harde the name of the scourge of God him thought
it was no tyme to withstonde that name by force, but that it war
bettir to put himself vndir by humilite. And that was the cause he
made opyn his ȝates, sayng that the scourge of God was welcome.
And so he wourshippid more the dyvine title thanne he ferid the
10 vnnaturall tyraunt and shewed that his cite was redy to receive
correccion in deseruing of mercye, like as the childe which yeldith
himself to the rodde of his fadir. And so the tyraunte entyrd into
the cite having no power to do any harme, but passed owt through
at anothir ȝate of the towne and abode no lengar, for the humble
col. 2 obeisau/nce of the good confessour toke away the ire of God and
16 closyd him from the execucion of Godis scourge. Thinke not but
the infinite power of God may make an ende of freyle power of the
myghty, prowde men of therthe and restore the feblenesse of the
humble, meke persones. For He is now as full of grace and of as
20 large confort as He was in the tyme of the birth of Philippe Dyeu-
done, which was Kyng of Fraunce, and he was called so bycause
he was borne by the yefte of God and ayeinst thoppynion of men
and come forthe in the tyme of dispeyre and was borne of a queene
that was past age of childeberinge, for to be the confort and hope
25 of the people of Fraunce, which war in grette turment through
burdon of the werr and dyvidid in diuerse affeccions within themself. Anothir tyme it happid Philip for his vertu to be callid con-
querour, and Lowys, his sone, which Almighty God fullfillid with
f. 99 wisedom of age in a yong body. Yette / had thei as grette trouble
30 duryng their reigne as he that þou seist now in thi tyme. For the
Emperour Othe, which was allied and holpen by the Erle of
Champayne, and on that othir syde the Kyng of Englond, which
was conforted and accompenyed with the Erle of the Marche and
of Brytaigne, went vpon them with ij hostis on ij partyes of the

1 more] *om.* NJ   2 that] *om.* N   named] called NJ   3 ȝendebus]
ȝendibeth N   4 and] the *add.* N *om.* D   whanne] *om.* J quant D
7 that] *om.* N   cause] that *add.* NJ   8 sayng that] NJ that *add.* R
10 his] the The N sa D   13 owt through] þurgh oute the cite N   14 at]
om. J   of the towne] *om.* ND   19 humble] and *add.* NJ   as 2] *om.* N
20 the 1] *om.* J au D   21 bycause] for because þat NJ   30 For] *om.* N Car D
31 of] *om.* N   32 syde] of *add.* N   33 and 2] *om.* N   34 hostis] hooste J

realme at one season with so grette hostis that it semed all shulde
be ouirthrowen at one stroke. Yet thei, with a fewe people departid
in two, in oon howre discomfited both hostis and all at oon tyme
with grette feer and litill brute gatte the wourship and the power
ouir them that proudely ded manace þem. But this was of an high 5
grace whanne at oone howre bothe the fadir and the sone gatte
þe victorie of their enemyes; and furst hough the fadir had þe
discomfitoure vpon the Emperoure, and the sone had the discomfiture vpon the Englyshe/men, which semyd one maner of col. 2
victorye. For the fadir had not suche leyser to send confort to his 10
sone of the grette victorye that he hadde vpon the Emperour but
that the sone rewardid him the same day with anothir ioye of the
victorye that he had ouir the Englishemen. So thanne be thow
remembird of thes newe ensaumples which bene of fresshe
memorye. And therfor I leve to the the recordacion of the case of 15
Kyng Charlys the Fyfte, [ayel to Charles Regnault], and the consideracion of the infortunable estate of the realme at the beginnyng
of his reigne and of the blisse[d]hed of Fraunce at the yssewe of his
lyfe. For yette at this day the olde men telle so certeynely what that
thei sawe in their days that it semy[th] bettyr to be a dede done in thes 20
present days thanne a storye writtyn of tyme passid. And if so be that
the othir ensaumples war to the derke, yette in this thou maist not
deny the trouth of the dede nor / mysknowe the party of th[i] case. f. 99ᵛ

For to bringe to mynde the high merytorye dedis and gloriouse
renowms of victories and also the evill dedis, for the edificacion 25
of owre wittis, writinges ben made as well of them that ought to
be accused as of them that ought to be recomended, for iustifiyng
of their dedis through the studye of clerkis, which liste to certifye
the mervailes that haue fallen, and for to meke vs vnto vertu and
that we may take ensaumple of othir mennes dedis. 30

[Vndrestondynge]

Thyine ensaumples ben right profitable and good to vndirstonde
so that thow wolt lerne me hough I shall hope. Wherefor I (pray)
the shewe me how and in whom othir men haue their hope.

1 one] ain J   2 one] a˘NJ   3 tyme] and add. NJ   11 vpon] of
NJ   16 Fyfte] first N   19 that] om. NJ   20 semyth] NJ semyd
R semble D   20-1 thes present days] this present tyme NJ   21 of] yn J
23 thi] J the R this N ton D   25 edificacion] edificacyons N   26 writinges
. . . well] writynge as wele ben made N   29 meke] make (a perhaps corrected
to e) N

[Hoope]

col. 2 In God, which is / the begynnyng and the vertu of all werkis and the ende and the perfeccion of all hoopes.

[Vndrestondynge]

5 Afore this tyme thou haste shewed me that God is soueraigne hoope, but we must furst serche owt lower hoopes which may conduyte vs to endeles hoope. Wherfor I woll aske the nough certeyn interrogacions to knowe who may helpe me to haue hoope and to dresse myn hoope to a poynte. And the furst interrogacion
10 shal be whethir prayer may conforte me in hoope. And whanne this is aunswerid I woll provide the othir interrogacions aftir their ordres and places according to pursute of the matir aftir that thou hast made thyne answere.

[Hope]

15 Iff prayer were not profitable and confortatyve, that God that
f. 100 stablisshid nothing in vayne wolde neuir / haue ordeigned it nor yeven þe maner of praying. For though so be that He is alone allmyghty to do His wille with the yeftis of His grace, yette is He iuste and rightfull for to employe them wele and will not graunte
20 His graces to suche as liste dispreyse them, but withdrawith them from suche vnkynde men as liste not to knowe Hym. For He will that men knowe the graces that He sendith them and to be taken as the patron of all good werkis, for witheowt Him no man is sufficiant to begynne nor ende anythiinge. Yette men may say
25 othirwise that He of His goodnes distributith His (tresours) in waste to suche as be not wourthy nor sette not therby as largely as to them that requer them and disserue them, which wer a grette wodnesse to speke ayeinste divine iustice or to revile the dignite of Goddis yeftis and to devye the free arbytriment of man, which
col. 2 may deserue meryte and vnme/ryte, to obteyne and to loose þe
31 yeftis of grace. The creacion of man proceded onely of Him that made all thing of nought, but the perfeccion and the saluacion of man procedith of humanite merytes and hangith vpon the dyvine

5 is] the add. NJ la D   7 nough] om. N   11 othir interrogacions]
tothirs NJ autres D see n.   12 to] the add. NJ la D   20 liste] will N
24 anythiinge] noþing NJ   26 not 2] nought N   26–7 as largely . . .
them 3] om. N   27 which wer] This is N   28 ayeinste] the add. NJ la D
33 humanite] of add. canc. J humayn N humains D

grace. For He that made the withowt the woll not do iugement
vpon the withowt the. To drawe the to Him withowt the may be
an open shewing of His powere and to iustify a man withowt
merittes it war a disordinaunce of His iustice. The makyng of man
was a werke of maistrye and of an absolut puysaunce, but the 5
iustifying of man is the werke of a iuge and of a rightfull ordinaunce. Owre Lorde gave þe inough whanne (He) gaue the abiding
and lyffe and vndirstonding for to iuge and free wille for to chese.
But and He had yeven the in dede that He put in thy power to
gette by thy witty excercyse, thou haddest not so perfightly ben / 10
create as thou arte. For the bestis and the plantis haue the state and f. 100ᵛ
perfeccion [of] their beyng ordeigned by nature, which they sewe
naturaly and go not owt of the wey; and thou hast [yn] þi fredome
and thi power, the conduyting of thi life and þin eleccion to do well
or evill. But the bestis be constreyned by þeir inclinacions and 15
appetites to þe dedis that thei ar made for, and thou maist restreyne
thin appetites and bryng them ageyne to reason by thin onely wille.
O what prerogatyve and hough [high] an excellence gave God to
man whanne He putt into his wille the redressing and the choyse
of his power. All othir that haue sowle have their power revled to 20
suche thingis as thei may do for the seruice of man, but the power
of man is rueled in that that he woll for the fredom and lordeshipp
that he hathe, through which he is lorde ouir the bestis. Thanne
the suffrage of prayer was not stablisshid / for bestis, which haue col. 2
their beyng and their ende determyned by the furst dethe, but it 25
is appropird vnto man, which is in the way of perfeccion and at his
owne choise wheder he woll turne to bonchef or to myschef, which
hath nede of helpe and sustentacion. Wherfor it is behouefull to
pray, through which, if he remembir his freelte, secheth helpe of
Allmyghti God and the redressing of Him that knowith all. For 30
though so be that the childe which is newe-taught to go and hath
power of him[s]elf to do the same, yette hath he his yghe allwayes
and cryeth on the modir for feer leste he shulde fall through his
impotencye and for because naturall affeccion yevith him cause and

2 vpon] of J   to Him] *om.* N   6 a 2] *om.* NJ   8 and 1] *om.* N & D
free] *om.* NJD   10 so perfightly ben] be so perfitely N   12 of] J *om.*
RN de D   18 an] and N   gave God] *tr.* N   19 into] in NJ
24 prayer] prayers N *sing.* D   25 their ende] the ende of her life NJ leurs
fins D   26 vnto] to N   27 to 2] *om.* N   29 of] to N   32 him-
self] himfelf R hymself for NJ   33 his] *om.* N son D   34 because]
that *add.* NJ   cause and] *om.* NJ *see n.*

vndirstonding to be susteyned by the modir. Also thou seest alday that the seeke man reioyseth and hopeth of helpe to be made hole whanne he haþe onely pleyned his greef to the leche. And whatso-

f. 101 meuir I haue / said to the byfore of bestis, yette thei in themself
5 haue a maner fourme of prayer and knowelage of Him that is their Maker, and that maist thou see by the synging of the birdis, which cast their voice and their crye towarde the hevene, and in like wise followe the plantis and the herbis, which bowe them toward the sunne which party that euir [it] removith, yelding by maner of a
10 signe a lawde to their Creatour, of the which natur hath taken away the speche wherwith thei wolde haue don their lawde and thei myght haue spoken. And to this accordith Dauid, which saith that the yong ravynnes cryen to God whanne their fadirs, for the straungenesse of their white fedirs, levith the feding of them at the
15 begynnyng, and wittenessith that God by their calling and prayer purveith at that nede for their mete.

Yette I telle the more that he, whatsomeuir he be, that entendith
col. 2 not to helpe and socour him/self by humilite, through pryde cannot knowe his impotencye in this lowe worde. For and man levith the
20 suffrage of prayer he disdeynith ayeinst God, like him that lesith his good for defawte of asking and yeldith him[self to] necligent of his perfeccion or ellis to presumptuouse of his merytes. And therfor knowe now that prayer doth grette conforte and profite, and this lerne at me that prayer was neuir presentid with good herte to
25 Allmyghty God but that it bar with Him grette fruyte.

[Vndrestondynge]

Howgh may this sentence be trwe seyng that many people make their requestis and yet thei obteyne them not? For oftymes aduer-sary pa[r]tyes requyrith of God victorye for themself and confusion
30 to there enemyes, which ben repugnaunte thingis and inpossible to obteyne.

[Hoope]

f. 101ᵛ God wyll / and suffreth the to praye aftir temporall affeccion and

2 seeke] meke J malade D   4 to the byfore] before to the N   5 haue a] in a N   6 the 1] *om.* NJ au D   7 the] *om.* J les D   9 of] or (*canc.*) N   11 wolde] *om.* N   13 their fadirs] þe fadyrs J the fadre N leurs peres D   15 and 2] a N   18 himself] *om.* NJ   19 lowe] *om.* N levith] leue NJ   21 defawte] fawte N lak J   28 them] *om.* N 30 there enemyes] his enemye NJ *see n.*   33 the to praye] to the preyde J the pride N *see n.*

humayne nature, but He woll enhaunce aftir His divine and eternall
reason. Thou maist not praye but in suche wise onely as thou
vndirstondist and felist, and He woll not enhaunce man but onely
as Him ought. Freelte and diffaulte ben the mocions of thi prayer;
power and perfeccion ben the sprynges of His yeftis. Thanne if 5
thou by thi disceiveable ignoraunce or by thi false, frowarde affeccion to do thi askyng, His invariable rightwisenesse and His infallible science shall not faile to do His disposicion. So God sewith
not thine appetite in thi werkes but rewlith His largesse by His
holy provydence and yevith him not all that euir him nedith but 10
suche as profiteth him, yet not suche as thou askest Him but suche
as thou oughtest to aske. Thi freelnesse causeth the to aske aftir
thine appetite, and His bounte maketh thi pray/er tourne to all thi col. 2
profight. And as touching this mater, my suster Feith, which spacke
furst afore me, gave the a good similitude. For the fesician gevith 15
not the seeke man to drynke as ofte as he askith it, but whanne it
is tyme and profight to his helth. Thanne thou that art ouyrcome
by the vices of the soule and askest victorye ouir thi bodily enemye,
it may fall so that God woll suffre the to have victorye of thi body
to thentent that thou shuldest meke thine herte, through which 20
thou maist ouircome pryde, which is the prynce of all vices. And
what shall fall of thine ouircomer, which God hath suffered to have
the temporall victorye which he asked? It is possible that vayne
glorye and presumpcion may putt him in seruage of synne, and
thanne shall pride have the triumphe ouir him through arrogaunce, 25
which shall make it fall vndir the as to þe / worlde and vndir God f. 102
in perdurabble damnacion. So thanne is this he that hath that he
wolle but not that he nedith. And as the Psalme saith, 'His prayer
is retourned into synne for because that þe entente is not ryghtfull.'
And thou that art ouircome with men and hast meked the vnto 30
them, hast thou not the victorye of that thou askest seing that thou
hast ouircome the prince of all vices and art made wourthi by thine
humilite to haue triumphe ouir þe men? Thou hast thi cownte
aftir the mesure and reason þat may not faile, and thyne aduersarye

2 in . . . onely] oonly in such but N only in such J   3 and felist] *om.* N
see n.   4 Him] he NJ   5 His] thi N ses D   6 by 1 . . . false] be
deceyvable by ignoraunce or N   6 false] fause J   7 His 2] *om.* N sa
D   9 rewlith] releueth N   10 him 2] he N   16 not] to *add.*
N   it 1] *om.* N le D   17 that] *om.* N qui D   20 through which] þat N
27–33 So . . . men] *om.* N   27 that 1] *om.* J   29 because] þe cause
J   entente] entencyon J

hath miscownted himself by worldely folye. Humayne prayers ben comparable to the requeste of a myghty man which axeth his way, for men ben as waygoers which entende alway to come to the soueraigne god and yet thei take their vyage by many wayes, and

col. 2 at some tyme suche as thei aske maketh them to go / owt of the way.

6 But God, which is [the] veray way, the veray trouth and the veray lyfe, is the Guyde that considerith and knowyth all the wayes of man, and suche as requerith Him bryngeth them into the right way that no man saf He can fynde nor knowe. For as muche as the heven

10 is enhaunced above therthe, likewise all the wayes of God be enhaunced above the wayes of man and hid and enstraunged from worldely men. If he thanne which asketh the way ought to be rueled by his trewe guyde and passe withowt sayng nay all the streytis wheras it ledith him, though that the way be right straunge aftir

15 his estimacion, thanne by a gretter reason the man that sechith helpe of God muste be guyded by the Maister of guyders, and though the way be ryght streight yet take it to the beste vndir the cunduyte of the dyvine prouidence withowt any murmur or gruge,

f. 102ᵛ and let him euir hope to bere with him the fruyte of / his prayer.

20 For knowe right wele that God wote bettir what is nedefull to man thanne man doth himself. For He which began to love afore or man lovid Him, His love procedith in chyerte all othir loves. Wherfor ther [is] non so sure as that which is confirmed in the wille of God whanne it is desyrid to the plesur of God, which is bettir pleasid

25 with owr welefar thanne our hurte may displeace vs.

[Vndrestondynge]

This solucion causeth me to haue a newe doubte. And I wolle founde me vpon Scriptur, which saith þat prayer appesith the ire of God. Thanne His wille is confirmed in our prayers and not

30 oure prayers to His w[i]lle seyng þat by them His indignacion is modred.

4 vyage] viages N *sing.* D   5 the] thair N   8 Him] he *add.* N   10–11 likewise . . . enhaunced] so ben the weyes of God N *see n.* 11 above] aboute J   and enstraunged] and estraunged J *om.* N & estranges D   14 it] he NJ   the] *om.* NJ   16 by . . . guyders] be God N au maistre des adresses D   17 way] weyes NJ   18 the] *om.* J la D 20 right] reght J   to] for N   21 He] the *add.* NJ   21–2 or . . . Him] or man lovyd J man N *see n.*   22 loves] lovers N   23 is 1] N nys J *om.* R est D   25 with owr] withoute N   our] with oure J withoute N   30 wille] NJ wolle R   them] bym N

[Hoope]

Thi argument procedith of ignoraunce.

[Vndrestondyng]

As hough?

[Hoope]   5

By as moch as thou knowest not the condicion and the difference
of qualitees and of the attribucions / of the names of God.   col. 2

[Vndrestondyng]

Shewe me thi[s] difference that disceveth me.

[Hope]   10

With a good wille. But note wele my wourdes and vndirstonde
this distinccion clerely.

[Vndrestondyng]

Procede forth.

[Hoope]   15

Summe names and titles ben attribute principally to God and
essencially and to men aftir by participacion and by dependaunt
goodnesse and wisedam. Furst thei belongen to God and He
enpartith them to men, suche parte as their feble condicion may
receive. And therfor He is of Himself trwe, wise and good; for   20
wisedome and bownte ben the shewyngis of perfeccion and all
perfeccion is in Him and procedith originally of Him. Yet some
qualitees that ben appropred to man principally ben attribute to
God by transsumpcion, amonge which I take ire and furour, that
thei ben humayne passions and titles of imperfeccion and therfore 25
thei compacte not, thes titles, to God truely. For He that is / all   f. 103
perfecte, all constaun[t]e and vnvariable, is neythir, to speke
propirly, yrouse nor furiouse.

6 and] nor N ne D   9 this] thi RNJ celle D   11 wele] will N
12 this . . . clerely] clerly this dystinccyon NJ   17 and 1] þan N
dependaunt] dyspendaunt J   18 belongen] been longyng N   21 and 2]
om. N & D   24 and] om. N & D   25 imperfeccion] inperfeccions N
sing. D   26 compacte] compecte NJ   27 perfecte] NJ is add. R om. D
constaunte] J constaunce RN constant D

[Vndrestondinge]

Hough is it thanne that Scriptur spekith so moche of His furour and of His ire?

[Hope]

5   O hough grette a difference is ther bytwene the eternall science of Allmyghti God, which knowith all thingis suche as thei be, and the litle vn[dir]stonding of man, which iugith the thingis aftir his opinione. God iugith of [the] divinly, which is a clere iugement and a true, but thou maist not of thiself knowe Him save onely in His
10 humanyte, of which thy knowelage is troubled and vnperfight. And syn thou maist not knowe Him in the perfeccion of His diuinite, thou hast non knowelege of Him saf onely in that that extendith to knowe the iugement of thin humanite. And therfor thou callest Him angry and furiouse as men be whanne thou felest
15 His punicions, and sayst that He is appesed as sone as He with-
col. 2 drawith His scourge. Good fren/dis, this chaunge is not in Him but it is in the which receiveth punicions or graces differenttely of Him which is withowt difference, lyke as the sunne schynith both ouir the good and ouir the evile. He that openith his wyndowe hath light
20 and who that closith his wyndowe ayeinst the sonne dwellith in derkenesse. Yet is the sonne for that neuir the derker nor the bryghter. Wherof he that lyeth and his wyndowes schette fast iugeth that it is nyght. Likewise aftir Scriptur ire is attribute to God, not for alteracion that is in Himself, but by the passions that
25 thou suffirst by His iustice, which come by the moveing of thyne owne self. And [yn Hym] abideth eternally the permanent con-staunce of [His] holy wille.

[Vndrestondyng]

Iff His wille be vnuariable and that He hath sette ane ordinaunce
30 and wille not [chaunge it], thanne me semys that prayer is of no valure. /

6 Allmyghti] *om.* NJ   7 the 2] all N les D   8 opinione] opinyons N   the] NJ thingis R toy D   10 vnperfight] ynperfite NJ   11 syn]
that *add.* N   15–16 and . . . scourge] *om.* J *see n.*   withdrawith] withdrawe N   19 ouir] *om.* N sur D   20 closith] shetteth NJ   21 is]
not *add.* NJ   neuir] neyþer N   21–2 the derker . . . bryghter] the bryghter
nor the derker NJ *as in* D   22 Wherof] wherfore NJ   25 come] comyn
J is comyn N   26 yn Hym] yn J yet N *om.* R à luy D   30 chaunge it]
NJ chaunged R *see n.*

[Hoope]   f. 103ᵛ

Thow secheste a thinge that no man may fynde and wolt be
acerteyned of suche thinges as God hath lefte doubtefull. Dyverse
doctours aftir their subtill wittes haue laboured to vndirstonde the
predestinacion of God with the [free] arbitracion of man. But thei 5
swomme above and foonde neuir the botoom, and flyen all abowte
and cowde fynde no place wherin thei cowde reste their traversable
myndes. The answers in this matere argueth ayeinste him [þat
shuld answer, and the argumentes returne ayenst hym] that argueth.
Thou wolt say in argument that God knowith all thinges afore or 10
thei falle. And syn it is so [þat] His knowing is certeyne and vnvariable, thanne suche thinges as He knowith for necessite must
nedis be done. Thanne in suche case He may not chaunge for our
prayours. But now let vs retourne the argument ayeinst thiself, and
lette vs say thus: If God may not chaunge / the beyng of thyngis to col. 2
come, thanne in that He were as not myghty, and if He hath no 16
power of suche thinges as He knowith that be to come, thanne
myght it be said that He knowith more thanne He may do, which
wer ane opyn errour, or ellis thou must confesse that He knowith
nothing of suche thingis as be to come. What availeth it to multiplye 20
argumentis in a mater that is stedeffast? Certeinly whatsomevir any
man argueth, aftir the trouth He hath the infinite power above all
thingis and knowith the invariablenesse of all thingis. Neuuirthe-
lesse the state of thingys that be to come be in themself chaungeable, and lyethe in the choise of man to chose whedir he woll the 25
good or the evile and make the myght of God inclinable to enhaunce
our prayers. Lette it suffice if we shewe the that the holy doctours
have wreten, and abide vpon that poynte wheras thei abyde. / For f. 104
though so be that their determinacion may not avoide all doubtes,
yette certeinly þei be voide of [all] errours. We believe stedfastly 30
that [God] is a symple and a souereigne essence which by Himself
and in Himself, as He that is all perfecte, knoweth all thingis. And

5 free] NJ freele R franc D   6 swomme] swymme N   flyen] fleen J
fledde N   7 traversable] transversable N   8 answers] onswere J *pl.* D
10 God knowith] *tr. (change probably indicated by vertical lines before and after
knoweth)* N   13 not] *om.* N ne D   16 hath] haue J   20 nothing
of suche] of no such N   20-1 What . . . stedeffast] *om.* N   21 whatsomevir any] whatso eny (*abbrev. sign over* n *canc.*) N   23 invariablenesse]
variaunce N   24-5 themself chaungeable] hymself chaungeable (*canc.*)
chaunable N   25 the 1] *om.* J   26 the 1] *om.* N le D   27-8 Lette . . .
abyde] *om.* N   29 their] the N leurs D   determinacion] of doctours *add.*
N *om.* D   32 perfecte] and *add.* RNJ *om.* D

we may clerely see that man is a substaunce compiled and inperfecte and hathe not the very knowelage of thingis. God knewe all thinges ere they were made, but man knoweth nothing in lasse thanne it be shewed him by his owtward wittes. And so the divine
5 science hath no maner proporcion with the knowelage of man, and [thu] oughtest not to iuge His vndirstonding for thyne. For thyne vndirstonding dependith vpon such thinges as thou knowest, but the thingis that He knowith dependen vpon His science and by that He knowith them, and thou knowest them in that that thei be.
col. 2 Their chaunge/yngis may not chaunge His vndirstondinge, for
11 their beynge procedith owt of His vndirstonding. If He knewe the thingis by themself, thanne the knowelage shuld followe the being of thingis. So shulde He knowe the possible thingis doubtefully and the necessarye thingis certeinly as thou knowest them. But syn that
15 He knoweth all thing of Himself, which is allway stable and perdurable, of necessite His vndirstonding may not be fallible. Beleve and doubte nothing but that He knoweth the thingis to come principally, the thingis temporall eternally, the thingis chaungeable invariablely, the thingis contingent necessaryly; nor chaungeable
20 nesse of thingis chaungith not His science nor strenghth not their contingence, for the being of them is of them thing chaungeable in them and by them, and the science which He hath of them is in Him and by Him stablely necessary suche whatkyns thay shal be.
f. 104ᵛ And / thei come contingently by their nature which of Him is
25 chaungeable suche whatkyns thei be. Be ye certeyn that all thinges arn present to His eternite, for He hath all togedir fro euir and for euir. His witte a[n]d all His being perfiteth and holdiþ togedyr the thinges corporellis, subiettes to mevyngis and to chaungyngis. Vndir the tyme thei haue neuir togedir their beyng passed nor their
30 estate to come, for passid is now taken from theim and to come thei abide for to come. Neuirthelesse all the tyme togedir is to Him more present thanne is to the the hour that is nough. I geve the

1 clerely see] tr. N   2 knewe] knowe N   5 and] þan N & D
6 thu] N om. RJ   His] J omits from here to p. 122. l. 9   11 owt] forth N
knewe] know N   12 themself] hymselfe N elles mesmes D   15 knoweth]
know N   stable and] om. N estable & D   19 invariablely] om. N inuariablement D   necessaryly] necessarye N necessairement D   nor] ffor N ne D
19–20 chaungeablenesse] chaungeng N   23 stablely] and add. N om. D
24 come] N come add. R   25 all] om. N toutes D   26 togedir] to
guyde N   fro] for N   28 chaungyngis] chaunges N   29 togedir]
to guyder N   30–1 for . . . come] om. N   31 togedir] the
guyder N

materiall exaumple: owthir the mydde parte of a compas, or more
grossely to make exsaumple to the axtre of a whele. Thaxtre, which
susteyneth the whele, abidith in oon estate and the parties of the
whele meven rounde chaungeably. He is of Himself euir in oon
mesured disposicion ageyne all parties of þe / whele, which of all   col. 2
sydes to Him arn present. But thei chaungen so that in them arn   6
their disposicions present to Him aftir whatkyns thei meve hye or
lawe. Thus for the mutacion which God create and vpholdith, His
beyng chaungeth not nor His science varieth not. [Sech] aftir the
variacion of the worlde in thingis which of themself arn variable,   10
and leve thou to God His stable abiding withowt scrupules or
doubtes. Mistruste not the auctorite of His power for the necessite
of His science and knowelage. For hough be it He knoweth thingis
for to come necessarily in Himself as they shal be, yett He may
theym lordely chaunge in them as it pleasith Him by our pr[ey]ers,   15
by His mercye or by our dese[r]vingis. And sothly His necessary
knowlage, His infinite power and His wille inexpugnable arn so of
acorde that He knoweth all that that He may and may all that that
He wille. Be ye content of this deduccion for [here beneth] thou
may haue no / more, and to myself, that am His doughtere, He   f. 105
hath no more promysed. So may thou know that if prayers and   21
des[er]uynges shuld not haue profited and God had so ordeigned
thingis that the fre wille of man war constreyned by necessite, I had
be create for nought.

[Vndrestondynge]   25

 Let vs presuppose that prayere was furst brought in to be a
meane bytwene the divine grace and humayne necessite and that
the high rychesses and graces of God haue no maner of proporcion
withe caytif mysery of mankynde if that som blissid combynacion
ne fynde a disposicion which reprocheth man of the clemence   30
divine, which iointur to make þou shall attribute the office to
prayer. Now herright to knowe it behovith the fourme of prayer.

1 parte] poynte N 3 estate] state N 4 rounde] aboute *add.* N of
Himself] *om.* N de soy D 7 disposicions] arn *add.* N whatkyns] wey
add. N hye] *om.* N haut D 9 Sech] *om.* RN Quiers D 12 doubtes]
nor *add.* N ne D 13 and] or N it] þat *add.* N 15 in them]
om. N en elles D preyers] N prowers R 19 Be ye] by þe N this] his
N here beneth] N he nethir R ca ius D 21 may] that N pues D
21-2 and deseruynges] *om.* N and desteu[? n]ynges R & merites D 22 haue
profited] aprofyted N had] hath N 28 of 2] *om.* N 29 caytif] the N
la chetiue D 31 to 2] of N 32 to . . . behovith] it behoueth to knowe N

[Hoope]

Who shall he be that shall [yeue] forme of doctryne ouir the
col. 2 souereyne Doctour, or what more agreable wourdis wold/dest thou
take for prayer to Hym thanne suche wourdes as He Himself hath
5 ordeyned for prayer? His iustice is thyne ordenary iuge, but His
mercy He made a party for the whanne He Himself taught the a
fourme of thy prayere and yave the a patron whereaftir thou
shuldest werke. Thanne aske non othir fourme thanne the same
that God hath yeven the and that the chirche techith the. [This]
10 is callid the Prayere Dominicall, said by the mouth of Him which
by doctrine and by ensaumple taught vs to pray whanne [He] Himself for þe needis of His humanite made prayere vnto His Fadir,
and wolde that His devoute Pater Noster shulde be registird in the
booke of the holy Euaungelys as a medi[ci]nall receyte for the
15 remedy of seeke soules. This wourthi prayere, which euery man
ought to lerne, conteyneth vij peticions, of which the furst iij ben
attribute to the honour and lawde of the Creatour, and the iiij that
f. 105ᵛ followen after / ben ordeined for the socoure and saluacion of the
creatur. The furst of the iij is the sanctificacion and thexaltacion
20 of the name of God. The second is the fruycion of the glorie of His
realme for the holy soules. The thridde is for the accomplisshement
of His rightfull wille, by the which as a very rule owre foryetfull
willes ben redressid. And thes iij demawndes God ordeigned not
for to haue by loving suche thingis as may breke His blissidhod,
25 but for to see the devoyr of the kyndenes of man. The furst of the
tothir iiij askethe the suffrage of norishing for sustenaunce of the
mortall body. The seconde procureth remission of fautes passed.
The thrid requyrith remedy ayenste the perill of temptacions that
ben present. The fourth requirith socour for the preseruacion of
30 evilles that be to come. In these vij partyes is founde the summe
of all prayers and the abbregement of suche thingis which causith
col. 2 the to aske. Yet not for / this these othir suffrages of the chirche
ought not to be lefte, for all springeth owt of the same founteigne.
God woll haue of þe a maner of trewage for thi creacion, and for
35 euery day that þou passiste vndir His warde thou oughtest to yelde

---

9 the chirche] J *resumes here*   This] *om.* RNJ Ce D   15 which euery]
om. N   16 lerne] it *add.* N   the furst iij] iij of the first N les trois prem-
ieres D   19 thexaltacion] þe exaltacyon J exalacion N   20 is] for
add. NJ   32 the 2] *om.* N la D   34 of 2] a *add.* J

Him a certeyne for a regoinessaunce. But He woll be payed with
the monye that He hath ordeigned, [and þerfore He gafe the
conages at the forge wan He ordeyned] the divine Pater Noster,
which is the ȝolke and þe ensaumple on which all prayers ben
forged. Nough thou has from a more high scole thanne the prynte 5
the fourme of the prayer in Him. It behouith the to enforme from
above [for] the disposicion of a suppliaunt. The mouth pronounceth
the wourdes, but God taketh hede of the herte. And therfor whanne
thou prayest to God thou shuldest pray with a brennyng desire of
thin hert, for ther is no graunte made frely if it be asked suche wise 10
as thei set not thereby. And moreouir loke that thi thought be
entierly and ententifly sette vpon thi requeste and for the / tyme f. 106
all othir thoughtes layde aparte. And take this for certeinte that and
all thi thought pursewe not thi prayer it tarieth in the way as an
arow shotte owt of a bowe that hath no feddirs. He also from whens 15
all yeftis come wille enteerely be requered with an hole thought.
In like wise also loke thou haue a stedfast abyding vpon that thou
prayest for [in]asmuch as the prayer profiteth not but [in] þat that
the feith of the requerer yevith him of merite. He ought wele to leese
a yefte that dispiseth the yever, and he is a fole that askith a thing 20
which knowith afore that it shall not be graunted. Thanne loke
thou kepe wele these techingis and þou shalt be sufficiently instructe
in thi prayers.

[Vndrestondynge]

I haue right wele vnderstonde thi techingis. Yet in this party I 25
wolde that ye holde the ordre that ye haue begonne and fortify your
reasons by ensaumples. /

[Hoope]

Thou callest me nough to a thinge of litell labour and of grette
effecte, for though so be the ensaumples of this matir be dewly 30
sowen all abowte in Scriptures and light for to fynde, yet ben thei
of right a grette mysterye. And thou shalt not fynde that the name

1 regoinessaunce] reconessaunce J recognicyon N   6 the 2] *om.* NJD
enforme] by *add.* NJ   7 for] N fro J *om.* R de D   10 is] nys NJ   made]
om. J fait D   frely] but *add.* N   17 also] *om.* ND   haue] hast
N   20 dispiseth] dyspyteth J se deffie D   21 that it] *om.* N
22 thou kepe wele] wele thu kepest N   techingis] thingis N enseignemens D
30 be 1] þat *add.* NJ   ensaumples] ensample N *pl.* D   31 fynde] NJ that
add, R   32 a] *om.* N

of the Deyite cam neuir so sone to the knowelage of man, but incontinent aftir prayer it sewed him. For prayere is so drawing a thing to
God, for suche gave He to dombe thinges forthwithall was yeven
þem the requeste of their prayer. Remembre the also of the saying
5 of Valerye in the booke þat he made of thinges wourthi to be hadde
in mynde. Saith he not ther that the people which war of panyme
religion made theire prayer to the ydoles and wolde nothing take
vpon them that was notable withowt thei made prayers, oblacions
f. 106ᵛ and obsecracions to their goddis? And if it so hap/pid that publikes
10 infortunes fall vpon them, the furst remedy was that thei wolde
seche to amende the comon defautes of their lawe and to appeace
the wrath of their goddis by sacrifices and obseruacions, by whose
vengeaunce the supposed to haue fall in their eville aventures. All
suche maner of people vsed suche obseruaunces and called their
15 goddes the avengers of evill dedis and rewarders of all good dedis.
And for to appeace the vengeaunces thei made sacrifices called
execracions, and this sacrifice was made with stones which thei
called obsecracions and war ordeigned whanne thei wolde pray for
prosperitees and victories. Agamenon, þe Emperour of Grece, did
20 sacrifice to the goddis his doughter named Effyginee vpon the see
syde what tyme that he wolde passe the see to ley seege to Troye,
praiyng Neptunis, god of the see, that he wolde helpe hym in his
col. 2 passage. Than / prayed he also to [E]olus, the god of wyndes, that
he wolde blowe his sayles with a moderate wynde to the porte
25 whereas thei desyird to londe. And Pyrrus at the comyng home
ageyne from the seege killid the fayr Polixene to make with hir a
sacrifice to their goddis notwithstonding she was the most noble
emprise that thei had within Troye. On þe othir syde Kyng Pryam
sent Calcas into the Yle of Delphos for to requer helpe and to haue
30 an answer of Appollo. And so in all their nedis thei neuir dis-

1 the 1] om. ND   knowelage] knoweng NJ   3 for . . . He] fo (canc.)
þat such as the Deite gaue N þat such as gave þem J see n.   6 he not] tr.
NJ   9 that] þe add. NJ om. D   10 infortunes] in/fortune N pl. D
10–11 fall . . . comon] om. N   10 was] om. J   11 seche] was add. J
and] for add. N   12 obseruacions] obseruaunce N see n.   13 to] NJ fall
add. R   14 of] om. N   obseruaunces] obseruaunce N pl. D   15 the
avengers] vengers J vengeaunce N vengeurs D   16 to] om. N   vengeaun-
ces] vengeaunce N pl. D   sacrifices] sacrifice N pl. D   17 execracions]
expracions J expiations D expiracions Fr. MSS. see n.   thei] were N   21 that]
om. N   22 praiyng] to add. NJ   helpe] om. N   in] of J   23 prayed]
prey N   Eolus] N Colus RJ see n.   24 a] om. N   26 a] om.
N   27 their] the N   28 emprise] Emperrise N emperyse J prise D
29 Delphos] Delphicos N   30 an] om. N

praysed prayer notwithstonding thei neuir knewe Him to whom thei shulde pray to or ought to haue made their prayer. And so in all their grette nedis thei sent their prayer byfore them. O thou Scipio Affrican, which for euirmore shalt be lawdid of all auctours, whanne aftir the sorowfull Batell of the Caves thou letteste ordeigne 5 in Roome at thentre of thi consulat that all the goddis shuld be wourshippid, and made to be / seced all [maner] of werkis of peace f. 107 and warr, both opyn and prevy, so that thei might furst vndirstonde hough the Romaynes myght be reconsiled to the favour of their goddis and to satify the eris of all the goddis by multiplieng of 10 requestis to stonde in their graces.

Yet þe ensaumples be not recited to thentent that ye shulde sew þem in the religion of their beleve, but for to meve you to the curiosite of deuocion. The auctorite of [the Olde] Testament woll not faile the in this byhalfe, but it woll shewe for his parte as many 15 ensaumples as the Bi[b]le of notable dedis which wer all bygune and conduytede by the meanis of prayer. But for to content thi desire I woll shewe the some thingis and of the surplus I woll sende the to þe bookes. And furst I say that Noe was preserued from the grette floode through the meanys of prayere. Moyses allso through 20 his prayers made the see to be devided in tweyne suche wise þat / all the people of Israell passed through withowt weting their feete. col. 2 Also at the requeste of Iosue the sunne stoode still and withedrough not his light from the childerne of Israell in the victorye that thei had at Gabaon. Vndirstondest thou not that the people of God 25 chased their enemyes in playne batailes as longe as Moyses lifte vp his hondis to hevynne, and as sone as he lette them fall downe the stroke of the bataile fell vpon his owne people? Through prayer also wisedom was yevin to Salomon, and by prayer was made the provisione of Dauid suche wise that Ihesu Criste shulde be borne 30 of his seede. And by prayer he ouircome all his enemyes. And this he shewith wele in his Psalmys, which ouirall ben fulfilled with lawdes and praysingis to God and suffrage of prayere. Certeinly ther ben no materiall armes so penetratif nor so vertuouse to breke

2 shulde . . . or] *om.* NJ   to 2] *om.* J   3 sent] sought N *see n.*   them] *om.* N   4 Scipio] Stypyon J   5 Caves] Taves N *see n.*   ordeigne] *om.* N   6 thi] the N ton D   7 maner] NJ manener R   16 Bible] N bille RJ Bible D   18 woll 1] *om.* N   19 the 1] *om.* N te D   20 prayere] prayers J s *canc.* N *pl.* D   21 see] rede see N mer D   to] *om.* N   22 all] *om.* N   weting] of *add.* N   29 to] vnto NJ   34 penetratif] penetrife N

f. 107ᵛ batailes and to gette victorye as [is] the / vertue of prayere. The
auncient prynces of Fraunce also shewith wele a preef in the same.
For thei that yaue themself most to God and entended to the
edificacion of chirches to thentent to gette the suffrages of prayers,
5 thei hadde the victorye of their enemyes, as Clouis, Clottorye,
Dagonbert and Charlemayn, which ben my wittenesse. And yet I
woll calle to mynde the good Kyng Robert, which was so muche
sette to prayer that he wolde wer a coope in the quier to begynne
the song and entvned the anthemes in the chirche. And on a
10 solempne day as he beganne [the] thrid Agnus Dei the walles of
a cite that his men had beseged felle downe evyne bifore them. So
thanne I woll yeve the no mo ensaumples of the Newe Testament,
for He that [is] Exemplier of all ensaumples yave the inough in
Himself like as I haue said byfore—that is to say, one ensaumple
15 for all. /

col. 2   Man that is made of erthe, feble and brotill as a vesselle of
glasse, growith and lyveth, travailith and goth abowte for to
seche the blissidhed and is sette as streite in the worlde as a man
of warre within listes. For þe flesshe mevith him and the evill
20 spirit temptith him; the worlde troubelith him on the tothir
syde. Wherfor he behovith to seche vertue and to requer the
grace of God, which may rewarde him for his merytes, and by
Him to conquer suche as wolde do him greff if he fell, if he
lacked or if he erred. Wherfor he hath nede to requer and pray
25 withowt sekyng of Hym that yevith the socours and lowsith them
that be bounde. For prayer is the ernest peny that God taketh of
man for to sette him in the high way.

[Vndrestondynge]

f. 108   Though I haue wele vndirstonde the auncient de/dis, yet obse-
30 cracions and sacrifice ben ioyned togedre, of which thou hast not
satified me. For thou hast determyned the matir of prayer, but
oblacion and sacrifice thou hast forgetyn vndetermyned.

1 batailes] a batayle N *pl.* D   2 the] this N   4 chirches] their
choise N Eglises D   prayers] prayer NJ *sing.* D   5 thei hadde] hadden NJ
6 wittenesse] wyttnesses J   yet] þat N si D   7 mynde] my mynde N
9 entvned] entevn N   11 a] þe J la D   12 mo] more N   18 a] *om.* J
19 within] the *add.* N   20 him 1] and *add.* N *om.* D   troubelith] trouble N
23 Him] allso *add.* NJ   24 and] to pay *add.* pay *canc.* N   25 withowt
sekyng of] without sekyng J beseching N sans cesser D *see n.*   socours]
socoure N   27 sette] see N   30 sacrifice] sacrifices NJ *pl.* D   31–2 the
matir . . . vndetermyned] *om.* N

[Hoope]

This argument is sideling to the askyng. So shall I make the in
this poynt a traversing discrecion withowt fourme of answer.

[Vndrestondinge]

If it be so that the matir be to my doctryne, to the be the 5
[ch]oyce of making of the fourme.

[Hoope]

The furst men that enhabited therthe serchid furst what was
most necessary to their perfeccion, for perfeccion drawith a man to
gete it ordinatly, but necessite enforceth a man to make his provi- 10
sion hastily. The rigour of necessite may not suffre the repugnaunce, his myght is so imperiall; but the perfeccion of blissidhed
suffreth withowt any constreinte whanne the pleasur that it yevith
him and the de/sier of the requerer be of one accorde. And though col. 2
so war that the bestiche people sought the sustenaunce of their 15
lyving before or thei sought the knowelage of God and of suche
thingis as had be necessary for them; and [hough] the beeng of
thingis and hough the crafte of thingis is enchayned, thei entird by
the knowlage of thingis that war necessary to them and desired to
knowe the profites of them. For at the furst tyme thei had but a 20
grosse vndirstondinge, naked of disciplyne and of naturall witte
and had no longe experience. Thanne whanne thei tastid of the
goodnesse which thei wele vndirstoode was neuyr made by them,
but as a thing newe-founde, thanne the remembraunce of their
necessite passed and the doubte of that was for to come mevid them 25
to enquere of the Werkeman that had made all these thingis. For
thei wolde fayne haue / ben nygh Him that myght fulfill them with f. 108ᵛ
suche goodis. For man was not borne to be maker of the cratures
of God but as a contemplatour of His werkes in loking vpon the
profitable thingis here byneth, having also in contemplacion the 30
mervailouse thingis of above. And therby thei had a maner of
knowlage in grette that their sustenaunce hing vpon a gretter power

2 sideling] sittyng N lateral D askyng] kyng N demande D 6 choyce]
NJ Ioyce R choiz D 8 enhabited] habyted NJ 9 man] for add. NJ
12 his] is his N 13 suffreth] suffre N 14 of 2] om. N 18–19 and . . .
thingis] om. N 20 profites] forfytes N 22 and] thei N 27 Him]
hem N 28 be] NJ made add. R om. D 30 having] haue N

thanne on the power of man [and fro þat tyme forth þer was no
man] that wold take vpon him that thei had any souereyne power
aftir that thei vndirstoode any parte of the Deite. In this furst
perceving, which was right derke, ben ooned all sectes and all maner
5 of vndirstonding in grosse what God is. But all folkes knewe not
what God is. But as sone as thes rude people perceyveden that the
necessaryes which longed vnto them rested in the power of some
persone both to yeve and to take away, thanne necessite compellid
col. 2 them to put / themself vndir for to knowe the Maker of all thing.
10 And therupon the made offeringis to God of His owne [goodes] and
not for neede that He had to take suche thingis as He yave Himself.
But thus beganne furst the sacrifices, oblacions and immolacions of
beestis and othir offerynges and sacrifices which thauncient lawe
auctorised aftirwarde, wheras it is wretyn and commaunded that no
15 man shulde apper before the awter of God withowt offeryng, and
that the sacrifice shulde be made to God, and tithes to be yolden
to Him of þe furst and beste thingis that grewe vpon therthe. And
aftir that thei knewe right wele þat it was needefull for them to
pray to Him. Lyke as the divine yeftis war knowen more and more,
20 the oblacions and the sacrifices wer employed vpon the ministres
of the temple, and by this introduccion cam in furst the ordre of
f. 109 the temple which aftirwarde was institute / serymonyously. And
thei were exempte from all vnworthy charges and fownded and
susteyned by the offeryngis that came to the awter. And therfor
25 preestes of the lynage of Levy had no possession of londe in the
cuntre of promission whan the heritage was departed amonge the
lynages of Israell, but thei received the dymes and offeryngis of
the vniuersall people. Their was no parte assigned them ouir the
hoole b[ut they had] their hoole thing vpon euery manys londe. The
30 lynages of Israell toke their partes aftir the porcion that was to them
lymyted. But this limitacion myght not touche Him which had
lordeship ouir all therthe. Thanne syn it is so that He haþe yeven
them all thinges to them necessary, reason wolde that His ministirs

---

1 þat] J the N　　　4 ben ooned] aboue N　　　8 persone] persons J
aucun D　to 2] *om.* NJ　　10 His] her N　goodes] J goodnes RN dons D
11 for] no *add.* NJ　　12 sacrifices] and *add.* N *see n.*　　16 made] *om.* N
fait D　and] as N & D　　17 and] the *add.* NJ　　21 this] his N ceste D
23 and 1] *om.* N & D　　25–6 of londe . . . cuntre] in the contre of þe lond
N　　28 them] *om.* J leur D　　29 but they had] by R by thei NJ
mais ils eurent D　　30 partes] so *add.* N　porcion] proporcyon NJ por-
tions D　　31 Him] *om.* N

shulde of euery thing [be] rewarde[d] agayn suche as myght pleace
Him. For equite and kyndnesse might not suffre but that He war
put in þe egalnesse of parting with oþir / which departid all amonge   col. 2
othir; in signe wherof that all was His, of all maner of thingis offering is made to Him.   5

Now hast thou the institucion of the sacrifices. [þan leueth þer
to declare the qualite of sacrifices.] It is to [be] vndirstonde and
noted tha[t] doves and lombes war presented to God, but the good
devocion made the preasent wourthi to be received. For the preestis
etyn the lombes and lyvyn vpon the offering of sacrifices, and God   10
receivith the hertis of them that doth the sacrifices. The shewing
of him that doth the sacrifices is in suche thingis as thei offre, but
the very sacrifice is in the conscience. Wherfor it is wretyn that
obeysaunce of herte is more agreable to God than the sacrifice of
beestis. The Creatour that fedith euery man is not noryshed with   15
the feding of thyn offeringis. For He that fullfillith euery man with
mete hath no suche hongre þat Him luste to ete any flesshe of
lombes nor of othir beestis. The lyght of thi candelles may / not   f. 109ᵛ
yeve so grette a light as the light of the souereigne sunne. Wher is
thanne the vertu of thi sacrifices save oonly in þi iuste obeisaunce? 20
For the oblacions that ben shewed owtwarde is but a figure apparent, and the misterye of the wourship that longeth to the divine
magnificence. But that man makyth a rightfull sacrifice [to God]
which offerith and submittith himself with an enteer thought to
obey His commaundementis. Through suche sacrifices was He   25
sende down to therth. For the herte that yevith him all to God may
not faile of the yefte of hoope. Harke what Dauid said vnto the,
which was right brennyng in sacrifice and stedfast in hoope. For he
did sacrifice to God, sacrifice to iustice, and in him was a good
hoope.   30

O thou man that makest thi sacrifice of goodis rauisshed and
offirst to God suche thing as thou hast taken away from thi nygh-
bour, what hoope oughtest / thou take in thi sacrifices? For suche   col. 2

---

1 be rewarded] N rewarde RJ *see n.*   3 departid] departe N   4 that]
om. N   of 2] *om.* N   5 is] was N estoit & deuoit estre D   6 the
1] *om.* N la D   the 2] *om.* NJ des D   10 offering] offrynges J *pl.* D
11 sacrifices] sacrifice NJ   12 sacrifices] sacrifice N   13 in] *om.* N en D
16 He] *om.* N   fullfillith] fulfilled NJ   17 luste] lyste J   19 souereigne
sunne] *tr.* N   20 sacrifices] sacrifice N *sing.* D   23 that] *om.* NJ le D
25 sacrifices] sacrifice N *pl.* D   27 said] seith NJ   28 which] NJ he
add. R *om.* D   33 take] takest N   sacrifices] sacrifice N *pl.* D

as thou hast take away by force is not wourthi to be offird and also
that maner of offeryng may not take away þe divine indignacion.
And whan thou offirst suche [good], thou dost thi sacrifice to the
yghen of men þat looke vpon the. But yelde ageyne that thou hast
5 take away, and thanne thou dost thi sacrifice byfore the yghen of
Allmyghty God. O good God, what thei be grettely disceved which
in their olde age make theire offeryng of suche goodis as wer
vntruely gotyn in their yong age. O thou slowe and tarying knowelage, evil couerid with feyned sacrifice, thou hast taken from God
10 by rapyne the obeisaunce of His commaundementis and the drede
of His name and wenest to appeace Him with suche goodis as be
not thyne. Knowe for trouth that the swetnesse of thyn encence
stinckyth byfore Him and thyn sacrifices ben to Him more annoy-
f. 110 eng thanne plesaunte. The Scrip/tur tellith hough our Lorde haþ
15 oftentymes dispraysed the sacrifices of synners of His mageste for
the abhominacion of theire synnes. Harke what He saith to the
people that ben of harde herte, which ben drawe away from His
perfite obeisaunce. 'Ye dispreyse', saith He, 'my commaundementis and woll that I take your offeryngis. Ye put away my
20 discipline and woll that I accepte your oblacions. Your sacrifices
noyine me; your solempnytees ben to me grevouse to her. Wherfor
I woll turne my face whanne ye wene to appese me through your
sacrifices. For I perceive wele that thes people which honour me
with their mouthe haue their hertis ferre from me.' God forbed
25 that the sentences that wer said to the Iewes which ben dede longe
agoo may be [avowed] vpon the Cristen people that lyven noweadayes. For I doubte me that the courages of men now beyng on
lyve ben ferre goon away from Him which above all thing hath a
col. 2 speciall / love to all Cristen people, which noweadayes ben most
30 ferthest from His obeisaunce, and namely suche as shulde be next
Him at His aultar. Somtyme masses war stablisshed by suche
people as dispraysed the temporall thinges, and thei war ordeigned
for the mystery of sacrifices. But nowadays thei seche all secular

2 of] *om.* N   þe] *om.* N la D   6 what] *om.* N   12 encence]
entent N   14 plesaunte] plesaunce NJ   15 sacrifices] sacrifice NJ
pl. D   of 2] to N de D   17 that ben] *om.* ND   18 saith He] *tr.* N
19 offeryngis] offrynge N *pl.* D   20-1 sacrifices noyine] sacrifice noyeth
N   23 thes] the N ce D   25 sentences] sotylnes N sentences D
that 2] whych J   26 avowed] N avowched J avenged R auoiries D
27 now beyng] þat now been N   27-8 on lyve] alife N alyve J   32 the]
om. ND   33 of] the *add.* N des D

operacions and make the spirituall mysteryes as a thing þat is
repreveable. For nough no man asketh what he ought to do in his
office, but the woll aske a question, what the benefice is wourth.
A, thou cursid introduccion! A, disordinat abusours! Ye haue made
of Goddis chirche caves of theves, and the saintuarye ye haue made   5
a place of trechery. The holy Euaungelys be put away and the
constitucions ben full of barat and of questions. Profite hath wonne
the victorye. And the holy doctrines of the olde fadirs might suffice
to euery ministir in the chirche. But euery man / woll take now a   f. 110ᵛ
newe forme.   10

Long agoo there was a newe statute of the Latyn Chirche which
shall departe from þe ordre of holy mariage vnto the dignite of
preesthode vndir the colour of clennesse. Now the statute renneth
that he hath drawen them to the worldly estates and [fowled] them
of the charges temporalles. This fu[r]st statute departed the Chirche 15
of Grece from [the] Latyn, and anon he sette an auaricioux disordinaunce of prestis to departe the people of Bohaymne from the
Chirche of Roome. What say I of Bohaimn? Ȝa, Cristendome
nerhand all! For the people of the chirche ben suche wise diffouled
with vylanny that at this howre thei be had in dispite as wele of the 20
leest as of the moste. For mennys hertis ben enstraunged from the
obeisaunce of holy chirche for the straungenes of his mynisters.
For nowadays thei be not weddid, but thei vse vnlawfull and dissolute leche/ryes, whereof I woll no more speke at this tyme. Foras- col. 2
muche as thei haue suche constitucions of place as therof the pleasur 25
is take, what importith the constitucion not to mary preestis but to
tourne lawfull generacion in advoutrye and honest cohabitacion of
[oon soole wyfe in] multiplicacion of lechery from sclaunder.

If I said all that I thincke, men myght doubte that the largenes
of temporall goodis medlyd with [þe] sulfre of envy and the he[e]te 30

1 a] om. N   3–6 but . . . trechery] om. N   4 A 2] and J Haa D
7 of barat] bareyn N de barat D   8 doctrines] doctryne N pl. D
12 from] om. NJ   vnto] than NJ   14 fowled] NJ followed R souilles D
15 temporalles] temporall N   16 auaricioux] avariaunte N auaricieuse D
17 people] peples NJ pl. D   Bohaymne] Nahaymie N   18 Bohaimn?
Ȝa] Nahymie Ȝa N minim or e after n under illumination R   21 enstraunged]
estraunged NJ   22 holy] the N saincte D   25 as thei] om. N   therof]
NJ as add. R of add. canc. N   26 is . . . importith] om. N   constitucion]
is add. N   27 in] into NJ   cohabitacion] habitacion N   28 oon . . .
in] oon sole wife is N oon soole wyf/ys (division ins.) J consoolewyse R vne seule
espouse en D   from] fro J for N   29 If] Hoope add. above as speaker's
name J   men] I N see n.   30 heete] NJ herte R chaleur D

of ambicion and of lechery hath made them redy for to sette fire
in the chirche. But this matir is to deepe to speke of, and the
determinacion therof is right doubtefull. Wherfor at this tyme I
woll holde my peese save I pray only to Him which hath hallowed
5 the chirche with His owne bloode that He suffre not to come suche
thingis as by lykelinesse shulde falle. Yet for all this let vs not blame
the good secular men which have yeven so grette poss[ess]ions to
f. 111 the / chi[r]che, for their soules shuld the more lightly come into
hevyn thanne the clergie. For þei haue taken so hevy a burden vpon
10 their shulders that it makith them stoupe evin down to ther[t]he so
that thei haue no power to looke vp towarde the hevyn. Sorow
makith me to say thus for I am half in despeir of their long dueryng
withowt a grette stroke. The shippe that berith a grette sayle saylith
in grette perill. Ther is no ryver durith long owt of his chanell.

15 So thanne I woll avise the to gadre the parties togedre of þat I
haue tolde the of the dignite of sacrifices and the [in]dignite of them
that don the sacrifices, and take this for a determynacion that
wheras the abhominacion of God turneth vpon þe sacrifices, persecucion beginnith sone aftir vpon the men. And for to satisfy the
20 shortely by ensaumples aftir the ordre accustomed, thi preef take
vpon Offny and Phynees, the sones of Hely, which war preestis of /
col. 2 the awter, whoos sacrifices wer abhominable to God. And the
debate of ther cace is dr[a]wen in Holy Scriptur as a thing passed.
But the prophecie of Danyell abidith yet for to come which desirith
25 the comynge of Ante-Criste and the tyme of persecvcion for the
abhominacions of the temple and the [distraccion] of the dayly
sacrifice.

By this disgression, which dependith to [þe] question aforesaid,
maist thou knowe that prayer and sacrifice profitith to conserue and
30 stable the prevy thingis and the opyn thingis. Yet take also for a
confirmacion the wourdes that Valere seid, 'The olde lordshippes,'
seith he, 'war allway stable as longe as thei seruid and did due
sacrifice to the dyvinite.'

7 possessions] J possession N possions R   8 for] *om*. NJ Car D   shuld
the] shul NJ   into] to NJ   10 them] to *add*. N   down] *om*. N   11 the]
om. NJ   14 ryver] þat *add*. NJ   15 I woll] *tr*. N   16 sacrifices]
sacrifice N *pl*. D   indignite] dignite RNJ indignité D   18 wheras] wer
N   20 thi preef take] take thi prefe NJ   22 sacrifices wer] sacrifice
were N *pl*. D   24–33 which . . . dyvinite] *om*. N   26 distraccion] J
distruccions R distraction D   31 seid] seyth J   32 seruid] god
add. J *om*. D

THE QUADRILOGUE INVECTIVE

PARALLEL TEXTS

OF TWO TRANSLATIONS OF

ALAIN CHARTIER'S

Le Quadrilogue Invectif

from Rawlinson MS. A 338
and University College MS. 85

To the ryght high and excellent mageste of princes, to the full
honorable magnificence of nobles, to the circumspection of clerkis,
and to the witty excercise of the people of Fraunce, Aleyn Chartir,
5 humble secretorye to the [Kyng], oure Souerangne Lorde, and of
my doubted Lorde, my Lorde Regent, as a ferre folower of oratours,
gretyng in the drede of our Lorde with submissione and humilia-
tion vndir His iustice, knowlegyng His iugementis and the retourne
vnto His grete mercy vndir the cownthenaunce of His punytion.
10 For like as the high digniteys of lordeshippes ben stablished
vndir the divine and infinite Power, the (which) reisith them in
florishing, prosperite and gloriose renome, it is to be belevid and to
be holdyn for veray certeynte that in like wise as their begynnynges
and their encresynges ben mayntened and adressid by the divine
15 prouidence, so in like wise is their ende and their disencresce aȝeine
col. 2 gevine by / sentence in the high counsell of the soueraigne Sapience,
the which subuertith some from their high trone of imperiall lordeshippes into the diepe pitte of thralldom and from their high
magnificence into ruyne, and makith also them that war victoriouse
20 for to be ovircome and them also to obey for drede which war wonte
by auctorite to commaunde. But whanne swete mercy, entermedled
with rightwisnes-iustice, yeuith ouir the princes and the people the
sentence of [atemprate] punytion, the pryde than of foles ouir-
trowed power that know nat Him is ouirthrowen by the high power
25 enemye; the superfluite of worldly richesse, which is norice of
discorde and murmur, ys chastised by His own norishing; and [þe]
vnkyndenes of receyvers of [Goddys] gyfftes vpon the people is
punyshed throwgh the withdrawing of His grace, which aftir good
amendement and lawfull correction sendith ageyn and redressith
30 the lordeshippes and the people in perfight peece and restitution

---

6 a ferre] after N lointaing D   7 with submissione] submyssyng N
and] with N om. S   11 them] thene S les D   in] into N   12 be]
om. NS   13 for] a add. NS   certeynte] certeyn N   14 the] om.
N la D   19 victoriouse] victours NS   21 entermedled] entremeldyd
N   23 atemprate] atempray N atemprar S blank space in R plus attrempee
D   the pryde than] than the pride NS   24 Him] þat add. N om. D
24-5 power enemye] power. Enemye R power Enemye NS   27 of 1] the
add. N   Goddys] goddes S goodys R goodes and N   vpon] of N sur D

The prologe of the tretye folowing entitled and
called the quadriloge of Aleyn Charietere secre-
tarie somtyme to the Kynge of Fraunce

To the moost high and excellent mageste of princes, to the right
honeurable magnificence of nobles, circumspection of clerkes and
good instruccion of the comon peeple, Alain Charietere, humble
secretaire to the Kynge, oure liege lorde, and to my moost redouted
Lorde, my Lorde the Regent, verey i[m]mitatoure of the oratours,
greting in the dreede of God and humiliacion vnder His iustice,
knowlege of His iugementes, and referring to His mercy vnder the
sharpnesse of His punicion.

How the high dignitees of lordshippes ben establisshe vnder the
diuyne and infinite Puissaunce, which exalteth theyme florisshing,
in prosperite and glorious fame and renoune, it is to be bileeuyd for
true affirmacion that as theire begynnyng and continuall increesinge
is may[n]teyned and addressid by the dyuyne prouidence, in the
same / wyse is thaire ende determined by sentence yeuen in the
high counseill of the moost souereyn Sapience, whiche sentence
som reuerseth and puttith down of the high trone [of] imperiall
lordship and dominacion into the lowe pitt of seruitute and out of
magnificence into ruine and destruccion, and maketh the mighty
conquerours to be vtterly discounfite and ouyrthrowen, and maketh
hem to obeye by constrainte that somtyme were commaunders by
auctorite. But whan swete mercy, medled with rightwysnesse of
iustice, yiveth vpon the nobles and comons the discreete and tem-
perate punicion for the pride of to presumptuous power, which
himself is abated thrugh mighty power of enmyes, the superfluite
of worldly thinges, whiche is norice of sedicions and murmure, is
chastised by His owne rod; and the ingratitude of the giftes of God
is punysshed vpon the men with subtraccion of His grace. And
aftirwarde good amendinge and true correccion settith in good
weye of redresse the lordys and the peeple in parfite peas and

5

10

15

f. 1ᵛ
(p. 2)

20

25

30

9 immitatoure] inimitatoure U

f. 1ᵛ of / their furst disposition. And so He meruelously diuidith His
graces aftur the diuersite of persones, of places and of tymes, and
[as] a masterfull lorde chaungeith, encreseth and amynushith,
maketh, vnmaketh in His werkes aftur His resonable wille which
5 no man [may] deceve.

And also afftur the rightes of nature, which hath their begynyng
in the diuine prouidence and the instrument of their workyng or
moving in the light and in the influence of celestiall bodies, as the
maisters shewen vs by the right inestimable science of astrologie,
10 which is writyn in the booke of large volume of hevenne of so many
diuerse printes and ymages, in which may be knowe the short and
longe abydinge of lordeshippes and citees, which the naturale
philosophures called peryode and haue their sekenes and their deth
in the ayre. So thanne He that all may departith and dividith the
15 powers, and He by His perdurable eternite movith the thinges
which renneth their course vndir the tyme. And He which (is)
col. 2 infi/nite in high power puttith the begynnyng, the myddis and the
ende in all His werkis vndir the moveyng of the hevynes, lyke as
dothe a potter, by moving of his whele maketh of one maner of
20 matir diuerse pottis of sundry factiones and gretnesse and ofttymes
brekyth the grete pottis if thei lyke him nat and maketh small pottis,
and of the matir of the small pottis he maketh ageine grete pottis.

And so we may haue knowlich of some thingis by remembrance
as in thaunciente bookis of owr forefadirs we may allday see and
25 knowe many grete mutationes, subuersions, chaunging of realmes
and principaliteys. For lyke as childern encresin and growe till thei
come vnto the perfect age of man and aftirwarde decline to grete
age and so to deth, in lyke wise the lordeshippes haue their begin-
ning, their encresing and their declyne. O wher is now the royall
30 cite of Nynive, which was in compas thre dayes iournay? Wher is
become also the noble cite of Babilone, which was edified by
f. 2 crafte / of masonrye so stronge that the makers supposed neuir to
haue failed, and now it is enhabited with serpentis? What shall men

1 diuidith] deu[?n]yeth N   5 may deceve] NS deceiveth (i *and* th *ins.*)
R *see n.*   8 of] þe *add.* NS des D   10 of 1] the *add.* N   11 printes]
princes N empraintes D   12 which the] the which N   13 philo-
sophures] phylysofyr S philosophie N   called] callen NS   14 the ayre]
theyr S them N leur endroit D   19 maner of] *om.* N   20 sundry]
diuers NS   factiones] fassions NS   21 maketh] þem *add.* N hym *add.* S
22 grete pottis] þe grete NS les plus grans D   24–5 and knowe] *om.* N
25 mutationes] invitacyons N mutacions D   27 vnto] to N   the] *om.* NS
33 it is] *tr.* S

restitucion of thaire good and first disposicion. And so the good
Lord deuideth His grace after the diuersitees of the persoones, the
tymes and the places, and as a maister and chief lorde chaungeth,
encreesith and dyscreecith, maketh and vnmaketh in His werkes
aftir His pleasire and moost resonable volunte, whiche no man may 5
deceyue.

And ferthermore aftir the rightwisnesse of nature, whiche hath
begynnynge of the dyvyne prouidence and instruccion of the
corages and meevinges in brightnesse, the influence of bodyes
celestiall ben shewde vnto us by the maisters of the moost inestim- 10
able science of astronomye, that in the celestiall book of the firmament, whiche is writen in so large volume of so many empreentid
ymages, by the whiche may be knowen the cours and lastinge of / f. 2
the lordshipps and citees, the whiche the naturiens callen the (p. 3)
periode, and that they haue sekenesse and deth as mankynde in 15
thaire nature. And so He that is allmighty departeth and diuideth
the worldy lordshipps by His perdurable eternite and chaungeth
the erthly thinges here, and He that is infinite in high power settith
in a meene, bigynnynge and ending in all His werkes vnder the
celestiall meeuing, and by oo rude ensaumple, as the potter by the 20
compace of oon molde makith diuers pottes of different bignesse
and facions, bothe more and lesse; and yf the grete pottes whan
they be made be nat to him agreable he brekyth hem and of the
same matiere maketh little pottes; and in the same wyse he maketh
of the little pottes the grete. Whiche memorye may somwhat 25
remembre us and the auncient bookes of oure forefadirs may yeue
us knowlege of oure dedes by thaire dedys that be passed, for all
maner of olde scripture is full of mutacions and chaunges of
reaumes and lordshipps. For as children encreece to parfite men
and than decline into age and deth, in the same wise haue the 30
lordshippes begynnynge, encreecinge and [fin]all declynnyng.
Wherfore is Niniue, the grete citee that was of lenght .iij. dayes
iourney? Whereynne is bycome Babilon, that was edified of
artificiall matere for longe lastinge, whiche is now inhabite with

31 finall] small (f *not crossed*, i *not dotted*) U

say of the grete renowme of Troye and of the riche castell called
Yllion, which was withowte pere, wherof the yates were made of
yvory and the pyleers of siluir? And now vnneth shall ye fynde any
parte of the fundation bycause of the grete multitude of bushis and
5 breres there growing, which takyth away the syght thereof fro the
people. Thebes also, which was foundid by one named Cadmus,
sone of Aginor, wherein were most plente of people in his dayes
above all othir citees, where shall a man fynde any such fruyte
nough comyng thereof through which a manne might be releued?
10 Lacedemoyne also, whens the lawes came fro vnto diuerse natiouns,
whereof some ben vsid yet at this day, made by Ligurgus through
his grete vertue, but in processe of yeris thei were extincte. Also
noble cite of Athenes, which was the veray founteyne of sapience
col. 2 and the spring of high doctri/nes of philosophie, is it nat nough in
15 subuersion and the fresch brok of his scoole dried vp? Yes certeyn.
The noble cite of Cartage, wherin were the good fighters and wise
men of warre, of which somtyme the Romayns had grete doubte,
where is nough become the grete excellence and glory therof?
Sothly by force of fyir it is turnid into asshes. Yet let vs speke of
20 the royall cite of Rome, which [was] last in souerangne mageste and
excellent vertue, and let vs noote right wele the wordis of Lucan,
which seith that the grete weight and peice of the said cite hath
causid his own fall, for hevy dedis mak grevouse falles. And so by
thes meanys euery man in his turne and aftir his ordir chaungith,
25 rebateth or subuertith from the happy fortunes and grete brute of
realmys, like as the grete monarchy of the worlde and souerangne
dignite of thempyre, which was somtyme translated fro the Asse-
riens vnto the Perciens, and from the Perciens vnto the Grekes, and
f. 2ᵛ from the Grekes vnto the Romayns, and from the Romayns / vnto
30 the Frenshmen and Germayns. And though so be that thes matirs
ben opinly knowyn, yett moche people woll not vndirstonde them.
For though the dedis ben tolde them which opynly apperith afore
their yghen, yet dwellyn thei in the vnknowyng of the cause. And
forasmoch as the iugementis of God, withowt whom nothing is but
35 as a diepe derkenes which no man may clerely vndirstonde, and
also that oure wittes ben so feble, oure yeris so shorte, and our

3 shall ye] *tr.* N   8 a man fynde] a fynde now N affynde now S
9 nough] *om.* NS   12 Also] the *add.* NS   ⌐13 veray] *om.* NS
14 of 1] the *add.* NS des D   15 brok] brookes NS *pl.* D   19 it]
om. NS   30 the] *om.* N   35 as] *om.* ND   and] *om.* N et D

serpentes? What shall we sey of Troy, the moost famous citee, and of
Ilion, the moost ryche castell withoute piere, where the yates were
of iuery and the pillers of siluer and now skantly restith the foot
of the fundacions, whiche be now enclosid with high busshys from
the sight of the peeple? Thebes, whiche was founded by Cad[m]us 5
and the best peeplid citee vpon the erthe while it endured, yit
natwithstanding it may nat by founde by true euidence that any
man is come of / that se[d]. Lacedomon[e], wherof the lawes come　f. 2ᵛ
to dyuers nacions, of the whiche yit we vsen, might neuyr so　(p. 4)
streightly kepe the lawes of the rightfull Ligurgus, which were 10
made for his perpetuite to thentent his vertu shuld nat be attained
nor brought to nought. Athenes, welle of sapience and springe of
high doctrines of philosophye, is it nat in subuercion, and the
streames of his scoole be broken and drye? Cartage the bataileuse,
which went with olifauntes in bataille and that was of olde tyme so 15
sore redouted by Romayns, where is now become that glorious
might but oonly in the asshis of the brennyng fyre? But now speke
we of Rome, which was last in souereyne mageste and excellent
vertu, and note we the woorde of Lucane, that seid that the seid
citee shuld be cause of his owne dekay and ruine, for the to grete 20
and heuy burdons causeth the grete and greuous falles. And by this
meene all erthly lordshippes and citees, ichone in thaire cours and
ordre, ben chaunged, enlowed and subuertid by the operacions of
fortune and the brute of the reaumes, and lyke as the monarche
of the worlde and the dignitee of the souerayn empir was of olde 25
tyme translated from the Assiriens to the Perciens to the Grekes,
from the Grekes to the Romaynes, and from the Romayns to the
Frensshmen and Germaynes. And how be it this is euident ynough,
yit many oon erryth therynne. For in rehersinge the deedys that
thei knowe by the sight of the yie they rest so, nat vndirstanding 30
the cause. And forsomiche as the iugementes of God, withoute the
whiche nothinge may be doo, be of so depe profoundenesse that
mannys vndirstandinge may neuere atteyne to the grounde, for
oure wittes be to feble, oure yerys to short, and oure affections to

5 Cadmus] Cadinus U　　　　　8 sed] seth U semence D　　　Lacedomone]
Lacedomons U　　　16 now] where is now *add.* U　　　26 Perciens] *possible*
om. here U *see n.*

affections to frele, we therfore compleyne vpon fortune, which is
a thing veyne and voide and may nat revenge the iuste vengeaunce
that our Lorde taketh on vs for our defaultes, for as Valere saith,
'Good come but lately, yet the long abydyng is recompencid
5 through the gretenes of the peyne.'

 Lyke as in the yer a thousaunde foure hundred and twenty of our
Lorde God I sawe the Kyng of Englonde, auncient aduersarye to
lordship and howse of Fraunce, glorifye himself to oure vttermest
col. 2 re/proche, and made himself riche with our goodis and dispreisid
10 oure dedis and oure corages, and of our people also he hath drawen
vnto him, fortefienge the willes of his allyaunce, and also I se our
vices daily growe to our confusion, wherefore I conclude in myn
opinyon the hande of God hangith ouir vs and hath put in vre for
His displesaunce the scourge of persecution. For I haue sought owt
15 curiously by the course of holy scripturis the defaultis and punycions of oure forefaders and feerfully debatid in my mynde whethir
this ferefull punycion be the rodd of the fadir for our chastising or
ellis a rigorous iugement for our vttirmest vndoynge. And amonge
othir scripturis whanne I rede the thridde chapitre of Ysaie, myne
20 herte was for verey feere sor troublid and myne yghen made derke
with multitude of terys whanne I sawe ouir vs the stroke strikin
which ben wourthi the deth and yeuith vs ensaumple of diuine
indignation in less that we fynde soone a medicyne. And he that /
f. 3 will vndirstonde ferther, rede the chapitre, which is the woourde
25 of God, whereas no tong nor writynge of mortall man may atteyne.
Than I, mouid of compassion to bringe to mynde the state of our
infelicite and to remembir euery man of suche thinges as towchith
him, I therfor have compiled this litill tretice which I call 'Quadri-
lougue' forasmoche as this matir is comprised in foure maner of
30 persoones in maner of moote or plee forasmoche as it procedith by
the maner of trauersing wourdis. Wherfor let no man rede the one
parte of this booke withowt he rede vp the tothir to thentent that
all the blame sholde not lye vpon oone of the persones.

 2 thing] NS a *add.* R 6–7 of . . . God] *om.* NSD 7 to] þe *add.* N
10 and 2] *om.* N et D also] þat *add.* NS 13 opinyon] þat *add.* NS
16 whethir] werfore N 18 vttirmest] vtmest S 22 of] þe *add.* NS
la D 28 tretice] tretee NS 32 vp] *om.* NS 33 not] oonly
add. NS

fraile to conceyue the seid iugementes, we trust in fortune, which
is full feynt and vayn. / But the iust vengeaunce that God takith for   f. 3
our defaultes may nat be reuenged, the whiche, as Valere seith,   (p. 5)
comyth ofte to late but the longe abode is recompensed thrugh
greuous payn.   5

And hou than in the yere of our Lorde .M¹.CCCC.xxij.ᵗⁱ I sawe
the Kinge of Inglonde, auncien aduersarie to the seigneure, himself
glorifie in our dispitouse reproche, enriche him with oure lyuinges,
dispreyse oure dedys and corages, and of oure men drawen vnto
him to fortifie the voluntes to his aliaunce, and also I see our vices   10
encreece with the tyme and to our blynde affeccions allweye somwhat sett therto to oure confusion, I haue concluded in my thought
that the hande of God is vpon us and that Is furore hath put in
execucion the flaile of persecucion. Wherfore I haue curiously
encerched in the discordes of the holy scriptures the defautes and   15
punisshementes of oure forefadirs, and in grete dreede troubled
and conquestioned in myn owne thought [i]f this sorowfull affliccion shulde be in chastisinge as a fadirs rod or ell in reigueur of
the iuge for oure determinacion. And amonge othir scriptures as
I sawe the iij.ᵈᵉ chapitle [of Ysaie], myn hert is troubled with fere   20
and myn yien wex derk with teeris whan I see vppon us light the
strokes that ben digne of deth, yiving tokenyng of divine indignacion but yf we seek bref remedie and medicyne. And who that
ferther will vndirstande let him rede the chapitle that is the woorde
of God, where the penne nor tunge of mortall man may neuyr   25
atteyne. And therfore I, meeuid of compassion for to bringe ageyn
to memorie the estate of oure infelicite and to ych man remembre
that that touchith him, I haue composed this litle tretys whiche I
call 'Quadriloge' bycause that in .iiij sondry maters is this operacion
comprehendid, and is seid 'Inuectyf' inasmiche as i[t] procedith by   30
maner of plesaunt woordes and by the fourme of repreef, and also
that / no man rede the oone part withoute the othir to thentent men   f. 3ᵛ
deeme nat all the blame vpon oon astate. And yf anythinge   (p. 6)
hereynne be worthy of lecture, lat it auaile for to yiue som space
of tyme to visite and rede the surpluse.   35

17 if] of U se D   20 of Ysaie] I seid U de Ysaïe D   30 it] is U il D

[Incipit Quadrilogum Inuectum et Comitum ad
morum Gallicorum correccionem]

[The Auctour]

Aboute the sprynge of the day whanne the sune shewyth his furst
5 light and nature content through kyndly rest of the nyght, which
callith vs vp to wordly labour, and nat long aftir I fonde myself
sodanly awaked. And like as the vndirstonding of man presentith
col. 2 aftir his rest suche / thinges as most lyen vpon the hert, [fell]
sodeingly to my ymagination the soroufull fortune and the pituous
10 estate of the high lordeschip and the glorious house of Fraunce,
which bytuene distruction and rysing agein roylith soroufully vndir
the honde of God lyke as the dyvine power suffirth it. And as I
brought vnto my mynde the diligent power of our enemyes, the
vntrouth of diuers subiectis, the losse of princes and chiualrye,
15 which our Lorde by vnhappy bataile hath left this realme gretely
vngarnisched, causith me nough to doubte vpon thisswe of this
infortune, thanne thought (I) ageinward vpon the greete largenes
of the realme and on the grette distaunce of parties being in the
same, wheras I sawe clerely that the enemyes myght nat suffice to
20 kepe, to maynetene nor to enhabite the fourth parte of the seide
realme. Also their fell vnto my mynde the merueylous noumbre
of nobles and defensable people that myght be founde therin, the
grette richesse also which habunden yet at this day in diuersse /
f. 3ᵛ places, the subtill wittes, the prudence and witty policie of people
25 of diuerse estates which haue their norischyng, state and liffe (in)
the same. And aftir that I had this [wise] debatid all thes maters
on this wise afore rehersed, me semid that fault of yeuyng and
receyving of goode ordre, discipline and rule hath putt in vre the
misusing of the power that God hath sent vs, which is cause of
30 the long enduryng of our persecucion. And it is [to] doubte that the
yerde (of) diuine punicion hangith ouir vs for our sinnes and that
the derknes of our lyuyng and corrupte manerys blindith in vs the
iugementes of reason and our parciall desiers maken colde thaffec-
tions of the comon wele. And thus we dwell in the vnknowyng of

1–2 Incipit . . . correccionem] NSJ J *begins here, see n.*   4 furst] fressh
N premiere D   6 labour] labours NS *damaged MS.* J *pl.* D   8 vpon]
on SJ   15 left] lost NSJ laissié D   18 distaunce] dystaunces SJ *sing.*
D   19 wheras] wher þat N   sawe clerely] *tr.* NSJ   20 parte] *om.* J
21 their] þan N   27 on this wise] *om.* NSJ   28 ordre] of *add.*
ins. N *om.* D   30 that] lesse (*ins. on line after erasure of* þat) N *see n.*
33 iugementes] iugement N *sing.* D

Incipit Quadrilogum Inuectuum et comitum
ad morum populorum correctionem

The Acteur

Aboute the dawnynge of the day whan the first cleerte of the sun
and nature, is content of the rest of the nyght, calleth us agayn to 5
worldly laboures, nat longe ago I fande me sodenlye awaked, and,
as vndirstanding aftir rest presentith first that that is moost in
herte, came in myn imaginacion the doloreux fortune and piteous
astate of the high lordship and gloriouse hous of Fraunce, which
betwene destruccion and releef is tremblynge in the moost wofull 10
wyse vnder the hande of God, as the divyne puissaunce hath suffred
it. And how I called to my remembraunce the power and diligence
of the enmyes, the vntrouthe of many subgites and the losse of
princes and nobles, wherof God thrugh vnhappy bataille hath left
this reaume disporveyed, whiche causith me sore to dreede the 15
comynge oute of this fortune, I thought agaynewarde to compare
in the contrarie the gretenesse and distaunce of the parties of this
land, where the said enmyes shulde nat souffise to / kepe the f. 4
iiij.ᵗʰᵉ parte, the merueilous nombre of the nobles and defensible (p. 7)
men that therynne might be founde, the grete richesse that yit 20
therynne doth habounde in diuers places, the subtile engynes,
prudence and industrie of peeple of diuers estates which therynne han [birth], lyuinge and astate. Aftyr the which parties
so debated in my thought, it seemyd me that defaute of yivinge
and receyuyng ordre of discipline and regle, set in due ordre the 25
mighty power that God hath left us, is cause of the longe lastinge
of oure persecucion. Soo it is to doute that the rod of the divyne
punission shulde be vpon us for our synnes and that the derknes
of oure lyues and corrupt condicions makyth blinde in us the iugement of reson and oure parciall desires cooleth the affeccion of the 30
publike well. And so rest we in disco[ni]saunce of oure fortune

23 birth] bright U naissance D   31 disconisaunce] discorusaunce U
descognoissance D

[oure] fortune that is to come, and to our enemyes thorough sympilnesse and fayled courage haue yeue theme corage and victory ouir vs mor thanne theire owne prowes hath don.

And the meane while that my vndirstondyng was thus troubled bytwene hoope and dispare, a [light] / slombir fell vpone me like as aftir the hevines of the furste slepe fallith oftentymes it comith towa[r]d the day. And as I laye thus half sleping me thought I saughe in a waste cuntre a lady of whom the high poorte and the lordly countenaunce shewed that she was com of royall lygne. But she was so soroufull and so soor bewepte that she semid a lady that was fallen from a gretter worschip than at that tyme hir estate shewid. And it semid wele by hir countenaunce that she was dowtefull and sore aferd of a gretter inconuenience and sorow that was to come, in tokenyng wherof ye might see hir her, which shone as the golde, was cast aboute hir shuldirs, not dressid but vnarayed; and on hir heede she ware a crowne of fyne golde which by diuerse punchingis was so soore brwsid that hit hynge ryght soor on the one syde; and specialy of the mantell that couerid hir body, of which the mervelous werkmanship ought to be remembrid, for it was wrought of thre maner werkis. And furst the high/est part was of auncient enbrowdour enrichid with many precious stones, wherin war figurid the noble flour-de-lyce sowen all abrode, and also banaris, penovns and sygnes of othir auncient kyngis and princis of Fraunce in remembraunce of [their] victorious renowns and of [thair] worshipfull enterprises. And in the myddes of this mantell was shewid diuers lettirs, carectis and figuris of diuers sciencis which lightnyd the vndirstondingis and workyngis of men. And in the lowest part of the saide mantell, which was next the erthe, men might see many diuers portraturis entirmedled with bestis, with diuerse plantis, with fruytis and seedis stretching vpward their braunches and growing from the bordwr byneth as it ware from the

---

2 fayled] fayling (ing *ins. after erasure*) N *damaged MS.* J   corage and] *om.* NSJD   4 And] in *add.* N   5 hoope] *om.* N   light] NS litill R *damaged MS.* J legier D   6 as] NSJ I *add.* R *om.* D   7 toward] NSJ towaid R   9 lordly] lady N   10 semid] as *add.* NSJ *om.* D   12 it] *om.* J   14 wherof] herof N   ye] I (*ins. after erasure of* ye) N   15 the] *om.* NSJ   vnarayed] vnrayde J   17 punchingis] pusshinges NSJ hurs D   18 syde] *possible om. here* RNSJ *see n.*   of 2] *ins.* the *add.* N   22 noble] *om.* J nobles D   23 penovns] pendvttys (*after erasure*) N   othir] *om.* ND   25 thair] NSJ othir R leurs D   this] the J   26 diuers 1] NSJ mantelles *add.* R *om.* D   sciencis] science N *pl.* D   30 seedis] sedyd N

comyng, and to oure enmyes through cowardnesse and failed
corage we yeue theym vpon vs victorie more than theire prouesse
and manhoode requirith.

In the meene tyme that my thought labored in this debate betwix
hope and dispeyre, a litle sleepe toke me liche as full ofte is likly 5
aftir the first rest towarde the mornynge; and as I was slombrynge
me thought I sawe in a dredefull cuntre a lady wherof the high
poort and ladyly countenaunce signified the right excellent extrac-
cion. But shee was in so grete heuynesse and weping that it seemyd
well that she was fallen from higher noblesse and honeure that than 10
her estate shewyd outewarde. And it appeerid well by her sem-
blaunt that shee was in grete fere and doute of more heuynesse and
mischeevys comynge. And in tokenynge therof hire faire here of
golden coloure ye might se spred and cast abrode in pitouse wyse 14
aboute hir shulders, and / a corone of fyne golde she bare on hir f. 4ᵛ
hede, whiche be diuers hurtes was so sore shakyn that it was (p. 8)
alleredy on the oon syde enclynynge downeward. Of hir clothing
I most reherce, and namely of the mantell that hir body cured,
wherof the merueylous and artificieuse werk it is to be remembred.
Of .iij. sondry werkes it seemyd that it was tissued and assembled. 20
First the ouyr partie of auncient enbrowdringe wherynne were
figured the noble floure-de-lyses and enriched with many precious
stoones, with baners, standardes and othir ensignes of the noble
kynges and princes auncient in remembraunce of thaire victorious
fame and renoun and of thaire laudable enterprises. In the mydell 25
part were entayled lettres and carectes and figures of dyuers sciences
which clarifien the vndirstandinge and redressen in rightwisnesse
the operacions of the men. And in the lower partie, which was
hanginge towarde the erthe might men see many diuers portratures
and entyrmedled bestes, plantes, frutes and seedys strecching out 30
the braunches alofte and growing out of the bordure byneth like as

plentuous erthe. Thenne what shuld I sey more of so precious and
so riche a werke as was made in the seid mantell and also of the long
processe and peyne of the workmanship therof? For ther was neuir
seene vndir hevyn non therto lyke, had it be so that enuyous fortune
col. 2 wold haue suffird it to have a/bydyn in his freschnes. But the
6 duryng of so excellent a werke so moch was displesaunt vnto the
seid fortune that she turnyd therto hir shrewed left side and openid
such wayes wherthrough this [saide] mantell, which was made by
soueraigne wisedome of the predecessours, was at that tyme by
10 violent handis brwsid and brokyn into diuers pecis so that the
highest parte therof was right derke to looke vpon and few apperid
of the flour-de-lice but all thei war brokyn or soylid. And therefor
let no man thinke but that the myddill partye was as well defa[c]id
as the tothir, for the lettirs, carectis and fyguris war so brusid and
15 brokyn that vnnethe might a man vndirstonde eny sentence in the
same. But and we come to speke on the lowar partie of the seid
mantell, it was so vsid in waste and in distructione by [s]oor strokis,
drawyng and halyng that in diuerse placis the ground of the same
mantell apperid vncouerid and the treys and seedis semyd as thei
20 had ben pullid vp by the rootis, casten hiddir and thiddir vppon
f. 4ᵛ hepis that no man cowde vn/dirstonde non ordynaunce ne fruyte
growyng. And so this mantell was in such wise empeyred both of
colour and of feyirnes that vnneth the workm[e]n that made it
cowde nat know their own werkmanship.

25   But now at this tyme I woll leve the spekyng of this mantell, for
bycause I woll nat tary long therupon and forasmoch also as it is
not thende of this 'Quadrilogue'. Yet notwithstondyng for aplying
of myn entent I woll in shorte processe declare the maner and
countenaunce of this said lady. And as me semed she stode nigh an
30 auncient paleys solempnely edified with feire walles and high
towres, compassid and enuirouned with diuerse habitacions by the
soueraigne witt and wisedome of werkmen, richely corvyn and wele
peyntid with many goodly thingis plesaunt vnto the yghe. But

2 was] NSJ so displesaunt *add.* R *see n.*   5 haue] a N   have] *om.* N
6 so moch was] was so NSJ   8 saide] N side RSJ   9 was] NSJ
and was R estoit D   that] a N   12 of] vppon N   all] at SJ that (th *ins.*) N
13 defacid] NSJ defatid R   15 might a man] a man myght N   16 come
to] shuld (*ins. after erasure*) N   on] of NSJ   17 so] *om.* J tant D   vsid
in] browth to (browth *ins. after erasure,* to *ins. above line*) N   soor] NSJ foor R
23 workmen] NSJ workman R ceulx D   24 nat know] knowen N knowe SJ
26 bycause] the cause J   28 and] þe *add.* NSJ *om.* D   31 envirouned]
bylyd (*ins. after erasure*) N   32 witt and] *om.* NSJ   33 vnto] to NSJ

land fertile and plentefull. What shulde I sey? Of so preciouse and riche ourage was wrought this mantell and by longe continuell labour was assembled the parties wherof it is composed so that vnder heuyn was neuir seen hi[s] piere, and fortune, annyed of longe prosperite, had [s]uffred it in his beaute to stande and 5 remayn. But fortune was so gretly displeased of the excellent lasting of so parfite a werk that she turned hir peruerse and wronge syde, and openyd weies whereof the seid mantell, assembled by the souerain instruccion of the pr[e]decessours, [was] allredy through violent handes broken and brosid and defouled. And the meeyne 10 partie was nat left hole nor conioined the oone to the othir, nor the lettres fourmed nor sett in thaire ordre, for they were departed and diuided / so inordinatly that right fewe might of hem gader ne f. 5 assemble that might bere any profitable sentence. But and we come (p. 9) to speke of the lower partie, it may be a thinge alone, for men may 15 see it so ferre worne in waste and destruccion through rude strokes, drawing and sliding so that in many parties the preent of the erthe is naked and discoueryd and the trees and seedys lyke as vnroted, cast awey and hanging ouerthwert by palles so that men may vndirstande noon ordinaunce nor hope to haue frute. And finally so fer 20 was that habite chaunged by enpeirynge of coloure and beaute that they that suche made it first, with payne shulde they knowe thereynne thaire owne werk.

Of this mantell I will passe ouer, for it is nat the ende of this present 'Quadriloge'. Neuyrtheles for to dispoose and to my princi- 25 pall intencion, I will in breue declare the gestes and countenaunces of this lady. A riche auncient paleis was beside hir curiously edified with wallys exalted and high toures compaced, comprehendid and enuirouned with diuers and different habitacions thrugh engynes of souereyn werkmen, enriched with entailed pictures, armories 30 and many othir thinges to the yie right plesaunt. But by the

4 his] hire U   5 suffred] fuffred U   9 predecessours] prodecessours U

thorough the necligence of the maister werkmen and defawlte of
good reparation, the wyndes and the watirs had (don) such harme
therto that in diuerse places it was like to foundir and fall downe, /
col. 2 and in right fewe placis apperid eny reparation but here and there.
5 Wherefore the mischyff semid gretter and the perill more nygh.
But whanne this lady byhilde this royall and lordly beldyng so nygh
to fall, thenne she, which in the same place royally was norishid in
grete habundaunce of goodis and worship, discouerid owte of hir
mantell (oone) of hir armys which was enbrowdered with flour-de-
10 lice medled with dolphyns, and with hir seid arme bar vp the wall
wharas she supposid was moste lykely to fall, thorough which she
was gretely travaylid by the long supporte of the same. Thanne she,
tornyng hir visage abowte, with yghen full of teeris, as a woman
constrayned of veray nede to desyre socour, furthwithall apperid
15 vnto hir thre of hir childern, which the toon stoode armyd, lenyng
on his axe, ferefull and pensif; the tothir was in long clothing,
sittyng in a chayer, herkenyng and holdyng his peese; the thrid was
in a poor habite, lying platte vpon the erthe, compleyning and full
of langour. But whanne she sawe them byfor hir, she, as a woman
f. 5 having to them an / indignation, spake with an high corage and
21 reprevid them of their ydill slewthe by queinte and straunge wordis
with sorowfull syghes, seing to them aftir the maner followynge:

[Fraunce]

O ye men owte of the way of good knowlych, femynyne of
25 coragis and of maneres, ferr from vertue and forlynyd owte of the
constaunce of your forefadirs, which for delicious lyuynge cheese
the meanys to deye shamefully, alas what dulnesse or what caytif-
nes of herte aylyth yow, which that have your hondis close and your
will mayte, that ye debate within yourself, in seyng byfor yowre
30 yghen your comune distruction, and muse as abiding on what party
or whennese the bourdon of your naturale herbergage shall fall or
subuerte, which might all tobruse yow and ynclose youre rvyne

---

1 maister werkmen] werkman mayster N   of 2] and J de D   5 semid]
om. J sembloit D   7 royally was] *tr.* SJ royally *om.* ND   9 with]
the *add.* N *om.* D   11 supposid] thought N   18 vpon] on NSJ
19 she 2] NSJ was *add.* R   21 slewthe] slowthe NSJ   24 knowlych]
knawynge J   25 forlynyd] forlyvyd J far (*ins. on line after erasure*) N
forlignez D   26–7 cheese the meanys] chesyn N   28 close] ckoyse J
28–9 your 2 . . . mayte] þat he (*ins. after erasure*) wyll mayten N   29 ye]
om. N vous D   31 whennese] when NSJ   your] of youre *add. canc.* R

necligence of the maistres and in defaute of good repara(cion),
the wyndes and watyrs had do therto so grete hurt and domage that
in diuers parties it was redy to synke and falle downe, and soo
appeerid no refeccion nor help sauf only a fewe estayinges of feble
and little pillers, whiche for to passe ouyr tyme in haste nat for to 5
endure were sett there whan the ruine and trouble was grettest and
the parill all ther moost. And whan she sawe this [l]ordly edifice
and royall hous well nygh fallen down, she that therynne was
noryced and brought vp in habundaunce of goodes and worshippes 9
discouerd from vnder hir mantell oon of hir / armes, whiche was f. 5ᵛ
couerd and poudrid with floure-de-lices and dolphynes quarterly, (p. 10)
that staied that side that was moost hanging, and by the grete
weight it enclyned downward, drawing grete parte of the surpluse
in ruine; and was hold vp with that arme the principall quarter of
the walle, whiche bare the braunle of the surpluse. And neuyrtheles 15
was the walle brosten oute in diuers parties and the principall pillers
enclined to the erthe ward, nat likly to recouere. Whiche lady was
right sore agreuid of so grete trauaile. And than she turned aboute
hir visage couerd with teeris, desiring som socour and constrained
by neede. And therwithall she apperceyued .iij. of hir children, the 20
toon standinge armed, lenynge vpon his axe, affraied and abaisshed;
the tothir in longe clothinge sitting in a sett, herkenynge in silence;
the .iij.ᵈᵉ in foule habite reuersid vpon the erthe, playnynge and
langwisshing. And as she had chosen hem at the yie, turned in hir
corage to hem warde, repreeving theym of their ydell lachnesse by 25
woordes full ofte brokyn with doloreus sighinges, whiche with woofull hert meeuid hir, saying in this wyse:

The Land

O men forvoied of the wey of good knowlege, femenyns of hertes
and corages, fer from vertus, forloyned of the constaunce of your 30
fadirs, whiche for to lyf deliciously ye cheese to dye in shame and
disworship, what musinge or caytyfnes of hert holdeth youre handes
bounde and the willes so mate and abaisshed in ferfulnesse, seeinge
before your yien your comon desercion and destruccion, musing / 34
as in abidyng on whethir side the burdon shalle falle of this your f. 6
naturall herbrurgh and [   ], the whiche might vtterly destroye (p. 11)

1 reparacion] repararacion (racion *canc.* cion *ins. in margin*) U   7 lordly]
wordly U seigneurieux D   33 and 1] and *add.* U   36 and] *blank space
follows* U

vndir his? Yet woll not ye put to your hondis by your travale and
labour, thorough which I myght be socourid. Who is he that canne

col. 2 sufficiently blame your slow and delicat conditions wherin / yow
be norisched? And yet it semith me that ye woll continue in the
5 same. What sharpe wourdis might I speke to repreve the grete
vnkyndnes that ye have shewed vnto me? For I may wele lay byfore
yow that, aftir the feith Catholike, nature byndith yow to fortefye
(þe) comon wele of the londe wherin ye wer borne and to defende
the lordeship [vndyr] the which God hath lent the grace to be born
10 vnto [and haue lyfe]. Alas hough grete war the coragis of our elders
byfor vs rootit in the naturale love of theire cuntre that their bodyes
desire to retourne in euery parte as into their propir place, for their
hartis war yovin to it as [to] that habitacion which is most agreable
to him. Wher his lyff and helth growith and amendith the man
15 sekith his suerties, his peece, his refuge, the rest in his age and his
last sepulture. Thanne forasmoche as the lawe of natur hathe estab-
lisshid so to be don it must be seide that [no] maner of labour ought
be vnto yow grevous nor no maner of aventur sholde be to yow
straunge for to susteyne and save the cuntre and lordeschip that /

f. 5ᵛ from your birthe vnto your dethe is of himself opyn to yow to all
21 sustenaunce and that fedith and norishith [yow] amongist the
quycke, and amongist the dede recevith yow into sepultur. For it
may right wele be seide that suche people ben vnnaturall that woll
not enforce themself for the susten[ta]tion of the comon wele and
25 levir suffir themself to be lost with the comon wele thanne dispose
themself to perile for the same, wherthrough it shulde seme that
naturall lawe, which bindyth all thing vndir hevyn, shulde be more
perfightly accomplisshid in dombe beestis thanne in any of yow and
also yow shal be founde more vnkynde thanne thei which have no
30 reason of vndirstonding. For the briddis of the eyre with their
beeke and talons defendyn their nestis; the lyouns and beeris also
kepe their cavis, defending them thorough force of their tethe and
clawis. Nough let vs retourn ageyn (to) the dedis of men and let vs

3 slow] slouth N   yow] ye NJ   om. S vous D   4 that] om. N   9 lent the
grace] ordeynd you N ins. J om. S fait D   10 vnto] om. NSJ   grete] gretly
SJ   our] your N   12 propir] prople S   14 and helth] om. N et la sancté D
15 the] to N le D   17 seide] syde N   21 yow] to do RNSJ vous D
22 dede] the dede add. R thi dede add. NSJ om. D   24 and] had add. NSJ
25 levir] to add. N   with] for N avecques D   26 themself] hemselfe J
hymself NS   29 yow shal] ye schull SJ ye shuld N   31 beeke] beekys
N sing. D   and 1] thayre add. NSJ   talons] taylns J   32 kepe] kepyn
and defendyn NSJ   defending them] om. NSJ   33 to] vnto J

you and enclose your ruine vnder his? And natwithstanding at alle
theise mischeeuys ye will nat put you in deuoire that I may be
socoured thrugh your laboure and trauaile. What is he that suffi-
sauntlye might blame and repreeue your slaughfull and delicious
condicions, whereynne ye be brought vp and will wex olde in the 5
same? Ner what sharpe and bittyr woordys may I haue to repreeue
your ingratitude against me? For I may ley to you that next aftir
the bonde of the feith Catholike nature hath obliged and bounde
you before all othir thinges to se the saluacion of the comon wele
of the cuntree that ye be borne ynne and to the defence of the same 10
seigniourie vnder the whiche God hath made you to be brought vp
and haue lyuing. And yit I sey that he aught litle to preyse his birth
and well lesse desire the continuacion of his lyf that passith his
dayes withoute som frutefull labore to the vtilite of himself and the
well publique, whiche I may like to the man whos remembraunce 15
dyeth with his lif. Elas so miche is in the auncient corages nygh and
inseparablely rooted the naturall loue to his cuntree so that the
body euyr entendeth to retorne of any partye as to his propre place,
the hert is yeuen as to that habitacion that to him is moost greable,
the lyf and the heele amendith therynne and encreecith. Man 20
seekith there is sikernesse, his pees and refuge, the rest of his age,
and his last sepulture. And sith it is so establisshed by the lawe of
nature, it most be said that no labour aught to be to you greuous,
that noon aduenture aught to be to you straunge to bere for (to)
saue that land and seignieurie whiche from your birthe to youre 25
last day as of itself is open to your sustinaunce, feeding and norissh-
ing / amonge the livers, and amonge the deede receyueth you in   f. 6ᵛ
sepulture. Than it may be seid that thei be vnkynde and vnnaturall (p. 12)
that will nat enforce thaire power and might to the defence and
saluacion of thaire cuntree and haue leuir be lost and destroied with 30
othir th[an] for to dispose hem to any pareill. And so it might seeme
that the lawe of natur, whiche all thinges vnder he[v]yn byndeth
with bonde indissoluble, shulde be more parfitely fulfilled in the
dom beestes than in you and that ye shulde be founde more vnkinde
than they that haue noone vndirstandinge of reason whan the birdes 35
with thaire billes and clees defende thaire nestes and the beerys and
lions kepen theire cavernys with the might of theire teeth and feete.
Retorne we than to the mennys astate and iuge oureself by othir

iuge owrself by othirs and remembir such thingis as may be wit-
col. 2 nessid in the auncient stories. And / furst hough the Troyans, [in
defendyng of] their cuntre, maynteyned the seege of Troye the
space of x yere ayeinst the Grekis, and the people also callid Scytis,
5 which helde warre ayeinst Kyng Darye of Perce, put hymself allwaye to the flight tyll tyme that thei come to the place wher their
fadirs and predecessoures had made their sepulturis and in that
same place thei fought evyn to the dethe like men that had naturell
pyte of theire frendis and cuntre, constreynyng themself to resist
10 and kepe the place wherin thei war borne and the sepulturis of their
formefadirs.

Alas this is to me an hard thing thus to compleyne. Yet it is to
me a mor hard thyng and lasse comfort to se yow which ought to
susteyne, defende and releve me ben most aduersaries vnto my
15 most prosperite, and instedde of my reward ye sechin my distruccion for the avauncement of your singular desiris. Myne auncient
enemys maken warr on me withowte by fyre and sworde, and ye
f. 6 make me warr withinne by your / vnstaunchable couetis and cursid
ambicions. The naturall enemyes sechin to put me from liberte and
20 ke(pe) me in their miserable subieccion, and ye mak me bond
thorough your des(or)dinat and slowe vsage, wenyng to be [de-
lyueryd] from the daungers of my fortune. Myne owtward enemyes
don me daunger and hurte as partye contrarye by the enterprise of
knyghthod and armys, and ye vndir the shadow of frendis, and
25 namely of frendelynes and defendours, ye put me in grete losse of
myne enheritaunce thorough defaulte of covenable gouernaunce.
Now me semith or thinckith that thes wourdis shuld seme to yow
bothe boistous and full of rigour, but and thei shulde be comparid
vnto your werkis and my necessiteis thei be of lesse cruellenesse
30 thanne (þe) casse that suffirth requyerith. Turne your yghen and
conuerte your iugement vpon yourself, vnknytt your thoughtis
from all affeccions that steren and meve yow owtward, and thanne
col. 2 shall ye knowe that many of yow / levyn the lordshipis whervndir

2–3 in defendyng of] NSJ defendid R pour . . . defendre D   3–4 the space
of x yere] x. yere and more N   4 also callid] *tr.* N   5 Darye]
S[?]arye SJ   6 tyme] hym N   10 sepulturis] sepulture NSJ *sing.* D
15 most] *om.* NSJD *see n.*   20 me 2] *om.* N me D   21 desordinat] de-
sidinat (or *ins.*) R   21–2 delyueryd] NSJ declined R delivres D   26 coven-
able] conuenable N   27 semith or] *om.* NSJ   thinckith] thing N   to yow]
om. N vous D   29 werkis] werkysse J   necessiteis] necessite NSJ *sing.* D
30 suffirth] or *add.* J   31 yourself] and *add.* N *om.* D   32 steren and]
om. NSJD

deedys, and remembre, as seyn the auncient stories, how the
Troiens for to defende thaire cuntree susteyned and suffred the
seege of the Greekes .x yere before thaire citee, and also of a peeple
called Scithiens, the werre that they had with Kynge Darye of
Perse, which were euer fleeing till they came to the place where the 5
grauys and sepultures of theire fadirs and predecessours were,
where they taryed, and there they faught to deth, as they that
naturall pitee had of thaire frendys and cuntrey, whiche constreyned
hem to resiste and kepe the place of thaire birthe and sepultures
of theire kynne.   10
   It is to me right harde that I most thus compleyn, but miche
harder and of harder recounforte is that ye that aught me to susteyn, defende and releeue ben aduersaries to my prosperite and in
place of rewarde ye seeke my destruccion and the auauncyng of
your singuler desires. Myn auncient enmyes make me werre out-   15
ward by fyre and glayue, and ye make me werre inwarde by your
couetyse and ill ambicions. My naturall / enmyes seek and laboure f. 7
to take my libertee for to kepe it in thaire miserable subieccion, and (p. 13)
ye serue me to the vsage of youre disordinate laschenesse, wenyng
thus to dwellen quite of the daungers of my fortune. They doo me 20
damage as myn aduersaries by thaire entreprises of armes and
knighthode, and ye vnder the coloure of frendis and the names of
frendis and defencers make an ende of my losse and destruccion
through defaute of couenable gouernaunce. Right rude and rigorus
my woordes may seeme to your liking, but for to compare theyme 25
to youre deedys and my necessite they be of lesse auctoritee and
sharpnesse than the cace that it suffrith requireth. Torne your yien
and conuerte your iugement vpon yourself. Ennake your thoughtys
of all maner affeccions whiche meeve you aparte. And ye shall
knowe that many of yow leuyth the seignurie to whom ye be 30

11 most] o *made into* v U *see n.*

ye be subiectis withowte diffence and pute owte of all goode fortune
lyke as a shippe is possid or tossid hiddir and thidir by tempest of
the see, which goth with a vaylid sayle and suffirth it to flete suche
waye as the wynde and the wawis likith to dryve it. So ye greve and
5 warr and greve your enemyes by wischis. Ye desir also their dis-
comfitur by prayers and by wourdis, and thei purchasse thorough
the enterprise of theire manly dedis. Ye couneseile to chase them
owte, and by þeir travaile thei chase yow owte. Their labour and
besy desire to conquer abashith your corages, and the necligence
10 that ye mak in your defence makith hardy the corages of youre
enemies. The teeris of women nor the syghys of men cannat purchace the helpe of God neythir the acomplyschemente of their
desiyrs, but our Lorde sendith His grace from hevyn vnto suche
as wittely and besely travailid to purchace prosperiteis and honor-
15 able worshippis. Thinke right wele that wille, [helth], liberte and
f. 6ᵛ desyre to / destroye your enemyes suffisith nat inow to recouere of
your grete hurtis, but and ye woll atcheue ye must put your hondis
to the werke for of the werkis comon the thankyngis and rewardis.

But wher ar noughadayes men of suche condicion that sekkin by
20 knyghthode theire renown and their perfeccion, whanne it cannat
appere in tyme of nede? Among all, fewe suche shal be founde.
Neuirthelesse suche as do wele be wourthi to have grete lawde and
preysing. O wher is now the grete prudence of clerkis and counsel-
lours, which by their grete wysedomes have ofttymes preseruid and
25 relevid many realmys from perilous aventuris? O wher is now
bycome the grete constaunce of the people of Fraunce, which of
long tyme have perseuerid trewely, stedfastly and entierly toward
their naturall lorde in grete wurship withowt seching of eny newe
mutacions? I dowbte me sore that all thre shal be subdewed from
col. 2 the dignite of (þeir) estatis. Diuers knyghtes and nobles cryen / 'To
31 harneyce', but thei seeche meanys of couetice how thei may en-
croche lyvelode and goodis. The clergie and the counceillours
spekyn vndir the semblaunce of two visagis, and yet they lyven
amonge lyvers. The people wolde lyve in fredom and suerte, and
35 yet ben thei impacient to suffre the subiection of lordship.

2 shippe] that *add.* NSJ   or tossid] *om.* NSJD   3 a vaylid] a valed N
avaylyd J avalyd S   4 the 2] *om.* NSJ les D   6 thorough] *om.* N
par D   7 Ye] he (*corrected from* the) J   14 travailid] trauaylen NSJ
15 helth] NSJ hath R salut D   16 to 2] þe *add.* NSJ   18 the 2] tho N
19 sekkin] sechyn J sethyn NS   23 and] of *add.* NSJ *om.* D   30 of]
from N   31 seeche] serch NSJ *see n.*

subgittes withoute defence, exposid to all fortunes, liche as the ship
that is cast to and fro by tempest of the see, which goth with lowe
veile thereas the wynde and wedyr dryueth it. Ye make werre and
greevyn your enmyes with wysshes, ye desire thaire discomfiture
thrugh prayers and woordys; and thei purchase yours by enterprise 5
of deede. Ye take counseill to chase theym, and thei labour to chase
you. Theire traueill and grete desire to conquere abaisshith your
corages, and your necligence of defence yiueth thaim hardinesse.
The teris of wommen and wysshis of men getith hem nat the helpe
of God ne the fulfilling of thaire willes, but to the traueilous, wise 10
and curyous comyth of the yiftes celestiall, and of thaire good
purchasing the high prosperitees and releevys. Than thinke verily
that it suffise nat to wille and desire the saluacion and publique well
and the confusion / of the enemyes; the hande most be sett actuelly f. 7ᵛ
to the deede for of the deede-dooing comyth the laudable rewarde. (p. 14)

But where ben they now that in theise knyghtly condicions 16
seeken theire fame and actuell perfeccion, whan thei appere nat and
auaunce theimself with the deede-dooing? But now amonge alle
right fewe may be founde suche, that they that doo well arn worthy
to haue laude and price. Where is the prudent wysdome of the 20
clerkes and counsaillers which bi thaire wittes haue preserued and
releeued many landes out of grete pareilles and aduentures? Where
is bycome the constaunt trouth of the peeple whiche so long tyme
hath had name of perseueraunce in trouthe, feerme and hoole
toward thaire naturall lorde withoute seekynge of any mutacions? 25
I doute me that all .iij. ben enlowed and abated of the dignitee and
deuoir of thaire estates. Many of the nobles cryen 'To harneys', but
thei renne to the couetise of the siluer. The prelates and counseillours speken with .ij. visages and thus passe ouer living with othir
lyues. The peeple will be free and kept in sauf garde, and yit arn 30
they vnpacient to suffre the subieccion of thaire souereyn.

O hough perylous and doubtable ben the customes of will and easis! O ye agid pompis rootid and noryshed in delices, ye have so gretly turnid vp so down and made softe the courages of French-men that this subuersion, thorough the meanys of fortune, hath
5 made vs of vnkyndly discord. For ye sitt vs so nyghe that [oure] hartis ben so wrappyd by yow that the peryll of lordeship ne the peryll of themself nor the doubte of their nygh dysheryteson cannat call them from their delicate customes. Ageyne suche is the naturall condicion of delicious willis, namely of suche as ben vnpacient
f. 7 ayeinst all labours, contrary to all vertuous willis / and werkis,
11 stepmodir to diligence and noryse of cowardise. They leese yow a(n)d yet woll nat ye lees them. Thei have ben and been the rebat-yng of your strengh and the confusion of your power, and in seching your helpe and releef ye kepe them and [hold] them with yow.
15 Wherfor I see wele that it is an hard thing to leve an olde custome. But who that woll vse the honorable dedis in tyme of nede he shall fynd that ther is nothing so plesaunt a travaile as suche a[s] wour-ship and renown springith of. For Scipion Affrican, whanne he had furst his hoost into Affrik, commaundid that all maner thingis that
20 prouokid eny man to voluptuosite within his legions that anon [yt] shuld be cast away and voydid owt of the hoost. Also Hanyball, aftir that the cite of Cappue was yolden vnto his subieccion, wherin he was richely recevid with all delicatis or delicacyes that might be founde, thorough which the knyghtis of the seide Haniball wer
col. 2 chaungid from their furst vertu of manhod into / ydelnes, into
26 plesaunt desyrs and lust of their bodyes. And for that ensaumple euery grete prynce shuld eschwe the lyke case. It happid falle so to Alisaundir aftir the conquest of grete Babilonye and also to Sarda-napallus, thorough thes vices afor rehersid lostin bothe lifes and
30 lordshippis. Thanne forasmoche as so grete conquerours regnyng in the glory of their grete victories haue bene ouirthrowen by voluptuous lyvynge, what suerte thanne may thei haue that be vndir the contrarious daunger of fortune, which harden themself in delicious lyvynge and corruption of their goode maners? Yet suche

1 perylous] perlious N   2 easis] ese N *pl.* D   5 oure] J *om.* RNS les D   7 doubte] dewte N nee the doubte *add. canc.* R   8–9 is . . . suche] *om.* N   9 vnpacient] inpacyent NSJ   10 willis and] *om.* NSJ *see n.*   11 to] all *add.* J *om.* D   of] to NJ de D   12 woll nat ye] ye will not N   17 as 2] NSJ a R *see n.*   19 maner] of *add.* NSJ 20 eny] a N   yt] J he RNS   22 vnto] into NSJ   23 delicatis or delicacyes] delicacyes NS delycatyes J *see n.*   25 furst vertu] *tr.* N

O moost redoutable and parilous custume of ease and voluntary
will, o anaged and enrooted norycing of delites and pompes, soo
long haue ye mysturned and made soft and tendre the corages of
the men that this subuercion, wherof fortune hath made vs a chesell,
hath wel nygh conveid us to ruine. And yit through you be thaire 5
hertes so enlapped with delicatiues condicions that the pareill of the
seigniour and of theimself ner the doute of theire nygh destruccion
may nat withdrawe hem from thaire ill and dampnable custumes.
For the naturall condicion of delicious voluntees is / suche that they f. 8
be impacient of any labour, whiche is contrarye to vertuous werkes, (p. 15)
stepmodre to diligence and norice to superfluite. They lose you and 11
yit ye will nat lese theyme. The(y) (c)ause you and suffre you to
perissh, and ye will nat suffre thaim from you. They haue be and
yit be the abating of your might and the confusion of your power,
and in seeking your helpe and releue ye kepe hem still and drawe 15
hem to you euer more and more. For right hard it is to leeue long
continuaunce and custume. But he that at the neede will dispose
himself to vse and endure in deedys of worship, he findeth aftirwarde noon soo parfite trauaile as that is wherof the prosperous
fame and renoun comyth to theim that ben vertuous. Scipion the 20
Affrican, whan he first had his hooste in Affrike, he commaunded
that all maner thinges prouoking uolupte and self will in all his
legions shuld be incontinent put down and throwen out. Hanyball
aftir that Capoue the citee was redu[c]ed in his subieccion and aftir
that he was therynne highly receyued and deliciously entreetid, he 25
fande his knightes hertes chaunged and mate of thair first vertu.
And for an example in cace like of an high prince byfell to Alexander, aftir the conquest of grete Babiloyne, and Sardana Pallus, he
lost therby his seigneurie and hys lyf. And sith it is so that the
mighty conquerou(r)s in the chief glorie of thaire victories han be 30
defouled and lowe brought through vsing voluptes, what [suerte]
than may they haue that vnder the daungers of peruerse fortune
enroote theimself to delicious lif and coruptible condicions? And

12 They cause] y *ins on line,* c *perhaps ins.* U   14 be the] bethe U
31 suerte] smert U sceurté D

ther ben that gon nyght and day to the feldys and woodis an
huntyng [and] an hawkyng to chase the bestis and bryddis, which
tak litill hede of their grete distruccion. And some ther be that
kyllen ther horses and peynyn their bodies to conquer estates,
5 offices and goodis and all othir maner of plesurs, and woll not putt /
f. 7ᵛ themself in daunger to diffende their naturale lordeshippis nor (for)
the rest of oone nyght woll nat suffir the daunger of one lityll
mysease.

O ye Frenchmen, which seke owte the goodly tastis of metis and
10 long restis of the nyght and of the day, the oultragious array of
garmentis and of iuellis, withowte takyng eny heede of the differ-
encis of estatis or degreys to whom suche thyngis shulde long vnto,
and also of the fair shewyngis of femynyne delices, ye slepe as
hoggis in the myre and filthe of horrible synnes which hathe
15 brought yow full nye thende of your goode dayes. Ye stop your
erys from all good amonycyons. But yet this shal be done vndir
shuche condicyon that the lenger ye dwelle in this lyf afor rehercid
the nerear shall ye be the [dredfull] daye of your exterminacion,
and so long ye may vse it and take so moche therof that ye may for
20 euermore be in daunger. But Semiramys, the noble lady of Babi-
col. 2 lone, lefte that one (half) of hir / heer vnkempte while she was in
kembyng for cause of a messaunger that came to hir and tolde that
a cite of hirs rebellid against hir; [and] whanne she had wele vndirstonde the messaunger which was come into hir closette, she lefte
25 that othir parte of hir heer vntressid and owte of ordinaunce vnto
the tyme that she had by veray force and myght of armys put the
cite ageyne vndir subieccion. Also the ladyes of Rome aftir the
pituous Bataile of Caves chaunged the richesse of their array and
the queyntise of their estatis. Also the [cuntre] of Langdok, whanne
30 it was takyn and put vndir by Kyng Iohn, chaungid their goodly
array, both men and women, levyng all maner signis of plesaunce
and ioye. O what men be ye or what hardnes restithe in your coragis
that woll suffre yourself willefully to be lost and wolle nat leve
suche thingis as b(r)ingith yow into perdicion?
35 Lerne to know your infelicite by the happy fortunes of your

6 nor] not N   9 and] the NSJ les D   11 of 2] on (ins. on line) J
11–12 differencis] difference N sing. D   16 amonycyons] monyciouns (ha canc.
before word) N   18 nerear] ner NSJ   be] to add. NSJ   23 and] NSJ
a R   24 she] scho SJ   26 that] om. N   27 vndir] hir add. NSJ
om. D   29 cuntre] NSJ counte R pays D   Langdok] lanloke N
30 their] thei N   31 signis] fygurs N remonstrance D

som there is that nyght and day by wo[o]des and feldys take thaire
pleasirs in hauking and huntyng, and othir ther is that will slee
horses to purchase the couetise and worldly rychesse and othir
pleasirs, the whiche for to gete worship and to acquite thaire /   4
naturall trauth and dutee thei wold nat lose the ease and rest of oon   f. 8ᵛ
nyght ner [suffer] the daunger of a straite or diseasid herburgh.   (p. 16)

Than ye seeke diligently the swete sauours of meites, the longe
restes borowed of the nyght vpon the day, the outrageous clothinges
and iuells, taking no kepe to the estates and degrees to whom thei
be longinge; and the plesaunt woordes and delites femynyns causeth   10
you to slepe as hogges in the ordure and filth of the horrible synnes,
which haue brought you so miche to the ende of your dayes. Stoppe
your earis to alle good excitacions, but it shall be vpon suche condicion that the lenger that therynne ye dwelle the more shall approche
the doolefull day of your determinacion, and so longe may ye vse   15
it and so miche that it will bringe you to the miserable perpetuite.
Semiramis of Babilonye left half the heere of hir hed vnkemyd and
vndrest whan the rebellion of hir citee was anuncied hir. And so hir
hed abode half vndrest till suche tyme as by might of armys shee
had brought hir citee in subieccion. The ladies of Rome aftir the   20
miserable Bataile of Cannes chaunged the richesse of there habites
and fresshnesse of thaire estates. The cuntre of Languedoke aftir
the taking of Kinge Iohn chaunged thaire clothing, both men and
wommenne, in leuing all demonstraunce of gladnesse and festiuite.
What maner men be ye ner what hardinesse haue ye in your corages   25
that suffre and endure thus to be lost wilfully and will not leeue
that that bringeth you to perdicion and draweth you to deth, your
armes aboute the nek?

Lerne to knowe your infelicite by the happy fortunes of your

1 woodes] wordes U bois D   12 haue] *word probably originally* han,
e *somewhat apart from* u U   28 nek] Nota bene processum *add. in red* U

enemyis, and remembir yow wele that the yse of wyntir nor the /
f. 8 scarcete of mete ne the pestilence of contagius maladies, the long
[travaile of] weryng their harneice as wele by nyght as by day lettith
them nothing of their strong enterprises nor it lettithe them not to
5 ley seegis nor to kepe the feelde. But all your dedis be voydid away
thorough euery light encheson or particular wille. Euery good
tydingis seme to yow a victorye, and euery euile tidingis abaschith
yow as people discomfited in bataile. For your vicious and your
fleing coragis be not affirmed to eny maner of goodnes; your wittis
10 be travailid for to accroche grete goodis and thorough your vanyteis
wastyn them ageyne; your vndirstonding is occupied in assemblyng
and gettyng the same, but ye have nat the wisdom to employe them
to the best entent.

Wold God it war wretyn in your mynde hough moche myght
15 profite the good gouernaunce of lordis in departyng their rewardis
to the goode men and to do punicion vpon the evill doars withowt
col. 2 fauo/ur of eny singular affeccions. For the correccion of evill folkis
takith away the boldenesse of evill doars, and the comfortyng of the
good doars is the doublyng of their good dedis. Moreouir I dar
20 wele say that the veray knowyng of the good people from the eville
most affirmith and mayntenith princes in their lordshippis and
magesteis. It was nat withowt cause that the noble Romayns made
ymages of brasse (and) of othir metallis in remembraunce of suche
wourthy persones as increscid their lordshippis and the comon
25 wele of their cite.

Now lette vs holde our peece at this tyme to speke eny more of
suche thingis, notwithstonding I cannat blame them to moche. For
nough I am come to that poynte to shewe yow shortly the encheson
of the quarell which owght to putt in yow the hardnes of corage.
30 For lette vs furst vndirstonde what people thei be that mak yow
this warre. And yf ye serche wele thei be come of the lyne of
f. 8ᵛ Forgestus and / Engestus, Saxons which as souldiours comen to
reskew the Kyng of Grette Brytaigne, which was oppressid with
long werris, and eftirward toke the londe and kept it to their own

1 of] your add. canc. R   3 travaile of] NSJ travelyng and R travail
des D   weryng] NSJ of add. R   5 to] om. NSJ   6 or] of J ou D
8 as] a add. NSJ   your 2] om. NSJ   9 eny] no NSJ   11 in]
a add. J   12 the 2] þat N   16 vpon] to N   17 correccion] correccions N sing. D   18 the 3] om. NSJ   26 at] as J   28 I am] tr.
NSJ   29 corage] couragys N pl. D   30 mak yow] maketh N
32 Forgestus] horgestus N Forgestus D

enmyes, and remembre that the frostes of wynter ner the scant
diminuacion of vitaill, the pestilence of the contagious seknesse ner
the longe trauaile to bere harneys nyght and day breketh nat the
grete / entreprises ner thay let nat to ley seeges and kepe feeldys.   f. 9
And all youre dedes shall be lettid and lest for euery litle occasion   (p. 17)
or particuler volunte. All maner of good tydinges abaisshith you as   6
though ye were discounfite in bataile. For your volage hertes and
viciouse corages be in nothinge ferme ner stable; your engynes
labour to gete richesse, and your vanitees wastith theim; youre wytt
is occupied to gadre theym and assemble, but your wysdome is lost   10
as to their dispoosing.

Now wold God it were writen in your remembraunce how miche
it is profitable in the exaltacion of seignurye for to departen the
guerdon of the good and to punisshe theim that ben yll withoute
folowinge the singuler affeccion. For the correccion of the yll   15
dooers withdraweth the boldenesse of yll doing, and the knowlege
of the good deedys double the corages in goodnesse. And feerther-
more I dar well say that well vndirstandinge and knowinge the good
men, whiche seldom can preece or boost, and to vndirstande the
yll, that will drawe bak at neede, is the principall and souereyne   20
cause that confermyth and maynteynyth the princes in theire
seignuries and magestes. Also it was nat withoute cause that for
memorye and laude the Romayns were wont to make ymages of
diuers metalles with artes and werkes triumphous of suche as lyued
in vertuous disposicions for to encrece the regaltee of the Romayns   25
and for to augmente the comon wele of thaire citee.

Than let us cesse of all theis maters rehercing, hou be it that I
cannat ouermiche blame ne repreeue your deedys. But come we to
declare briefly that the iust querele, though it were so that therynne
ye coude finde noon othir encheson, it ought to renwe the hardi-   30
nesse of your corages. First vndirstande what they be and against
whom ye most make werre. And yf therof ye enquere truly they be
of the / kynne of Fergestus and of Angestus, the Saxons whiche as   f. 9ᵛ
saudoiers came to the Kynge of Grete Brytayne whan he was   (p. 18)
oppressid with werrys, and aftir that they toke and o[c]cupied the   35

---

6 tydinges] *probable om. here* U *see n.*   20 will] *that will add.* U
32 most] o *made into* v U *cf. 153/11*   35 occupied] oocupied U

vse whanne thei founde the kyng dispurveid of his good knyghtis
thorough meenys of the werre, and vndir a feynid colour [of] peece
slowghen the remenaunt of the noblest of the londe. Thes ben of
the lyne of him that putt owte and slewghe his soueraigne lord,
5 Kyng of Englond, and tyrauntly vsurpid vpon his lordshippis. Also
thei be the same that oftentymes haue made werre vpon your fadirs
and predecessours, brent and wastid your feldis and townes and
vtterly haue desiyrd to destroye and bryng to nought your noble
generacion. It be thei also that be ioynid and alyid with your rebellis
10 and vntrue people of this realme, and in fortifiyng of their vnresonable quarelle thei haue ioynid them to the sustentacion and mayn-
col. 2 tenaunce of your vntrue subgettis. / Yet on that othir parte I woll
shewe yow reason which ought to enflame your coragis and geue
yow suerte and confidence. Remembir yow wele that your olde
15 naturall enemyes, assailing yow by their own enterpryse, which
come and chalenge your contrey and londe vpon yow, thei ben the
people that maken on yow asawlte, and ye be the defendours.
The(y) woll tak away your liberte, and ye be bounde to defende
yow from thraldom. Thei desyir your distruction and dethe, and
20 nature byndith yow to defende your suerte and your life. [Thei
enforce hemselfe to ravysshe and take away be strenkith the lyf]
and [the] substaunce of your wifis and of your childern, which
nature constreynith yow to norishe swetely and love them tendirly.
Also thei woll put owte your rightfull prince and naturall soueraigne
25 lorde, which ye be bounde to defende bothe with body and goodis.
Thei entende also to ocupye the royall seete, puttyng yow to
myschef by their grete tyrannye. Now call ageyne to yow the
conquestis of your noble predecessours which subdewed a grete
f. 9 partye of Grece / and brought it vndir their subieccion, and yet by
30 this day is by their name callid Gallo-Grecye, and conquerid Rome
evin to the Capitale. Yet ye which dwellyn in this realme and have
your lyvyng in the same liste nat to socour nor defende yourself.
For ye suffir to be as a people exilyd from your own countrey,
which ye be lothe to leve and yet ye woll not kepe it. What maner
35 of thing thanne is that that makith colde and abaschith such wise
your courages? Parde your enemyes be nat inmortall nor lengar of

2 peece] pitee N paix D   4 of him] om. ND   6 the] om. N
9 It] yet N   13 reason] resons NSJ pl. D   to] om. NSJ   16 and
chalenge] and chalengynge SJ chalengyng N see n.   17 yow] a add. N
22 the] NSJ your R la D   28 conquestis] conqueste J pl. D   29 it]
om. J   by] at NSJ   32 to] om. N

cuntre for theimself at suche tyme as they founde the kynge dispurueid of knyghthode thrugh fortune. And thus by treason vnder
feynynge of peas they slwe the surpluse of the nobles of the lande.
It is the lyne of him that put downe and slwe his souereyn lord, the
Kynge of Ynglond, for to vsurpe tirauntlye the seigneurye. They 5
ben thoo that often han made werre to your faders and predecessours, brent and wasted your feeldes and townes. And they ben
descended of suche lyne that thaire naturall desire is holly to bringe
to nought your generacion. They ben thoo that ben ioyned and
allied to your vntrue rebellys of this reaume, and [to] querele 10
vnresonable they haue ioyned vntrouth, supportinge the false and
vntrue deedys of thaire allies and felawys. On the othir partie I will
declare the resons that aught your corages to enflamme and put you
in suerte and confidence. Your auncient and naturall enmyes saute
you by entreprise of armes, chalenginge your land and your cuntree. 15
They ben assailinge and ye ben deffendinge. They wold bringe
your libertee into seruitute, and ye aught to defende yourself from
thaire seruage. They seeke your deth and perdicion, and nature
bindeth you to defende your suerte and your lyf. Thay doo thaire
power to take and rauissh by force the lyf and substance of your 20
wifes and children, whiche nature constraineth you switely to
noryssh and tendrely to loue. They will put oute your rightfull
prince and naturall lord, the whiche your bodyes with handes and
feet aught to defende. And they entende to occupie the royall seete 24
for to / def[oule] you vnder tirannye. Right lothly ye wold take in f. 10
hand the conquestes of your predecessours, whiche gate grete parte (p. 19)
of Greke in thaire subieccion, which cuntre is called yit Gallo-
Grecide. And also they conquerid Rome vnto the Capitolle. And
the erthe wherevpon ye enhabite and feede and susteyne you ye
cannat socour nor defende. And ye suffre you for to be as in exile 30
in your own cuntree, whiche ye may nat leeue nor ye cannat kepe
it. What thinge is that that so miche c[oo]lith and abateth your
corages? The enmyes ben nat made of erthe inmortall nor

25 defoule] defende U defouler D   32 coolith] callith U refroider D

lyfe thanne ye be. Thei haue none othir speris ne harneys but ye
haue as good, nor thei be nat of so grete noumbur but ye ar as
(grete as) thei or gretter. Their vre shall nat alweyes be fortunable
in their dedis forasmoch as fortune is alweye variable. Thanne of
5 veray force if thei have eny avauntage more thanne ye haue, it must
nedis be in the hardines of their coragis. But and ther be enythinge
col. 2 (þat) / puttith you vndir them it is nothinge ellis but the mul[ti]tude
of your synnys, which puttith your hertis to flight and causith the
schynyng of your glorye to be quenchid and made derke to the
10 destruction of your lordeshippis withowt seching of any remedye
in lesse that Almighty God put to His graciouse hand, whereto me
thinckith ye put yow in no devoir for to gette His grace, and therfor
it may nat long tarye but that the name of Fraunce shal be caste
downe to your pardurable shame and malyson.

15 <center>[The Auctour]</center>

    This full soroufull lady with right a wroth harte spake full egrely
to the thre persones afor rehercid, the teeris rennyng downe by hir
yghen as lytill smalle brokis, with a ferefull looke, as a parsonne
hauyng by the seid thre grete wronge. Thanne thes thre, which of
20 long space aftir had holde their pees, bygvnne to grugge, and
f. 9ᵛ namely he which / laye flatte on the erthe full of sorow and hevinesse
and soo atteynte with all evilles that no maner of vertu nor strength
was lefte in hym save onely a sympill voyce and crye, which ganne
to speke and answere as hereaftir folowith:

25 <center>[The Peple]</center>

    Allas modir, which somtyme haddist grette habundaunce of
plenteuous prosperite and now full of anguysch and hertely sorow
and in maner of declyne from the royall ligne, I beleve right wele
and take in gree thi correccion, knowing that thi compleintis be nat
30 vnreasonable ne withowte cause. Wherfor I take a bittir displesaunce
in the same forasmoche as the grete myschef, the repreef and hurte
lyeth vpon me, and therfor ye ought nat to haue me suspecte. But
inasmoch as I bere the blame and the scharpe penaunce of othir
col. 2 personis, I may be wele likened [to] the asse that / berith the inport-
35 able chargis, and am betyn and prikkid to do [and] suffur suche

2 of] in NSJ en D   5 it] is N   6 enythinge] any N   11 that]
than SJ   15 The Auctour] *at bottom of f. 11 and top of f. 11ᵛ in scribe's hand* S
18 a 1] *om.* NSJ   19 seid] side N   wronge] wronges N   20 aftir
had] *tr.* N   26 grette] *om.* NSJD   31 forasmoche] inasmoch N   34 be
wele] *tr.* N   34–5 inportable] ynpotable S

indeuiable more than ye be. They haue nothir glayues nor harneys
but ye haue of the same, nor they ben nat of so grete nombre but
that ye be as many or more. Thaire happe shall nat be fortune
allweyes to be to thaim propice, whiche of hir nature is euer
chaungeable to alle maner of peeple. Than most we say yf they 5
haue auauntage and ben exalted vpon us, it comyth of manhode
and hardinesse of corage. And yf ye be deprimed and vnderlaied
be of your enmyes it is through the multitude of your synnes,
which conuerteth and turneth your cowarde hertes to flitte. And
so ye suffre the luminarye of your glorie to be skonched and put 10
oute, and your seignurie be destrued beforn your yien withoute any
seekinge of remedye saf oonly that the grace of God werkith of
itself, the whiche to des[erue] ye seet litle payn ne deuoire. And
thus may it nat longe endure but ye shall see the name of Fraunce
in dekay and ruine to your perpetuell schame and malediccion. 15

The Acteure

Theise wordes right egyrly and with angry hert this woofull lady
seid vnto the .iij. persones be/foresaid. And of hir faire yien, wherof f. 10ᵛ
the streames of teeris were rennyng, she lokid so affrayingly vpon (p. 20)
thaire disaraye and countenaunce that it seemyd well that she felt 20
hirself by theim iniuried and disknowen. And aftir that that yche
of theim had kept silence a longe space of tyme, he that lay reuersid
vpon the erthe, pleynyng and languisshinge and so fer ataint with
importable doloure and care that in him was left no vertu sauf
oonlye the vois and the crye, began to speke in the maner folowinge: 25

The Peeple

A, a, moder, of olde tyme habundaunt in plentefull prosperite
and now full of anguissh and heuinesse for the decline of thy noble
lyne, I receyue well in gree thy correccion. And I knowe well that
thy complayntes be nat vnresonable nor withoute grete cause. But 30
it is to me right bittir the displesaunce that I haue of this myschief,
the losse and reproche also, and that thou shuldist holde me suspect
whan of othir mennys gilte I ber the moost sharpe penaunce. I am
as thee asse that berith the fardell importable, and I am beten and

---

1 indeuiable] Nota bene *add. in red in margin by passage* U   13 deserue]
desire U deservir D

thyngis as is nat in my power. [I am allso the butt ayenst whom]
euery man shotith the arous of tribulacion. O vnhappy and soroufull caytif, from whens comyth this false vsage that thus turnyth vp
so downe the ordir of iustice, which euery man hath ouir me as
5 moche power as myght woll geve him. The labour of my hondis
norischith the slowthe [of] idill people, and thei rewarde me ageyn
with persecucion of hungir and of sworde. I susteyne their lyf with
my swete and travaile of my body, and thei make me werre with
ther outragis, which hath brought me to lyve as a begger. Thei lyve
10 vpon me, and I dey for them. Thei ought to kepe and diffende me
from [the] enemyes, but allas thei kepe (me) wele inough from
etyng my brede in suerte. O Lorde God, hough myght eny man in
this werke haue perfight pacience whanne to my persecucion may
f. 10 nothing / be ioyned but deth? I dey evyn as I go on the erthe for
15 defaulte of myn own goodis that I haue gotyn. Also I see wele that
labour hath lost [his] hoope; marchaundise canne fynde no [redy]
way to have his dew course; all goodis ar takyn away save onely
suche as is [defendid] by the spere and the sworde. Wherefor I haue
non othir of hoope in my lyve save by dispeyr leve my staate and
20 do as thei do that haue dispoiled [me], which louith bettir the pray
than honours of the werre that is in this realme. But it is a pryve
robbery, a thefte which takith awey by foorce the comon wele of
realme vndir the colour of armys, and is ravischid away by violence
for defaute of iustice and good gouernaunce. The werris ben
25 cried and the standardis be reysid on hight ayenst the enemyes,
but the exployt of their dedis be ayeinst me to the distruccion of
my powr sustenaunce and of my wretchid lyfe. Thei feyght with our
col. 2 enemyes with langage / and wordis, but with me thei fyght with
dedis.

30   O modir, beholde and avise wele my sorowfull affliccions, and
thow shalt knowe wele that alle comfortis and helpis failyn me. The
feldis haue no fredom to kepe me in suerte nor I haue nat whereof
to labour therinne to furnisch suche fruytes as shulde be gaderid to
the norishyng of my life. Alle is put in othir mennes handis, closid

---

1 I . . . whom] NSJ and anempst me R Je suis le bersault contre qui D *see n.*
7 their] the N leur D   8 my 1] the SJ *om.* N la D   11 the] NSJ their R
des D   13 my] perfight *add.* RNSJ *om.* D *see n.*   18 and] be *add.* N
19 othir] trest *add. ins.* J *see n.*   save] but N   staate] astate N   21 honours]
the honours NS the honour J l'onneur D   werre] *possible om. here* RNSJ
see n.   22 of] the *add.* NSJ *om.* D   31 thow shalt] than shalt thu N
34 Alle] þis *add.* N Tout D

constrained to do that I may nat doo. I am the quyntyne agains
whom iche man shootes arowes of tribulacion. A, a, woofull caityf,
from whens comyth custume whiche hath so frowarde(ly) turned
the ordre of iustise so that iche man hath right vpon me aftir that
he is of power. The labour of myn handes susteyneth the cowardes 5
and noughty whiche persecute me with hunger and glayue. I hold
vp thaire lyues with swete and trauaill of my body, and they make
me werre which bringeth me in beggernesse. They lifen by me, and
I dye for theim. They aught to defende me from the enmyes, but
elas they kepe me well from etynge my brede in sikernes. Hou 10
shulde I now / be in parfite pacience whan to my per[s]ecucion may f. 11
nothinge be likned sauf oonly deethe? I dye for defaute and neede (p. 21)
of the good that I haue truly gotyn. Labour hath lost his esperaunce. Marchaundise may fynde no wey sauflye to goo and come
and to be preserued in stablenesse. Nor I haue noon othir hope in 15
my lif sauf oonly to lyue all in dispeire, for to doo as they doo that
ben enriched with oure goodys, the whiche louen bettir to take a
praye than the worship of the werres. I see all that is taken with
riall power is well taken. What called I werre? For it is no werre
that is kept in this land; it is a pryue robberye, a theft out of alle 20
mesure, force publique vnder shadowe of armes, and violent rapine
through defaute of iustice and good ordinaunce. Men cryen to doo
armes and the standardys ben displayed agains the enmyes, but the
verray deede is agains me to the destruccion of my pouere substaunce and of my miserable lif. The enmyes ben foughten with by 25
grete woordes, but I am foughten with by deed.

A, a, modre, considre and see my sorowfull affliccion, and than
shall ye knowe that all refuges faille me at neede. The feeldys haue
no fraunchise to ministre sure dwellinge, nor I haue no more wherwith I may labour theym for to gader the frute of oure sustenaunce. 30
All that is nat enclosid and fortified with walles and dykes is getyn

withinne the wallis and diches that I may nat come ther nygh. And
now we must leve the feldis deserte and abandone them to wylde
bestis and to them that be dispurveid and owt of all confortes,
lesing their livis aftir their goodis for hevinesse. The schare and
5 cultre, which were wont to eary the londe, is turned vnto the
mortall sworde, and myne handis that of long tyme haue borne the
chargis whereof othir men hath gotyn their easis and takyn awey
f. 10ᵛ all that I haue and yet wolde haue more thanne I may gete. / Wherfor it is force that the body fall into declyne and myserye for default
10 of good, and so in sorow vndir disperpulid lordeship and charge of
household I begge. I live in deying, seing byfore [me] the deth of
my wyfe and of my powr childern, which daily aschyn me sustenaunce, and liyth nat in my power to confort them, and I myself
as a man lokeing hevyly and sorowfully for hungir and defaulte,
15 abydyng my last day. Of the surplus a man nedith to aske no questions, for the werkis ben wittenessed so opinly of this inportable
famyn which [re]nnethe and shal be vpon the people so bittirly that
it wol be to late to call ayein to mynde the habundaunce of tyme
passid. And this shall follow: that natur, which that techith euery
20 man to susteyne his lif through the which recreation of mete, must
slake the brydill and yevith them licence to ravisch and to take it
col. 2 by force whersomeuir thei goo, which now beginnyth / right
mervelously and the conclusionis shal be soo dowtefull that thei
shal be more ferfull to se thanne it shal be me(r)veylous to
25 ymagine.

O it is a full noyous thing to speke of this, but (it) is a more
[grevous] thing to susteyne my [pituous] desolacion, for I am put
in exile, prisoner in my howse, assailid of my frendis and of them
that shold be my defendours, and I werre with souldiours wherof
30 the payment is made with my propir goodis. And for to make an
abhominable some of my evill and infinyte mischaunces, I se non
othir exploit in the warres of this realme but onely londes forwildid
and contreis disenhabited, multitude of wedowis and orphelyns,

4 The] of the NSJ *see n.*   5 eary the] eeryth N   vnto] into N
8 and . . . haue] *om.* N *see n.*   9 is] no *add. ins.* J *om.* D   into]
in NSJ   15 nedith] not *add.* N   17 rennethe] vnnethe RNSJ   shal
be] shall NSJ courra D   18 to 2] NSJ to *add.* R   19 that 2] *om.* NSJ
20 which] wyth (*ins.*) S   24 to se] *om.* N a veoir D   merveylous] *two r's
ins.* R   27 grevous] NSJ pituous R griefve D   pituous] SJ pitevous N *om.* R
piteuse D   30 an] *om.* J   31 abhominable] abhomynale SJ   mischaunces]
myschaunce N *pl.* D   32 realme] royaulme NSJ   forwildid] forweldyd J

and purchasid into othir mennys handes with othir grete losse that
men may see dailye. Now most the feldys be lefte deserte and
vnhabited and habandouned to the wilde bestes. And they that by
true trauaile of marchaundise haue socoured and holpen many
oone, most now stande with the losse, dispurueid, and with greu- 5
ouse, thoughtfull sorowe lose theire lifes. The soc of the plough is
turned into mortall glayue. And myn / handes, which han doon the f. 11ᵛ
laboure wherof othir men gader the ease in habundaunce, ben full (p. 22)
oft distressid vnto brestinge oute of blood because I gif nat that
that I haue and that I haue not. And thus the body most decline 10
for defaute of goodes, and that, langwysshing vnder lordship
destrued, charged with beggyng hunger, thus to lyf in deyinge,
seeing the deth of my pouere wyf and my little children and daily
desiringe my deth, whiche were to me nothinge soo leef for short-
inge of my payne, as he that with sharpnesse of hunger and defaute 15
of counforte is laid in the moost doloreux wyse to his last day. Of
the surpluse it neede nat make nother enquest nor demaunde, for
the deedes ben soo publique and the witnesse is hunger intollerable,
whiche rayneth and shall rayne so bitterly to euery man that all to
late shall the grete habundaunce passed be remembred in soroufull 20
wepinge and defaute of resonable departing of the remanent of
goodes, whiche ben consumed by outrages. And it will ensue that
nature, which techith iche man to conserue his lif by recreacion of
meites, shall slake the bridell and the licence to take it by force,
wherof the begynnynges ben allredy right merueilous, and the con- 25
clusions shall be so redoutable that it will be more dredfull to see
than it is merueillous to the ymaginacion.

Right ennoyouse and miche more to susteyn is my pitouse
desolacion, for I am in myn owne hous as in exile, prisonner by
myn own handes, sauted by my defendours and werride to the 30
raunsoms wherof the paymentes ben made by my propre castell.
I see noon othir weye actuell of the longe werrys of thys reaume
sauf oonly land in destruccion, cuntre inhabitable, in multitude of

caytivis, beggers and wretchis, and mutacion of goodis from the
handis of suche as haue rightfully gotin them into the hondis of
suche as be myghty and mischevous men. And in suche wise is
chaungid [the] comon welth and put owt of his naturall course so
f. 13   that / dueryng the fersenes of werre the lawe holdith his peaxce and
6   iustice hath lost his seete of iugement wherin he was wonte to sitte,
and nough wille rewlith and iugith as maistres and makith such
commaundement that what force willith and shewith by power she
fulfillith, an what she fulfillith she alowith, and what she approwith
10   she enhaunsith, affirmith, auctorysith and nat punyschith. And so
the policie of vs Frenschmen may be likenyd to the feble house-
holder[e] which sparpelith and wastith his possessid substaunce
afore a newe prouision had. Thei ete ther lande or it may growe and
voyde their garners owt of season with so grete mesures that at the
15   most nede the brede failith. The ampte purueith and sparith his
store in the season of somer anempste the hardnes of the colde
wynter and ordeyneth all his necessiteys or nede come. Ha, ye
Frenschmen, ye do euyn the contrarye, for ye waste and spende
col. 2 afore the hande / all suche as shulde helpe yow in your grette
20   necessiteis, and putte the chargis of your werre vpon the powr
people, which oughte to live vndir yow in suerte and to be socourid
ayeinst the contrarious fortunes.

   Yet and I sawe that by knyghtly hardines of the warre, wherof
ye make so grette a brute, that the enemyes myght fele the losse and
25   hurtis, thanne my herte warre the more [easy] to be susteyned, but
all tymes to suffure and fele no maner of goodenes maketh mannes
corage to fall in dispeyre and entirly lose his pacience; and whanne
pacience failith, which susteyneth the coragis ayenst the hardines
of fortune and holdith the othir vertues alyed and ioyned vnto him,
30   but doubte ye nat but thanne thei be disseuerid and departid. For
oftetymes it fallith that whanne pacience failith, all obeisaunce,
subieccion and constaunce failen, and turneth the ordir of vertue
into disordinate confusion, as we may note and take exsaumple
f. 13ᵛ of / Kyng Roboam, which for the grette oppressions of his people
35   wolde nat make lesse ne ceesse his malice ne vse the councell
of olde wise men, but sewed the opinyons of the vnlerned yong

      1 caytivis] and *add.* N *om.* D   2 as] y *add.* J   4 the] NSJ to R
11–12 householdere] NSJ householders R *sing.* D   16 anempste] ayenst
NSJ   18 and spende] *om.* NSJD   21 to 1] *om.*NSJ   27 whanne]
his *add.* J *om.* D   28 the 1] his J les D   30 but 1] *om.* NSJ   36 of 1]
his *add.* NSJ des D

wydowes and orphenys, caitifes, beggers and desolate, and mutacion of goodes taken from theym / that haue truly goten theyme and   f. 12
brought to the gretter and mightier rauysshers. And all thinge is so   (p. 23)
lad and chaunged out of kende that thrugh the impediment of
armes the lawes ben cessid and iustice hath left his tribunall seete   5
wherynne sitteth voluntary wyll, whiche hath made suche an acte
that that he may doo bi force he willeth, that he willeth he fullfilleth, that he fullfilleth he prouueth, and that that he prouueth is
alloude, exalted and vnpunisshid. By a right comparison the
polecye of this land may now be likened to the hous of an yll   10
husbond, the whiche destrueth his present substaunce or he make
purveaunce of that is comynge. He etteth his vigen in vergeus and
auoideth his garners out of season in hepyd mesur so that bred
failleth him at his neede. The pyssemyre porueieth himself in
somyr agains the hard and colde ceason and he maketh his pur-   15
ueaunce or he be sodenly taken with neede. Ellas men out of regle,
ye doo me contrarye and waste before the hande that that shulde
socoure you in othir grete needys, and ye put the burdon of youre
werre in the charge of the peeple, the whiche shulde vnder you
dwelle hole and sounde as a sparynge for socours at a grete neede   20
and for to haue recours in peruerse fortune.

Yf I might see that through knyghtly hardynesse in the werre,
whereynne ye make grete brute, the enmyes shulde fele som losse
or domage, myn hurtes shuld be the more easy to bere; but allwey
to suffre and endure, hauyng no hope of comfort, causeth a mannes   25
corage to falle in dispeire and vtterly lose pacience. And yf so be
that pacience faile, alle maner of obeisaunce and counstaunce most
needys faile, and turneth the ordre of vertu into disordinate confusion. And good exaumple / may be taken by the Kyng Roboam,   f. 12ᵛ
whiche for the oppression of his peeple, the whiche he wold nat   (p. 24)
ceese nor amende, setting apart the counseill of the auncient, sage   31

27 pacience] *probable om. here* U *see n.*   30 whiche 2] whiche *add.* U

men. He loste therefor [of] his lordeshippis x lignagis and ane half.

The people of a realme ben full feble whanne the nobles and the clergy may nat suffice to kepe vp the body of policie ne susteyne
5 their lif and ther estate. And yet I mervaile not that it is thus abandoned to all infelicite, for I se no similitude to this body but that the policie of Frenshmen may be likenid vnto a wodman which with his tethe bitith and raseth away his own membres. Wherfor the auncient Romayns purueid them wele ayeinst suche grette
10 inconueniences; for kepyng the parties of their commynte, euery man in his dignite and in his ordre, stablisch[ed] the tribus of the people, whoos office was to susteyne, defende and kepe in fredome
col. 2 the comons ayeinst / the senatours and the power of þe nobles. But her it is nat so, for I am lette fall in the handis of robbers takyng
15 their praye, which constrayne me to crye vengeaunce to Allmyghty God for the inportable and soore affliccions which thei haue putt vnto me for lacke of helpe. For it is oftentymes founde in the olde writyngis that for the myserye of the powr people [and] the wep- yngis and sorowis of them that must nedis suffur, the diuine iuge-
20 mentis hath yevyn full egre and sharpe punycion. Wherfor I counseile euery man that fyndith hymself gilti in this trespas that he bewar, for it is not to thynke that the turmentis of so many coragis and the pituous and lamentable voice which addressyn their cryes, wepyngis and compleintis vp to the high hevyn move nat
25 with pite the mekenes of the right mercifull and all-puysaunt Creatour[e], that His iusti[ce] procedith nat to the confusion of theim þat cause the iniquityf wikednes.

f. 14   And I, abydyng my deth and in dis/payre of my lif, can seche no ferther for my recoueriere. And in thes wise, my right doubted
30 modir, I discharge myn herte and exempte myself from the grevous blame of which I ber the peyne. And I reporte me to thi good iuge- ment whoo ought to bere this blame. I may be holde as excused and put owt of this repreef and blame, for sorow and mysease chasen

1 of] *om.* RNSJ de D   lordeshippis] lordshipp and NSJ seigneurie D
3 realme] royaulme SJ royall lyne N royaume D   full] but N   6 abandoned]
haboundyd N   this] his N ce D   7 vnto] to NSJ   8 bitith and]
om. N mort et D   9 purueid] purveyth J   10 inconueniences]
inconvenientes NSJ   19 and] the *add.* NSJ   26 Creatoure]
Creatours RS creatures NJ createur D   iustice] NSJ iusticie (ci *roughly
made*) R   to] *om.* J a D   27 the] theis NSJ   iniquityf] inyquytes
N iniquytyse S inquietyse J   29 recoueriere] recouerere N   30 exempte]
exempe J   32 ought] hought N   33 mysease] myschefe N mesaise D

men and folowing the assottid oppinions of the yonge menne
vnwytty, he lost of his seigneurie .x. kindereddes and an half.

The peeple is a notable membre of a reame withoute the whiche
the chirche nor the nobles may neuir suffise to make a body of
policye nor to susteyne theire estates nor thaire liues. Nor I haue 5
no grete merueile that the peeple shulde be abaundouned to sorow
and infelicite and persecu[t]ed by the tothir membres, subgites to
the same chief. Nor I can see no bettyr similitude to this purpose
but that the policie of this lande is like to the furious man which
in a woodnesse biteth and renteth his othir membres. Right well 10
purveid to suche an inconuenient the auncient Romayns whan that,
for to kepe the parties of thaire comonte iche in thaire dignitee and
ordre, they establisshed the tributys of the peeple, which had
officers in the same to susteyne and defende his fraunchise agains
the senat and puissaunce of the noble men. But so it is nat with me, 15
for withoute helpe and socours I am bilafte in the handes of
rauisshours as a praye to thoo that constreyne me aftir thaire will.
A, God, I desire vengeaunce vpon theim for the importable and
hard affliccion that they gyf me. For it is often seen in the scriptures
for the miserye of the pouere peeple and the weping of the sufferers 20
the diuine iustice yiueth sentence of right egre punicion. Than let
him beware that knoweth himself gilty, for it is nat to (thinke) that
so many turmentid corages and vois moost piteable, the whiche as
in dispaire addressen theire kryes and playnynge to heuyn, but 24
that they shulde meeue to / pitee the clemence of the moost mercy-   f. 13
full and allmighty Creatore and that Is iustice [shulde] socour (p. 25)
thaim to the confusion of thoo wherof procedeth suche iniquitees.

And I, that is abiding my deth and dispaired of my lyf, can no
ferther to recouer in no partye. And thus I discharge myn hert
agains the, modir moost redoutable, exempt of the gilt and of the 30
grete harmys wherof I bere the payn, and rapoort me to thy good
iugement to knowe in whom is the blame. For I aught well to be
holden excused and left as a caytyf withoute putting to my miserye
blame and reproche. For sorowe and vnease chacen me to deth so

2 half] Nota bene *add. in red in margin by paragraph* U   7 persecuted]
persecuced U   22 thinke] tkink *canc.* thinke *ins. in margin* U

me to the dethe so straitely that I am dryed vp in þe brest withowte hoope of any amendement. Wherfor I canne no more but cursse theym that don me this cruelle, pleynyng my hert sorow owte of the which Almyghty God for His grete pyte sende me shortely an
5 ende, for I may nat dwelle therin longe (but) as a wretche owte of all conforte.

[The Auctour]

Thanne sodanly he helde his pees, which, for mysease of his body and lacke of mete, his speche and his spiritis wer woxen feble, and
col. 2 as a man fulfilled with sorow myght vnne/the speke. Thanne he
11 that was armyd toke vpon him for to speke with an high and wroth herte suche wourdis as heraftir folowis:

[The Knyght]

Nowgh may a man clerely se the litle constance of thi chaunge-
15 able corage, [peple] dissaveable and light to dissave, whanne thou const nat suffre the ease of pees nor thow may nat susteyne nor ber the hardnes of the werre. For as soone as thow waxest riche and plentuous of good thow canste nat lyve with[oute] murmour and blamyng thi bettirs, but as soone as the hardnesse of the werr,
20 which by thyne owne purchase cometh vnto the, anone thow art enclyned to all seducions and maist not susteyne nor bere theim, but sodanly goost from the wey of true obeisaunce. Thow pleinest vpon me and cryest vengeaunce to God of þe evils and hurtis that
f. 14ᵛ thow thiself hast purchasid, nat iuge/ing thiself nor thin owne
25 defaultis, but makest noyse and clamour vpon thi present losses and affliccions withowte remembring thyn owne fawtis of tyme passid, which is the cause of thyne owne myschef and of many othir. Remembre the also by hough many vnkyndnes [and] iniurious willes thow hast suffird to passe away the grette swetenes of pees,
30 the suerte of iustice and the grette habundaunce of goodis, which byfore the begynyng of the warres haue endured by long processe in this royalm. Wer nat thow that tyme fulfillid with rychesse,

3 don] haue done NSJ   owte] *om.* N   11 him] *om.* J   and] a
add. NSJ   12 heraftir] *om.* NSJ   14 Nowgh] how J Maintenant D
14–15 chaungeable corage] *tr.* N chaungeably corayge J   15 peple] *written*
as character heading within text NSJ *om.* R peuple D   dissave] us *add.* N
om. D   17 the 1] that N la D   22 true] truth N   26 owne] olde N
28 vnkyndnes] vnkyndenesses SJ   and] NSJ of R et D   30 which]
the *add.* N   32 royalm] royall lyne N royaume D

greuouslye that I drye standing, withoute hope of bettyr. Nor I can
no more sauf oonly curse and banne thaim that doo me this, playnynge my grete dolour, wherof God for His mercy will soon cast me
oute, and briefly to deliuer me out of this languerous lyf sith that
from hensforth I may therynne no lenger dwelle but in miserable 5
orphent[e].

The Acteure

And whan he had said and tolde his complaynte, he heeld his
peas, for thrugh (disease) of body and defaute of meyte his wordys
and his spirites were full weyke, and as he that full soore is en- 10
graiued with sorowe with grete payn might speke a woorde more.
And so he that was in harneys tooke the langage and began to
answere alle on high with angry hert, saying in this wise:

The Knyght   14

Now may men see clierly the little counstaunce / of thy chaunge- f. 13ᵛ
able corage, peeple seduys and light to deceyue, whan thou cannat (p. 26)
suffre the ease of peas nor thou may susteyne the hardnesse of the
werre. For whan thou art in richesse and plente of good, thou
maist nat lyue withouten blaspheme and murmure; and as soone
as the grete presse of the werres comyth vpon the, thou art enclyned 20
to all sedicions, whiche thou maist nat bere withoute foruoyeng of
true obeisaunce. Thou playnyst vpon me, cryeng to God for vengeaunce for the harmys whiche thou hast purchaced, but thou
iugest nat thyself for thyne owne gilte, makyng thy clamoure and
slaunder of thy present losses and affliccions withoute remem- 25
braunce of thy defautes that ben passed which ben therof causers.
Call to thy memorie in how miche ingratitude and iniurious volunte
madly thou hast suffred and passed the grete swetenesse of peas,
the sykernesse of iustice in grete habundaunce of goodes, the
whiche sith .xxx. yeris into the entree of the werres hath endured 30
in this roialme. Was nat thou than replenysht with richesse,

6 orphente] orphent U orphanté D   9 disease] diease *canc.* disease *ins.*
in margin U   20 art] nat *add.* U *om.* D   25 of] of *add.* U   27 miche]
and *add.* U

enuiround with delites and with all fraunchises to vse theim at
thyne owne pleasure? Thenne know thiself atte leeste wey that
thow, thi wif and thi childern ete your brede in suerte, euerych
oone in his place vndir the lordeship [which] was fulfilled with all
5 goodis and pleasaunces and withowte any losse or daunger. Where-
col. 2 for thow oughtest to haue that tyme in thy remembraunce, / for
God knowith what rumour and shamefull sclaundirs thow shewdist
theime that gouernyd the [at] that tyme in vnion and plentuous
tranquillite, which may be callid a grette vnkyndenesse bothe [to]
10 God and to thi prince. But now at this tyme thow must prayse that
thow blamedest so egrely afore this tyme.

O hough daungerous a thyng is it to a corage that knowith nat
his owne condicion whanne he livith in prosperite of worldely
goodis. Yet it is a more harde thing them to endur in ease which
15 cannot remembir themself that fortune may lightly chaunge the
eases into sorowfull myseases. [And] to this purpose a man may
fynde in the Romayns hystories that the long pees vnknowen, the
plente of goodis which make prowde the coragis of vnkynde people,
and the deliciouse idilnesse also, which was occasion of euile dedis,
20 caused the grette batails, the vnlawfull werres and grette discordis
among the Romayns in the tyme of Catilyina, of Silla and of
f. 11 Marrious, / through whom the lordeschip of the Romayns was
more hurte and greuid thanne by straunge enemyes, which is seene
at this day by the grette rwynes befallene in the seid lordeship. An
25 so the folish people which desier nothinge but newe chaunges sech
(and) couet oftymes suche thingis as be vnto them most contrarious. Wherfor I tell the that thi rumours and particular affeccions,
thi lesingis, thy evill wordis and thi light bileve have brought vnto
the this bittir diuision through thi folishe meyens and obstinate
30 willes that thou hast susteyned, which causith the now to fall in
daunger of the werre. For thow woldist neuir ceasse vnto the tyme
that thi perfight peace was trowbelid and chaungid into cruell
diuision, wherof thow hast now more than thow maist bere. And

1 fraunchises] fraunchise N *sing.* D   theim] þen N   2 atte] at the N
at J   5 pleasaunces] plesaunce N pleaunces J   7 shewdist] schewest J
shewethst N   8 theime] then NS   at] NSJ ant R   vnion] vnite J
12 is it] *tr.* N   14 which] þat *add.* N   16 myseases] myschefys N
mysche *canc.* myseases S mesaise D   And] NSJ A R   17 hystories]
storyes NSJ   24 befallene] þat ben fallen NSJ   25 so] *om.* N Ainsi D
27 particular] particulers N   29 thi] the NSJ   meyens] moyens SN
31 woldist] wulst S   32 thi] the J ta D   into] vnto NSJ

enuyrouned with delices, with alle fraunchise to vse theim to thyn
owne pleasir? Be now aknowe that thou, thy wyf, and thy children
were wont to eyte your brede in suertee, ich man vpon his own
place, heped with all maner goodys withoute daunger of losse. Of
that same tyme maist thou haue remembraunce, and God knoweth 5
the brute, the rumore and slaunder opprob[r]iouse whiche at that
tyme thou gaf to theim that reuled and gouerned the in plentefull
vnion and tranquillite. That same ceason thou blamed and held for
yll in right grete ingratitude agains God and thy prince that that
now thou most praise and desire, the whiche beforetyme thou 10
blamed so / egyrly.   f. 14

O what daungerous thinge is in the corage of man that disknoweth (p. 27)
his owne condicion for to lyf in multitude of wordlye good. But yit
more payn it is to endure grete ease to theim that cannat thinke
that fortune may lightly transforme thaim into doloreux disease. 15
To this purpose rehercen the Romayns stories that the longe peas
vnknowen, the plenitude of goodys that causeth presumpcion in
the hertes of thaim that ben ingrate, and the delicatyue ydelnesse,
whiche yiueth occasion to be subtile in yll disposicions, were
causers of the batailes, werres and dissencions amonge the Romayns 20
in the tyme of Catilina, of Silla and of Marius, wherof the seigneurye of the Romayns is more abated and fallen withoute releef
than by straunge and naturall enmyes, whiche seigneurye was
suche and so high, as the stories declaren it. And so the made
peeple that desiren euer mutacion seekith ofte and coueiteth that 25
that to him is most contrarie. Wherfore I tell the that thy rumors
and particuler affeccions, thy lesinge wordes and light beleue haue
sett vpon the this moost bitter diuision. And thrugh the parties that
thou hast madly chosen and susteyned with obstinate volunte is the
werre spronge and agraued. Nor thou woldist cesse till thy parfaite 30
peas was troubled and chaunged into moost cruell diuision, wherof
thou hast inough and more than thou maist bere. And sithen thou

6 and] and *add.* U

forasmoche as thow hast provokid and callid this myschief vnto the, thow muste nedis suffre the pryckyngis of the same, for he that

col. 2 purchasith the werr / shulde gette it vndir suche condicion that he submit himselfe vnto all evile aventours that growen of the werre.

5 So werr of his owne propir natur comyth for lacke of iustice. For and we war all iust and true we had no nede to (þe) power of armys. But and thow wold seche [þan] all good ordir, mesur and reason in the werre thow traveilist in veyne, for and the most rightwous man that euir vas borne made werre it myght not be but he must greve

10 some man. And forasmoche as thow hast leid vpon me this charge aforetyme, I woll tell the more. Thenkist thow to scape from the hand of God, to whom thow requirist vengeaunce vpon vs, whanne through thy veyne indignacion, thy folisch thoughtis and thyne errours bene thoccasions and the rootis of the evils that we haue

15 done? Haue in mynde the punycions of the childern of Israel that fell vpon them in the tyme of Moyses and Aaron for their vn-

f. 11ᵛ pacience and / murmours that thei had ageinst their hedis and rewlars, wherefor som of theime sonke evyn quycke into the erthe and the remenaunt war devoured with serpentis and with fyer that

20 fell from hevyn and brende into powdir. And therfor confesse anone thes thingis which thow maist nat deny, and beate thi brest for thi fowle synnes that thow hast lived in, and remembir thiself that thow crydest 'Nowell', makyng grete fest [and ioye] for the sorowfull dedis that thou didist in thi prosperite, for the which now

25 thow cryest 'Alas' oftentymes of the day. But I counsell the to requyre Almyghty God that He pardonne the of thy grette blynd-nesse and foly, nat in such wise that He punysch not othir that suffirn peyne with the in the same errour, through whom many a good man hath ben beryed in the feldes and murdryd in townys by

30 some of yow at diuerse tymes withowte mercy, for the which your

col. 2 sclaundir is ronne into othir realmes to perpetuall shame / and diffame to the people of Fraunce, which in tyme passid war re-nomed of all benignite and goodnes. So all thes thyngys be notyd and knowen which I reporte me to God that seeth all thinges.

3 the werr] *om.* N guerre D   7 seche þan] N *tr.* SJ þan *om.* R doncques D
8 rightwous] rightuous SJ right noyus N   13 thoughtis] thought NSJ *sing.* D
14 errours] errour NSJ *sing.* D   18 evyn] *om.* NSJ *see n.*   19 the] *om.* N
les D   war] *om.* NSJD   20 brende] þem *add.* N   22 thi] the NSJ
tes D   23 crydest] cryest N   and ioye] NS ayore R and þore J joieuse
leesce D   25–6 'Alas' . . . pardonne] now to allmyghti god to perdon N
see n.   31 realmes] royaulmes SJ

hast prouoked it an(d) called it to the, thou most needys suffre the
charge and prikkinges therof. For who that euyr pourchasith werre
he aught to seeke it by suche condicion himself to submitte to the
infortunable aduentures therof growinge. Werre of his propre birth
comyth thrugh defaute of iustice, for and we were all iust we shuld 5
haue no neede to the might of armes. / And therfore yf thou will f. 14ᵛ
in werre haue ordre, mesure and reason, thou labourest in vayn, (p. 28)
for yf the iustest man that euyr was shuld make werre it may noon
othir be but som shall felle by him greuaunce. For all suche as ben
of ill disposicion, the whiche in tyme of peas dar nat put thaire will 10
in execucion, they take [bolde]nesse to doo it vnder colour of werre.
Aboue alle this, seying thou chargest me so sore, I shall tell the
more. Weenyst thou to slide from the 'hande of God, whos vengeaunce thou requirest vpon us, whan thy vayn indignacion, thy
mad thinkinge and thyn erroure by the occasions and routes of the 15
ill deedys that we doo? Haue in memorie the punisshmentes
whiche, for the murmure of the peeple of Israel and inpacientes
agains thaire [chiefs], that fell vpon thaim in the tyme of Moyses
and Aaron, of the whiche peeple som sanke sodeynlye withynne the
erthe, som were deuoured with serpentes, and som were brent with 20
the fire that descendid from heuyn. Confesse now that thou cannat
denye, and bete thy culpe for thyn ill synnes. Remembre thyself that
kryedest 'Nowell' for veray ioye and gladnes of the dolereux deede,
for the whiche thou saist now an hundred tymes a day 'Ellas'. And
therfore beseche God to pardone the thy blynde folye and nat to 25
punissh othir whiche for the same errour suffren with the, wherof
so many good men haue so horriblelye ben beried in feldys and
deede in townes at many and dyuers tymes withoute mercy so that
the skaundre therof is allredy in othir reames to the perpetuell
diffame and shame of the peeple of this land, the whiche in tyme 30
passed was renownd in alle goodnesse and benignitee. And that alle
theise thinges be clierly knowen I repoort me to God that seeth it.

11 boldenesse] borldenesse U

Notwithstondyng I woll lette them passe ouir, for thei be full
bittir to remembre, save onely I may nat holde my peece to tell
that the light feith, the chaungeable and litle trouthe of subiettis
to this lordship, tha[i] ben the movyngis and the causes of the
5 comyngys of our enemes vpon vs, and ellis durst nat thei haue
takyn suche hardines. But sithe it is so that I must speke ferther
of the same and that þou hast reprived me of grette sleuthe, I dar
right well sey that thyn vnstablenesse and litle constaunce is the
grette cause that our matyers be in suche case as we see. For in
10 dyuers placis but nat in all, who that takith not hede as grettely to
the as to thenmyes, thi folye and thi litle feithe wold do so many
f. 12 grette harmes that thow and othir sholde af/tirward sore repent.
Fertheremore forasmoche as thow pleynist so sorowfully, which
semith that no man hathe disease but onely thow, and (þat) thow
15 takest no hede of the sorowfull fortune of othirs, though so be that
euery man compleyne there owne diseases, thinke nat the contrarie
but the grette men in their estate suffirn as moche and moche more
thanne thow dost. O hough many worshipfull men and grette ladyes
haue ben exiled owt of (þeir) cuntrey and full evill receyued what
20 with the and with othir, that ben dispurveid of all goodis and
goodnesse, fer owte of conforte, fulled with sorow for acquyting of
their treuthe! O hough many eville nyghtis and lacke of mete and
drynke haue thei endured that hauntyn the labours of the werre,
chargid [with] harneys bothe in wynde and reyne withowte eny
25 coueryng save onely the firmament, and oftetymes loose their
col. 2 horses and goodis and put their lyvis in iuberte, and at the last / be
slayne! And many their be þat peynyn themself to the seruice,
which haue leyde their londe to morgage and aftirward haue fallin
in grete pouerte. And þe [grete] burgeses, that accompten their
30 mony for lacke of othir occupacion, or the riche chanon, that
spendith the most parte of his tyme in mete, drynke and slepe,

2 onely] þat *add.* NSJ   4 thai] that RNSJ   movyngis] moye-
vynges SJ   5 comyngys] commyng N *sing.* D   7 that] *om.* J   grette
sleuthe] grete slouther SJ slaughter grete N lascheté D   8 that] that *add.* N
9 be] *om.* J   9–12 For . . . repent] *om.* N *see n.*   10 hede as grettely]
as grete hede S a grete hede J *see n.*   16 there] his N   diseases] disese
NSJ dueil D   18 and] NSJ and *add.* R   21–2 fer . . . treuthe] *om.* N
21 fulled] fulfylled SJ   23 hauntyn] hath awnted N   24 bothe] bot
N   reyne] ryne N   26 horses] horse SJ harneys N chevaulx D   and 1]
their *add.* NSJ leur D   iuberte] ieoperte N iuberte iuperte SJ   the] *om.*
SJ   be] *om.* N   28 to] in NSJ   30 mony] vndre lokke and kay
add. canc. N

But neuyrtheles I passe ouir for they ben so bittyr / to remembre, f. 15
sauf oonly that I cannat kepe me from sayinge that the light, (p. 29)
chaungeable feith and litle trouthe of the subgites to this seigneurie
was mocion and encheson of the comyng of oure enemyes vpon vs,
the whiche elles wolde neuir haue taken the boldenesse nor hardi- 5
ment. And sithen that it most be spoken so fer and that [thou]
yevist me reproche of lachenesse, I dar well say that thyn infirmite
is litle constaunce, is chief cause that it is no bettre with us. For
in diuers parties, yf men shulde take no kepe as well to the as to
the enmyes, thy foly and litle feith might cause grete damages, the 10
whiche thyself and othir shulde bye right dier aftirwarde. And
eftsones because thou playnyst so deeply, seemyng that noon othir
suffre doloure nor disease sauf oonly thyself, setting at nought the
fortunes of othir how be it iche man playneth his sorowe, wenyst
thou that the noble men haue nat as miche to suffre as thou hast? 15
How many high men and nobles ladyes ben exiled of thaire cuntre
and ill receyued amonge you! And othir there is dispurueid of all
goodes and counforte and engraiued with sorowe for thair true
acquitaill and preseruynge of thaire trouthe. How many ill nyghtes
and defaute of meyte and drinke full ofte they endure that usen and 20
frequente the occupacion of werre, charged with weight of harneys
in wyndes and raynes withoute any othir coueringe but heve[n] and
ofte lese thaire horses and castelles, settyng thaire lyfes in aduenture
of deth, and so in deed so to dye! And many diuers, for to put
thaimself in poynte arayed well for to serue, haue sold and mor- 25
gaged thaire landes, the whiche aftirward fallen in grete pouerte.
And a grete burgeys, that rekenyth his money for defaute of othir
occupacion, or a riche preest, the whiche spendeth the moost parte
of his / tyme in etinge, drinkinge and slepinge, shall krye vpon us, f. 15ᵛ
(p. 30)

22 heven] hevee U ciel D

cryen vpon vs and asche vs why we fyght nat and chase nat [oute]
owre enemyes like as men myght chase dovis from a pese reke and
like as it war as light to do as to speke therof. Neuirtheles thei that
so iugen of the werris list nat leve one day of their pleyasur nor
5 woll [not] ley owte of their purs the valew of a peny but with com-
pleint and sorow, semyng vnto theym as it wer a thyng lost, whanne
the prynce with his power must lay to his handis; also and we haue
nede they woll do vs litle mor ease thanne and thei warr owr
enemyes.

f. 12ᵛ   And of suche folke come the clamours and the / compleyntis
11 which liven most at their ease, but the affliccions ben vpon the
powr labourers and we haue the peynes and the travels. But yet
I speke nat generally of all people, for ther be many that be right
good and constaunt. Yet thei that I haue afore rehersed bringin vp
15 the murmours, the compleyntis and the rumours, of whome ther
be so many that at this tyme I woll holde my pees. For many of
them rekke neuir who rwle the lordeship so that thei may be nygh
their own profightis and ferre from their lossis; and many of them
had rathir disavow their naturale lorde for thencressing of their
20 richesse thanne for to suffir any lossis of goodis in the keping of
their trouthe. Wold God that euery man had vsid the comon wele
and the honour of the prince and that their coragis had ben stablischid as thei owght haue ben of right. Allas thanne had nat we
col. 2 fallen to this grette inconueniens. O yf fortune / had be so myghty
25 ouir the trew and entier coragis that she myght haue put vs into
a litle prosperite atte lest wey, we sholde the sonner haue risen vp
by the vnyon and stabilnesse [of] owr willis. But it is nough all
othirwise, for lyke as oone maladye engendirth anothir, sembla[b]le
wyse comyth affliccions vnto the people whanne thei haue newe
30 chaunge. Exaumple hereof is clere: for we haue sought dyvision
amongist owrself, we haue eftsonis put withowt vs and from withowt vs ayeinst vs. And it apperith wele that by the sustenaunce of
an outrageowse and vntrwe folye we have don so moche, what with

1 vs 2] *om.* NSJ   2–3 and . . . therof] *om.* N   4 leve] not *add.* N
8 and] *om.* N   11 affliccions] affleccions SJ affeccions N affliction D
14 thei] *om.* N   15 the 2] and N   19 rathir] leuer NSJ   21 Wold
God] *tr.* N   24 grette] *om.* NSJD   inconueniens] inconuenyent SJ
myghty] myght N   25 haue] a N   26 lest] last N   haue] a N
28 semblable] J semblale R semlable S semeable N   29 wyse] wisedam N
comyth] aftir *add.* N *see n.*   31 owrself] *possible om. here* RNSJ *see n.*
31-2 withowt] *om.* N   32 vs 1] and *add.* N *see n.*

askyng why that we fight nat, saying that we chasse the enmyes as
men dooues out of a peese feeld, as though the deede-dooing were
as easy to us as the tellinge of a tale vpon the elbowe sittinge at the
wyn. But neuyrthelesse they that thus iugen of the werre at home
by thaire fire wold nat leese a day of thaire ease or vnpurse a peny 5
but with mykell sorowe and as looth departinge as though it were
lost, whan the might of a prince most lay to his hand; and yf we
haue neede, with as grete payn they wold receyue us allthough we
were enmyes.

Of suche comyth the clamours and playnynges whiche ben more 10
replete of ease than we be, but the affliccion is vpon the comyn
peeple laborers, and to us is the payn and trauaile. I speke nat of
all, for there is som that ben good men, constaunt and stable. But
the condicions that I speke of be more often founde in theim that
sittith forth thaire complaintes and murmure. And so miche there 15
ys wherof I holde my peas that dyuers rekken neuer hoo hath the
seigneurie so that they be next to the profites and fer from the
losses, and sonner wold cheese to forsake thaire naturell lord for
to kepe and encreece thaire richesses than to suffre losse for to
dwelle in trouth and worship. Now wold God that iche man shuld 20
alwey han the publique well and honeure of the seigneurye before
the yien so that the corages had ben stablelye confermed as the
aught. Elas we had nat fallen than in this inco[n]uenient. Or yf
fortune had be so mighti vpon the true and entier hertes that
somwhat we had be put bakke of oure prosperite, at the leest we 25
might the sonner haue ben releeuid thrugh the vnion / and stable- f. 16
nesse of oure voluntes. But elas it is all othirwyse, for like as oon (p. 31)
seekenesse bringeth anothir, soo growen the affliccions of the men
and encreecen in chaungeable mutacion allwey more and more.
The exaumple therof is to clierly knowen, for we haue sought 30
diuision withynne oureself for to finde muta[cion] of the gouernour
amonge us, and from amonge us we haue put him from us, and
from vs agains us. And now it apperith that, for to susteyne an
outrageouse and vntreue folye, we haue so long goon to and fro that

31 mutacion] mutacicion U

one partie and ane othir, that we haue put the gouernaunce of owr
soueraigne lorde into the handis of his mortale enemyes. O constaunce, a vertu full notable, worthi to be hadd in perpetuall
memorye, by the which the lordeshippis be made long to endur,
5 and the people, whatsomeuir thei suffir, thei sckape with honour /
f. 15 the daungers of contrarious fortune, thow hast wele founde but
fewe coragis of Frenshemen that haue fulfillid thi doctryne in the
mereveillous daungers of thes warris. But blessid mut thei be that
in suche grevous tempestis and trouble confusions haue mainteyned
10 the warres withowt reproche. Yet whatsomeuir that (hath) befall in
this seasons we ought to haue lernyd inough to affirme our coragis
to suche thyngis as be to come and helpe to redresse by our bettir
advise suche thingis as we haue turnyd vp so down by our symple
folyes. Wherfor no man ought to spar perill of body, traveile of
15 thought nor dispence of goodis.

For we fynde in the Romayn histories of many evile aduentoures
fallen vnto them which fortune oftymes haue brought full lough,
but thei, constraynid by wisedam, haue vertuousely rysen vp ayein
with their labour an peyne into grette honoure and worship. For
col. 2 whanne thei lost their knygtis thei made newe / of [the] strengest
21 that thei coude fynde of euery degre, as wele bonde as othir, and
put them to excersice of armes. And by the good ordinaunce that
thei made thei helpid themself in their batailes and bycome wor-
schipfull men and hardy in their dedis, for in all maner thingis
25 vsage makith men sevre in their werkis. Ferthermore whanne thei
sawe their cite vngarnyschid of richesse and the comon treasour
was failid, euery man wold liberally yeue of his own, bothe of
iuellis and othir goodis, for the socour of the comon wele, and this
wold thei bye ageyne the tyme of prosperite with [þair] propir
30 goodis, for þer was nothing so ioyfull vnto them as the restoryng
of their lordeship and the comon wele of their cite. Yette for to
shewe vnto you ensaumple that for the comon nede of the Romayns
ther was no particular thing sparid ne hidd, wer thei neuir so

1 ane othir] with oþer N   2 his] oure N son D   5 thei sckape]
om. N griefve D   6 wele] om. N bien D   8 mut] myght N   9 grevous]
om. N griefve D   10–12 withowt . . . come] om. N   10 that hath] þat
haue SJ (ins. S)   11 coragis] corayge SJ pl. D   16 Romayn histories]
Romans storys NSJ   17 oftymes haue] oftentymes hath N hath ofttymes SJ
23 thei helpid] to help N helpe SJ   and] om. N et D   24 and hardy]
om. N et hardiz D   maner] of add. NSJ   28 this] þus N   29 ageyne]
NSJ in add. R om. D   of] NSJ their add. R om. D   30 vnto] to N
32 vnto] to N   you] an add. N om. D   that] om. N que D

oure souerain lord is yeuen to gouerne us in the handes of his
mortall enmye. O constaunce, moost laudable vertu and digne of
perpetuell memorie, by whom the lordshippes be made longe to
endure, and the men, though they suffre, thei skape the daungers
and pervers fortune, right fewe corages hast thou founde in this 5
land the whiche haue folowed thy doctrine in theise meruelous
daungers. And right eureuse and right happy ben they that in so
grete tempest and troubled confusion haue maynteyned thaimself
withoute r[e]proche. But whatsoeuyr is fallen in tyme passed we
aught inough to haue lerned to reforme oure corages agains that is 10
comynge and helpe to redresse by better aduise that that we haue
misturned by wronge byleeue, whereynne noon aught to spare
parill of bod[y], trauaile of thought nor expense of richesse.

Inow finde we in the Romayns stories of ill aduentures sodeinly
growen to the Romayns and hou that fortune had brought thaim 15
right lowe, but they releue thaimself more mightyly at the neede
thrugh thaire stedfast stablenesse. And yf they had lost of thaire
knyghtys they wold make nwe and sett vp som out of euery estate
and degree, and namely of the seruauntes, whiche shulde lerne to 19
exercise the deedys of armes, and / by the curiouse labour and f. 16ᵛ
ordinaunce that they put therynne preeuid well in manly prowesse (p. 32)
in tyme of bataile, for in all maner thinges vsaunce maketh men to
be seure and ferme in the deede-dooing. And on the othir partie
yf the treasour of Rome was vngarnysshid of money, yche man
liberally gaf of his owne tresoure or his iuellys preciouse for to 25
socour in publique neede and to be agayn the good tyme of prosperite and comon well of thaire propre castell. Nor nothinge was
to theim soo deere as that that they dispoosed to preserue the
seigneurie and publique well of thaire citee. And ferthermore for
to shewe by example, to the comon well of the Romayns no par- 30
ti[c]uler thinge, were it neuyr so precious, was nat spared nor

9 reproche] roproche U   13 body] bodily U corps D   30-1 particuler]
partituler U

precious, the noble man callid Vegece tellith how in the defending
f. 15ᵛ of the Capitole of Rome cordis and ropes / failid them in their nede,
and forthewith all the ladyes of Rome made kytt of the feyr heir
of þeir hedis and toke it vnto the workemen to make newe cordis
5 in sokeryng of the comon wele, and co[n]sentid also to yeve away
their best kerchewis and their best array and take themself to
boistous garmentis and labored with their hondis as thei had be
powr people for the comon profyght of their cite.

But o alas now [me semyth] I see the contrarye, for nowadayes
10 the fadir sayth to the sone and oone neyghtbour to anothir, 'Fayer
frende, this tyme is mervelous, for I canne nat vndirstonde hough
the state of this present thingis shall turne. Wherfor I cannat see
but we must hyde and bury vndir erthe or transport into anothir
cuntrey bothe our goodis and all othir thingis that we shulde lyve
15 by.' What menith this? Ought ellis but in wenyng to save hymself
col. 2 aparte withedrawe them from the besinesse / of the comon wele and
put themself owte and [the] comon profite also from the vsage of
suche goodis as issewen owte of the same? But thei be suche wise
disseyvid therin that oftetymes thei lose their good forasmoche as
20 thei eschewe to entende the profit of the comon wele. But I suppose
that the moche speche therof chargith. Yet this I may seurly sey, that
neuir wourship, vertue nor þe vniuersall welthe of the comonte,
that shulde sownde to the lordeship, was neuir so litill enpryntid in
their coragis as it is at this tyme. Turne your yghen aboute to
25 knowe the condicions and the maners of euery estate, and ye shall
see that eche of them dreme aparte in their owne myndes vndir a
singular forme hough thei may gette their welth. O Lorde, th[at]
arte most myghty, if it so were that all suche as thus muse and
29 ymagyne by themself wolde ioyne their vndirstondynges togeddre
f. 16 and serche owte the newe arreysing of their lordeship, / thei shuld
fynde the comon prosperite and the welthe of their estate and of
their lyvis, wheras nough by their parciall desyirs lette their lordeship fall into pardicion.

1 man] men J   3 made] om. N   the 2] þair N   4 toke] take J
7 labored] labour N   9 o alas now] now olas N   me semyth] SJ om. RN
m'est advis D   10 to 1] vnto J   anothir] and othir N   13 vndir] þe
add. N om. D   transport] it add. N   14 bothe] all N   15 hymself]
themselue N   17 and] of N et D   17–18 also . . . same] om. N
see n.   20 eschewe to entende] entend to eschew N   21 this] om. ND
27 that] NSJ thow R   31 the 1] om. J   32-3 lordeship] lordshippes N
sing. D

recelled, Vegece reherceth that as to the engynes of werre, wherof
the Romayns defended the Capitole of Rome, was failled the
cordage, the ladys of the citee did kutt thaire faire here of thaire
heedys for a publique necessitee and con[s]ented thaire naturell
and deerest ornamentes to be conuerted into the rude operacion and   5
to be wrought by the harde handes of the workemen, the whiche
heeris fro the day of thaire natiuite they had keped and spared and
curiously laboured.

But now elas me seemyth I see the contrarye, for the fadir seith
to the sonne and oon neyghbour to anothir, 'Freendes, the ceason   10
is right merueilous nor we wote nat hou all present thinges shall
falle and turne. Than most we hyde or berye in the erthe or ellys
transporte in othir cuntrees oure goodys and richesses.' What
meenyth this sauf oonlye wenyng for to saue thaimself aparte, fore-
cloose and stoppe the helpe of his goodis fro the comon neede and   15
depri[u]e thaimself and the vsage publique from the goodys whiche
ben growen of the same? But they ben deceyued and / abused that   f. 17
they leese thaire castell and goodys for to eschewe the profite of the   (p. 33)
comon well. And I beleeue that to miche speche in charge or
accusacion of othir is nat laudable. I may well say that neither   20
worship, vertu nor vniuersall saluacion of the seigneurie nor of the
comonte were neuir lasse empreent in the corages than they be
now. Turne your yien aboute for to knowe the condicions and
disposicions of men of all maner estates, and ye shall see that many
there is that dremen by thaimself to seke a wey for thaire singuler   25
saluacion. A, a, God Allmighty, yf all thoo that sekyn this subtil-
nesse wold ioyne thaire wyttes togider for to seek the releef of thaire
seigneurie, they might gete, to the comon prosperitee, the saluacion
of thaire estates and thaire lyfes, the whiche by thaire parciall
desires they lose with the lordship that they lyue in perdicion.   30

4 consented] constented U   14 meenyth] meeu[?]yth U   16 depriue]
deprime U priver D

Now playne the people vpon vs. Now murmur and crye the comon people ayeinst the lordeship for the money that at sum tyme is leveyed among them for þe defence of the cuntrey. They wolde fayne be kept and diffendid, and yet many of them grutchyn to be
5 oonys contributorie to their own saluacion, like as thei wolde haue all their pleasuris withowte suffering of any disease and leve to vs the perille and the charge, and (þei) nat helpe therto. We may nat lyve by the wynde, nor our revenues may nat suffice to susteyne the mereveillous chargis of the warr. For and the prince gadird nat
10 money of his people for to paye vs for our seruice, we must of very necessite leve of suche goodis as we fynde with concience, and [þat] col. 2 I reporte me to / God.

Thanne forasmoche as aduer[c]i[t]e is com[en] to all the realme, it is of necessite that euery man suffre that God sendis him. And
15 the most glorious Lorde aboue knowith whethir we be quyte [or exempte] in this case. For and any man compleyne and axe wher we be, thei that come and passen thorough our londis and reuenewis do vs no lasse harme thanne we do to othirs. Wherfor and all this war weyed in a iuste ballaunce, the travails and the periles that we
20 suffren, the burdon, the dispencis and the grette hurttis that we susteyne, and on that othir syde the grette evilles that wee doone, we shuld nat haue lasse parte of the trouble thanne the people that cryen vpon vs. But it may well be that vndir our shadew many grete outragis be don, for in the warre, wheras force reyneth and the
25 sworde is lorde, right may have no power. But who that wold trewly serche oute this case, it shold be founde that þe people of f. 16ᵛ lowe estate that be / sette forthe vndir the name of a man of armes ben gilty of this fowle and horrible excesse, and the evile growith of the people which reboundith to themself ageyn. Why(for) all
30 thise chargis ought not to be leyede vnto the noble men, which love moche bettir to live in their howses lyke lordis thanne to [be] harberowed in diseasis and [an hoste] in anothir mannys daunger.

And though the people compleyn and be sor diffowlid and hurte,
35 yet I call God to wittenesse that we be not all clere but haue right

1 vpon] on NSJ   2 at sum tyme] *om.* N aucunesfois D   5 oonys] *om.* NSJ   11 necessite] necessit N   13 aduercite] NSJ aduertice R comen] NJ comon S come R commune D   16 and 1] an *add.* N   20 dispencis] dispence N *pl.* D   23 vs] *om.* N nous D   27 forthe] in suerte N 28 fowle and] *om.* NSJD   30 thise chargis] this charge N *sing.* D 32 an hoste] NSJ oft R comme hostes D

Now playneth the peeple on us. Now crieth and murmureth the
comons agains the seigneurie for the money whiche at som tymes
is rerid vpon thaim for the defence of the cuntree. They will be
keped and defended, and yit dyuers of thaim will be by force constreyned to be tributaries to the sauf garde, like as they wolde haue   5
the goodis for thaire parte withoute suffring of disease and that we
shuld bere the parilles and the paynes and haue noo good. We may
nat lyue oonly with the wynde, nor oure [reuenues] may not suffise
us to susteyne the werres withoute the prince rere of his peeple for
to paye us, and in seruyng to the comonte we lif with suche goodys   10
as we fynde, and to God I reporte me for to haue oure consciences
excused.

And sithen it is soo that the aduersite is comon to all the reame,
it is force that iche man suffre that that God sendith him, and God
knoweth yf we be therof exempt. For and we playned theron as we   15
goon, they that goon and come / vpon oure landes dooth us noo   f. 17ᵛ
lasse greeuys nor dommages than we doo to othir men. And yf all   (p. 34)
were weyed in a iuste balaunce, the trauailes and parelles that we
suffre, the dispence and dommage that we bere, and on the othir
side the harmes that we doo, we shulde [not] haue lesser part of the   20
doloure than the peeple that cryeth so vpon vs. It may well be that
vnder coloure of vs many grete outrage[s] be doon, for in werre,
where force is and reigneth and the glayue hath dominacion, there
may rightwysnesse haue no cours. But for to enquire well, it shall
be founde that som of the peeple and of lowe degree whiche put   25
thaim forth vnder the name of armes ben culpable and gilty of
theise horrible excesses, and amonge som of the peeple breedyth
the mischeeuys whiche vpon thaim redo[nd]eth. And therfore all
the charge aught nat to be put vpon the noble men that had leuyr
lyue as lordis vpon thaire goodes than for to be logged vnthan[k]-   30
fully like as hostes in othir mennys daunger.

Than yf the peeple playneth and is defouled and hurt, I call God
to wytnesse that we be nat all hoole and that we haue inow to oure

8 reuenues] reames U revenues D   22 outrages] outrageous U
28 redondeth] redouteth U redonde D

inough for our parte. And syn it is so we must compare evill to evill,
yet þis avauntage haue the comon people, for their purse is as a
cisterne which hath gadird and gadirth the watirs of all the richesse
of this realme, for the cofirs of the noblis and of the clergy be gretly
5 amynusid thorough the contenuaunce of the warre, for the feblenesse of their moneyes makit their paymentis the lasse of suche as
col. 2 shuld growe of hir rentis / which is owing by the comonalte. And
what by outragious derthe and withe their labours, dayly thei en-
groce vp the richesses, and now haue thei among them our catall
10 and goodis. And yett thei crye ageinst vs and blame vs that we
feight nat at all howris as thei that doubte full litle to put in aventure withowte reason and ordre all the noblesse of the realme. For
thei woll yeve the noble bloode grette chepe, and whanne all is lost
thanne woll thei wepe aftir.

15   God diffende but that we shuld annoye and greve our enemyes
and to feight with them in place and tyme wher any avauntage may
be founde. For ther be many worshipfull knyghtis and esquyers in
this realme that wolde desiyr nothing ellis but that the kyng wold
yeve them licence to put them in their devoir. But ther is as well
20 wisedom in armes for to abyde and delaye for their avauntage as
their is in marchaundise or in othir lasse occupacions, and it ought
f. 17 to be reputid and / takyn for a gretter worship and laude a[t] the
ende of a bataile to withdrawe and wisely save his host and kepe
them togedir whanne it is requirid of necessite thanne thorough
25 thaduenturous hardines leve aparte the wisedom of attemper-
raunce and mesur, wenyng therby to gete right a worshipfull
name.

And to this purpose me nedith nat for the confirmacion of my
reason to serche oute the auncient stories off tyme passid, but we
30 may take to our lesson that hath be seen late and in our dayes.
For we may recorde in our hertis the cruelte of the vnfortunate
Batale of Agyncourt, which we have full der bought. And yet we
pleyne vpon the sorowfull fortune and bere vpon vs all [þat evyll]

1 for] to NSJ   so] þat add. NSJ   4 this] the N ce D   5 contenuaunce]
contenaunce N longueur D   5-6 feblenesse] scarste N fieblesce D
6 their 1] the SJ om. N des D   moneyes] moneye N pl. D   8 by] þurgh
the NSJ   12 the 2] þis NSJ le D   16 feight] feyght J feyght feight S
18 ellis] elles J ellis elles S   22 at] and RNSJ au D   23 wisely] savely N
26 right] om. NSJ   30 that] at NSJ   and] om. N et D   31 vnfortunate]
ynfortvnat J   33 the] þat NSJ la D   þat evyll] NSJ the sorowfull
R celle malle D

part. And sith we most compare ill to ill, yit this avauntage hath the
comon peeple that is as the cisterne that receyueth the watirs and
droppinges the whiche of all the richesses of this reame, that were
in the cofirs of the nobles and clergye, ben spairboilled and lessed
by the longe continuaunce of the werre. For the feblenesse of the 5
money hath diminued the paiementes of the dutees and rentes that
were due vnto us. And also the outrageous derth that they haue sett
in vitailles and werkmanship encreecen thaire goodes, the whiche
daily they gadre and assemble. Now haue they with thaim oure
castell, and yit they krye agains us, blamyng us that we fight nat at 10
euery / tyme, as they that putteth litle doute to sett [in] auenture f. 18
withoute reason and ordre the nobles and the reame. For they wold (p. 35)
gyf grete cheepe the blood of the noble men, the whiche blood and
reame, and it were destroied, they wold weepe thaire deth aftirward.

God defende that I shulde meene or say but that it is needefull 15
to greeue and make werre to the enmyes and fight with thaim in
suche tyme and place as they may be taken at avauntage. And many
there is in this lande of knyghtys and squiers that wold desire no
bettyr fortune than for to be put in place to fight and doo thaire
deuoire. But in armes there is wysdome and conduit for to abide 20
a good tyme and to take his auauntage as well [as] in marchaundise
or in othir besinesse. And in a chief it aught to be reputed for a
grete laude and worship in the ende of a victorie wysely to can
withdrawe and saue his hoost and kepe it hoole in tyme of neede
than it is [by] to auenterous hardinesse to expose it to losse and 25
leeue temperaunce and mesure in weenyng to gete the name of
manhode and knyghtly prowesse.

It is no neede to conferme my reason to seeke stories of tyme
passed. But let us take for a lesson that we haue seen now late and
remembr well in oure hertys the verray dreed of vnhappy bataill 30
that we haue dier bought. And yit we playne the sorowfull infortune
wherof we bere vpon us the vnhappy mischaunce, of the whiche

2 that 1] *possible om. here* U *see n.*   10 yit] yit *add.* U

myschaunce owte of which we cannat sterte withowte diligent travaile and wise sufferaunce in chastesing our perilous hastinesse by
the seuirte of good attemperaunce.

Ther is a grette difference in the counseill of a prince that is vrous
and in prosperite, that woll kepe the / same and deffende it, and
anothir prince which fortune sheweith nat his fauour vnto and yet
wold fayne ryse ageyne and take awaye the victory from the victour. To this caase ar we brought wherin lyith gretter watche and
gretter wisedom thanne the werkis of hasty buffettis, as in lyke
caase the wourthy Romayne named Fabius Maximus shewid ful
well in the tyme that he occupied the office of dictatour aftir the
innumerable losses þat the Romayns hadde thorough the folisch
enterprise of Varo, which was a consull of Rome, at the grete Bataile
of Caves ayeinst Haniball, which at that tyme was reisid vp in grette
pryde thorough the highnes of his victories, in the which bataile
ther wer so many noble men slayne that for to magnifi his victorye
the seid Haniball sente vnto Cartage thre tonnefullis of ryngis of
goulde which war take of the fyngirs of dede bodyes. But aftyr that,
this noble Fabyus helde his hoste / togedir and costeyed his enemyes
and grevid them litill and litill, bothe of their men and of þer
vitailles. And though so were that Haniball provokid hym to bataile
and that the people murmurid ayeinst him for bycause he wold nat
feight with hym, yet for all that wold nat he þat the Romayn
cheualry, which wer somtyme grette victours, shuld be myschevid
all at a tyme, but helde his men so long aback that thei, contrary
in a maner to his wourship, arraysid and made anothir dictatour
namyd Munycious and made hym master of the horsemen. So
thanne he that was subget befor was made a fellowe to Fabius,
whervpon the seid Municius thought that he wold fullfill the will
of the people to feyght ayeinst Hanyball. But he was shamefully
discomfited and had lost all his legions if Fabius had nat socourid
hym and put away his enemyes. And thanne was he feyne to yeve
thankingis to him which he had sclaun/dird before and toke for a
grette vertu the constaunce of Fabius which afortyme callid hym
latches and slowe. But thorough his meanys thei war so streight
vpon Haniball that with a litle losse of the Romayne knyghtis þe

col. 2
6

10

15

f. 17ᵛ
20

25

30

col. 2
35

1 of] the *add.* N   6 and] *om.* N   7 fayne ryse ageyne] agayn ryse N
11 of] a *add.* N   13 grete] *om.* NSJD   17 tonnefullis] tonnefull NSJ
21 though] þurgh N   22 ayeinst] ayent SJ   bycause] the cause J
25 but] he *add.* N   28 made] as *add.* NSJ *om.* D   to] of N   29 that]
om. N   32 yeve] yelde NSJ rendre D   33 toke] it *add.* N

we may neuyr come out [but] by grete diligence of trauale and wysely to suffer and to chastise our hastinesse by the suerte of good and sad temperaunce.

There is grete difference or aught to be in counsaile and in deede betwix the prince happy to prosperite, whiche will the same kepe 5 and defend, and him that out of peruerse fortune will releeue and take the victorie out of the handes of the conquerours. Su/che werke f. 18ᵛ haue we for to leede wherynne needith more awaytinge wysdome (p. 36) and conduit than hastiuenesse of hoote corage. And in cace like it shewed by the Romayn Fabius Maximus in the tyme of his dicta- 10 ture, aftir the grete innumerable losse that the Romayns had by the mad enterprise doon by Varo, the consule, in the Bataile of Cannes agains Haniball, than exalted in pride thrugh the highnesse of his grete victorie, in the whiche bataile were lost so greete numbre of noble men that the said Haniball, to magnifie his victorie, he sent 15 into Cartage .iij. quarters of golden ringes which were taken of thair fingers in the bataile. But Fabius, aftir that, held his hoste togedyr and keped it besyde of his enmyes, euermore awaiting to doon thaim hurt and domage by litle and litle, both of men and of vitailes. And t[h]ough he was prouoked to bataile by the seid Hani- 20 ball and that the peeple murmured agains him because he wolde nat fight, neuyrtheles he wold neuere suffre that the knighthode of the Romayns, depri[m]ed by the victorie of the aduersaries, were all at onys disposed to the parelles of fortune, whiche at that tyme was fauorable to his enmyes, and so longe held him in this wise that 25 his peeple, in deregacion of the title of his worship, the[y] exalted in dictature and as his felawe Municus, the maistre of the horsmen, and he that was vnder him and his subgiet was egall and felawe to him. The whiche Municus for to fullfille the pleasir of the peeple faught agains Haniball, but he was shamefully ouerthrowen and 30 discounfit, and he had lost his legions and Fabius had nat socoured him and put abak his enmyes. And so was Municus constrayned to yeue laude and thanke to him whos worship he had slaundred and blasphemyd before, and / to holde for vertu the counstaunce of f. 19 Fabius, whiche before he callid cowardes, by the whiche constaunce (p. 37) the worthy Fabius with litle domage or losse of Romayns knyghtys 36 lad his enmyes so hard that with grete losse and hurtes, aftir all

23 deprimed] depriued U deprimee D   26 they] thex U

seid Haniball was chasid oute of Ytaly into Affrike and at the last
ouircome and shamefully slayne.

And if it pleasid God I wolde suche grace myght fall to vs, and
so it woll do if it be nat long on ourself, for any harme that we suffir
5 for our synnes and the diuision that [is] among vs, Frenschmen,
which encresith the strenghe of the aduersaryes, we may wele see
that our aduer(ser)ies or enemyes have putte themself in merveillous
daunger. Wherfor and we coude do peyne wisely for to greve them
and also to suffir paciently our tribulacion, it wolde be moche the
10 mor lightar to vs to chase them away thanne it is for them all to
[conquere us].

Wherfor, modir, take in gre þat the people constreynith me to
f. 18 answer, and be ye the iuge [of] oure / debate at your own pleasure,
for (I) suppose touching my parte I am dischargid.

15   [The Auctour]

Unnethe had þis person endid his tale but he (þat) spake furst
beganne to replye by maner of inpacience to here that he was so
repreued of his fawtis and seid:

[The Peple]

20   Now I see wele that lyke as vyolence makith right by force wheras
it hath non, in like wise wolde pryde confound trouthe thorough
high and grette wourdis and discharge himself of his shamefull
werkis and [put] it to them that leest may do. O good Lorde, what
mannes affeccion is [a] vayne and a chaungeable thing, whanneas
25 fortune in hir chaungeable werkis maketh the vntrwe wey, seying
in this wise, that and it myshappen to wretchis, thei ber on honde
that he hath deservid it, like as he that wolde kill his dogge and for /
col. 2 to colour hymself berith on honde that his dogge is woode. Thou
sayest that I am causer of this vnhappy werr and that I haue pur-
30 chasid it and kept it to myself by inpacience of the [high] prosperite
of pees. Thow saist also that thorough my folische errour and the
parties tha[t] I haue vntrwely susteyned is [this] confusion and

3 if] om. NSJ   myght] scholde J   6 wele] om. N clerement D
7 aduerseries or] om. NSJ   8 for] om. N   9–10 the mor] more the more N
10 all] om. NSJD   11 conquere us] NSJ wynne on vs (ins.) R   13 the]
om. ND   17 by] the J   21 thorough] þugh N   22 himself] hemself NSJ
25 chaungeable] varyable NSJ variables D see n.   26 myshappen] myshappe
NSJ see n.   30 by] the add. J om. D   32 this] NSJ the R ceste D

thaire victories, they were dryuen and chased out of Italye into
Aufrike, where Haniball was miserablely discou(n)fit and so died.

Please it the good Lord that thus it may falle vnto us, and so
shall it be but yf the faute be in oureself, for what harmes that we
suffre for oure synnes and the diuision that is amonge vs, whiche 5
encreeceth the power of the aduersaries, men see clierly that thaire
losses ben grete and thaire daungers right meruailous. Wherfore
yf we can sett payn wysely for to greue thaim and paciently to
suffre, it is miche more lighter and easier to us, as infortunate as
we be, for to driue thaim out than it is to thaim, as exalted as they 10
be, to conquere us.

And therfore, modyr, take well in gree that the peeple constrayn-
eth me to answere, and iuge of oure debates aftir thy good pleasir,
for as for my part I weene that I haue suffisauntly discharged me.

The Acteure   15

Skantlye had the knyght concluded his reason whan he that first
spake toke the langage, full of impaciens for to here repreue his
defautes, saying in this wyse:

The Peeple

Now I see well that as violence yeueth itself forced right thereas 20
it aught nat to be, in sembleable / maner will presumpcion put down f. 19ᵛ
and destrue trouth thrugh high and grete wordes and himself dis- (p. 38)
charge of his owne shamefull deedes vpon thaim that may nat
redresse it. A, God, how miche is wordly affeccion wayn and
chaungeable whan fortune hath sett so vntrue a weye in his variable 25
operacions that, as soone as a mischief fallith to the caityffes, men
put vpon thaim that [it] is thrugh thaire deseruynge, like as he that
will slee his dogge and for to colour his own mysdeedys puttith on
him that he is woode. Thou saist that I am cause of this cursid
werre and that I haue purchaced it through the impacience of the 30
high prosperite of peas. Thou saist that my mad erroure and the
parties that I haue holden ben causers of this confusion and

2 discounfit] 2nd stroke of n ins. U

[this] vnhappynes fallen vpon vs. Whervpon I ansuer the that the foly of the poor men is foundid [vpon] the owtrage of the grette men. Also the synnes and the disordinate thingis descende from the grette to the smale, for like as the princes and the high men be
5 gouernid in their estate and in their lyuynge, right so [the peple] take ensaumpule and ruele of them, be it good or evile, pees or sclaundir. Wherfor I tell the that the grete plente of goodis and richesses of tyme passed whanne pees was among vs, thenne the grette men and the nobles vsed them in wast and dissollucion of
f. 18ᵛ lyving and in vnkyndnes / of the mysknowlege of God, which hath
11 now reysid ayeinst him murmur of the people, which is causid by your vnmesurable lyuyng and your disordinate gouernaunce and dryvith vs to inpacience, which is the beginnyng of our evile. For when the goodis and the rychesses multiplyed in the realme with
15 haboundaunce, as watir that comyth owt of a qvick spryng, right so your vnmesurable pompes, youre ydill slouthe applyed to all maner of delytes and to the disknowlegyng of yourself hathe suche wise turnid youre sheldis that the grette ambicion of estatis, couetise to gette good and envye for to governe hathe brought you
20 to the confusion wher ye be at this howr. And by thes thre thingis was and is consumed the royall money, and [the] treasour of lorde-shippis wastid in the tyme of plente. For neithir the multiplicacion
col. 2 of the goodis which at that tyme war for to come on euery / parte nor the consideracione of necessite that was for to come myght
25 neuir move your corages to knowe that it was expedient to reserve to the prince nor to purvey for him at his nede, but at all tymes it shulde be spendid afore or it myght come in. For lyke as drynke aug-mentith and encreasith the drynesse of the ydropique, likewise who that had most was most sette on couetice. So is the voice of the
30 people like as the voice of tyteleris which by their crye denouncen the comyng of the see floode. For our talis which thow callist murmurs signified at that tyme the myschevis that war for to come. Novgh it is soo that thorough outrage and discorde comyth mur-mur, vpon murmur rumour, vpon rumour diuision, vpon diuision

---

1 this] NSJ the R   that] NSJ that *add.* R   2 the 1] grette N vpon] NSJ vpopon R   11 now] *om.* ND   him] hym þe N ceulx D 14 the 2] *om.* N les D   rychesses] riches N ryches be J   17 delytes] delices N   18 grette] *om.* NSJD   25 was] were NSJ   27 drynke] drynketh N   28 ydropique] ydropisyn N   who] ho J he N qui D 29 So] it *add.* N   30 of] the *add.* J   31 see floode] flode of þe see N *see n.* callist] caldest SJ   34 murmur] a *add.* N   vpon rumour] *om.* N

vnhappy mischeefes. Wherfore I answere the that the folye of the
pouere peeple is founded vpon the outrage of the grete men and
that the synnes and disordinate gouernaunce ben descended from
the gretest to the lowest. For as the princes and high men maynteyne thaimself in thaire lyuyng and estate, the peeple taketh of 5
thaim regle and exaumple, be it good or ill, of peas or of slaunder.
And therfore I tell the that of the grete plentee of goodes and
richesse in the tyme of peas, the mighty and noble men haue thaim
vsed in waste and dissolucion of lyf and also in disknowing and
ingratitude of God, whiche hath caused the murmure of the peeple 10
agains thaim. And soo is your vnmesurable lyf and disordinate
gouernaunce the causer of oure impacience and begynnyng of
myscheefes. For at suche tyme as the goodes and richessys were
multiplyeng in the reame and the treasours were habundaunt like
a springe of qwyk watyr, your vnresonable pompes, your tendre 15
idelnesse anoynted with delices, and the vnknowing of / yourself f. 20
hath allredy mysturned your wyttes so that ambi[cion] of estates, (p. 39)
couetyse of goodys and envye to gouerne hath brought [you] into
the confusion wherynne ye be now. And by theise .iij. myscheevys
is the royall money consumed and the tresours of the seigneurie 20
vasted in tyme of habundaunce. Ner than the multiplicacion of
goodys comyng and growinge in euery parte nor the consideracion
of the neede ensewing might nat meeue your corages to vndirstande
that it was expedient som of the goodys to reserue for the prince
at his neede, ner to make any purueaunce or it be rather spent than 25
receyued, and lik as drynes of thurste to thaim that ben in the
dropesye in drinking encreeceth and augmentith, and so he that
had moost richesse more coueyted for to haue. Thus was the vois
of the peeple as the see mawes, which by thaire krye denonceth the
floodes of the see. For oure woordes that thou callest murmure 30
betokened than the mischief whiche for theise causes was for to
come. Than it is soo that thrugh outrage and disordinate reule
comyth murmure, of murmure rumore, of rumore diuision, of

17 ambicion] ambicicion U

desolacion and sclaundir. And who that is causer of suche begyn-
nyngis ought nat to be dischargid of the sequeles. Thanne and thow
blame [me] for the aduercite that I am in and I may nat kepe
f. 19 pacience, / it is more shame to the that whanne thow wer in thyn
5 high prosperiteis thow [cowdest] neithir have attemperaunce ne
moderacion. Thyne inconstaunce ought to be callid more thanne
myne, and thyne excusacione lasse receueable thanne myne forasmoche as thi witte and thyne auctorite is gretter.

Lete vs speke of the folische errour and of the parties which thou
10 accusist me of and saist that I haue susteyned them. And if it wer
as grette nede to tell as it is honeste to holde our peece of this vice
and the grette shame that myght falle therof, I cowde wele say ther
wer many that long to the that may nat wasche ther handis therfrom
no more than I may. [And] forasmoche as the werkis and the dedis
15 goon byfore thaffeccions and the light wourdis also of the smalle
people, I report me (to) the now, which of vs is most chargid. Yet
I may say this moche: what thorough lettirs, predicacions and
exortacion of presumptuous clerkis, I haue belevid suche language
col. 2 as thei [haue] put in my / eeris, and if thei haue errid the question
20 may be axid them, and [I] wote wele thei cannat be excusid. Wherfor I wolde the vengeaunce shuld fall vpon them forasmoche as
vndir colourable shewing of trouthe thei haue brought vs into this
deepe derkenesse.

Yete in anothir thing I am by the constrayned to answer foras-
25 moche as thou dedist noote me by suspeccion that ther was defaulte
in me and that I refusid to helpe the and thyne, and thow affirmyst
also that the powr people which vndir thi colour be sette alofte
make the delyte[s] wherthorough thou gettist an evill name. At
fewe wourdis I dar right wele afferme that thy dedis, which euery
30 man knowith, yevith me mor cause of defiaunce ayeinst the thanne
is yevin confyaunce to the prince. And for to shewe this defaulte,
I woll shewe exaumples instede of reasons and woll name the places
and townes wher diuerse of thi folkis haue duellid and abyden as
f. 19ᵛ long as thei / myght gete eny vitaile, takyng away the goodis which
35 thei neu[i]r labourid for. But whanne [the] vitailles war spendid

1 causer] cause ND   1–2 begynnyngis] begynnyng N *pl.* D   7 receu-
eable] reseyvable N ressayuable S resoynable J *see n.*   11 it is] *tr.* J
16 now] *om.* NSJD   17 this] thus NJ   lettirs] lettre J   17–18 predicacions and exortacion] *as in* D exhortacions and predicacions N   18 suche]
maner of *add.* J   28 delytes] NSJ delyte R *pl.* D *see n.*   wherthorough]
werby N   At] as N   33 and 1] the *add.* NSJ les D

diuision desolacion and slaunder. And whosoeuyr is causer of suche
begynnynges aught nat to be giltlesse of the sequeelys folowinge.
Therfore yf thou blame me that in so hard aduersite I may kepe
no pacience, and in thyne high prosperitees thou mightyst nat kepe
temperaunce ne moderacion, thyne inconstaunce aught to be called 5
lesse than myn and thyne excuse lesse resonable forsoomiche as thy
wytt and auctorite is gretter than myn.

Come we to speke of the mad erroure and of the parties wherof
thou accusest me that I shuld susteyne. Yf it were as nedfull to 9
declare it as it is honestee to kepe it of suche obpro/briouse vice as f. 20ᵛ
therynne may be, som of thyn might no more cleere theim nor (p. 40)
excuse than I may. And sithe that the operacion of dee[d] goth
before the affeccions and light wordes of the comon peeple, I
reporte me to th[e] to conclude who is moost charged. Soo mich
may I say: that I haue beleeued what by lettres, by renomme, by 15
predicacions and exhortinge of presumpcious clerkes it hath ben
put in myn earis. Therfore I haue erred; let thaim bere the blame,
and vpon thaim be it the vengeaunce sithe that vnder coloure to
declare us trouth they haue brought us in this obscure derkenesse.

Of anothir thinge I am by the constreyned to answere whan thou 20
notyst me suspect of defaute of helpe and refuge or doute of receyuyng the and thyn, and also that thou affermyst that som of the
peeple whiche vndir coloure of the sett vp thaimself doon the
harmes wherof thou berist the slaundyr. At fewe woordes I dare
well say that thyn deedes, whiche all men knowen, yiven me more 25
cause of diffiaunce agains the than they yiue confidence to the
prince. And yf it most needys be shewed, I shall lay exaumples
instede of resons and reherce the places and townes where many
of thyn haue inhabited as longe as the vitailes and rape of goddes
might susteyne thaim, but they haue left the places whan thaire 30
pray and rape and felony was failed. And they haue taken of the

12 deed] deeth U fait D   14 the] thy U toy D   16 presumpcious] 2nd
u closed at top like n U

and goon, thanne toke thei of their frendis suche as thei durst nat
take of their [enymyes], but lefte the places to their enemyes which
thei wer chargid to kepe. Yet I woll holde my peece and nat say to
moche of this mater. But forasmoche as thou saist that som of my
5 folkis don all the grette evils vndir colour of the, suche as thei be
thou hast made them. For thou art their shadow to bere owte (their)
iniquitees and thei make the a shadowe for to multiplye thi vices
and for to encrese thi companye with theves, for to gete more sowde
and for to gete a gretter name, through which thou distroiest the
10 people and thyne own wourship. And so thi companye shewe þi
synnes in horrour and cruelte, which be nat wourthi to haue grace
to do wele, but as folkis discoragid for to haue victorye of thyn
col. 2 enemyes. And at the / last ende thei woll bryng the to confusion
in lasse thanne thou maist be bettir aduyse haue a nerre remedye.

15   [The Auctour]
Thanne he that was in harnes musid a litil and sodeinly brayde
owte and saide in the maner that followith:

              [The Knyght]
Bi thy wourdis I vndirstonde the wille of thi corage, and as ferr
20 as þou maist and darist, thy dedis and thi wourdis be sette all in
rygour; but though so be that feer takith away thyn hardinesse, yete
there restith in the egir and p[o]ignaunte wourdis of detraccion
ayeinst them that be bettir thanne thiself. Thow makest thy com-
pleintes of the vanytees of the pompes and dissolucions of our
25 estates, and it semith that thou makist moche sorow for the wasting
of goodis, which dispensis come owte of the purses of the nobles
and the treasours restith in thi cofirs. Wherfor displeace the nat
f. 20 though / I blame the the more. Yete I aske the a question: whethir
is more greuous vice or more hurte that we abate our estatis oute
30 of mesur, or to the to take suche thing as longith nat vnto the. And
for to conclude vpon this poynte, þe tyme that thou spekist of and
the tyme that now is, I call all lyving men to wittenesse that thow

2 enymyes] NSJ enenymyes R   their 2] the NSJ aux D   6 to] for to
NSJ   7 iniquitees] inequytees J   thi] þe N tes D   8 thi] the N
ta D   20 darist] draryst SJ oses D   21 takith] take SJ   22 poignaunte]
NSJ prignaunte R poignant D   23-4 compleintes] compleynt NSJ pl. D
28 Yete] þat N   30 to 1] for (corrected from to, r ins.) N   32 tyme]
NSJ the tyme add. R

frendes that that they durst nat chalenge on the enmyes for to leeue
the places to the enmyes which they had taken in charge to kepe
for the frendes. And of all this langage shall suffise me. But whereas
thou saist that som of myn doo and committe the fautes vnder
colour of the, suche as they be thou hast made thaim, and for thaire 5
misdeedys thou aughtist to bere the burdon. Thou art to thaim
coloure to / performe thaire iniquitees, and they make the membre f. 21
to multiplie thy vices and to encrece thyn companye of theevys for (p. 41)
to haue the more saude and wages and for to [get] gretter name,
wherby thou destruest the peeple and thy worship. And so they 10
yeelde the—thy synne and the horrible crueltes of thy felawship—
vnworthy to haue the grace of good deedys-dooyng, defied and
discoraged to haue victorie vpon thyn enmyes. And in the eende
they will bringe the to confusion but yf be a better aduise thou seke
som good and nygh remedie.   15

The Acteure

A litle while mused he that was in armes, and than he began to
speke saying in this wise:

The Knyght

By thy saying I vndirstand well the will of thy corage and that 20
as miche as thou maist or dare thy wordes and deedes be in reigueur.
But whan drede taketh from the hardinesse, yit restyth thy langage
egre and bytinge, allwey redy by de[t]raccion to renne vpon him
that is thy better. Thou makest thy complaintes of the wayn pompes
and dissolucion of oure estates, and it seemyth by thy wordes that 25
thou berist outrageous greeuys of the consumpcion of the money
wherof the expences is vpon the purse of the nobles and the tresours
therof ben in thy coofers. Neuyrtheles take it for no displeasire yf
I tell the that aboue all othir thou art / moost to blame. I make the f. 21ᵛ
a question: which is moost domageable vice, to us for to abuse and (p. 42)
maynteyne oure estates ouere that that mesure yiveth vs whan they 31
apperteyne vnto us, or elles thou to take suche aray of estate that
is nat to the longinge? And for to conclude vpon this present tyme,
I call all the lyuers to wytnesse that thou hast passed thy degree in

23 detraccion] decraccion U   33 this] *possible om. here* U *see n.*

arte in thyne estate moche bettir thanne we be. Whervpon thou maist see an open preffe dayly in thi own syght, for take me a taylours man and wom[a]n of powr degre and loke whethir thei be nat bolde to wer suche arraye as dothe a wourshipfull knyght or
5 a noble lady, which for honour of princes ought richely to be arrayed. This fawte that is right sclaunderous comethe of higher than thou or I, for thei in whose hondis r[e]stith the rewardis, which shulde be yevin to them that hath deseruid them, thei haue put them into gownes and into suche thingis as shewyth fayr and
col. 2 fresch in apparaunce owtward; / wherfor euery man hath suche
11 wise lernyd this conseite that it is an harde thing to knowe þe states of persones by their array or to knowe a wourshipfull man from a craftis man.

Yete thou speketh of the waste and consumpcion of goodis which
15 to me liyth nat to answar; for the profight hath nat be myne, wherfor the reprefe ought nat to be leyd vpon me. For euery man knowith wele that the cite, which aboue all othir hath be tachid with murmur and with disobeisaunce, hath swolowid vp all that money that thou hast spokin of hertofore, and the people of the
20 same haue receued and gaderid vp the grece of the labore and of the conquest of othir parties of the realme and [the] last sparyngis of the nobles, lyke a swolow in the depest parte whedir all is descended. Now hath he yolden suche wise his rewarde that the postom of his pryde, swollen with to grete goodis, is brokyn all abovte and dis-
f. 20ᵛ par/pulid, castyng owte the poyson of cruell and horrible seducion
26 and the [werkes] of vnmanly tiranny. Lo here is the encheson of the murmur and the moving of thyn inpacience. Lo here the dissolu-cions which thou reprevst vs of and puttist by fore the appesing of thy cowert ymaginacions, saiyng with thi mouth which thow hast
30 in dede discouerid. Thou hast made crye ayeinst enlarging of dis-pencis and ayeinst þe lightnesse and the ioye o(f) the yong noble men, but [thu] hast nat caste [oute] thy rebukyng voice ayeinst the vntrwe effusion of bloode which hath brokyn the place of iustice

3 woman] women RNSJ femme D   5 richely to be] to be richely N
6 fawte] faught N   sclaunderous] sclaunderours S   8 them 2] it NSJ
9 them] it NSJ   into 2] in NSJ   11 states] estates N   16 the] to N
18 disobeisaunce] disobedyaunce N   hath] haue NSJ   that] the N celle D
20 receued] reseyved N reysseyved SJ   22 all is] tr. N tout est D
24 pryde] is add. N om. D   to] so N trop D   24–5 disparpulid] disparlyd N
28 by fore] be fore NSJ see n.   the appesing] the thappesyng NS   30–1 dis-
pencis] dispence N pl. D   33 brokyn] brought N froissié D

thyn araiement miche more than we. And yit daily maist thou see
that a seruaunt-tailoure or the wyf of a pore man of lawe degree
bere or dare bere the araiement wherof a manly knyght and a noble
lady were wont to be right well beseen in the court of a mighty
prince. This right s[c]andalouse defaute is come from an higher 5
than othir thou or I, whan they that haue had for to departe and
dele the rewardes of the good deedys and worshippes hauen youen
thaim to the gownes and apparaile outward, wherof yche man hath
taken suche instruccion that it is harde to knowe the estates of the
men by thair habites nor to cheese a noble man from a werkman 10
or a iourneyman.

And ferthermore thou spekyst of wast and consumpcion of the
money, wherof but litle it apperteyneth me to answere, for the
profite hath nat ben myn nor I aught nat to bere the reproche. So
well all men knowe that the citee, whiche aboue all othir it hath 15
ben spotted with murmure and disobeisaunce, hath englouted and
swellid all this pecunie whereof thou spekyst heretofore, and that
the peeple of the same haue entowned and gadred the fatt of the
labore and of the conquestes of othir parties and of the reame, and
of the last spared of the reame and of the noble men, like as a 20
botomlesse coofre and abysme wherynne all is descended; and than
after this it hath yelde this rewarde / that the enposteme of his f. 22
pride, swollen with to miche goodys, is brosten out on euery part (p. 43)
and hath casten abrode the venym of horrible and cruell sedicion
and the deedes of vnmanly tyrannye. This is the encheson [of] the 25
murmure and the meeuing of thyne impacience. These ben the
dissolucions that thou puttest before the to our reproche for to
pollisch and couere thy malicious soteltees by thy mouthe, whiche
thou hast shewde ynowgh by deede. Thou hast made clamore
ayenst the large expenses and the myrth and reioysinges of the 30
yonge noble men, but thou hast nat cast thyne obprobriouse wois
agains the vntrue effusions of the blood of mankynde which han

5 scandalouse] standalouse U   18 of the 1] of the add. U   24 of] of
add. U   25 of 2] and U des D

and made opyn the waye of abhominacion. Thou hast accusid youþe and the grete ioyousetees therof, but [thu] excusid and susteynid [the] tresons and the cursid conspiracions wher[for] thou arte in þe ruynous partye. Of thyn errour and that partye which

col. 2 thou hast susteyned thow maist nat excuse the foras/moche as thyn

6 obstinate will aforetyme past the lawe insomoche that whosoeuir said the contrary to thi fauour and pleasur his sentence was iuged wourthy deth and thy iugement was gyven afore the vndirstondyng of the case. And though opyn exortacions have mouevid the to this,

10 I reporte me to them that publisch the matir what caused (the) to say and to beleve, and lette the wronge rest wher it ougtht. But of evile affeccion comyth blyndnesse and light beleue, for he that is corrupte byfore with evile thoughtis by the wourdis of othir may soone be holpyn to be disseyvid.

15 Wherfor thou maist nat by reason compleyne. Thou wolt nat alowe no good dedis ne thou wolt sett no brydill vpon thi desiyrs saue onely will to the contrary of that thou shuldest do. And all þe evill dedis that be doon thou tellist them forth, but the good dedis

f. 21 be soone forgotyn, haueyng no remembraunce of the / wourshipfull

20 and fair aduentures which diuerse honorable men haue doon of tyme past in the werr. Thei might nat at one stroke scomfyte them all, for like as the ev[i]lles that we haue and the werres that we susteyne was nat sette at the poynte in ane houre oonely, so the geynrestoryng thereof cannat be founde at oon tyme, but we must

25 go owte of this mischief in suffryng grette sorowfull discomfortis and doubtis, medlid with hope.

And thou wol be answerid to the charging wourdis which touche the placis that haue be abandoned withowte any defence, I tell the for certayne that thou shalt fynde right many that [full] wourship-

30 fully and myghtely haue be defendid withowt socours. Neuirtheles it cannat be but in suche an entremedled and daungerous werre but there must be bothe good dedis and grette fawtis. Yet I cannat see that at all tymys that the good dedis be rewardid nor the euille

col. 2 dedis duely punyschid. / Wherfor I cannat vndirstonde whethir is

35 more shame to them that kepe nat ne diffende nat their wardis or in them that shuld yeve socour and sloughth it by necligence. But

9 though] the *add.* NSJ *om.* D   the 2] them N te D   10 publisch] publysshed N   the 2] them NSJ toy D *see n.*   16 wolt] not *add.* NSJ sett] *om.* N   21 them] *om.* NSJ   25 this mischief] theis myschevys N *sing.* D   28 abandoned] habounded N   33 that at] at NSJ *see n.* the 1] *om.* J   35 wardis] wordes N

broken the bonde of iustice and open the weye of abhominacion.
Thou hast accused youthes lustinesse and mery gladnesse, but thou
hast excused and susteyned the treasons and vntestable conspiracions whereof thou art in this ruine partie. Of thyn erroure and thy
parties whiche thou hast susteyned thou maist nat excuse the whan 5
thine obstinacion hath at som tymes ordeyned suche lawe before
the hande that who that tolde the contrarie of thy fauoure was
before this woorde iuged worthy to dye and his sentence yiven
before the cace. And yf publique exhortacions haue meeuid the
herto, I reporte me to the publiquers of the sayinges and to the to 10
beleeue thaim, and so let the wronge rest thereas it aught to be.
But of the ylle affeccion comyth the blynde and light beleue. For
it may helpe self to deceyue through the woordes of othir, whiche
withynne himself is allredy corrupte by yll thoughtys.

And so by reason thou maist [nat] complayne the, nor thou maist 15
nat preyse thyself of good deede-doinge, nor thou canst nat refreyne
thy desires, but allewey willinge the contrarie of the duetes. / The   f. 22ᵛ
yll deedes, as miche as there [is], is well remembred, but the good   (p. 44)
deedys ben in litle space forgetyn, hauyng no remembraunce [of]
many faire aduentures and honorable deedys that diuerse noble 20
men haue actuelly doon herebefore in this werre. They may nat all
at [oon] stroke disco[m]fite the enmyes, for like as the harmes that
we haue and the werre that we susteyne was nat sett forth all in an
houre, also shall nat the releef be founde all at onys. But we most
come oute of this mischeef in sufferinge payne and dolours of 25
counforte and doutes, medlid with good hoope.

And yf thou will haue an answere to thy chargeable woordes
touching the places habandouned withoute defence, I tell the that
in the contrarie thou shalt finde som place that mightily hath ben
keped and defended withoute any socours, as needys most in werre 30
so entermedled that there ben both good deedys and defautes. But
I haue nat seen the good deedys to be rewarded nor the defautes
punisshid. And so yf ther be shame, I wote nat who aught moost
to wax reede, of thaim that faile to kepe suerly and defende thaire
wardes, or elles they that failleth hem of good socours. And in 35

aboue all othir the most shame is to them which make the good
doers and the evill as it were all one thing save [þat] the good men
be content in þeir herte by vertue, though in iugement of the people
ther is but litle difference bytuene the good and the evill. And this
5 is for none othir cause but for lacke of knowlege insomoche that the
high and myghty men amonge the grette haboundaunces aboue all
othir thingis haue grette despite whanne men tell them trouthe, and
among all othir besines they be wery and dull to here whan trouthe
is shewed vnto them. Yet the singular properte of trouthe is, the
10 more it is defoulid the more it openith and shewith himself, for the
f. 21ᵛ beginnyng therof is harde and sharpe / to susteyne and suffre, but
the issew therof is agreable, swet and fruytfull. Yet the wilfull mysknowlege of estates woll nat suffre the entre of the said trouthe ne
list to knowe the fruytfull ende and isswe of the same. The con-
15 trarye therof, that is to say vice, takith anothir way, for thentre
therof is attractyfe and pleasaunte, but the conclusion is hevy and
full of bittir sorow and repentaunce which oftetymes cumith to
late.

[The Auctour]

20   The debate and stryffe of thes two men was right noyous and
sharpe for the sharpe and bytynge wourdes þat were bytwene them.
And withowte spekyng of any wourde the thrid [þat sate besyde],
which at no tyme had opynd his mouthe till he sawe the multipliyng
wourdis approche to the dedis, and whan he felt hym priked with
25 the charge (þat) thei bothe layde from them and by cowarte meanys /
col. 2 wold haue leyd vpon him the charge, (he) thanne byganne to speke
and said suche wourdis as [hereafter] followeith:

[The Clergye]

Inough and more thanne our wittis may redresse or oure pacience
30 may suffre we haue vpon vs discordis and debatis, and we be pursued with dyvisions bothe withinne and withowt though this dis-
sencion be nat movet amongist vs. And we woll resemble them that
seith the fyre bren their habitacions and debate among themself

1 them] the *add*. N   2 þat] yet RNSJ   3 in 2] by N   the] *om*.
NSJ des D   14 list] not *add*. NSJ   16 pleasaunte] plesaunce N
19 The Auctour] *at bottom of f. 25 and top of f. 25ᵛ* S   20–1 and sharpe for
the] for the J for he S for he (he *canc*. to here *ins*.) N *see n*.   24 wourdis]
NSJ that ware bytwene them *add*. R *om*. D *see n*.   25 layde] ley SJ   them]
by *add*. NSJ   meanys] moynes NSJ   26 haue leyd] alayde N

especiall is the shame to thaim whiche putteth both the fauty and
good doers alle in oone rowe, sauf oonly that vertu yiveth to the
good men the contentinge of thaire hertes to the iugementes of the
men. And for this litle difference whom maist thou put in defaute
sauf oonly lak of knowlege, and also that the high and mighty men, 5
whiche haue grete habundaunce of all thynges, they haue moost
disdeyne and despite to heere the trouth? Yit neuerthelesse trouth
hath this propirtee that the more that it is defouled so miche more
it is exalted and releeuid; and his begynnynges ben hard and sharpe 9
to suffre, but the yssue is / agreeable and fructuouse. But the dis- f. 23
conysaunce of the high lordships may nat suffre his entree and (p. 45)
disdeyneth to knowe the frute of yssue in the conclusion. His contrarie holdith anothir veye, for his entre is plesaunt and agreable,
but his conclusion is dolorouse and full of bittir repentaunce, which
comyth all to late.   15

The Acteure

Longe and to annouse more than it needith was the contencion
and debate of theise tweyn, strivinge togedir by byghting woordes
ful of hate. And with silence was the thrid sett beside, herkenynge
what the seid, the whiche had nat yit openyd his mouthe till suche 20
tyme as he sawe the langage multiplye ouermiche and touche him
and whan he felt himself sharply prikked of the charge whiche yche
of thaim put from himself for to turne it on him couertly. And the
entree of his speche was suche:

The Clergye   25

Ynow and more than oure wittes may redresse or our paciences
suffre we haue on us discoordes and debates, and we ben persecuted
with diuisions both withynne and withoute ouermiche, withoute
meeuing of this nwe contencion and stryf. And yit we will resemble
thaim that seen the fier fast brennynge by thaire places and habita- 30
cions and ben in questions and debate amonge thaim to knowe who

and aske questions, who hath sette the howse on fyre and to whom the sclaunder shall perteigne of the same dede, yet all this meane while the fyre brennyth their howses through their necligence, which shuld renne to quenche the fyr and to save their own howses and their neyghburs from distruccion. I cannat se that oure stryvis and debatis langage sawyn opinly or in sewerte amon[g]st vs may cast vs owte of da/ungier. And therfor it behouith vs to drawe by the coller and to take the bridell with the tethe vertuously, and as the horse through beting and scourgynge and the oxe by force of prikyng mightely drawith owte their chargis and lodes owte of evill passages, likewise I beleve that the scourge of the divine iustice, which strikith vs by this present aduersite, ought to stere and move vs to gadre corage to put vs owte of this infortune. Let Hym take this enterpryse which is of power, for the aduersite þat we suffre ought be to vs more agreable thanne we canne vndirstonde or knowe which of His pite is sent to vs for punycion. Yet I doubte it is [not] grette inough for the misknowlege of God and defawtis that reste amonge vs. And if we passe this nat knowyng the power of God, we shall fall into gretter perilles, which shall teche vs bettir what God may do and also of what myght we be. Of this matir I seese for this tyme / and [to] returne to this difficulte þat we serche, I say that like [as] the membris ar altrid and corrupte by long malady, may nat retourne to helth withowte diue[r]se actes and marvelouse chaungis and residwacions, likewise we may nat be cast owte of this grette entermedlid tribulacion withowte sufferyng many dowbtefull assawtis and mortall perilles vnto þe tyme that the (contagyous) infeccion which reynith amongist vs haue accomplischid and fulfillid his course and vnto the tyme [þat the thyng hyt]self may retourne to his own nature. And so lette no man othirwise beleve but amongste suche enbracementis of warre no werkis may be don withowte complayntis, to the pleasur and contentyng of euery man. And if thou seche or wold fynde vttirly reste of herte

1 on] a NS of J   2 shall] shuld NSJ   3 their 1] the NSJ la D
necligence] neglygences S neglyegences J   6 amongst] amonst R
amonges NS amonge J   8 coller] coleer SJ coloure N   11 passages]
passage J *pl.* D   12 stere] us *add.* NSJ   13 to put] for to cast NSJ
gecter D *see n.*   14 this] his N   16 for] oure *add.* NSJ   17 it] it *add.*
N   21 this 2] þe NSJ aux D   22 I] and y (y *ins.*) J   that] *ins.* S *om.* N
23 diuerse] NSJ diueise R   24 and] of J et D   25 grette] *om.* N
tumultueuse D sufferyng] of *add.* N   28 vnto] to *ins.* J to N   28–
9 þat . . . hyt] that the thyng SJ þat thyng hyt N que . . . les choses D *see n.*
31 to] of J au D

put therynne the fyre and who aught of due/tee to put him in f. 23ᵛ
deuoire for to skonche it; and in the meene tyme the houses ben (p. 46)
brent thrugh thaire difficultee and necligence, where yche man
withoute question aught t[o] renne as to the fyre to eschue the
destruccion of his owne house and purchacing the saluacion of his 5
neyghbours house. Than I see nat that oure strifes and woordes,
sauen openly or secreelye the oon agains the othir, may kast us out
of this daungerous pace, but men most drawe to the coler and take
mightilye the bytt with the teeth. And yf the hors thrugh betinge
and flaielinge and the oxe with harde prikkinge drawe out thaire 10
cartes of the deepe and foule weyes, also I beleeue that the flaiell
of the diuine iustice, whiche strikith us by this present aduersite,
shall meeue us to take corage for to bringe vs out of this infortune.
He that hath the power to take this aduersitee in gree that we suffre
he is happy, for, though it suffiseth to punissh oure trespaces aftir 15
the divyne mercy, I deeme that it is nat grete ynough after oure
defautes and ingratitude that we haue. And yf we passe this withoute knowlege of the grace of God, in a gretter mischeef may we
entre which shall teche us bettre what God may doo and what we
be worthie. Hereof than will I cesse for to retourne to the diffi- 20
cultees that we seeke, that as of a longe seekenesse, wherof the
membres ben alterned and corrupte, may noon retourne to heele
withoute accesse and merueilous mutacions and paynes, also we
may nat bringe us out of this sorowfull tribulacion withoute suffring
many doutefull assautes and mortall parilles and that the con- 25
tagious infeccion that reigneth amonge us haue finallye ended his
cours so that aftirwarde all thinge may retourne to thaire naturall
kyn/de and that no man beleeue that in suche enbrasing of werre f. 24
may any actuell deedys be doon withoute complayntes and con- (p. 47)
temptes of many men. And yf thou seeke or will haue rest of herte 30

4 to] te U

and pece in thi concience, thou mast be likenid to hym that sechith
reason amongst woodmen.

And nat long for to tary aboute this matir but to retourn to the

grounde and possibilite / to putte thes grevouse dissencions, which
5 answer nat in dede nor in werke to the willfull desiyrs of hasty men,
considre we therfor that a prince that maynteynith the warre and
hath power ovir grete people ougtht to haue in hym thre principall
thingis—connyng, richesse and obeysaunce: connyng to knowe his
own dedis and the dedis of his enymyes, richesse to susteyne (his)
10 warre and also to drawe his enymyes to hym, and obeysaunce for
to spede redely in tyme and place both thavauncement of his
profight and the eschewing of his hurte. Thanne lette vs see
whethir we have thes poyntis or noo. Yet it suffisith vs nat onely
to haue them withowte that we woll and can wisely helpe ourself
15 withe them. As towching conyng, euery man knowith wele that
there be among vs people of grette witte and clere vndirstondyng.

Yet in them may be an obstacle aftir the wo/urdis of Isai, which saith
that the counsell of wise men is oftentymes turnyd and ouerthrowe
for fawte of due knowlege of God. Anothir obstacle is this, that
20 whatsoeuyr grace God hath sette in the hedis of yong men, othir
of good vndirstondyng or of discrecion in iugeyng, yette their
compacite may nat welle condyt ne comprehende the particulare
consideracions ne the witty and subtile cawteles that belongith
to so high a werke.

25 O werre of enemies and diuisione of frendis, discor[de] of
realmes and cyuile batailles and more than cyui[l]le batailes both
withinne citees and lordeshippis, by you is yevin [yoke] of servage
ouir the right high and myghty men. By yow is yevin (to) mortale
men knowlege that God inmortale regnith vpon them, which may
30 represse and thurst downe the pryde of þeir ferce powere and make
them to serue othir that be of lesse power thanne themself and /

chastise the vanyte of their grette habundaunces and bryng them
to indigence and necessite. Let vs se thanne the grette awaytis

1 that sechith] to seche N qui quiert D   4 thes grevouse] the grevys N
ces griefves D   5 answer] answerd N   hasty] haste S   7 grete]
þe N om. SJD   8 thingis] poyntes NSJ choses D   9 enymyes]
enemye SJ sing. D   12 the] om. NSJD   13 vs nat] tr. NSJ   17 Isai]
Isay ysai S Isay Isay J   20 whatsoeuyr] what ins. J what N   23 ne the]
nor the SJ nor to N   25 discorde] NSJ discordede R   26 cyuille]
NSJ cyuible R   27 yoke] om. RNSJ joug D   28 is] also ys SJ is allso N
29 inmortale] immortable SJ   31 to] om. NSJ   32 chastise] chasteth J
habundaunces] haboundaunce N pl. D   33 to] grete add. J om. D

or peasible conscience, thou resemblest him that sekith reson amonge the mad and woode men.

And for to nat occupie longe aboute this matere in vayn and for to come to the fundacion of possibilite to sett an ende in theise greuous discencions, whiche restith nat in the deede nor operacion 5 of the willfull and hasty men, therfore considre that to a prince that hath werre in hande and hath puissaunce of menne, he most haue iij. principall thinges—wysdome, moneye and obeissaunce: wysdome for to knowe what he hath adoo and to vndirstande the deedys of his enemyes; money for to drawe to him warde his contraries and 10 for to susteyne his helpers; and obeisaunce for to doo redyly actuell deedys in tyme and place to the auauncyng of his profite and in eschewing his dommage. Enquere we most yf we haue theise .iij. thinges. But yit and we haue theim it suffiseth nat oonly to haue thaim withoute that we can and will wysely demeene thaim. And 15 as to the wysdome yche man knoweth that in this reame there is men of clier vndirstandinge and of hygh wysdome and naturall wytt. Neuerthelesse there may be an obstacle aftir the woordys of Ysaie, that seith that ofte the good counsaile of the wise men is withdrawen and taken by God for defaute well to knowe His grace. 20 The othir obstacle is this, that who that euer hath grace of good vndirstandinge or discrecion well for to iuge that God hath put in the heedys and comprehencions of the yonge men, thaire capacite might neuer the regardes particulers and cauteles ingeniouse 24 whiche longeth to soo high a / werke well to guyde nor to com- f. 24ᵛ prehende.   (p. 48)

O werre of enmyes and diuisions of frendys, dyscordes of reames and vnhappy batailes withynne the citees and lordshipes, by you it is sett the yok of seruitute vpon the high puissaunce. Be you is knowlege y[i]uen to the mortall men that vpon thaim reigneth God 30 inmortall, whiche the pride and mighty power may take awey and make thaim thrall to a lesse and lower man than thaimself. And the vayne glorye of thaire grete habundaunce He can chastise and reduce to indigence and necessite. Than let it be remembred how

8 obeissaunce] for to doo redily actuell deedys *add.* U   14 nat] nat *add.* U

of our enemyes that thei haue vpon vs, the grette daungiers of ser-
vauntis and of soldiours that be evill payde, indignacion of peop[le]
that be cast owte, murmur of subgettis, plaintis of people and of the
comune, diuerse reportis, suspecious tonges, and ryotes among
5 themself, a prince, conditor of the werris, is constreynid to here, to
dowbte and to refreyn. And euery man shall knowe that there hathe
bene more suertye, liberte, sufficiaunce and power a man to leue at
his pleasur in the powere litle howse of a schepeherde thanne in the
grette and high palayes of princes, for the grette auctorite of lorde-
10 shippis hath causid many of them to fall into bondage [by þe desire
of the same and yet more than bondage] whanne thei ar comppellid
of force to diffende the same. Now is to be iugid aftir the forsaid
col. 2 writingis hough the state and / infelicite of princes, whiche, for the
geting of lordeshippis and for abydyng of the same as to them
15 belonge, be now made subgettis and bonde to men of diuerse
affeccions and contrary wille. Wherfor it may follow clerely that
and the grettest and wisest prince that euir God sette vpon erthe
were envirouned with grette and wighty necessitees and prikkid
wiþe sharpe prikkis to releefe of the same lordship, it were right
20 harde to purveye a remedy for the welth of the said matere and
follow thentente and appetites of the people. The resonable vndirstondyng and knowlege growith with the yeris of long lyvyng, and
experience makiþe the certayne iugementis, and the [wisedom is]
sought and founde owte in them that haue most seen and lyve
25 longest. Neuirthelesse lordshippis haue had allway yet hiderto nede
to haue wisse princes and helpe also of suche as haue grette vndir-
f. 23ᵛ stonding medlid / with experiens. And though so be that in tyme
of werres past men myght make reporte withowte vauntyng and
pryde of the good dedis that thei didd for þeir princes, it is so nough
30 that within a fewe dayes men might see a prince that was but yong
of age estraunged from his enheritaunce and royall house by furir
and sowing of discorde; he was also werried with his enemyes,
assailed with the swourde and evile sayng of his propir subgettis,
sympely obeyid of his people, forsaken of his principall helpers

1 of . . . thei] that oure enemyes NSJ *see n.*   2 people] peope (l *ins.
after final* e) R   6 and] *om.* N et D   14 abydyng] l *ins. after 1st* y N
15 made] *om.* N faiz D   18 wighty] wytty N   prikkid] were *add.* N
om. D   19 prikkis] thornes N poinctures D   releefe] relese N relever D
20 purveye] purvaye N purvoye SJ   23 wisedom is] NSJ wisedomes R
est la savance D   25 yet] *om.* N   27 in] the *add.* NSJ ce D   29 princes]
prince NSJ   31 estraunged] enstraunged N   furir] furye N furour D

many awaitinges of enmyes, daungers of seruauntes and ill content
sowdiours, indignacions of men that ben nayed and put oute, murmure of subgietes and complaintes of comon peeple, diuers and
suspecious repoortes, longe riottes amonge his men, prince ledinge
werre is constreyned to herken, to doute and to refraine. And yche 5
man shall knowe that there is more happe, fredam, suertee, suffisaunce and facultee of liuinge to his pleasir in the looge of a litle
gardeyne than in the high paleys of the princes, the whiche grete
and mighty power hath made thaim to be thrall. Therfore it may
be iuged aftir the premisses the estate and infelicite of the princes, 10
the whiche, for to encrece in lordshippes or for to kepe still that
that is to thaim longinge, be made thrall and subgites to men of
diuers affeccions and contrarie voluntees, and for to purveie and
haue an yie to the thinges repugnynge to the cas that sodeinlye
falleth on thaim, be it in thaire auauntage whan they can best take 15
it or in thaire preiudice yf they cannat remedye it. Than it may
clierly enswe that yf the wysest prince that euer God made in the
erthe were enuirouned with the heuy thinges and smerte prikkinges,
the whiche for to releeue this oppri/med seigneurie fallen daylye, f. 25
right harde it were to him to purveye to the publique well and to the (p. 49)
diuers appetites of the men. The resonable witt encreeceth with the 21
yeris and the longe lyf, and grete experiences maken the certeyn
iugementes, and so is the wysdom sought in thaim that moost haue
seen and lengest haue lyued. Neuerthelesse this lordship hath had
neede hiderto to a wyse prince and of assistence of men that had 25
wysdom and kunnynge. And yf [of] the deedes passed in this tyme
of werre may be made rapoorte withoute auauntynge, in fewe daies
might a prince be seen in yonge age put afer by furoure and sedicion
out of the royall house wherof he is sonne and heyre, werred by his
enmyes, assauted with glayues and woordes and of his propre sub- 30
gites, and douteouslye obeid of the surpluse of his peeple, and bileft

which of right ought most to haue eyded him, dispurveyed also of
treasour and besette rounde with rebelling fortresses. And whosoeuir he be that hathe vndirstonde and comparid the hevynesses of
thingis in tyme past vnto this tyme, though so be the dedis of this
5 high lordship be nat as euery good herte ought to desiyr, yet it hath
col. 2 nat be withowte peyne, thought and / grette diligens but that men
have [done] their parte and labour to sette it vp ageyne from the
lowe poynte that it stoode in vnto such a poynte as ye see it stonde
at this hour. And I take God to recorde that the symplest of the
10 realme may right wele iuge it and they that be most rude may
clerely vndirstonde it, for it is nat yet thre yere that I haue seen
diuerse men of all estates brought so lowe and so enpouerisched
that the most parte of them in their coragis fledde from the dewte
they ought haue done to their lorde and from the supporting also
15 of their lordshippis, like as a thing that war loste and like also [as]
a sike thing iuged to the dethe and abondoned withowt remedy,
which aftirwarde haue take harte ageyne and good trust of their
amendement and releef. Lo thanne in suche people be the vertues
affirmed and preved, [as] whanne men be in extreme perilles and
f. 24 yet the grette wisedomes res/tith with them, notwithstondyng the
21 grette doubtis and trowblis that thei stond in, as who seith, in the
myddle of their feeres and [dredfull] aventures.
   Wherfore me semith that the comon wele ought nat to be lefte
though our infortunes be grette, for at that tyme haue we most nede
25 to put it fourth and avaunce it with all oure powere and might. And
lyke as owte of vs reboundith the prosperite of the comon wele,
lykewise ought we to susteyne and helpe bere owte the infortunat
aventures bothe in dede and corage whanne necessite requierith.
And thereof may we take ensaumple of the vertuouse and coragious
30 man namyd Mathathias and his chyldern, as whanne the Machabees, in the persecucion that the Kyng Antiochus didd vpon the
childern of Israell thorough the instaunce and grette vntrough of
certeyne of the same people, which warr turnid to the kyng afore

2 treasour] treson N tresor D   3 hevynesses] heuynes N hyvenesse J
pl. D   4 be] þat *add.* NSJ   6 grette] *om.* ND   8 stoode]
stody J   12 enpouerisched] enporysshed N   13 dewte] þat *add.* NSJ
14 ought] to *add.* N   15 that war] that was SJ was N   17 trust] tryst SJ
18 releef] relees N   19 as] NSJ and R ou (when) D   21 as . . . in]
om. N *see n.*   22 feeres] speres N   23 to] *om.* SJ   27 helpe] to
add. N   29 thereof] herof NSJ   may we] *tr.* N   33 the 2] same *add.* N

without his principall helpe in whom he shuld truste, disporueied
of tresoure, enclosed with rebellions. And who that hath alle weyed
and remembred the heuynesse of all thinges into this day, though it
be so that the deedes of this seigneurie be nat so well as yche good
hert aught to desire, it hath nat ben withoute paynefull thought and 5
diligence for to bringe thaim agayne, as lowe as they were, in suche
plight and estate as we may see thaim now present. God is therof
wytnesse, the symplest men might iuge it, and the rudest clerlye
knowe it. And yit is nat .iij. yere passed that diuers men I haue seen
in alle maner of estates, som so vnstedefaste and litle feith that 10
diuers in thaire corages fled the adhesion and presence of thaire
lord and the helpe of thaire seigneurie, like as a thing that is cleerly
lost and as a seeke man iuged to dethe and abandouned withoute
remedye, the / whiche sith hath taken hert and good hope. There f. 25ᵛ
is founde the stablenesse and the vertu approoued whereynne be (p. 50)
the extreemys and dawngerous perilles, whan the wytte restyth 16
amonge the grete doutes and the constaunce in the myddys of the
terrible aduentures.

Than aught nat the publique well to be left whan the infortune
of the same yeldith it more besy in trust of good socours. For as in 20
us redo[nd]eth the well of the publique prosperite, also aught we
to helpe and susteyn the infortunes of his aduersite and nat to faile
thaim in deede nor corage at a grete neede. This weye helde the
vertuous man, and of hole corage, Mathathias and his children
the Macabees in persecucion that Kinge Antiochus made vpon the 25
peeple of Israel through the vntrouthe of som peruerse men of the
same peeple whiche turned to him warde. For aftir the citee of

21 redondeth] redouteth U redonde D

col. 2 rehercid; but aftir that the cite / of Ierusalem was by treason
robbid, pillid and brente withe grette and lamentable occision of
people and brought in seruage and some disperpulid hidir and
thidir where thei might fynde any place to reste themself in, this
5 wourshipfull Mathathias and his sones afore[s]aid, which ware
withdrawen into the mowntaynes, wente and gadird togedir them
þat war fledde and destitute, which war right fewe in numbir, and
affermed them suche wise in their coragis that [they] chose rathir
to suffre dethe thanne to see the grette affliccion and fall of their
10 people and of their brethirn. Wherupon thes folkis that wer hidde
in the mountaignes, whanne they wer gadered togedir, thei war so
vertuously gouerned that thei, thorough schedyng of their bloode
and suffryng of deth, bought agayn [the] servage and desolacion of
their people and restorid ageyn the realme of Iuda vnto his olde
f. 24ᵛ fraunchise / and also to his high dignite. What ensaumple haue we
16 also in this case of [the] grette magnanymyte of Scipio Affrican,
which ought to be remembrid what tyme that the Romayn lordeship was gretly defowled by Haniball, aftir þe grette victories that
he had, to se corages of the Romayns, hough in them was no maner
20 of comforte but as dispayred what meanys myght be founde for the
savacion of their cite, for the most parte of them were condiscendid
to take their shippis and leve the cite for to dwell in othir regions.
Thanne this said Scipio, which vndirstoode his own perill and
othirs also, and had an vndirstonding of the will of the senatours,
25 he by his grette wisedam ouircome the doubtes of his own herte for
the tendir love that he had to the comon wele, and sodeinly pullid
owte his swourde among all the conseylours and with a sterne
countenaunce made his othe and said that whosoeuir wold speke
col. 2 eny more to leve the cite and / abandone it [to] their enemyes, shuld
30 fele the sharpe bityng of his swourde, which shulde be [the] rewarde to them that wold forsake the comon wele for their singular
wele. Thanne all suche as were of goode wille and corage acceptid
grettely his wisedam and grauntid to do theire powere in the same.
Wherupon thei bidin still in Roome and come agayne to grette
35 auctorite.

2 lamentable] lamentale S   4 reste] hide NS hyde (*corrected from* byde) J
5 aforesaid] NSJ aforefaid R   8 them] in *add.* N   they] SJ *om.* RN
9 and] þe *add.* NSJ le D   13 deth] thei *add.* NSJ   the] NSJ their R la D
17 that] when N   19 corages] þe corages N the courage SJ couraiges D
24 the 2] *om.* N du D   26 that] *om.* N   28 that] *om.* N   30 bityng]
bydyng SJ   the 2] SJ *om.* RN le D

Ierusalem was by grete treson taken, robbed and brent by grete
confusion and lamentable occision, and the peeple in seruitute and
dispeire, Mathathias and his children, whiche were withdrawen in
the hilles, gadred the woofull fliers in litle nombre, establisshing in
thaire corages to cheese the deth rather than to see the affliccion 5
and decline of the peeple and of thaire brethren. And so uertuously
gouernyd and so fewe men in the hilles were hid that they redemyd
and bought with thaire blood and deth the seruitute and desolacion
of thaire peeple. And by this meene was putt agayn[e] the reame
of Iuda in his freedom and high dignitee. What exaumple haue we 10
in this case of the manly, magna[n]i[m]e Scipion, which is worthy
to remembre hou in tyme that the Romayns lordship was so hard
defouled by Hanyball aftir his grete victories, / whan the Romayns f. 26
had no manere of esperaunce nor trust in the saluacion of thaire (p. 51)
citee and that the moost partie of thaim wer entendinge to take the 15
see and abandoune the citee of Rome for to goo inhabite in anothir
region, he that knewe the comon parelles as well of him as of othir,
vndirstanding also the Senate was willinge to departe, he vain-
quyssht and ouercame the doutes of his hert for the publique
affeccion, and drwe out his swerd in the myddes of the counsaill 20
and sware with a grete othe that he that shuld speke any more of
abandounynge of the citee shuld feele with the sharpenesse of his
swerd what the reward was of thaim that wold leeue the publique
well for thair singuler saluacion. And to his volunte folowed all
suche as were well-wylled, and aftir that dwellid in Rome and 25
releeuyd thaimself in thair grete auctoritee.

Wherfor it followit that conyng and constaunce is to them necessary that woll drawe themself owt of evill fortunes, and we that be
in the same estate now at this tyme haue nede of more helpe þan
we haue deserued. But and we haue by any meanys vsid amysse
5 grette wourkes, and, now sumwhat amendid of our infelicite and
mischef that we haue stond in, yet our helpe failith, it ware right
necessarie to guyd vs vndir suche maner a fourme that we fall no
more into the grete perilis, for the falling in ageyne may be to vs
f. 25 a peyne mortall. Wherefor this worde / ought [wele] to be noted,
10 but yet it ought moch more to be dradde forasmoche as the vexacion and travaile ought make clere the vndirstonding and encrease
þe sentence, for who that doth contrary it is a tokyn of a harde
herte and a derke will, whenne afftir aduersite men woll nat take
a knowlege of the occasiones and the offences don byfore tyme, but
15 whanne thei be [a litle] brought owte therof woll renne therto
ageyne, as the hownde dothe to his vomyte. And whosoeuyr woll
followe this waye, hopyng therby to come to a gretter prosperite,
myght lightly retourne ageyn to a gretter confusion than is passid,
which God forbeede that euir it shulde so fortune.
20   Forthermore we must somwhat vndirstonde and know the difficulte of the dedis that we do and to know also whethir our goode
wold extende to bere oute oure necessitees. Neuirthelesse I woll not
put myself to ferfurth in this matere for it is full harde [for me] to
col. 2 yeve therin very iuge/ment and also it is full harde for many that
25 speke therof for to comprehende it in their myndis or for to know
it perfightly. For the fynaunce [or] goodis that the prince receyuith
is nat takyn nor levied of his revenewes, but thei be gotyn by
industrye and diligence; and the dispenses and paymentis that he
makith [for] our necessitees is nat as a thing lymyted, but it is a
30 verey swolow wherin all the goodis be founderid and dispendid.
For who that maynteinith the werres may nat nombir and make ac-
compt of goodis, whethirsomeuir his receytes be small or grette. Also
the demaynes, parte of them (is) occupied by thenmyes, and on that
othir syde thei be wastid by them that lyue vpon the countrey. So

4 and] þan N   5 grette] goddys N grans D   7 vs] om. N   a] of NSJ
9 to] om. NSJ   12 doth] the add. N   14 and the] and NSJ et des D
18 retourne] turn N retourner D   than] that SJ þat (t canc., abbrev. sign
of n ins.) þat N   20–1 difficulte] dyffulte S dyffaulte (corrected from dyfficulte) J
21 the] om. J du D   22 wold] wyll N   24 very] true add. N   26 or]
SJ and N of R   28 dispenses] dispence N sing. D   29 for] NSJ of R
pour D   31 and] nor N ne SJ ne D

Than it folowyth well that wysdom and constaunce ben needfull
to thaim that will drawe thaimself out of peruerse fortune, and we
that ben in such estate haue had therof and yit haue greete neede,
more than God yiueth us and more than we des[erue]. And yf we
haue somwhat vsed it at our grete neede, and now after a litle 5
amendinge of the first infelicite we begynne to faile, and the myscheefes wherynne we haue founde ourself haue ben right yll, but
for to fall therynne agayn will be to mortall. This woord aught well
to be noted and miche more to be drad because the vexacion and
trauaill aught to cleere the vndirstandinge [and] good will encreece. 10
And the contrarie therof betokenyth hardnesse of hertys and obstinate willfulnesse, whan aftir the grete aduersite men will nat knowe
the enchesons and offences which hath brought thaim in suche
myscheeuys, but as soon as they feele thaimself somwhat easid / 14
and dyscharged they turne agayn to thaire first custumes, like as f. 26ᵛ
the dogge that goth to his vomyte. And who that wold folowe this (p. 52)
weye and leeue the hope that is of bettyr prosperite lightly might
falle in wors cace than the brute of the first confusion that with so
grete dolour we haue passed, whiche God defende.

And aftir this we most entende to knowe the difficulte of the 20
deedys that we haue in hand and yf our money may strecche aftir
oure necessite. And in this weye I will nat put me ouerferre, for it
were [hard] to me therof well to iuge, and to many othir that therof
spekith yll to knowe or comprehend it. Yit I may knowe that the
sommes of money suche as our prince receyueth, it is nat taken of 25
noo re[uenues], but it is come by policye and diligence; and the
grete expenses that he dooth for our needys, it is nat limited but
it is more like a verey abisme whereynne all synketh and wasteth.
For who that ledith werre may make no compte nor mesure in
expence, be it hys receyte litle or mykle. Now is grete parte of the 30
demaynes occupied by the handes of the enmyes, and on the othir
partie wasted by suche as lyuen vpon the cuntree. Also the aydes

4 deserue] desire U desservons D   10 and] of U et D   26 reuenues]
reames U revenue D

by thes meanis the aydes that war wonte to be leuyed for the feete
of the werr be now sessed and vttirly put away for the releuyng of
the people. On the tothir syde if men wold aske a question, what
f. 25ᵛ helpe the prince / hath of his subiectis, the ansuere therof is clere
5 inogh, for the trouthe is knowen to euery man. And who that wolde
compare the pees of tyme passid to the tyme that is nough, a man
shulde fynde a grette difference bitwene the helpis that was at that
tyme done to princes in the peasible tyme ouir that is doon in tyme
that now is, which is a full besy season. Yet and so were that we
10 had as moche good, as moche helpe and as grette revenewis as we
hadd at that tyme, ther be men and necessitees inough wherupon
it myght be enployed, as in w(a)ges for men of werr, keping vp also
the state of lordis an grette charge of abilementis for the werre, the
costis of harneys, costes of viages to the see for embassadurs,
15 presentes that be yevin [to] straungeris, yeftis to them that haue
done goode dedis, and many othir thingis wherof at this tyme I
col. 2 holde my peece. For thei that ben most boun/den to do seruice
make themself derest to be bought, takeyng no consideracion to
their trouthe. Many mo suche fawtis ther ben longyng to thes same
20 werkis, for iustice and liberalite bene two vertues þat take hede to
largesse and to rewardis, for thei peyse and mesure them egally
aftir the reason of mennys desertis. But I dowbte me that in this
case their rewlis be nat wele kepte and I suppose that there be
errour in the distribucion in to grette dispence and large yeftis to
25 suche as haue nat wele deseruid them and [on] the othir syde nat
wele recompensid suche as haue truely deseruid. And so the ouirmoche that goth on that one parti hath no countrepeise, wherfor
the balaunce may neuir be guyded egally nor mesur dvely kepte.
Yet diuerse men enforce themself to assoile this argument, sayng
30 that it hath ben so at all tymes, for it was neuir but that in courte
f. 26 of princes wharas men haue / don right good seruice but oftentymes
thei haue ben right symply rewardid, and suche as haue don right
sympill seruice haue benne sette vp in grette welthe and prosperite.
Yet contrary to this reason I say in maner of replicacion that suche
35 as holde this opynion ben but of symple vndirstondinge, for that
vsage that hath in hymself any preiudice, the vsinge therof ought

1 leuyed] leveyed NJ leuyed *canc.* leueyed S   3 tothir] thodir N
4 therof] herof NSJ   11 wherupon] wheron NSJ   12 enployed] employed
NS empleyed J   23 their] the N leurs D   24 the] to J   25 as]
þat N   27 that 2] *om.* N   31 but] *om.* ND

ben cessid that were wont to be reysed for the payement of men
of werre and all is for the releeuing of the peeple. And yf men desire
to knowe what helpe the prince hath by his subgittes, the answere
therof is cleere ynow, for yche man knoweth the trouthe. And who
shall compare the tymes of pees that is passed to this present tyme, 5
a grete difference may be founde betwixt the aides of that tyme
passed and the aydes of this besy tyme and needfull. And yf more
large were the moneye, aides and revenwes there is needfull besinesse ynough / to employe it, as in saudes of men of armes, estates f. 27
of lordys, expences vpon engynes of werre, armees in the see, viages (p. 53)
of enbassadours, presentes to the straungers, giftes to the ser- 11
uauntes, rewardes to the helpers and to corrupt the grefauntes, and
more there is wherof I holde my peas. For they that ben moost
beholde to serue makyn thaimself to be deerest, and many there is
that by largesse most be brought to doo thaire deuoire where trauth 15
and duete cannat bringe thaim therto. Of othir fautes there may be
ynowgh vpon this poynte, for iustice and liberaltee be two vertus
that ouerseeth the rewardes and largesses and weyeth thaim by
mesure egallye according to right and to the deseruynge. Wherof
I doute me that in this cace the reules ben nat well kept and that 20
erroure be in the distribucion by outrageous expense and to shewe
largesse where it is nat worthy, and yll to yeue and recompense
him that well hath deserued it. And so the ouermiche that goth on
the oon part hath [no] countrepeyse, and thus the balaunce may nat
hold right nor kepe no mesure. 25
　　To this argument som enforce thaimself for to yiue solucion,
seying that so hath it euyr ben, for it was neuer but in the court
of a prince there hath ben seruises ill knowen and vndirstanden,
and of the good deedes ill rewarded deserued. But for to replie
agains this abusion I sey that euer is come therof ill conclusion 30
where the vsage aught to haue no place whan the vsing berith

haue no place, namely whanne the tyme and scharpenesse of nede
constreyne to refreyne the haboundaunces of goodis, which aforetyme the idilnesse of grete hertis hath openid and throwen at large.
And though so be that this streight rewle shewe hymself contrarye
5 to the vertu of liberalite which belongith to princes and haue nat
the power at all tymes to be kepte to þeir honour, yet may I right
welle fortifie that the said vertu through circumstaunces hath a
regarde and a tyme to rewarde in placis conuenable. Yet must ther
col. 2 be vndirstonde a difference / betwene the tyme of plente and the
10 miserable tyme that nough regneth, for dew and honorable yefftis
that were yevyn in tyme of prosperite shulde now be callid prodi-
galite. Wherefor euery man ought take hede to suche thyngis as
hathe ben aforsaid, for the synne and charge of suche as ouirlargely
purchase for themself wol be reputid more vpon themself thanne
15 on their prince, whos fredom and noblesse of corage is made to
doubte to say nay. For (who)so woll entende to enriche himself
vndir a prince that stondith in necessite and hath but litill shewith
that his prive affeccion and his corage endeinith nat that the comon
wele shuld prospere. But the olde Romayne fadirs war right ferre
20 from this custome, for diuerse of them admynusid their householdis and the magnificence of their estates for because thei wolde
nat charge the comon wele in tyme of necessite.
f. 26ᵛ   Yet I cannat holde my peece but I must nedis speke / of anothir
inconuenience, for ther be som of the cheueteynes that be condi-
25 tours of the warre which take away the wages of the souldiours and
yeve them but litill or nought, which causith them of necessite to
live vpon the poore people. Wherefor vpon suche capitaynes may
well renne a foule tatche of thefte farced with grett vntrouthe, and
so continuyng as strong theffis which done grette shame to the
30 lordis, for thei norisch and susteyne a nest of theffis onely for to
robbe þe people. Now woll I departe from this purpose saving only
that I woll ioyne this conclusion in suche wise: that euery trwe subiecte ougtht nat for the profight of the warre only leve wourship.

1 and] þe add. NSJ la D   6 power] to be add. NSJ   to be] canc. S
om. NJ   7 circumstaunces] circumstaunce N pl. D   8 conuenable]
covenable N conueable J   ther] þis N   9 vndirstonde] and add. NSJ   a]
and J and a NS a perhaps canc. N   14 reputid more] tr. N   15 on their]
an (a made from o) oþer N   16 enriche] euerich NSJ see n.   17 and hath
but litill] om. J and is in necessite add. NS see n.   18 that 2] to N om. SJ
19 shuld prospere] om. NSJ see n.   20 for] far N   24 inconuenience]
ynconvenyent SJ   26 of necessite] om. ND

preiudice, and namely whan the tyme and the sharpnesse of the
smarte needys constreyne to refreyne that that plente of goodes and
the ydell prolonginges of the grete thinges had caused to be openyd
and abandouned. And though it be so that regle so streight aught   4
nat / to be had but that the liberall vertu, whiche is so well settinge   f. 27ᵛ
in high lordship, haue allwey his effect as in the noble persoone of   (p. 54)
the prince, natwithstandinge I may susteyne that the said vertu for
circumstaunce aught to see tyme and place of yevinge and that in
tyme of habundaunce and ydelnesse suche donacion shuld be
called deede of largesse the whiche now shuld be called prodigalitee.   10
Well aught they to haue regarde to that is said, they that in court
purchase for thaimself more than for suffisaunce. Mich more synne
and charge is vpon thaim than on the prince for his liberaltee, for
nobles of corage causeth him to doute for to sey nay to his own men.
And whoso will enriche himself with a nedy prince and encreece   15
to gretely his substaunce and estate of his goodes that hath but litle,
he shewyth by his privey affeccion that his corage is indigne of
publique seruise. Fer from this custume were reuled and gouerned
the Romayn faders whan many of thaim lessed thaire houses and
power and diminued the magnificence of thaire estates for to be out   20
of charge in the thinge publique in tyme of neede.
   Of anothir inconuenient I may nat holde my tunge: that there is
som capteyns and guydes of peepele that taken the siluer of the
saudeours wages and will nat departe it amonge thaim, but maketh
thaim to lyf vpon the comon peeple, wherof folowith the shamefull   25
spott of theft farced with vntrouthe. And thus continuinge as the
grete theevis that stelyn from the seigneurie, they noryce and susteyne a nest of othir smale theeuys for to robbe and reue the comon
peeple. Than of this purpose now will I cesse sauf oonly that I lay   29
therto this conclusion: that a true subgite aught nat for the / profite   f. 28
of the werre leeue the worship therof. And they that the well of   (p. 55)

And thei that leve the goodnesse of vertu and the welthe
publike and woll nat take vpon them the enterpryses of warre for
the same, but entende on nothing but to gette goode, may nat be
col. 2 callid the wele-/willars of the comon wele. For the prosperite of the
5 goodis that thei gette makith their affeccions light and variable
insomoche thei dar nat put themself in aventure of the warre. But
the wourship and trouthe of vertuouse folkis bringith the harte, the
witte and the vndirstondyng to declare and shewe all suche thingis
as may sownde and helpe the comon profite, of which men may of
10 diuerse storyes drawe owte touching this mater many grette ensaumples of diuerse grette and wise men that willefully haue lost
their livis for to recouere the [prosperite] of suche thing as hath
longid to the comon wele, like as did Codrus, the Kyng of Athenes,
which was answerid by the goddis suche wise: and so were he were
15 slayne in bataile that he ledde, the victory shulde rest vpon his
party. The enemyes of Codrus fortuned to haue knowlege of the
same answar whervpon thei made an ordinaunce vndir grette peyne
f. 27 that no man shuld / come nygh ne towche the said kyng in bataile.
But the said Codrus, havyng a speciall loue to the comon wele,
20 chaungid his royall array and put himself in pore harneys that no
man shulde spare him more thanne anothir to thentent that through
his deth victorye shulde growe to his people and to the citee that
they myght from thensforth live in suerte from their enemyes.
Marcius Currius also, dyd nat he lepe into the profounde swollowe
25 which sodenly openid in grette largenesse and came to the market
place of Rome, through which all þe said cite was in perill and
cowde nat be remedied, aftir þe sayng of their divyne counceillours,
in lesse thanne the most noble thing of Rome wer d[e]scendid
therin? Thanne this noble Marcius, which was in his florishyng
30 youthe, knowing that prowesse of noble harte was the most wourthy
thing that myght be, toke an horse clene armyd and lepte into that
col. 2 inestimable depe / pitte full of derkenesse, and as soone as he was
in the pitte it closid [agayn], through which the cite was savid.

2 enterpryses] entreprise N *pl.* D   3 goode] NSJ wherefor thei *add.* R
see n.   4 the 1] *om.* NSJ   wele 1] wyll N   6 insomoche] þat *add.* NSJ
10 touching] to *add.* NS of *add.* J   11 haue] hufhath (huf *probably canc.*) N
12 for] *om.* N   prosperite] prosperite propyrte N psperite *canc.* prosperyte
? *canc.* properte S properte RJ prosperité D *see n.*   14 goddis] in *add.* N
were 1] þat *add.* N   were 2] was N   16 the] this NSJ ceste D
24 Currius] Cursius N *see n.*   30 prowesse] promysse N proesce D   of]
a *add.* N *om.* D   31 clene armyd] armed at clene N   33 it] *om.* SJ

vertu and the publique saluacion, namelye in thenterprises of
werre, desire nothinge ellys sauf the gettinge of goddes, they shall
neuer doo at the longe wey no soluable ne actuell deede. For the
profite and the pray ledyth the affeccions light and variable of the
couetouse men thaim to put in aduenture, but the worship and 5
trouthe of the vertuous men ledith the hert, the wytt and vndirstandinge for to expose thaire lyues to the publique well and saluacion of thair lorde. Of exaumples herof may be had of diuers stories
and put forth many high and wyse men whiche wilfully haue lost
thaire lyues for to recouere the prosperitee of the well publique, lik 10
as Codrus, Kynge of Atheniens, whiche had in answere of the
goddes that, and he died in the bataile where he was going to, it
shuld be to him a victorie. And though it be so that his enmyes had
herof knowlege and made defence that no man shuld strike Codrus,
neuerthelesse he chaunged his royall aray to thentent that noon 15
shuld spare him, and by his deth his peeple had the victorye and
his citee suerte of the enmyes. Marcus Tulius, dede he [not] lepe
in the deepe profundenesse of the erth that was open in the market
place of Rome wherof the citee was in parill, nor it might neuer be
hepid, as the aruspices saiden, withoute that the more digne and 20
noble thinge of Rome shulde therynne descende? But the yonge
man, vndirstanding that prouesse of noble hert was the moost
digne of erthely thinges, lepe, on hors bak and armede, withynne
that inestimable profoundenesse for the saluacion of the citee, after
the whiche lepe the [er]the closed again togedir. Decius avoued his 25

Ther was anothir named Decius that avowed hymself for to deye
for sauacion of the legions that were vndir his condite. Sampson
forte also for to distroye the Philistiens, which wer enemyes to
the childern of Israel, through his grette myght kest downe the
5 paleys whanne the Philistiens war most in their royalte. Othir
stories men may fynde inow, but it suffisith me to shewe that goodis
and richesses ben but accessaryes and bounde to vertue and as
chaumberer that mynistreth suche thingis as ben necessary to the
freelte of man, and yet thei be harde to gette, daungerous to kepe,
10 perilous to distribute, sorowfull to lose, and necessary to princes
and lordis for the condite and acheving of their werris. So withowte
this we may nat wele perfourme nor acheve oure werkis and in dede
f. 27ᵛ the sufficience / of this failith vs at all tymes, through which lakke
owre dedis may come to no profight.

15   Now woll we [go] to the thredde poynte wherin we haue to
declare what obeisaunce ought to be kepte to a prince that is in the
werre for his knyghtis and for his subiectis. Whereupon I woll
grounde me on the right grevous sentence of Valere, which saith
that knyghtly disciplyne, streitly holden and rygorously kepte,
20 mayntenith the lordshippis that be goten and it gettith ageyne also
suche lordshippis as be diffendid ayeinst them. Now I aske a question: what is knyghtly discipline? Nothing ellis but to kepe the
lawe that is ordeigned in excersyseing of armes and of batils vndir
the commaundement of him that is chief and for the profight of the
25 comon wele. Wherfor all suche as laboured euir to gette wourship
and victory by prowes of armes kepte the lawe so curiously that
col. 2 thei wold do nothing / contrary to suche thingis as longid to
knyghthod. And on that othir side who that offendid the commaundement of the chief ther was non othir meane but onely to deye
30 therfor. And this was wele provid by Mavlius Torquatus, which,
in the tyme þat he coundited the Romayne legions, made smyte of
the hede of his owne son for bycause he did fight with his enemyes
ayeinst the commaundement of his fadir notwithstonding that he
had obteyned the victorye, and yet this yong knyghtis victorye

1 for] *om.* NSJ   6 it] *om.* N   7 to] vnto NSJ   as] a *add.* NSJ
10 perilous] perlyous SJ   11 their] the N leurs D   13 sufficience]
suffycyente SJ   14 may] not *add.* N   22 to] *om.* NSJ   23 in] the
add. NSJ le D   25 as] þat euyr NSJ   laboured] labure N   euir] *om.*
NSJ   26 lawe] lawes NSJ   27 to 1] of NSJ   28–9 the . . . chief]
the þe cheef commaundment N   32 bycause] that *add.* SJ   34 knyghtis
victorye] knyght notwithstondyng his victorye NSJ *see n.*

own deth / for to saue the legions that he had in conduit and f. 28ᵛ
guydinge. And Sampson the mighty, for the Philistiens confounde (p. 56)
and destrue thaim, that were enmyes to the peeple of Israel, he
brought down [by] his grete might the hous vpon thaim and him
bothe wherynne they kept thaire counsaile. Of othir stories men 5
might finde ynow, but it suffiseth me to haue shewed that money
and worldy goodes ben no more than accessaries and seruauntes ai
to vertu, as the wommen seruauntes the whiche ministre the neces-
saries of mankyndes fragilitee. And yit by the richesses ill to gete,
daungerous to kepe, perilous to distribue, doloreuse for to lose, and 10
needfull to the princes and lordes for to guyde and perfourme thaire
werres, withoute the whiche this werk may nat we lede nor susteyne. And neuerthelesse they faile us as to furnyssh in suffisaunce,
and we faile thaim as in thaim disposinge to profite.

Now goo we to the thrid poynt that we haue to declare, that 15
obeisaunce aught to be had and preserued toward the prince in
tyme of werre by his knyghtes and subgites. I make my premise
after the greef sentence of Valere, which seith that discipline of
knyghthode, straitely [retayned] and rigorouslye kept, maynteneth
the seigneuries that ben had in possession and conquerith thaim 20
that ben defendid in the contrarie. And what is disciplyne of
knyghthode sauf oonly lawe ordeyned and preseruy[d] in the
excercinge of armes and batailles vnder the commaundement of the
cheef and for the publique vtilite. This ordre hath curiously be
kept by all thoo that euer gate worship and victorie by proesse of 25
armes so that nothinge was doon agains the right of knyghthode or
agains the commaunde/ment of the chief but the payn was capitall f. 29
and mortall, where it appeerid well by the memoriall deede of (p. 57)
Manlius Torquatus, the whiche that, in the tyme that he guyded
his legions Romaynes, he made his sonnes hed to be striken of 30
because that he had foughten with the enmyes agains his fadirs
commaundement natwithstandynge that he opteyned the victorie.
And in this cace the victorie that was doon by the manhode of the

19 retayned] retrayned U retenue D   22 preseruyd] preseruyng U gardee D
29 that 2] the *add.* U

myght nat hide the disobeisaunce that he had don, but was put
to dethe as a transgressour ayeinst the lawe. And so the rigorouse
discipline of knyghthode ouircame the naturall pite of the fadir,
for he that nature gaue to be a fadir mercifull shewed hymself
5 at that tyme as a rigorouse iuge egrely obserued in fullfillyng the
noble lawe of armes.

Many diuerse storyes may be shewed of grette punycions and
f. 28 scharpe iustices / doon for lack of keping the obeisaunce and ordre
of the full notable lawe of armes. Moreouir of suche as for that
10 cause haue lost their hedis men may fynde in the Romayne stories
and othir writingis diuerse grette thingis. And also for smale
offences and diuerse necligences knyghtis war tyed to a stake and
beten with roddis and put from the feliship of knyththode to the
degre of fotemen. Vndir this fourme was punyschid Aurelius by
15 the counseile of Cocta, for he was betin with roddis and aftir that
put to the fotemen as oon of their numbur for because he had
necligently by the enemyes suffird to be brente parte of the closyng
of a feelde which he had in gouernaunce. Also Lucius Tucius was
condempned to go barfote through the ooste withowt companye
20 and the horsemen that war vndir his rewle war comaundid bere
stones to the werkis forasmoche as thei did yelde themself shame-
col. 2 fully to their enemyes / withowt diffence.

Wherefor lette vs iuge the grette and difficulte thingis by the
doubtis that we fynde [and perceyve] in the lasse thingis, and
25 thanne shulde we knowe that comunalte ne companye may nat be
maynteined withowt iustice, for among thevis in the continuaunce
of their being togedir and departing of their prayes, ther must be
a maner of iustis kepte oon to anothir though so be þat iustice be
nat ther propirly for thentencion of the same matir, but it is shewed
30 thus by maner of similitude. Thanne if it be so that the familiers
of an householde faile to kepe ordir and obeisaunce ayeinst their
hede, hough shulde thanne endure an hooste of men of werre which
be moevit in their coragis? Nor also I wote neuir hough the seurte

4 that] by *add. ins.* S   gaue to be] to haue bene NJ owght to haue
ben (owght *ins.*) S *see n.*   8 iustices] iustice N *pl.* D   keping] kepynke
of J   10 men] we N on D   12 necligences] negligence N *pl.* D
13 the 2] NSJ the *add.* R   16 as] and N   18 gouernaunce] kepyng N *see n.*
20 horsemen] men of horsbake NSJ gens de cheval D   that] which N
23 difficulte] dyffycul NSJ   25 shulde] shul N   26–8 for . . .
iustis] *om.* J *see n.*   26 continuaunce] countenaunce N   32 thanne]
om. ND

yonge man as a conquerrour might nat skonche the disobeisaunce
that he did as a transgressoure. Wherfore the rigoure of the knyght-
lye discipline ouercame the naturall pitee of the fader, for he, whiche
nature excited to be mercyfull fader for to acquite his deuoire as to
his blood, shewed himself as a rigorouse iuge egrely to obserue the 5
lawe of armes.

Many diuers histories might be produced to this purpose of
othir sharpe punysshmentes and iustices doon for defaute of kep-
inge obeisaunce and ordre of the moost honeurable crafte and
deedys of armes. Morrouer as for suche as for theise causes haue 10
capitally ben punysshed, might many be founde in the Romaynes
scriptures the whiche for smale and litle necligences haue ben
beten with roddes at a stake and put downe from the worship of
knyghthode in the degre of seruing footmen. And in this manere
was punisshed Aurelius by the counsaile of Cocta, for he was beten 15
with roddes and sett ageyn with the footmen bycause that necli-
gentlye he suffred the enmyes to brenne a parte of the closture of
the lowginge that he aught for to kepe. And Lucius Tucius was
commaunded to goo barefoot withoute any felauship through the
hoste, and the horsemen that with him were for to serue with stonys 20
the wer/kemen because that they were shamefullye yolden to thaire   f. 29ᵛ
enmyes withoute defence.   (p. 58)

Iuge we the grete defautes by the doutes that we apperceyue in
the litle defautes. So shal we knowe that no felauship ne comonte
may nat endure withoute iustice insomiche that amonge theevys, 25
for to continue togedirs and departe thaire prayes, they most kepe
amonge thaim a maner of iustice, though it be so that it is no
iustice, yit it is so called by similitude. And sithen it is that in oon
houshold most be kept ordre and obeisaunce, how than shuld
endure an hoste of men, garnysshid with harneys and meeuid of 30
corages, nor hou may thaire suerte be kept agains thaire enmyes

of the lordis myght be kepte ayeinste their enemyes and peace
among themself and their frendis in lasse than their willis were
vndir the power of a hede and their power lymitid vndir the obei/-
f. 28ᵛ saunce of a commaundour, which may kepe ouir them iustice of
5 armes and knyghtly disciplyn.

What shall I thanne say of vs, ne what hope may I haue in our
e[n]terprise and armes in lasse thanne knyghtly discipline and
rightfull iustice be dewly kepte? Othirwise cannat be said in this
caas but that we go as a shippe withowt gouernaunce an as an horse
10 withowt a brydill. O Lorde that art almyghty, Thou knowist verily
if dewe correccion shuld be made, mo shulde be founde gilty
thanne othirwise, for euery man wold be maister ouir his maister.
And yet have we, and it be serchid, but fewe good prentyces, and
many their be that woll gadyr felischip togedir and make themself
15 capiteynes. Of thes ther be so many what capiteynes and maistirs
that vnnethe a man shall fynde a seruaunt or a fellow. But sum-
tyme it was othirwise, for ther was no man callid a squyer lasse
col. 2 than / he were knowen of souereyng prowes. On the tothir side ther
was no man callid to take wagis as a man of armes in lasse that he
20 hadde take a prisonner with his owne handis. But nowadayes euery
man that canne gird hym with a swourde and were an haberioun
dar boldely take vpon himself to be a capiteyne. And oftetymes it
happis that certein enterprises be taken, as segis to be leyde to suche
a place or such, and thervpon the crye is made and the day is sette.
25 Thanne to see hough the people come therto, it is pyte to see, for thei
come more for feere and shame thanne for any good wille they haue
to do wele, and yet thei make it as it were in their chose whedir they
woll come late or erely, the turnyng ageyne or the abydyng. Othir
ther be also that love bettir the easis of their howses than thei loue
30 noblesse and wourship, which when thei be constreyned to go from
f. 29 their house, they wolde fayne do as the snayle which ca/rieth his
howse [with hym] whersoeuir he goo. But and thei wold kepe their
houses as thei shulde do, they wold nat alway abyde in them, for

1 and] the *add*. NSJ leur D   6 our] your N noz D   7 enterprise]
emterprise R entreprynses SJ entrepryses N *pl*. D   and 1] and of N and *ins*. of
canc. S   thanne] þat NSJ   9 that] at SJ   16 that] than J   a man
shall] shall a man NSJ   a seruaunt or a fellow] a felawe or a servaunt
NSJ   19 that] þan NSJ   23 to 2] in N   24 is 2] *om*. NSJ
25 pyte] for *add*. N   26 more] *om*. N   27 as it were] is NSJ *see n*.
29 easis] ease NSJ *pl*. D   32 whersoeuir] wheresomeeuyr SJ wherfor-
someuer (for *perhaps canc*.) N   33 they wold] þen wolde þai N   abyde]
byde N

and thaire pees amonge thaimself and thaire frendes sauf oonly by
that that thaire voluntes ben in the puissaunce of oon chief and
thaire powers limited to obeye the commaundement of him that
vpon thaim may kepe iustice of armes and cheualrye?

What shall I than say of vs, nor what hope or trust may I haue 5
in oure enterprises of armes withoute knyghtly discipline and
rightwysnesse of iustice of armes be kept and obserued? As in this
cace it may nat be nayed but that we goo as dooth the vessell in
the see withoute sterne and as the hors withoute bridell. A, God
Allmighty, Thou knowyst that whosoeuer in theise parties wolde 10
correct the abusions, there shuld be more of the culpable and giltye
than of the correctours. For yche man will be a maistre of the crafte
wherof we haue as yit right fewe of good prentices. All may skantlye
suffise for to greue thenmyes and yit yche man wold make a felauship and be a capteyn himself. And so many there be of chiefes and 15
maistres that with payn they may fynde / felawes and seruauntes. f. 30
Somtyme was noon called a sqwier but yf [he] had ben in deedes of (p. 59)
souerain prowesse, ne noon was called to the wages of a man of
armes withoute he had honestlye taken prisonner with his owne
hand. But now [to] can guerde a swerde and doo vpon an habirgeon 20
suffiseth to make a nwe capteyn. And yf it falle that any enterprises
ben made or seeges seet or the banne of the princes cryed and the
day often named for to kepe the feeld, where at diuers tymes men
come more for the manere sake than for doute to faile and for
dreede of shame and reproche than willing well to doo, and yit is 25
it in thaire choyce of erly or late the comynge, the goinge home or
abidinge. And suche there is that so miche louen the ease of thaire
houses more than the worship of the nobles so that at suche tyme
as they ben constreyned to departe, right fayne wold they bere
thaire houses with thaim, lik as the snayle that draweth with him 30
the shelle wherynne he harburght and restith. But and they wold
kepe thaire houses in suche maner as they goten, that shuld nat be

13 right] right *add.* U   20 to] two U

the olde awncientes with the travaile of their bodyes and iupardye
of their lyves haue goten honours, noblesses and suche as longith
to their right. We see our prince that neuir ceassid this iiij. yeris
day to take vpon hym viagis and grette labours, having full litill
5 rest nor abyding. We also see the straungers which be allied with
owr realme that put themself in iupardy to passe the fortunes of the
see for to com to our socour and to be partineris of our aduersite
and peyne, but many of them that [ben] bownden to diffende abyde
and harke hough the werkis shal be guydede and drawe hymself
10 along from the strokis. This ignoraunce and fawte of harte is cause
of the hardnesse and rapyne on which the people compleyne, for in
defaulte of suche as shulde helpe and put to their honde we be
col. 2 fayne to take suche as we / may fynde for yeftys to maynteine and
supporte our lordeship, which haue nat withinne the same nowthir
15 howse ne londe, instede of theym which be bounde of veray duete
to maynteyne and ber owte to their power the charges, for fawte
of which straungers and suche othir as maynteyne the warre be in
a maner constreyned to live vpon the poore people. Neuirthelesse
our chargis ouircomith vs suche wise that of force we must nedis
20 suffre it, and also the penaunce that longith to this hath nat as yet
sufficiauntly chastised vs. Also whenne the noble entreprenours, of
whom, our Lorde be thancked, we fynde in this realme many and
diuerse that be wele apprevid, and wold fayne put themself to doo
wele, thanne be they in suche wise delayed that vnnethe thei canne
25 gette forewarde. And yet whanne they be fourth, as faste thei high
to come home ageyne. Wherfor it is grette peyne to begynne any /
f. 29ᵛ good thing, but yet it is a gretter peyne to kepe all thing togedir and
to perfourme our entent.

　　Yet there is a worse necligence thanne this, for notwithstonding
30 the litill wille that restith in diuerse of them ther is founde so grette
pryde, which of theire own wisedome can no maner of coundyte,
that thei disdeyne to do othir men seruice thorough whom
thei myght haue goten grette wourship and woll nat. Wherfor our
infortune is the more.

　　2 honours] and *add*. N　　longith] longed NSJ　　3 prince] allso *add*.
NSJ *om*. D　　5 also see] *tr*. NSJ so *add*. J　so *add. ins*. S　　with]
to N　　7 aduersite] aduersion (adversyte *in different hand in margin*) N
8 but] and N et D　　9 hymself] hemself N　　12 as] os J þat N
13 for yeftys] *om*. N par dons D　　14 lordeship] lordshippes N　　15 which]
of verray ryghtwysnes *add*. NSJ *see n.*　　veray] *om*. NSJ　　17 as]
þat N　　18 a] *om*. NSJ　　19 nedis] nede S　　20 this] þat *add*. N
21 entreprenours] entreprysers *ins. as gloss* N　　24 canne] not *add*. N

with ease nor rest, for the auncient noble men with the trauaile of
thaire bodyes and parill of thaire lyues gate the worshippes and the
rightys of noblesse. Wee see oure prince whiche this .iiij. yere day
hath nat ceessid to trauaile withoute rest or ease. Wee see the
straungers allied to oure reame passen the fortunes of the see for 5
to come to oure socours and to suffre part of oure aduersite and
payn. And many of thaim that ben bounde to defende vs herken
and abide what the conclusion shall be and rather wold suffre to be
chased and laden with the burdon of the werre vnto the dryuinge 9
oute of thaire houses or thay wold put payn to releeue thaim/self f. 30ᵛ
nor to chace the werres ferre from thaim. This ignorance and faute (p. 60)
of hert is cause of the hardnesse that we suffre and of the rapes
wherof the peeple complayneth, for, in defaute of thaim be whom
we shuld be holpen, neede hath caused to take suche as might be
goten to make his werre of men goten by giftes and praiers instede 15
of thaim the whiche deuoire and trouth aught to exhorte thaim of
veray dutee to doo it. Thus is the werre made by men that haue
nothir house nor lande and for the moost parte suche as neede
constreyneth to lyue vpon othir men. And our grete neede hath
caused us to suffre it, and as yit hath nat the penaunce of this synne 20
chastised us. And whan the manly men, wherof, blessid be the good
Lord, there is yit in this reame that be right well approued, doo
thaire labour to bringe to the feeld the noble men for to doo som
good deede, they make so longe delay and ben so loth to departe
outwarde and hyeth thaim as soone as they may hastily to retourne 25
home agayn so that with grete payn may anythinge be put in
the wey of good begynnynge, but with miche more payn may it
affectuelly be performed.
    Yit is there wors than this necligence, for [withe] the litle good
will of diuers is therof founde a so grete arrogaunce and lettinge 30
that they that can nothinge guyde nor conduit will bere noon armes
vnder othir capteyns and they hold it for a disworship to be subgite
to him vnder whom they may haue the good fame, to the whiche
thei might neuer atteyne by thaire owne guydynge nor polecye.

29 withe] whiche U avecques D

O thou folisch and blynde pryde, having litill knowlege of vertu, o hough perilouse an errour thou arte in! The fete of armes [and] of batailes through thi cursidnes be broken and put owte of ordre; the grette and myghty powers of the grette powers arn disioyned
5 and diuidid whanne euery man woll trust his own witte and [s]ewe his opinyon. [And] suche folkes, wanne thei may compare with their bettirs, oftetymes don suche fawtis that thei be put vndir
col. 2 them / that be of lowest degre. Yt comyth also to my mynde that (I) [haue] hard diuerse men say that thei wold nat goo vndir the
10 penon of suche a man an suche 'for my fadir was neuir vndir hym'. But lo, hadde thei peysid wele this wourde the wolde rathir haue kepte it in thanne haue spokyn it. For the linages be nat the hede of the warris, but suche to whom God, their wittis or their wourthines, and the auctorite of the prince hath commytted of his grace
15 and commaundement to be obeyed, which obeysaunce is nat only yevin to the parson but to the office and ordre of armes and to knyghtly disciplyne, which euery noble man ought to proferre aboue all othir honoure.

And to this we may wele be moevid by the stories of our auncient
20 fadirs, but yet we shuld be rathir constreyned by the myscheves and foliship that we see byfore our yen for lacke of obeisaunce. Wherfor and reding of stories may profight them anythyng ayeinst
f. 30 suche pryde, latte vs rede Titus / L[iv]ius, and we shulde fynde that the dictatours and consulis of Rome which had the condyte of
25 Romayne batails were oftentymes chosen and take owte of the feeldis from their labours, lyke as it is founde of Fabricius, Lucius Quintus and of diuerse oþer which war streightly obeied. For and any faulte war done ayeinst the disciplyne of armes, pyte myght haue no place, lignage ne high porte had no favour, and prayers
30 myght nat be herde. Suche wise were their werkis that through their dedis and their techingis thei taught [to] suche as were men

2–3 and of] and NSJ of R *see n.*   4 of . . . powers] *om.* N *see n.*   arn]
om. NSJ   5 sewe] J sue N fewe RS suivre D   6 opinyon] oppynyons S
unclear J   wanne] as whenne J as when that NS   10 hym] men N   11 the]
thei NSJ   haue] *om.* N   12 it 1] *om.* J   haue spokyn] a spoke N
13 warris] werrers N querres D   13–14 or . . . hath] *om.* N   16 yevin]
yolden NJ yeuen *canc.* yolden S rendue D *see n.*   and 1] þe *add.* NSJ
17 proferre] preferre N   20 be rathir] *tr.* NSJ   21 foliship] felyshipp N
see n.   that . . . byfore] afore N   our yen] þer yen N then J yen *canc.*
yyn S *see n.*   22 them] *om.* NSJ   23 Livius] Lucius RSJ Lucyvs N
Livius D   shulde] shall N schul S scholle J   24 and] þe *add.* NSJ les D
consulis] counseles J   27 and . . . For] *om.* N

O arrogaunce, mad and blynde, and litle constaunce of vertu, o moost parillous erroure in deedes of armes and of batailles, by thyne maledicion ben / broken and disordeyned the mighty puis- f. 31 saunce and the armes disioyned and diuided at suche tyme as men (p. 61) will beleeue thy will and thy oppinion. And so for to compare 5 thaimself with the best they doon often suche defautes whiche causeth thaim to be deprimed vnder the lowest. It falleth in my memorye that I haue oftentymes herd dyuers men sey in this wyse, 'I wold for nothinge go vnder the penon of suche oon, for my fader was neuer vnder his.' But this woorde is nat well weyed or it be 10 said, for the cheefes of werre comyth nat by heritage, but suche as God yiueth wysdome and manhode, hauing the auctorite of the prince, there aught so to be taken and obeyed, the whiche obei- saunce is nat yiven to the persoone but to the office and ordre of a[r]mes and discipline of cheualrye, the which yche noble man 15 aught to proferre aboue all othir worship.

We may be meeued this to entende by diuers olde stories, but to the same aught to constreyne us the grete harmys whiche by pre- sumpcion and faute to obeye ben fallen and yit falle in oure lyues before oure yien. And yf stories ben profitable to repent this pride, 20 rede we Titu Liuius, and we shall finde that the dictatours and senatours that guyded the Romayn batailes were full often chosen at Rome by eleccion of the manly men whiche were sent fore out of the cuntree where they labored the erthe, as it byfell of Fabri- cius, of Lucius Quintus and of many othir, the whiche were so 25 dreedfully obeied that whereas the defautes were agains the disci- plyne of armes pitie had no rome, ne lynage nor high poort might haue no fauore, nor prayers be herd. For suche was thaire opera- cion that by deedes and by / t[e]chynge they gaue knowlege to the f. 31ᵛ

(p. 62)

29 techynge] touchynge U ensaignemens D

of warre that thei shulde dowbte their cheveteignes more thanne
their enemyes, also þat thei shulde rathir dowbte [the] peynes of
their shamefull defawtes thanne the woundis that thei bere away
from their aduersaries. Suche thingis may nat be hydde that trewe
5 affeccion constreynith to be shewed, and though so be that this
matir [tuch to] the high dedis and to the high persones, yet I speke
col. 2 but aftir my sympilnes, / for ther was neuir seene at yghe ne redde
in writing lasse disciplyne ne more lacke of iustice longing to armes
thanne [we] see now kepe among our knyghthode. Who is that can
10 shewe byfore me that for his vertuouse seruice is honorablely
rewardid aftir his desertis? On the tothir side wher is any correccion don vpon the infynite delictes which nowadayes be vsid ayeinst
all ordinaunce of armes and reuers of the lawe and also ayeinst the
customes of all wourshipfull men? Wherfor if ther be any man that
15 woll desyer the ignoraunce of oure people, hough many may we
fynde that haue disobeied the commaundementis of the capiteynes,
also come whenne þem liste and go whanne them liste and lette for
no displesaunce? Also thei abandon their wardis and withowte
[leve] deliuir their fortreisses for deliueryng of þemself. At nede
20 also thei faile, and whanneas nede nat thei putte away their felli-
f. 30ᵛ ship to live sen/gelly for their profight.
　　And yet among all thes thingis who that cowde shewe me any
punycion doon, wherof ensaumple myght be had for the doctryne
of any amendement of this, thanne shulde the rigour of my wourdis
25 be the more mollified. But I reporte me to God [and] all suche as
knowe it hough it is. Yet ther is a thing that gruggeth me more
thanne this that I haue rehercid, for I se hough the nobles and
wourshipfull men take so litill hede to themself that (there) is no
difference of rewle and condicion bytwen them and the mys-
30 gouerned folkis, nothir in their willis nor in feere of their soueraignes, ne taketh no hede hough evill name thei gette, ayeinst
which euery noble herte ought make more mortall werre thanne
ayeinst their enemyes, for thei ought suche wise to guyde hemself
that their werkis myght make them to be knowe from othir

2 the] NSJ their R les D　　4 their] the N des D　　6 the 1] om. NSJ
the 2] om. NSJ　　12 delictes] delytes NS delyces J　　13 and 1] þe add.
N au D　　17 also] þei add. ins. J　　and . . . liste] om. N see n.
19 leve] ins. J om. RNS cause D　　20 whanneas] nede not thei add. nede
not canc. N　　nat] om. J　　21 sengelly] singeerly (1st e corrected to l) N
synglerly (le perhaps orig. ee) J　　22 me] of add. NSJ　　32 ought] to
add. N

peeple which did bere armes that the cheftayne was more to dreede
than the enmyes and the shamefull paynes of the shamefull defautes
more cruell than the wowndes that thei brought from thaire aduersaries. It may nat be hid that that true affeccion constreyneth for to
say, and though it be soo that it toucheth to the grete deedes of the 5
high men I speke therof accordinge to my smallnesse. But it was
neuer seen with yie nor red in no scripture lesse discipline ne more
fraile iustice in armes than is this that we say that we kepe vpon
oure cheualrye. What shall he be that shall lay forthe an high
worship doon for vertuous seruise, nor oon [s]oule correction for 10
the infinite delites committed in chefe, contrarie to all maner of
ordinaunce of armes and to the reuerse of the lawes and custumes
of the manly and worthy men? And yf any man enquere to knowe
that that no man may ignore, how ma[n]y han be seen disobeye the
commaundementes of the prince, breke the defences, come whan 15
it liketh thaim and goo agayne, who that euer be displeasid, haban-
doune and leue thaire wardys for to kepe thoo that ben left and
habandouned withoute cause, deliure the straunge places for to
deliure thaimself out of strenght, at a neede to faile and yelde
thaimself, and withoute neede make a peeple to departe and kepe 20
a companye aparte.

     And yf any man of all theise defautes might shewe me a punis-
shion wherof the exaumple might be doctrine of amendinge and
redresse, somwhat it wolde swage the rigoure of my woordes.
But to God I repoort me hou that it is, and to yche man that 25
knowyth it. And more it greeuith me that the noble men take so
litle kepe therto that they suffer thaimself to slide in / ordinaunce f. 32
of othir men withoute difference of condicions or voluntees, nor (p. 63)
they will nat constreyne ne correct suche as purchace ill fame and
renoun, contrarie to the whiche noblesse of hert aught to haue more 30
mortall werre than agains thenmyes, for suche amonge othir aught
to bere suche a marke that thaire deedys may cause thaim to be

col. 2 mysgouerned people and that in / noon of them may be founde any
spotte of reproche in lasse that thei make therfor a remedye, like
as did the Sipiouns at Rome whanne thei toke away from oon of the
eyres of Scipion Affrican a rynge wherin was enprentid the ymage
5 of the wourthi Scipion forasmoche as he followed nat the werkis of
hym of which he bare the tokyn. It is wreten also of Marcus
Staurus hough he gaue a fadirly and a vertuouse answer and also
shamefull to suche people as be of faylid coragis, for it was on a
tyme shewed him hough his sone came shamefully from a bataile
10 home towarde his fader. But whanne the fadir vndirstode the meene
of his comynge, said these wourdis, that he more gladly wolde haue
goon ayeinst the ooste if thei had brought hym wourshipfully dede
thanne to receyue hym into his house aftir so dishonorable a faute.
Lo her the saying of a constaunte fadir which kepte intierly the /
f. 31 ferme honour of his house and of his noblesse and was the sentence
16 of a veray wourshipfull man. Also in like wise I rede of a woman
which is of freile natur, yet she surmountid the saying of Marcus
whanne she went ayeinst hir childern, which fledde away from a
bataile, and for to confounde their repreuable shame of cowardnes
20 left the comon shame of womanhode and opened hir clothis byfore
[hir], saying to them this wise: 'Syn ye woll nedis flee [reentre]
againe into the wombe that hath borne yow, for I vndirstonde ther
is non othir place to save yow', in lyke as [she] wold say that it had
be bettir thei had neuir be born thanne to come owt of hir bely
25 to grette repref to them and all their lyngnage.
 Suche ought to be disciplyne of knyghthode to feere shame [be
kept] in the house of nobles as in the hoost of pryncis, for the
reuerence and the s[a]vable doctryne of the wourshipfull fadirs and
col. 2 olde men of a lienage may moche [more] profight to / yong men in
30 vertu thanne the feere of iustice of suche as ben theire heedes. For
and so wer that the wisedam of Salamon, the prowes of Ector, the
constaunce of Macabeus, the stre[n]gh of Sampson, the subtilte of
Vlixes, the multitude of legions which wer conditid by Dayre or
Yerces, and the gret riches of Ostomyen wer put in a host that is

2 reproche] reprosche SJ reprove N   that] than SJ   4 wherin] were
as N where ys S   13 hym] *om.* NSJ le D   14 a] *om.* JD   15 the]
a NSJ *om.* D   21 them] in *add.* N   reentre] SJ entre N and entre R
see n.   23 she] NSJ ye R elle D   24 bettir] þat *add.* N   to] *om.* NSJ
26 be 1] the *add.* NSJ *om.* D   27 as] and N comme D   28 savable] NSJ
(1 *ins. after* v N) seivable R salvable D   29 a lienage] Alienage R alynage
SJ a lynage N   32 strengh] NSJ streigh R   34 a] and N

knowen from other men so that noon of thaim leeue no spott of
reproche in his sembleable withoute remedie, like as the Scipions
did at Rome whan they tooke from oon of the heires of Scipion the
Aufrican a ringe wherynne was empreented the figure of the manly
Scipion for because he folowed nat the steppes of him of whom he 5
bare the remembraunce. And also of Marcus Staurus is writen an
answer of a uertuous fader and shamefull reproche to thaim that
ben of fauted hertys and corage, whan it was tolde him that shamefully his sonne was comyng from a bataile to him ward, wherto he
answerd that more gladly he wold go toward his enmyes and his 10
sonne had manfully be slayn in the bataile and that he wold neuer
receyue him in his house aftir a shamefull reproche. This was the
saying of an entier stable and ferme constaunce to kepe worship of
his hous, and it was sentence yeuen of an noble and high hert. But
yit by the mouthe of a womman of fraile sexe was this woord passed 15
and surmounted in cace like, whan a lady of high noblesse cam
agayn hir sonnes that were fleing from a bataile warde, and for to
put awey theire vituperable shame and lachenesse she lefte the
comon shame of womanhede and discoured h[er]self before, saying
to thaim, sith that they wold flee that they wolde come agayne into 20
the belye that / bare thaim and that shee had noon othir place to f. 32ᵛ
saue thaim, as though shee wold say that they had ben bettyr ben (p. 64)
vnborne than for to haue comen out of hir belye to the reproche
both [of] thaim and of thaire lyne.

Than aught knyghtly discipline to be kept as well with worship 25
in the noble mennys houses as in the hoste of a prince, for the good
fame and saluable doctrine of the manly faders and auncient men
of a ligne may be more profitable to induce the yonge men to vertu
than it is to dreede of the iustice of the cheef. And as in a somme,
yf the sapience of Salamon, the prouesse of Ector, the constaunce 30
of the Macabees, the strenght of Sampson, the cautele of Vlixes,
the multitude of the legions of Dayre and Xerses, and the havure

3 Scipion] Scipions (s *erased*) U   19 herself] himself U   25 with]
with *add.* U

owt of ordinaunce, withowt iustice and dis[c]ipline of knyghthode,
the wisedom may nat availe but be as a thing voide, for the prowesse
is mollified, the constaunce broken, the strenght feblischid, subtiltees an[e]antisid, the multitude distroyed and þe richesse wastid.
5 Wherfor and if it speede wele it is more by fortune thanne by
reason.

   Thes thingis and our othir defautis be nat to speke of for makyng
debate among oon and othir and vttirly say no more but to suche as
lust vse this matir more for correccione thanne [for] reprefe. And
f. 31ᵛ yet I recite nat this for to charge with / any persone but to thentent
11 that men shulde therof take good avise. So at this tyme me thinkith
that this suffisith inough to euery man and more þan I can say, for
though so be that it is of litill effect yet it procedith of grette
haboundaunce of good wille.

15   [The Auctour]

   Thanne he which was in harneys made a request that he myght
make a shorte replicacion and saide as hereaftir folowith:

            [The Knyght]

   Off the vndirstonding and knowlache which ought acompanye
20 the mageste of princes and of lordis, nor how thei dispose their
goodis in many maners, of all suche thingis I woll holde my peace
at this tyme and leve the language to them that vndirstond the
burdon and the daungier therof. But to the obeisaunce of knyghtly
discipline, wherof our estate is at this our moche reprevid and
col. 2 gretly chalaungid. Yet / which is he of vs all that may kepe the
26 ordre of armes or knyghtly discipline aloone? Or [ho] may receyve
it and kepe it in lasse thanne it be putt to him wrongfully and also
mainteyned? How shulde this beginne among the membirs if it
faile in the high persones, and hough may the subiectis kepe it if the
30 soueraingnes breke it? But who that woll atteyne the roote of this
malady must begynne at the fundacion and the spryng wherthrough
suche knyghtly ordinaunce owght to take the continuaunce and

1 ordinaunce] and *add.* N *om.* D   discipline] NSJ distipline R
4 aneantisid] NSJ andantisid R aneanties D   5 if] *om.* NSJ   8 vttirly]
to *add.* N   10 to 1] no N   13 is] but *add.* NSJ *om.* D   14 good]
go S   16 that] that *add.* S   19 acompanye] A Companye R a companye
SJ a Companye N   24 at . . . reprevid] moch repreved at þis houre N
26 ho] S he RNJ qui D   27 wrongfully] *om.* NSJ   28 shulde] shal NSJ
29 if] giffe NSJ   32 to] *om.* NSJ   the] *om.* N

of Octauien were in an hoste disordinate, out of iustice and knyghtly discipline, the sapience in conclusion shuld be void, the manhode swaged, the constaunce broken, the strenght brought in debilitee, the wyles and cauteelys made noughty, the multitude distiped, and the good and haueure wasted. And yf any good happe byfell to thaim, it shuld be more reputed by fortune than by reson.

All theise withoute othir defautes ben nat to reherce for to entre in contencion or strif of oon agains anothir, but rather be to remembre tho that will no lenger vse thaim more for correccion than for reproche. Nor I reherce thaim nat for to yive any charge but therynne to take aduise and that this litle that I haue seid may suffise to yche man, for though it be of litle effect it proceedith of grete habundaunce of good will.

The Acteure /

Oon soule replike to speke required he that the armes bere and thus began to say:

(The Knight)

Of the wysdom and kunnyng that aught to felauship the princes and lordes, and thaire richesse to conuerte in diuers disposicions, I may wel hold my peas and leeue the woordes to thaim that haue therof the deedes and daungers; but of mageste to the obeisaunce and discipline of cheualrie, wherof oure estate is now reproched and greeuouslye repreeuid, where is any of vs that may kepe the ordre of armes or knyghtly discipline by himself? And who shall receyue it or kepe it but yf it be to him youen and maynteyned? How may it begynne amonge the leest whan it is fallen amonge the highest? And how may the subgites kepe it yf the souerayns breke it? And who that will come to the roote of this seekenesse he most come to the fundacion and springe wherof the knyghtly ordinaunce

growyng, and [þat of] the maistirs myght come the patron and
exsaumple wherof their helpers and their apprentices myght fynde
to werke vpon. The right excellent techingis of Aristotill and prac-
ticke of dedis made all thingis subiectis to Alisaundirs knyghtes.
5 The constaunce and coragious amonycion of Kyng Priamus dowbled
the prowesse of the wourthi Hector. The watches and the wele-
f. 32 aduysid gouernaunce of Haniball made / his people to passe the
Alpees and the grette maresses and þe merveillous passages withowt any grette hurte. The enterprises and the excersises of armes
10 that was in Kyng Charles the Grette gaue vnto Rowland, Ogier and
Olyuere their grette name which endurith yet to this day. And the
goodly behavyng and high looke of Kyng Charles that last died,
which oftintymes made Bertrame ouircome his enemyes so gloriously þat he brought the realme, which was at grette myschief,
15 sodainly he raysid ageyne vnto gret welthe and peace. This same
Bertram lefte in his tyme suche memorye of knyghtly discipline,
wherof it is spokyn at this day, that what knyght or wourshipfull
man had don a thing to his grette reproche, on shulde come as he
satte at his mete and shulde kytte the clothe that lay before hym.
col. 2 Wherby may be vndirstonde that the streighte keping of wour/ship
21 made the wey large of knygh[tly] prowesse to them that lived in
thes dayes, for the opyn punycion of the rigorouse vengeaunce
closid vp all suche weyes as touchid any dishonorable dedis, for
execucion was don forthwithall vpon all shamefull offences by the
25 prince and by othir high persones, which at that tyme was thought
equite but [now]adayes it shulde be take for cruelte. Notwithstonding pyte and bountevousnes longen singularly to princes
forasmoche as their grette powere maketh them to be redoubted,
but pyte and mekenesse makith stable and firme, and of the meke-
30 nes and humanyte of a prince growith confidence, [disconfidence],
seurte and disseurte, hardines to take vpon hym, and constaunce
for to conduyte. But to the contrary of mekenesse growith
suspeccion, of suspeccion growith vengeaunce, [of vengeaunce]
rancour, separacion and murmur.

3-4 practicke] praetyk SJ   4 thingis subiectis] þing subiect NSJ pl. D
5 and] þe add. NSJ om. D   amonycion] admonycions N sing. D   6 the
wourthi] om. N vaillant D   the 3] wy add. canc. NS   9 the] grete add. N
om. D   10 Ogier] Roger N   11 to] om. NSJ   15 he] be NSJ
17 it] om. NSJ   22 the 2] þis NSJ om. D   23 closid] closyn J   26 for] om. N
27 longen singularly] longyng singlerly N   30 and] of N et D
34 rancour separacion] as in D tr. N

aught to betake his birth and continuacion. For of the maisters
comyth the patroon and exaumples wherevpon thaire helpers and
prentices most werke. The moost excellent doctrine of Aristotle
practiked by wey of deede made alle thinges subgite and surmount-
able to the knyghtly prouesse of Alexander. The constaunce and 5
corageous exhortacion of the Kynge Priamus doubled the prouesse of
the worthy Ector. The good conduit and wyse gouernaunce of
Haniball caused his men to passe the streyghtes and grete marreyses
and merueilous passages withoute grete hurte. The enterprises and
the excercites of the Kynge Charles the Grete gaue to Rolland, 10
Olyuere and Oger thaire grete renoun, the whiche yit endureth.
And the ripe direccion and noblesse of Kynge Charles last des-
tressid / caused the good Bertram so many tymes vainquyssh and f. 33ᵛ
ouerthrowe thenmyes, and this reame out of greef mischeeuys (p. 66)
releeuid in pesible felicite. This Bertram of his tyme lefte suche a 15
demonstraunce in memorye of knightly discipline that any noble
man that had doon any forfeit reprocheable, at such tyme as he was
at his meyte the boord clothe was kut awey before him. This
streight keping of worship made the large wey of manhode amonge
the knightis and nobles that in tho dayes were lyuing, and this 20
openynge of rigorous vengeaunce foreclosed all we[y]es of dis-
honeurable dedes and reproche. In this behalue the redynesse to
reuenge quikly suche shamefull offenses longeth to the princes and
high men, to doo in equite which in othir caces shuld be reputed
for cruelte. Though it be so that to princes syngulerlye perteyneth 25
meekenesse and debonairte because that grete power maketh the
seigneuries redoutable, but mekenesse causeth thaim to be stedfast
and stable. For of the ientilnesse and mekenes of the prince breedith confidence, of confidence suerte, of suerte hardynesse to take
on hand, and constaunce of good conduit and guydinge. But to the 30
contrarie of mekenes breedith suspeccion, of suspeccion vengeaunce, [of vengeaunce] rancoure, of rancore separacion and
murmure.

21 weyes] werres U voyes D

So at this tyme I thincke to put myself no forther in this mater,
f. 32ᵛ but / I woll reporte me to suche as haue the rewle and gouernaunce
of the comone wele, praying God that thei may duely acquyte them
in their trouthe, for doubte [of] displeasur of persones ought nat
5 lette the comon profite ne the welthe of lordis. And who that yevith
counseill aftir the appetite and nat aftir reason, his opynion is nat
trewe but flaterye. Wherfor I say certainly that in the trouthe of
counseillours restith þe suerte of princes and the welefar of the comon
wele, wherin must be serchid owt the botoume of our defaultes and
10 the solucion of our debatis.

[The Auctour]

This replicacion endit, hough be it that euerich enforced themself to make gretter declaracion in othir thingis, but the lady afore
rehercid commaundid them to kepe silence and so made conclusion
col. 2 of their argumentis and questions, saying as hereaftir / followith:

16   [Fraunce]

I woll no lengar here youre excusacions nor offences, for in your
discordes and discharges oon ayeinst anothir lieth nat the rysing
ageyne from myn infortune, but only in that that euery man ought
20 rathir applye to his own chastesinge thanne to the blame or repreef
of his neyghboure. But yet the affeccion of the comon wele may
staunche the singular disordinaunces [i]f your willes myght ioyne
in one maner desyir for the comon wele, sufferyng your infortune,
and also if pacience be kept among yow ye may happe to come to
25 good fortune suche wise that through your wisedomes remedies
myght be founde. And syn that God and natur hath made you
more perfight thanne any othir thing that hath sowle, me thinke
that ye shuld nat be more disordinate thanne the beestis, but ye
f. 33 shuld enclyne to your own / saluacion, profight and diffence, lyke
30 as don the flyes that make hony, which iustely kepe their office and
their ordir, and for diffence of their lives labour sore to bring in
their mete in season of the yere, for keping togedir their assemble
and by their litill pollicey to kepe the lordship of their kyng þat
regnith among them vndir a litill praty roofe, [and] as it happith
35 othirwhile that their kyng be hurte in bataile whanne it fortuneth

3 thei] *om.* N   10 solucion] solucyons N *sing.* D   17 offences]
affences SJ affeccions N deffences D   22 disordinaunces] disdrdynaunce N
pl. D   if] of RNSJ se D   27 thanne] þat N   33 litill] *om.* N petite D

Furthermor I thinke nat to put me in the debates of this mater, but I reporte me to thaim that haue the publique thinges in thaire counseile and gouernaunce for to acquite thaire trauthe and conscience in playn maner. For doute to displease the persoones they aught nat to let the profitable thinges to the seigneuries and comons. 5 And he that yiveth no counsaile but oonly to the appetite and pleasir and nat to the reson, his oppinion is no counseile but / playn f. 34 flateringe. Wherfore I sey that in the trouthe of the counseillours (p. 67) lieth the suerte of the prince and the saluacion of the publique well, and there aught we to seeke the roote of alle oure difficultees and 10 the solucion of oure debates.

The Acteure

This replike finissht, though it be so that yche of thaim enforced thaimself to speke more, the ladie aboue writen commaunded thaim to kepe silence, and than she made conclusion in thaire argumentes 15 and questions, saying in this wyse:

The Land

I will no lenger here your excusacions ne defences, for in youre discordes and discharges lieth nat the releef of myn infortune sauf oonly that yche man aught to take it more to his owne chastisinge 20 than to the shame or repreef of any othir. But the affeccion of the publique well may auoyde your singuler disordinate reule yf the voluntees ben conyoined all in oon onely desire to the comon saluacion; and yf in suffering your fortune and that yche of you to othir kepe pacience, to you togedir may come all this gracious good 25 happe the whiche yche man seekith by dyuers remedies. And sith that God and nature hath formed you more parfite than othir creatures that haue soules, be nat more inordinate than the smale beestes ne more necligent or lesse inclyne to your comon saluacion, vtilite and defence than the litle bees, the whiche of thaim in thaire 30 swarme kepe thaire ordre and iupart thair lyues to kepe and defende thaire assemblees and litle polecie and for to kepe the lordship of thaire kynge, whiche reigneth amonge thaim vnder a litle hyue, that at / som tymes whan he is hurt in bataile with anothir felauship f. 34ᵛ

(p. 68)

19 of] of add. U

that oon company metith with anothir, thanne thei take and ley
hym on their wynges, and othirwhile suffir themself to be slayne
for mayntenaun[c]e of their kyng, of his lordship and of his right.
So at this tyme I haue herde inough of your chiding and debate.
5 Wherfor I woll that at this tyme ye holde your peace. Yet I woll
nat that all this season shulde be lost in [veyn], but I woll ordeyne
that your reasons shal be wretyn to thentent that euerych may
col. 2 know / his owne diffaulte by othir and such as shull rede it may
avoide suche errour of theire hertis which thei themself ar repreuid
10 of by ther neyburs. Wherfor I woll that ye make no lenger disputacion that is hatefull but suche as may be fru[y]tfull.

[The Auctour]

Thanne was I callid, for I was so nygh that I herde all their
saying. Thanne said the lady in this wise to me: 'Thou that hast
15 herde this presente disputacion made by manere of Quadryloge
Inuectif, take and write thes wourdis to thentent that thei may
abyde in memorye for the fruyte of theim that shall see this processe. And forasmoche as God hath nat yeve the strengh of body
nor vsage to wer harneys, I woll that thou serue the comon wele as
20 ferforthe as thou maiste. For the penne and the tonge of oratours
enhauncid as moche the glory of Rome as did the feighters.'
f. 33ᵛ Thanne thes persones / vanyschid owte of my sight and the
sleepe lefte me. And so through my litill vndirstondyng I haue
accomplisshid the comaundmentis of the said lady by this present
25 writyng. Wherfor I pray euery man that thei woll favourablely
declare and iuge to knowe rathir tha[t] I do it for good affeccion
thanne for glory of the werke. For I certify to you trewly that the
mocion of this werke was more labourid for compassion and necessite of the common wele thanne for presumpcion of vndirstonding,
30 and rathir for profiting by good exortacion thanne for any repref
to any persone.

1 company] om. N compaignie D   metith] mete oon SJ   thanne] theme S
2 hym] þem N   themself] self ins. J hem N   6 veyn] yow RNSJ
vain D   8 diffaulte] dyffame J faulte D   shull] shuld NJ   10 that]
om. NSJ   11 fruytfull] y either r or incomplete letter R   13 all] om.
N tout D   14 in . . . me] to me in þis wise NSJ   21 the 1] om. J la D
26 that] NSJ thanne R   good] om. N bonne D   27 to] om. NSJ
30 any] om. NSJ

of been they bere him and kepe him vp with thaire w[i]nges and
suffre deth for to kepe and maynteyne his seigneurie and his lyf.

I haue herd ynough of your chidinges and debates. Wherfore I
will that ye suffre and cesse from hensforth. Neuerthelesse to
thentent your ceason be nat wasted in vayn, I haue ordeyned your 5
resons to be writen so that yche man may therynne knowe his own
defautes by exaumple of othir, and because that thei shall reede
thaim, may put out the erroure of that is in thaire hertes, wherof
they shall fynde thaimself by thaire neighbours reproched in the
lettre, and that hereon be noon hatefull disputacion but vertuous 10
and frutefull.

The Acteure

At whiche tyme the lady called me, for I was there beside where
I had herd all that was said, saying to me, 'Thou hast herd this
present disputacion made by maner of Quadriloge Invectif, write 15
theise woordes to thentent they may be had in fructuouse memorye.
And sith that God hath nat yeuen thee strenght of body nor excercice of armes, serue the publique well of that thou may doo. For as
mich was exalted the glorie of the Romayns and thaire corages
enforced to vertu by the penne and the tunge of the oratours as by 20
the glayues of the fighters.'

Theise personages fled than from myn yien and the sleepe left
me. So haue I performed by my symple wytt the commaundement
of the seid lady by this present writinge. And to yche lectoure I
pray tendrely in fauourable interpretacion and thereynne iuge to 25
knowe the good affeccion more than the glorye of the operacion.
For I certifye for veray / trouthe that the meeuing of this werke is f. 35
more through compassion of publique neede than by presumpcion (p. 69)
of vndirstandinge and for the profite by good exhortacion more
than for any repreef.   30

Explicit

22 fled] than fled U

DATE DUE

GAYLORD   PRINTED IN U.S.A.